"Tobias has delivered an impressive anthology, especially so for its international scope. Nine sections cover every aspect of the documentary. A must for anyone working in the field today."

Bob Pest,
Hot Springs Documentary Film Festival 1998

"...a far reaching yet comprehensive consideration of the issues confronting non-fiction image making, from people who have been there; are there now, and are gearing up for what the future will bring. A very valuable collection of perspectives."

Timothy J. Lyons,
Editor, International Documentary

THE
SEARCH
FOR
"REALITY"

THE ART OF DOCUMENTARY FILMMAKING

EDITED BY MICHAEL TOBIAS

Published by Michael Wiese Productions
11288 Ventura Blvd., Suite 821
Studio City, CA 91604, (818-379-8799) (818-986-3408 fax)
mw@mwp.com
http://www.mwp.com

Cover Design, Art Hotel, Los Angeles
Cover Photos, Robert Radin and Michael Tobias
Director of Editorial and Production, Ken Lee
Book Layout, Gina Mansfield
Final Copy Check, Bernice Balfour

Printed by Braun-Brumfield, Inc., Ann Arbor, Michigan
Manufactured in the United States of America
Printed on recycled paper
Copyright 1998 by Michael Tobias

We are grateful for the many wonderful photographs from Ulli Bonnekamp, George T. Butler, Henry Diltz, Direct Cinema, Julio Cesar Fuerra D., Stuart Keene, NASA, Barbara Trent, S. Laffey, Jeremy Norgarth, R. Radin, Sebastian Richter, Vanessa H. Smith, Michael Tobias, and Pieter Vandermeer. All photographs are copyrighted by the photographers and used by permission.

ISBN 0-941188-62-0

Library of Congress Cataloging in Publication Data

The Search For Reality : the art of documentary filmmaking / edited by
  Michael Tobias.
      p. cm.
    ISBN 0-941188-62-0
    1. Documentary films--Production and direction. I. Tobias,
Michael
PN 1995.9.D6S37 1997
070.1'8--dc21   97-41448
                                                                                 CIP

Books from
MICHAEL WIESE PRODUCTIONS

Directing Actors
The Director's Journey
Producer to Producer
Inspirational Hollywood
Persistence of Vision
Film Directing: Shot by Shot
Film Directing: Cinematic Motion
Fade In: The Screenwriting Process
The Writer's Journey
Film & Video Financing
Film & Video Marketing
Film & Video Budgets
The Independent Film & Videomaker's Guide

To Jane Gray Morrison,
an extraordinary artist, my soulmate, editorial conscience, and true love...
without whom there is no reality.

THE SEARCH FOR "REALITY"
THE ART OF DOCUMENTARY FILMMAKING
Edited by Michael Tobias

TABLE OF CONTENTS

ACKNOWLEDGEMENTS   XI
INTRODUCTION BY MICHAEL TOBIAS   1

PART I - ORIGINS, HISTORIES, REFLECTIONS   5

Robert W. Wagner – One or Two Things I've Learned About Documentary Film   7
Malvin Wald – Desperately Seeking Marilyn   15
Ian Mutsu – Confessions of an East-West Filmmaker   23
Michael Rabiger – On Learning to Make Films (The Midwife's Tale)   31
Richard Leacock – A Search for the Feeling of Being There   43

PART II - THE "MOMENT"   51

Dyanna Taylor – Framing the Wind   53
Dale Bell - "Woodstock" – From Vision to Symbolic Reality   65
Bettina Gray – The Intimate Moment: The Art of Interviewing   87

PART III - VISIONS AND EXPEDITIONS   97

Jeremy Hogarth – "The Big Wet"   99
Nicholas Webster - A Passion For Truth   115
Bobby Carmichael – The Ice Climb Commitment   121
André Singer – Strange Bedfellows: The Feature Documentary, Television and Anthropology   133

PART IV - THE POLITICS AND POSSIBILITIES OF ADVOCACY   139

Sheila A. Laffey, Ph. D. – From Walden to Wao Kele O Puna to Wetlands   141
Stefan Jarl – A Manifest on the Subject of Documentaries   149
Barbara Trent – At Risk: An Anatomy of a Decision   155
Keyan G. Tomaselli – Sanity Lost and Found:
                The Travails of a South African Documentary Filmmaker   167
Michael Tobias – The Search for Reality   183

PART V - THE CHANGING TECHNOLOGY OF NON-FICTION 195

Robert W. Wagner – The Family Filmed 197
Godfrey Reggio – All Together, All At Once, The Rocketship 20th Century 205
James Brundige – Four Arguments for the Preservation of Television 219

PART VI - COMMUNICATING WITH A PUBLIC 223

Robert Radin – The Documentary: The Near Perfect Vehicle 225
Prof. Ren Yuan – A Comparative Study of Eastern and Western Documentaries 229
Martha Foster – Intercultural Documentary and the American Audience 237
Jens Meurer – The Elusive Art of European Coproduction 245
Joanne D'Antonio – The Audience Representative 253

PART VII - THE BUSINESS OF DOCUMENTARIES 257

Arnold Shapiro – Ten Golden Rules 259
Mike Fox - Art of Documentary 271
David L. Wolper - The Documentary: Entertain and Inform, Not Just Inform 285
Jillian Robinson – Maestro 289
Alexis Krasilovsky – Writing for Real 295
Christopher Fryman – Notes from Japan 303
Mitchell W. Block – Documentary Production and Distribution: Beyond the Year 2000 315

PART VIII - TWO INTERVIEWS 329

An Interview with Frederick Wiseman 331
An Interview with Albert Maysles 343

PART IX - THE SPIRITUALITY OF NON-FICTION 359

Mickey Lemle – Zen and the Art of the Documentary 361
Vanessa H. Smith – Answers In Blue 369
John Swindells – In Search of Soul 375
Eduard Schreiber – The Eye Swims in the Canale Grande 383

ACKNOWLEDGMENTS

I wish, first, to thank my parents Bill and Betty, who were key to the origination of this project. It was my father who insisted I take an "early retirement" from academia many years ago and head for the wilds of the film industry in Los Angeles.

To all the contributors, who gave of their hearts, their time, their inspiration, and their voice, my deepest appreciation.

I am indebted to my dear friend and co-producer, Robert Radin, who has voyaged with me on dozens of madcap cinematic escapades on every continent, in search of 1) a film, 2) the best espresso houses in the world, and 3) a glimpse of reality, whatever that may be.

To Marc, Jean and Alvaro, a special enduring gratitude which each alone can understand.

A very special thanks to the William Morris Agency, particularly Bill Douglas, Ray Solley, Mike Lubin and Claudia Cross.

And, finally, my deep appreciation is conveyed to Michael Wiese, for instantly "getting" this book over a phone call, and his dedicated production colleague, Ken Lee. Without them, there would be no book.

INTRODUCTION

THE SEARCH FOR REALITY - THE ART OF DOCUMENTARY FILMMAKING

EDITED BY MICHAEL TOBIAS

Throughout the world, documentary filmmaking is exploding, in the best sense of the verb. More nonfiction films are being made, and the audience for them is greater than ever before. That is not to say that all documentary filmmakers consider current trends in the marketplace to be positive ones—many do not, and with good reason. Yet, it is indisputable that the documentary has become a significant vogue in the artistic expression of a generation, and it gives every indication of growing in popularity and diversity.

A century of documentary filmmaking has, of course, preceded the present passions for nonfiction, beginning with social photography in the 1850s, and turning to film as the available technologies greeted the impulse.

But never has there been so voracious a broadcast and theatrical interest in the output of so-called "reality–based" productions, and serious documentary films.

Numerous books have explored the history and theory of non–fiction, one of the best, in my opinion, being Bill Nichols's *Representing Reality - Issues and Concepts in Documentary* (Indiana University Press, Bloomington, 1991). It is a work of complex philosophical, psychological, and thematic analysis that is essential reading for anyone concerned with the rudiments of the field of nonfiction.

But what about the passions, intentions, ruminations, and excitement of filmmakers themselves, whose words come from the heart of their own rich experiences as documentarians? The reader and fellow filmmaker has had little opportunity to see gathered in one place a feast of such viewpoints. Here, such a book has been fashioned. *The Search for Reality* comprises a rich chorus of documentary filmmakers from throughout the world probing the meanings, techniques and approaches, as well as the revelations and frontiers, of their craft.

1

Directors, writers, producers, executive producers, cinematographers, editors, distributors, and interviewers reveal and explore the complexities of documentary and reality-based filmmaking and presentation from their own personal experiences. Each contributor brings a distinctive professional and artistic career to the task of addressing what it is that makes a documentary or reality–based program satisfying.

Various aspects of realism, style, narrative, inquiry, the shades blurring objective reality and subjective approach, are probed in the light of what it is that lends nonfiction filmmaking its unique blend—at its best—of clarity, integrity, provocation, and "reality." The book includes within the broad approach to documentary both traditional nonfiction narrated or cinéma vérité films, as well as news documentaries, social advocacy nonfiction works, reality–based pieces, nonfiction art films, nature/adventure films, visual anthropology, history, and artistic expressions that defy all categorization. Some aspects of docudrama are also addressed.

Aspects of old and new technology are also treated, in addition to the past, the present, and the future of that technology's impact on the art, the message, and the opportunities for nonfiction.

Marketing is also a key theme running throughout much of the book—in the United States, South Africa, Japan and China, Australia, and all over Europe.

There are two primary areas of concern that surface throughout the many contributions. The first, and most important, deals with the filmmakers themselves, as they have undertaken to make a film, or get it out to a market. The book chronicles the countless gradations of perspective, through reflection, anecdote, the reliving of certain moments in a filmmaker's career, and carefully considered exposition. The broad range of contributors gives readers an in-depth overview of the art of documentary filmmaking, and a greater appreciation of its difficulties, distribution challenges (how do very serious, uncompromising documentaries get financed and sold?), its complexity, vigor and endlessly enriching possibilities.

In the midst of the collective adventures and personal stories from the trenches— be it in the field or an editing suite—the book hopes to convey the many nuances of artistic commitment to documentaries, from concept to distribution. What is the essence of nonfiction? Can the filmmaker influence the outcome of reality, as it is perceived by the audience, and what responsibilities, possibilities and concerns does this inherent power pose? Is it even possible to faithfully reflect the nature of reality? What does that mean? Is it relevant? Can there be objectivity? Is it possible, is it desirable, or does subjectivity rule nonfiction? Where does the documentary become "reality-based" programming? What is truth? Are the distinctions important ones? What are the basic canons of integrity for the director of photography, the editor? Where does social advocacy play a prominent role in the documentary arena, and if so, to what extent? Are all documentaries "advocacy" pieces in some sense? How is the audience affected by documentaries? Have there been changing perception and response patterns to documentaries over the last fifty years, and why, perhaps? Has the evolving digital technology in film and editing and transmission (i.e., Betacams and non–linear modalities and satellite feeds from the field) effected the message?

None of these questions are meant to be answered just like that, of course. But we hope the book should prove valuable to the general filmgoer who cares enough about film to read a work on the subject. For students of film, and aficionados of documentary, this will be a unique volume that profiles the many styles and approaches of nonfiction filmmaking that now account for as much as 40 percent of all network television, if one includes news, current affairs, and the large array of "reality-based" shows, in addition to the traditional documentary–specific networks.

Each contributor has been asked to write a very personal essay, an eye-witness account of a particular concern: that might be a saga, a behind-the-scenes blow-by-blow, a decisive moment in a film that reflects the problems, challenges, and possibilities for documentary; a theme, a point in a career, a moment in a film, or an overview of a general pattern of special significance that emerges from many films in the contributor's professional career.

It is my hope that readers will come away from this collection with an enhanced appreciation for the extraordinary range of involvements and projects by documentary filmmakers throughout the world, keeping in mind that this is the first volume in what promises to be a series of such volumes in coming years.

By juxtaposing so many diverse essays, styles, reflections and meditations, *The Search for Reality* should provide an invigorating approach to the art of documentary filmmaking, and an overview of its colossal energies, eccentricities, and importance.

PART I

ORIGINS, HISTORIES, REFLECTIONS

Robert Wagner making documentary footage for the Office of the Coordinator of Inter-American Affairs, Panama, 1944.

ONE OR TWO THINGS I'VE LEARNED ABOUT DOCUMENTARY FILM

ROBERT W. WAGNER

My lifelong involvement with film began with the homemovies shot by my father, and in movie houses on the south side of Columbus, Ohio, watching cowboys and Indians racing across the screen, and vicariously experiencing the exciting celluloid adventures of handsome gentlemen and beautiful ladies in exotic places around the world. I was awed by the reality of these larger-than-life moving images, enchanted with their romance, and filled with respect for the magic of those who made them, whether it was good old Dad or C.B.DeMille.

I learned that the camera changes the way people behave. As kids, the self-conscious feeling that we were being filmed, and possibly immortalized looking silly, was amplified by our father's loudly announced directions about how we should act. The result was that family movies showed us laughing, bonding, and happy—the way our old man wanted us to be, but not always the way we were. Even as dimly civilized teenagers we also recognized that our screen idols did not behave like most of the people we knew in real life.

Years later this distinction was clarified by the distinguished actor Alexander Knox in an article titled "Acting and Behaving," published in an issue of the old Hollywood Quarterly. Frank Capra, in a conversation about working with nonactors, described the difference more explicitly: "Put a camera on a short-order cook, and he becomes a chef!"

During the Depression, as a university student of the social sciences, I was impressed by the gritty black-and-white photographs by Dorothea Lange, Walker Evans, Arthur Rothstein, Ben Shahn and other Farm Security Administration photographers, and influenced by Pare Lorentz's visually powerful and poetic documentary films, *The Plow That Broke The Plains* (1936) and *The River* (1937). Like news photographs, newsreels, and home movies, documentary works of the time were in bald black-and-white, seemingly without artifice, which helped establish the monochromatic image as a reflection of "reality" and promoted the popularly held belief that "the camera never lies."

A small group of documentary filmmakers including Ralph Steiner, Willard Van Dyke, Paul Strand, Joris Ivens, Leo Hurwitz, Julien Bryan, and especially Robert Flaherty—the "father of the documentary"—seemed to be a breed apart. They made short films on low budgets with small crews, nonactors, existing light, and minimal equipment. They demonstrated how lean narration, supported by music of a Virgil Thomson or an Aaron Copland, could elevate to art and poetry tragic images of eroded land and portraits of dispossessed people who had no place to stop and no place to go. Driven by social and personal conviction, they had a love for films of the kind not being made in Hollywood, and a need to create them. Shortly after Flaherty's death I asked Frances Flaherty how her husband began a film project. "He made films just like he defecated," she said. "It was an organic, natural process."

During World War II as a motion picture writer-director with the Office of War Information, I became associated with another breed of filmmakers composed of people from Hollywood, the newsreels, New York's Film and Photo League, a few from the former U.S. Film Service, and members of film units of the Armed Forces. It was a concoction of different approaches to filmmaking spiced with talents at odds with Washington bureaucracy, Hollywood egos, studio politics, and differing personal, political, and artistic convictions.

The director of the O.W.I. was the respected radio network newscaster Elmer Davis who, in addition to riding herd on a collection of film writers, directors, editors, and cinematographers, was also in charge of the agency's press, radio, and graphic media departments, the whole of which he described as "a cocktail." His first directive to the chiefs of these departments was: "This is a people's war, and to win it the people should know as much about it as they can. This Office will do its best to tell the truth and nothing but the truth, both at home and abroad. Military information that would aid the enemy must be withheld, but within that limitation we shall try to give people a clear, complete, and accurate picture." Of course, it wasn't all that easy.

Persistent elements in Congress saw government—made films as political capital for the party in power; accusations of censorship came from the conservative press; and there was strong opposition from Hollywood producers who resented government "amateurs" going into the "film business" with public funding—war or no war. There was also competition between government agencies and between branches of the Armed Forces to the surprise of one whose experience with the inside machinations of Capitol politics was practically limited to what could be learned from a screening of *Mr. Smith Goes to Washington*. The O.W.I.

was my first realistic exposure to the deeper issues of documentary expression, information, politics, and propaganda.

Directing production in New York was playwright Sam Spewack who, with wife Bella, had written *Boy Meets Girl* and *Kiss Me, Kate*. Also working in the O.W.I.'s office at 35 W. 45th Street was documentary pioneer Ralph Steiner, Chicago realist-novelist Meyer Levin, and veteran newsreel assignment editor Bill Montague, from all of whom I learned much.

In the documentary tradition most of these government—made films were low budget one-or two-reelers. Some were scripted by Hollywood professionals such as Garson Kanin, whose *Ring of Steel* was narrated by Spencer Tracy, and realist-poet Carl Sandburg who wrote the narration for *Bomber*, which described the making of the B-24.

Orson Welles did the voice-over for the ten-minute film *Tanks*. The first and only major production of the domestic branch of the O.W.I. was a powerful but now forgotten compilation film titled *The World at War* written by Spewack. When Capra took over the documentation of the war with his *Why We Fight* series which was eventually distributed theatrically, the O.W.I.'s home-front production was limited to short films dealing with how to fight firebombs, scrap drives, the reasons and rules for gasoline, tire, and meat rationing, and the acquisition and theatrical and non-theatrical release of selected independent, Hollywood, and Armed Forces films related to the objectives of the OWI.

My assignments included several possibly important but dull topics to be cut into newsreel releases. Known as "poster films" they dealt with victory gardens, the recruitment of farm workers, a short titled *Free Labor Will Win* based on an O.W.I. poster with the same title, a one-reeler on *Wartime Nutrition*, and another titled *Black Market*, which was directed by William Castle who later gained attention as one of the "Kings of the B's" for his productions *Macabre* (1958) and *Rosemary's Baby* (1968).

Wartime informational and documentary film writing tempered the later work of both screenwriters who continued in the narrative tradition and those who went into nontheatrical film production—a field which boomed after the war. For example, Malvin Wald who scripted some thirty training and documentary films, later wrote the story for *The Naked City* (1948). Edward Anhalt who scripted Army training films later made *Panic in the Streets* (1950), *The Young Lions* (1959), and *Beckett* (1964). Documentary filmmaker Ben Maddow, a writer in the First Motion

Picture Unit of the Army Air Corps, later wrote the screenplay from the Faulkner novel *Intruder in the Dust* (1949) and coscripted *The Asphalt Jungle* (1950).

Experience making wartime documentaries was also reflected in the postwar films of established Hollywood filmmakers: William Wyler (*The Best Years of Our Lives*, 1946); George Stevens (*The Diary of Anne Frank*, 1959); and Frank Capra (*It's a Wonderful Life*, 1946), who also produced the educational TV series *Our Mr. Sun* and *Hemo the Magnificent*, 1956. The lesson was that all filmmakers are tellers of stories which have to both interest and inform their audience. That is the art of both the instructional and the narrative filmmaker. As George Bernard Shaw put it in his book, *Everybody's Political What's What*: "The honest artist does not pretend that his fictions are facts; but he may claim as I do that it is only through fiction that fact may be made instructive or even intelligible." In 1977, Lester James Peires, Sri Lanka's international award-winning director, in a conversation with the writer in Colombo, mused: "Sometimes I think there is more fiction in my documentaries and more fact in my fictions!"

When Congress closed the domestic branch of the O.W.I., Spewack, Montague, and others joined Robert Sherwood and Philip Dunne in the overseas branch in London. Others, like veteran *March of Time* and O.W.I. cameraman Carl Pryer, and I went with the Office of the Coordinator of Inter–American Affairs, the O.W.I.'s Latin American counterpart which was directed by Nelson Rockefeller. Pryer and Wagner believed theirs were the most "authentic documentaries" possible since they were shooting raw, unedited, silent (m.o.s.) footage—not making a "production."

Assignments ranged widely: Merchant Marine activities in the Caribbean and the Pacific; U.S. Medical Corps studies of tropical diseases in Guatemala; remote locations in Peru, Ecuador, Chile, Colombia, and the Amazon where the U.S. was searching for rubber, quinine, mineral, balsa, and other resources which had been cut off by the Japanese in southeast Asia, as well as recording projects designed to strengthen the economy and public health of our allies and as a response to extensive Axis propaganda in Latin America. We tried for objective documentation but, of course, every time we made a long-shot, medium-shot, and close-up of the same

Robert Wagner. Shooting films for the Office of the Coordinator of Inter-American Affairs. The location was a village along the Amazon on the eastern border of Peru. 1943.

10

subject we were creating a little story—not full of sound and fury, but certainly a small message told by a pair of American filmmakers from their point of view.

Hitler and Mussolini had their ministries of propaganda. Lenin declared all art to be propaganda. In 1622 Pope Gregory XV formed the "Congregatione de Propaganda," a college for priests to perpetuate the faith at home and abroad. In the U.S., however, "propaganda" was a pejorative word. The product of O.W.I.'s domestic branch, because it tried to follow Davis's directive to "do its best to tell the truth and nothing but the truth at home and abroad," became known inside government circles as "white propaganda." An overseas branch, the Office of Strategic Services (later to become the C.I.A.) under the direction of "Wild Bill" Donovan, delivered to the enemy negative and misleading information known as "black propaganda."

In the end, what became "propaganda" and what was "information" involved not only the filmmaker but also the collaboration of viewers. The ultimate censor and interpreter of the truth or falsehood of the message was in the eye and mind and background of the beholder. The only hope was that Lincoln may have been right when he figured that all of the people couldn't be fooled all of the time.

After the war, as chief of information for the Division of Mental Hygiene in the Ohio Department of Public Welfare, I wrote radio shows, made films, photographs, and published articles on mental health at a time when *Life* magazine and other popular publications and social organizations were crusading against poor conditions in what was still called the "insane asylums" of America.

Filming in antiquated locations, under hazardous conditions, with existing light and administrative red tape is standard procedure in many documentary productions. Working in a community of disturbed minds and an atmosphere of public prejudice and misunderstanding of mental illness were added dimensions. The culture of the mentally handicapped and their environment, like the culture of a foreign land, had to be understood to be filmed with any integrity, veracity, or even any credibility.

Respect for human subjects and the task of documenting the dismal plight of one out of every twenty Americans committed to mental institutions without violating their civil rights raised ethical and legal issues which would become even more critical in later years as ubiquitous, investigative TV cameras probed increasingly idiosyncratic human behavior, aided and abetted by the public appetite for scandal and sleaze. We could do our best to "get inside" our subjects but, whether shooting a documentary in a ward of psychopaths or recording the life of indigenous peoples in an Andean village, we realized that as filmmakers from another culture we would always be "outsiders."

As chair of the Department of Photography & Cinema at Ohio State University, I had the opportunity not only to teach cinema, but also to produce films on a great many subjects in collaboration with some of the best minds in the arts, sciences, and humanities. In a university film department equipped with sync-sound, high-speed, and animation cameras, lights, editing benches, a 16-35mm processing lab and a studio, I knew why Orson Welles, when he stepped onto the R.K.O. lot for the first time, exclaimed: "This is the biggest electric train set any boy ever had!"

In documenting the commonplace I found drama in visual experiences which transcended the thing itself. The time-lapse microscopic recording of the cell division of a single frog egg, slowly rotating like an orb in space, could be not only scientifically revealing but also, with appropriate music, as dramatic as a science-fiction scene from Clarke and Kubrick's 2001. The blast of color in the polarized light of a wind tunnel; the delicate touch of a surgeon's probe in extreme close-up; the slo-mo of dancers afloat in a perfect pas de deux; a comedic documentation of an entire college football game condensed into five minutes, seen as a piece of folk art supported with a background of country music; the icy, abstract growth of chemical crystals—all of these films were factual, yet fictional in the sense that they were not "the real thing." They were movies! And so I came to believe Emile Zola, amateur photographer and novelist of the realist school who, in 1900, told a reporter: "You cannot say you have thoroughly seen anything until you have got a photograph of it!"

In 1953, working on a script for the Turkish Ministry of Health to persuade villagers to use the services of government-trained midwives, I spent some time in Anatolia learning about Muslin culture and the traditional role of women. The film, titled *Saidye: Village Midwife*, was directed by Irvin Kershner who later directed *The Empire Strikes Back* (1980) and *Never Say Never* (1983). Another film, on how to build an outhouse, was well received by villagers who easily followed the instructions but said that what they really liked about the film were "the chickens!" Being farmers, they instantly spotted in the distant background a few white pullets which escaped the attention of the outsider-filmmakers.

We see what we know. The final edit in any production is the act of an audience. Respect for the viewer's existing knowledge and intelligence seemed to be more characteristic of documentary than of many Hollywood filmmakers, along with a special skill for balancing human compassion with the responsibility of revealing oftentimes awful truths.

James Agee described the camera in the twentieth century as "next to the unassisted and weaponless consciousness, the central instrument of our time." In the twenty-first century digital cameras in the hands of millions will document millions of moments of millions of human lives. Hidden cameras in every nook and cranny will record the corners of our closets and the corners of our mind. Once mainly a toy and a tool, the camera will be more often seen as a weapon, and its user as a shooter without a license. With digitalization the veracity of every image will be in dispute. In the virtual, interactive imagery of cyberspace, shadows have become the substance. Reproductions have overshadowed realities. I overheard one American tourist upon her first sight of the Eiffel Tower exclaim: "Look, Harry! It's just like the postcard!" As Susan Sontag observed: "The camera makes everyone a tourist in other people's reality and eventually in their own."

Will technology and the tawdry make paparazzi of us all? Or is a new breed of image makers emerging—artists with a fresher vision, storytellers of more creative and more responsible documentary expressions—a new generation of searchers for "reality" in a world of dissolving forms?

In the Prado in Madrid there is a small, black chalk drawing by Goya of an old man hobbling along on two canes. Remembering its title seemed a handy conclusion to a rambling essay on one or two things the writer learned about documentary. Beneath his drawing Goya had penciled: "Aun aprendo"—I am still learning.

DESPERATELY SEEKING MARILYN

MALVIN WALD

On Sunday morning, August 5, 1962, Dr. Thomas Noguchi reported for work at the Los Angeles County Morgue. As a deputy medical examiner, he performed autopsies on citizens who had died without a doctor in attendance and determined the cause of death.

Dr. Noguchi was used to working Sundays. As the song said, "Saturday night is the loneliest night" and lonely women, without husbands, friends or lovers, took their own lives on Saturday night and their bodies were brought to the morgue on Sunday morning.

As Dr. Noguchi prepared to work, he glanced at the report form for the name of the first case. "Ah, so," he remarked to his assisting nurse, "same name as star of movie I saw recently."

Then he pulled back the sheet covering the face and did the biggest doubletake of the decade when he saw it was *the* Marilyn Monroe, not someone with the same name.

He took his time, carefully gathering pertinent facts—her weight, height, color of hair and eyes, the presence of semen.

Then he picked up his scalpel and plunged it into the spectacular chest of the most famous blonde of the twentieth century.

Dr. Noguchi was the first of an army of scavengers who would profit from picking at the bones of the dead superstar. An entire cottage industry was born that day as human vultures hovered over her remains, ready to make a killing in the markets where her name spelled glamour, sex, and sensationalism.

One of the first to enter this market was Seymour Reed, president of Official Films, a New York based production company which had just concluded *Biography*, a series of syndicated documentaries, compiled from stock footage, a joint venture with David Wolper. The films were crisply narrated by a perceptive, charismatic New York television journalist named Mike Wallace.

Reed summoned me to his suite at the Beverly Hills Hotel the next morning. He admired the work I did as an early writer with the Wolper Organization, collaborating with producer-director Jack Haley, Jr.

Reed had in mind a half-hour documentary to be called *Marilyn Monroe*. He wanted me to write it because he was seeking the same dramatic approach to Monroe as I had taken in *Hollywood: The Golden Years* which told the story of silent stars Mary Pickford, Greta Garbo, Charlie Chaplin, and Douglas Fairbanks, Jr. Elmer Bernstein, who did the music for that film, would join us in this project.

As narrator, Reed was using Mike Wallace, with whom I had worked on three syndicated documentaries.

Reed had also hired an energetic young producer, Art Lieberman, and Phil Rosenberg, who had been film editor when I wrote *D-Day*, a Wolper special scooped up by NBC for network showing.

I wanted to be certain that this would be a serious biography, not a fan magazine type assemblage of gossip.

Reed assured me that artists with the integrity of Elmer Bernstein and Mike Wallace would not be identified with a cheap product, but he warned me that there would be difficulties.

For one thing, there would be a shortage of available Monroe film footage. He had heard that 20th Century Fox was planning a Monroe documentary, since most of her films were with them. Rock Hudson was signed to narrate.

Reed's former partner, David Wolper, was getting in on the act, too. He would have access to such United Artist films as *Some Like It Hot* and *The Misfits* with John Huston, director of *The Misfits*, narrating.

That was formidable opposition. Since Reed's limited budget wouldn't allow us the luxury of time, we would have to work fast and be on the air first. And we would have to use ingenuity to find enough footage to fill twenty-three minutes of screen time.

Since Fox and Wolper would feast on scenes from her important films, we would have to scramble among the leftovers to come up with a presentable compilation. It was a challenge which I found exhilarating—how to make something out of bits of nothing. Reed gave us a deadline of completing the film in December, allowing us four months to research, film, and edit the documentary, a task that normally required nine months.

I told my associates that there were two events in her life which were pictorial and major.

By hook or crook, we had to have those.

The first was for the opening of the film, a montage of Marilyn in a bare-shouldered cocktail gown in 1954 singing "Diamonds Are a Girl's Best Friend," before 100,000 freezing GIs in Korea. The footage was the property of the U.S. Army. To obtain it, I visited the local Army Public Relations Office and asked them to have the Pentagon grant us the rights.

The officer in charge was very friendly. I was well known to the military for I was a veteran of the First Motion Picture Unit and I had written the 1954 Sterling Hayden film, *Battle Taxi*, dealing with the first use of helicopters in modern warfare. Washington was so pleased with my script that they had supplied full cooperation, helicopters, pilots, the use of army facilities, and actual combat footage.

The local officers wondered if the Monroe project would reflect well on the army. "Gentlemen," I replied, "picture this. Marilyn is in Tokyo on her honeymoon with Joe DiMaggio. The army asks her if she would entertain the troops. She does so promptly, leaving her newly married groom all alone in their hotel room while she takes off to wiggle that magnificent body and croon her hit song before the troops who have selected her as their favorite pin-up. What greater love had an actress for her country that she should desert her new husband to do something for the boys."

The army was sold. They gave us the film gratis, with one caveat. They did not own the copyright to the song. We would have to negotiate with the publishers. When we explained that this was a low budget affair and that their song would open the film, they were most cooperative. For a few hundred dollars we were allowed to use their music.

Now we had the sock opening. But we also needed another piece of film which epitomized the struggling young actress arriving at the pinnacle of fame, the day in June 1953 when twenty-seven-year-old Marilyn placed impressions of her hands and feet in cement at the Grauman's Chinese Theatre along with Jane Russell, at the premiere of their costarring roles in *Gentlemen Prefer Blondes*, the film with the Diamonds song featured.

We knew that Fox Movietone Newsreel had covered that event exclusively and had been told there were no other movie photographers present.

I contacted friends in the field of fan magazines and one of them told me about a freelance still photographer named Jack Knox, who often took a 16mm movie camera to premieres.

Apparently Marilyn sympathized with the plight of freelance photographers like Jack. She got permission for Knox to do it for his private collection.

When I explained to Knox how vital his footage was to us, he consented to sell it to us for a modest amount and a screen credit.

There remained one additional hurdle. We had to obtain Jane Russell's permission to use her likeness. Rather than bargain for a fee, we suggested a donation of $500 to her pet charity for war orphans. She was delighted to sign.

As for Marilyn's feature films, the only one we could use was scenes from *Ladies of the Chorus*, a 1949 Columbia quickie musical made when Marilyn was twenty-three. It revealed her talent for singing and dancing, but failed to further her career, which suddenly came to a dead end when Harry Cohn failed to renew her contract.

We now had about eight minutes of film, but fifteen more were required. Like detectives on a manhunt, Lieberman and I sought out anybody who had known Marilyn and had personal footage on her. Bandleader Ray Anthony had once thrown a party to which Marilyn came and was taught how to play the drums by Mickey Rooney. Anthony gave us the film and Mickey Rooney generously allowed us the use of his image for free.

Our search next led us to the office of Emmeline Snively, owner of the Blue Book Model Agency in the Hotel Ambassador. She recalled how, in 1945, a busty nineteen-year-old brown-haired girl Norma Jean Dougherty came to her office, recommended by an army photographer from *Yank Magazine*. She had a wholesome, natural air, a lovely smile, and spoke in a girlish, breathless voice.

Mrs. Snively took her on as a client, had her bleach her hair blonde, gave her lessons in modeling, and then made a screen test. She explained that Norma Jean later became Marilyn Monroe and she was glad to sell us the screen test for use in our film.

I asked Mrs. Snively if she knew where there were any other Marilyn movie films. She couldn't suggest any, but she knew of a photographer who had about a hundred photos of her he never sold. His name was Andre De Dienes, but he was a recluse and hard to find.

Luckily a Las Vegas friend asked around and located De Dienes. He called the photographer who reluctantly agreed to see me and Art Lieberman.

De Dienes, a fifty-year-old man of Hungarian birth, was surly as we met him in his home-studio on Sunset Plaza Drive, above the Strip in West Hollywood. He protested that he wanted nothing to do with anything about Marilyn because none of the obituaries mentioned him or the contributions he made to her career.

But despite his hostility, he could not resist telling us about his first meeting with Marilyn in 1945. He had asked Mrs. Snively to send him the girl-next-door-type-model for an Easter layout for a family magazine. But when he saw Norma Jean in that tight sweater, he frankly told her that she was a natural for glamour or even nude photographs. She refused to talk about nudity, but changed into a form-fitting bathing suit which revealed a phenomenal figure.

De Dienes had a commitment from *U.S. Camera* for a series of bathing suit pictures at scenic locations such as Death Valley, redwood forests, and beaches. He informed her that this would mean traveling with him, but she had no objections. She said she was divorced, so she was on her own.

She later moved in with De Dienes, and he launched her on a career whereby her fantastic torso graced the cover of dozens of girlie magazines.

In August 1946, one of them on the cover of *Laff Magazine* caught the attentive eye of Howard Hughes, then recuperating in a hospital from a plane crash. He ordered his local talent scout to track down the girl. Fortunately she had used the pseudonym of Jean Norman and Hughes's man couldn't locate her. He went to Mrs. Snively who pretended that Jean Norman was one of those fly-by-night models who had just been in town briefly.

Then she called movie agent Helen Ainsworth and told her, "I've got a little blonde that Howard Hughes is hot for."

Mrs. Ainsworth took Norma Jean to Ben Lyon, casting director of 20th Century Fox who immediately made a screen test of the voluptuous model. The next day while running off his dailies, Daryl Zanuck saw the test and demanded to know who ordered it. When Lyon explained that he did, because of the Howard Hughes interest, Zanuck reflected. Hughes was the man who had discovered Jean Harlow. Maybe this girl would be the blonde bombshell of the forties. He signed her to a one-year stock contract at $125 a week, and Lyons changed her name to Marilyn Monroe.

Part of her dramatic training included study at the Actors Lab. De Dienes showed up with photos of Marilyn in some of her acting exercises. When asked to portray death, she put a black shawl over her head.

He also showed us a series of photos indicating how she transformed her once pretty face into one of extraordinary sensual beauty through makeup and proper hairdressing.

However, Zanuck thought she lacked acting talent and at the end of a year her contract was not renewed.

Ironically, in 1950, her success in a bit role in *The Asphalt Jungle* led to her return to Fox in *All About Eve*, and a new contract which propelled her to fame and fortune.

After seeing the hundred or so photos De Dienes had taken of the early Marilyn Monroe, Lieberman and I knew we had something special and intimate, something that the other documentaries might lack. But De Dienes refused to sell.

I argued that he was like the dog in the manger. He could hold on to the photographs and die, and the world would never know about them. But if he let us use them, then he would be sharing his art and Marilyn's developing beauty with the rest of the world.

Finally, he softened and agreed to make a deal for cash and a screen credit also.

We thought we had what we needed for a solid show special. We were able to accumulate sufficient footage from newsreel companies to complete the needed twenty-three minutes.

We were able to obtain footage of her funeral in Westwood. By now, the medical examiner's office had decreed that her death was caused by probable suicide.

Then we heard of an interview she had done with Edward R. Murrow for CBS on his famous "Person to Person" program. That was just the something extra to give the show more life. But would CBS sell film to a small syndicated company?

Lieberman doubted but I had an ace in the hole. The year previous I had met Murrow in Hollywood. Then head of the USIA in the Kennedy administration, he was seeking films about lives of blacks in America. I told him about *The Rafer Johnson Story* which I had written and Mike Wallace narrated.

Murrow was so pleased with the film that he bought it for showing in Africa and sent Rafer along on a personal appearance tour.

Murrow's associates at CBS granted us the rights, and having him in our film interviewing Marilyn added the right touch of class.

As the final cut was assembled and I was preparing the narration to accompany it, Seymour Reed suggested that I not mention the word "suicide." The medical examiner's office had decreed her death to be "probable suicide."

Reed reminded me that the leading advertisers on television were pharmaceutical companies. They might not favor a show in which the heroine dies from taking an overdose of their industry's products.

Another controversial item was the supposed affair between Marilyn and then President John F. Kennedy.

This was 1962. The president was still alive, extremely popular and very much married. We did not want to sink to tabloid journalism. So that too was bypassed.

By January 1963 the film was ready to be marketed. Seymour Reed had hoped to sell it in syndication. But such was the interest in the subject matter and the approval of our low-keyed portrait that the American Broadcasting Company bought it for two network runs. Critics hailed the work as poignant, dignified, and moving. Simultaneously overseas sales resulted in Japan, Great Britain, and Germany. All of that followed by syndicated sales throughout the world.

Mike Wallace's career started to skyrocket after the success of the film and today he remains the star of television's top rated *"Sixty Minutes."*

Later that year Kennedy was assassinated. Reed again was on the ball. He hired Art Lieberman to produce and was signed to help write and produce. We had no trouble persuading Cliff Robertson to narrate. He had just starred in *PT109*, playing the part of Kennedy as a naval officer and felt honored to be asked to be in the film.

My friend Jim Bishop, who had written a book about Kennedy in the White House, joined our show to recall anecdotes of his experiences living in the White House with the Kennedys.

Again we were faced with a dilemma. Should the Marilyn Monroe–JFK romance be mentioned. We elected to omit and leave it to future scandalmongers.

Today both the Marilyn Monroe film and JFK biography are on cassette and selling in video stores. Over the years I have received royalty checks on the sales of reruns and cassettes. And what is fascinating in terms of ratio, MM has outsold JFK, by seven to one.

But perhaps with the success of Oliver Stone's controversial *JFK* the odds may change.

Nevertheless, it does seem weird that fate ordained that I should be the film biographer of both MM and JFK. But in an even greater story twist, in 1962, a few weeks after her death, the U.S. Navy produced a short film called *An Answer*.

Kennedy starred in the film, and I was called upon to write the narration for the show which played nationally in movie theaters.

I received letters of appreciation from the Secretary of the Navy and the president's White House Naval Aide. But I never heard from Kennedy, because at the time, he was too busy playing brinkmanship with a Russian named Khrushchev.

CONFESSIONS OF
AN EAST-WEST FILMMAKER

Ian Mutsu
International Motion Picture Company
Tokyo

East is East and West is West, and never the twain shall meet, or so thought Rudyard Kipling. But in recent times East and West have come closer together, and as the days go by they are learning more about each other thanks to television on home screens. As channels multiply and become international, the opportunities for documentary filmmakers are bound to grow.

The Japanese public first came to learn about America and formed opinions about the people of the USA through films during the era of the first World War, the days of the good old silent black and white movies. Stars like Douglas Fairbanks, Mary Pickford, Harold Lloyd, William S. Hart, and Charlie Chaplin quickly became targets of Japanese admiration. Of all foreign countries, the U.S.A. enjoyed the greatest amount of friendly feeling and admiration because of its films. So much of what one succeeds in absorbing is visual. Even today at my advanced age I can vividly recall some of the scenes in movies I went to see in my middle school days.

These positive feelings continued until the mid -1930s when the military had tightened their grip on the nation enough to begin a ban on everything smelling of American culture. Gone were the movies and the accompanying newsreels which had been valuable sources of information on the world outside for the Japanese.

During the hostilities in China in the 1930s, it became compulsory for Japanese movie houses to show short "cultural films," most of which were propaganda designed to stir up patriotic support for aggression on the continent, initially termed the "China Incident." If documentary filmmaking's first aim is to report the truth, there was practically no soil in Japan in those days for any growth of dedication or talent in this area. Today the soil is of better quality.

I believe that my mixed blood launched me on my life's work of reporting what goes on in Japan to the outside world, first with the typewriter, then with the still and moving picture cameras. I was born in London in 1907 after a prolonged and heavily opposed courtship between my English mother (an accomplished writer and musician) and Japanese father (son and heir to the eminent statesman, Mutsu Munemitsu, whose statue continues to adorn the entrance to the Ministry of Foreign Affairs in Tokyo).

My boyhood coincided with the days when every Japanese from kindergarten to university was indoctrinated in the myth that Japan was the greatest country in the world, the emperor was divine and ruled over a race chosen to conquer Asia. My father employed private tutors so that, I now assume, I could avoid this indoctrination. Later, I was exempted from conscription in the army because of my foreign size and looks. This was a huge stroke of luck for me, and probably one of the main reasons that I am, at nearly ninety, still here today, pen in hand.

In 1930 I returned to Japan from studying English literature and music in Birmingham, England, and started working as a journalist. My first job was with the *Japan Advertiser*, an American newspaper published in Tokyo with a high standard but low circulation. Concurrently I served as Tokyo correspondent for the *London Daily Express*. My next step was to move to Japan's national news agency, Domei, building up and heading their overseas news desk, eventually employing about sixty people to send news reports in Morse radio telegraph to Domei bureaus around the world. These reports were then sold to the local press.

One morning I came to work early and learned of Pearl Harbor: war, incredibly, between the countries of my parents. I had no previous knowledge of such a possibility. Not long thereafter I quit my job and spent the remainder of the war at my family's summer cottage in Karuizawa, a small town in the mountains about ninety miles from Tokyo. There, at noon on August 15, 1945, 1 heard the emperor's voice for the first time, coming weakly through the radio speaker to announce that the hostilities had come to an end. The announcement, in my opinion, was far too late.

Back in Tokyo I was offered and immediately accepted a new job as newswriter for the United Press (now UPI), accredited to the headquarters of the Allied Forces. Imagine: a Jeep and a PX card; freedom to write and transmit my reports on the UP transmission network worldwide; weekly pay in U.S. dollars, plus an "overseas allowance" in Japanese money. Tokyo was largely a wasteland, but this was one of the happiest periods of my life. It also introduced me to the opportunities of documentary filmmaking.

At Tokyo's Foreign Correspondents Club, at which I am a life member, there were frequent film showings, and watching them—especially the World War II newsreels—led to my rather rash jump from the typewriter to the camera. I wrote the script of my first documentary, a compilation of newsreel footage to run a little over one hour. I sought out the technical expertise of Gene Zenier, a Warner Brother news cameraman, and bought the footage from my prewar friend Aeral Varges of MGM News of the Day. The film we produced, *Japan Awake*, was a message to the Japanese to acknowledge that they had been misled by the military into thinking that Japan was invincible. The production was sold to Toho Motion Picture Company, distributed nationwide, and was a financial success.

The success of *Japan Awake* was satisfying and misleading at the same time. It was gratifying to be able to put across the truth to the Japanese, but I was mistaken that documentary films could make me rich. To this day—after participation in over a thousand films—I've yet to come across a filmmaker that has made his millions through documentaries!

Nonetheless, *Japan Awake* led to my production of half a dozen more documentary films for the Japanese to view and digest. I quit United Press and became a cameraman for the U.S. newsreel pool, which took on film coverage of occupied Japan with MGM News of the Day at its core and also including Paramount, 20th Century Fox, Universal International News, and March of Time. It was lots of fun running up and down Japan photographing the emperor on his tours to meet and pacify the people. The 35mm black and white film that I was employed to shoot with Japanese cameramen I had hired was immediately flown to New York, where it was processed at Hearst Metrotone News and then distributed to pool members for showing at film theaters worldwide. Quantitatively, the moving picture news from Japan must have been relatively small, but the audience size must have been tremendous, and the work was therefore worth the effort.

However, the newsreel was soon to step aside and give way to home-based television news.

In 1952, I set up IMPC (International Motion Picture Company) in order to produce documentary films for overseas distribution. One morning, early in IMPC history, the phone rang in my bedroom. It was Kyodo News Agency. War had broken out in Korea. I rushed over, begging a ride in a small U.S. Army plane. I had with me a heavy model Eyemo camera, tons of film, and, in my inexperience and ignorance, a tripod. The first thing I did after landing in the battlefield was to throw away the tripod. Not too long after that I decided to withdraw myself, as it seemed that the hostilities would be terribly prolonged. The Japanese, after all, had earlier spent one and a half years bogged down in fighting on the Asian continent. What was I doing getting shot at while I had my own company to run?

Still, there was no U.S. news film bureau in Korea, so I organized the war coverage

Ian Mutsu with some of his documentary films on Japan.

from Tokyo, working with Japanese, Korean, Chinese, and American news cameramen whose film coverage was sent to my office via military transport, then transshipped to New York by commercial airlines. There was enormous demand for coverage and much work. Over time I found the American cameramen the best, and the Japanese the worst. At that time, they were far too timid.

The war in Korea injected new blood into Japanese industry, and this increased the opportunities for IMPC to find corporate sponsorship for documentaries on Japanese themes for overseas consumption. IMPC has always held to two guidelines: first, present a theme that is of interest to the market or to a specific segment of the market; second, be honest. Honesty always wins friends. Even the so-called PR films sponsored by government agencies aiming to improve international relations should present the truth and appeal for understanding, since trying to fox the audience is more likely to generate hostility than friendship.

One of IMPC's successful documentary series in the early days was *Meet the Watanabes*, a short film depicting daily life in a typical Japanese family. It was a visit to the little grandson's birthday party. I wrote the script almost overnight, and the proposal was swiftly approved by the Foreign Ministry. The film was shot on 16mm Kodachrome (which in those days could only be produced in the United States) at the Shin Toho Studios using actors and a name cinematographer. Yet it was not fiction. *Meet the Watanabes* had a successful run via Modern Talking Picture Services and led to half a dozen other films in the Japanese Family series.

Not everything IMPC has done has been directed toward bringing the East to the West. We gained valuable experience when given the task of versioning in Japanese many—I believe about thirty—masterpieces from the National Film

Board of Canada. These were wisely put into the hands of Japanese producers for Japanese voicing so that the pictures would gain maximum impact when shown in Japan. This was a very difficult task, since we could not alter the visuals. A straight translation of the voice track can often ruin a picture. We had to fit in narration that would be just right for local audiences.

The problems for producers interested in making documentary films in Japan for the overseas market today remain the same as the problems that hindered those of us similarly inclined forty years ago. The difficulty of gaining financial support is of course the first hurdle. Almost never is it possible to secure a grant for research and preliminary study of distribution plausibility. Very often, when the underwriter is a corporation, the producer must participate in what is sarcastically termed a "scenario contest." He sits at a table, along with another dozen producers aiming to win the business, listening to the client's desires and expectations. Then each producer must submit almost a shooting script for no payment. The winning script is not necessarily the best one, especially when the documentary is designed for international communication. Too many Japanese still tend to think that the planet is inhabited by only two types of people—Japanese and gaijin, or outsiders of all colors and creeds. This is no position from which to analyze the foreign market. In addition, too many Japan-made documentaries intended for the West are conceived by Japanese, written in Japanese, shot by Japanese, and then cut to a Japanese voice text which has been approved by the client who is paying. At the last minute a translator is called in to write the copy for the narration. This is an unfortunate system. (Our IMPC system endeavors to have staff writers prepare the English narration concurrently with the editing, so that a perfect balance can be achieved—with client approval—between video and audio.)

Fortunately, there have been exceptions (too few) to this state of affairs.

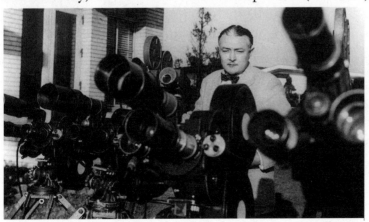

Ian Mutsu with Elmo cameras used to shoot news and documentaries in Japan.

Very talented bilingual American writer-producers (also too few) have been commissioned to do documentaries on Japanese themes for audiences in the U.S.A. and elsewhere, and this is obviously the way to go for future documentaries of this kind. The foreign producer needs to shoot in Japan with the help of a competent, bilingual Japanese assistant who knows the field, where to go, what to shoot, and how to cut corners.

The central theme of any documentary, and the methods for developing this theme, should come from the person who understands the market. Adding such a person to a team initially requires more money but, in the end, saves money. The Japanese client inclined to underwrite a documentary for the overseas market must be convinced that employment of an overseas writer-director is no luxury. Making a documentary that will languish on the screen and perish in the can is a sure way to throw away money.

Some time ago IMPC had an interesting experience working with a producer–director from the West on a film on a particularly Eastern theme. The film was to be about haiku, the short, seventeen-syllable poetry style widely practiced in Japan. My good friend Seaton Findlay was brought over to direct. During his three-week stay, some members of the Japanese crew criticized him saying they thought he was often missing things, shooting in the wrong direction, getting the story wrong. Although Seaton spoke no Japanese and was not a haiku poet, the excellent thirty-minute film, postproduced in Ottawa, won a gold prize in Japan.

I have encouraged IMPC over the years to seek financial support for our collaboration with foreign television teams coming to Japan. Although this is not as rewarding as producing your own film from script to screen, it is one of the best and easiest ways to find audiences in the West for documentaries shot in the East. Since 1979 IMPC has worked in the field assisting more than 200 TV teams from 78 countries.

Thanks to the trials and tribulations of making documentaries I am now covered with snow. In my final days, as television channels increase in number and quality, I am hoping that someone will come along to take over the helm and sail ahead into a new era in which opportunities for East-West documentaries are bound to grow.

Ian Mutsu, Tokyo 1996

Yonosuke Ian Mutsu

Born in London, England, on January 14, 1907. Japanese father and English mother who by marriage became Countess Iso Mutsu. Early schooling in Japan. The University of Birmingham and the Midland Institute of Music. Since 1931 newswriter in Japan with the American–owned *Japan Advertiser*, the *Daily Express* of London, Domei News Agency and, after Japan's defeat in WWII, Tokyo Bureau of the UPI.

After producing half a dozen documentaries, turned from the typewriter to the camera. Served as Tokyo Bureau manager to further U.S. newsreel pool, which, with MGM News at its core, distributed new film to theaters worldwide. In 1952 incorporated International Motion Picture Company in Tokyo, specializing in corporate-sponsored documentaries for audiences abroad. IMPC also works extensively with television crews filming documentaries in Japan. Ian is still owner and president of IMPC which so far has been involved in over a thousand documentaries.

ON LEARNING TO MAKE FILMS
(THE MIDWIFE'S TALE)

BY MICHAEL RABIGER

When I learned I had an *accoucheur* among my nineteenth century ancestors, I had to look the word up. Great-great-grandfather McCaul was, it turned out, a male midwife who migrated from Dublin to a poor part of London around the time of the great famine. He must often have wondered, as he supervised the mess and pain of childbirth, what future awaited this particular infant in a world where supply conspicuously outstripped demand.

I too am a migrant, do similar work, and have similar thoughts—but while delivering young filmmakers of their creations rather than babies of the urban poor. I too think about supply and demand, and ponder what makes so many young people throw themselves like moths at the flame of film's creative process. It seems that those who aspire to direct, whether fiction or documentary, do so partly to acquire a coveted form of influence, but more often they do so because telling stories, even more than consuming them, makes a person complete.

For most of this century people learned how to make films through apprenticeship, as I did. Schooling is recent and—compared with the teaching of literature, art, or theater—hardly more evolved than medicine was in my ancestor's day. Learning to direct is particularly difficult, and since virtually all film students want to become feature film writer/directors, you would expect film schools to concentrate on issues of control and authorship. But few go beyond reflecting the priorities and conditions of the film industry, which never set out to educate anybody.

My own learning path—as editor, documentary director, then fiction and documentary film teacher—seems worth recounting because I think it illustrates the obstructions and contradictions one encounters, no matter what route you take. As a teenager four decades ago, I never actually planned to go into the film business. Indeed, fortified with British fatalism, I had made no plans whatsoever. My school career had been undistinguished and, since I couldn't hack math or Latin, offered no hope of joining the 6 percent who made it into university. My father, a film makeup man, heard that his studios were taking in some apprentices, and suggested I apply either for the camera department or the cutting rooms. So at seventeen I entered Pinewood Studios near London as a trainee assistant editor. I remember being welcomed into the cutting room, looking around at the machinery and people crammed into the tiny space, and thinking, "I'll have this down in a year." In fact my learning curve took ten times longer, not only because of my profound immaturity but also because the film industry was, and still is, not a good place to learn.

Pinewood Studios in 1956 was the size of a small town and cranked out twenty features a year. Comprising the usual agglomeration of stages, departments, car parks, sheds, lots, and admin buildings, it had an awesomely powerful "front office," and no less than three dining places ranged by price and class. Britain then was unapologetically feudal, and the Rank Organization studios echoed this even in name.

I had been there only once previously—as a nine-year-old on a day visit with my dad. Magically different worlds unfolded behind each thickly padded stage door. On the set I obediently held my breath while Jean Simmons and Stewart Granger played and replayed a scene for *Blue Lagoon*. It involved dunking a borrowed infant in an elaborately fabricated rock pool. Afterwards we visited the sound recordist, sequestered with his huge photographic sound camera in a darkened truck. He let me wear his headphones.

Now eight years later, I was working there. A week after arrival they had me synching rushes for a features unit, scared shitless by the responsibility. The pressure on us five or six apprentices to each assemble one to two thousand feet of rushes in a couple of hours was so relentless that one dared not listen to each take's sound track. You eyeballed the clapper in the optical track (magnetic sound had yet to arrive), synched it rapidly to picture, spliced it on treadle cement splicers and rushed your rushes up flights of concrete stairs to the projection box. Your handiwork then appeared on a huge screen for upward of forty important people during their lunch hour. There was ample opportunity to make huge public mistakes, since the entire unit—director, crew, stars—would guffaw if you mistakenly synched the clapperboard to somebody dropping a hammer. If a splice came apart in the projector, it unleashed panic in the projection box, followed by an agonizing wait in the dark while the projectionists reloaded.

Whether we screened rushes or an assembly of the whole epic, every viewing was a stomach-churning cliff-hanger. Not just my piffling reputation was at stake, but those of the first assistant and the editor too. When reputation is everything, one learns not to take chances. There was in any case little time or will for instruction beyond the demanded tasks. When knowledge is earning power, there is no incentive to give anything away, so the knowledgeable conceal what they know, often by mystifying it. Even had there been time for instruction, we often worked sixty to eighty hours a week, striving to stay on our feet while feeling nearly brain-dead.

It took three years and six whole feature films before I more or less understood a film's life cycle. So many. people, so many specialties, so many processes like tributaries merging into the river of manufacture. Like every young person, I secretly believed I would one day direct but never even knew where ideas and form were planned. It was a factory, and factory workers don't need to concern themselves with the product's design. I'm not complaining; I loved being in a place where a whole circus might camp in the car park. It was exciting to eat your lunch within sight of famous actors, or surrounded by extras kited out as Bedouins, or with the same people a week later dressed as French revolutionaries. On the back lot one could marvel at a sizeable chunk of the Bastille, all ready for storming, or one side of the Titanic listing to starboard in two feet of murky water. Once my favorite parking spot was already taken by a phenomenal elephant turd. Life was never boring.

Learning was also crimped by a rigidly unionized labor system which meant one had to call an electrician to even change a light bulb (imagine the jokes). There was no hope of experimentally moving out of editing to another craft track. Because every echelon jealously guarded its turf and mystiques, you had to assimilate knowledge by stealth if you were at all ambitious.

I did, however, learn a lot about actors from the rushes and from seeing how an editor could shape quite thin and inconsistent work into a decently convincing performance. I worked on films with respected actors like Dirk Bogarde and Rod Steiger, and saw much good character work from the repertory actors of the day. For variety I served on a crummy Jayne Mansfield comedy (*The Sheriff of Fractured Jaw*) and can truthfully claim to have directed a tired and dowdy-looking Marilyn Monroe while she was making *The Prince and the Showgirl*—to the cutting room toilets.

I saw vast amounts of staging, acting, and directing—some good, some of it hack work. I assimilated approaches to dramatic criticism by attending discussions with the likes of Sidney Bachman, Tony Richardson, and the legendary Raoul Walsh, who predated the film industry itself, and began directing in 1915. During a discussion about how long a man who is shot takes to fall down, Walsh mesmerized us by recounting how a man he had seen shot in a western bar seems to stand for an eternity ("with about an inch of brains sticking out of the hole in his head") before crumpling to the floor. Discussions were heatedly partisan, and often went much deeper than might be expected from the undistinguished films we were making.

But the most profound experience was simply staying with the same movie for its six or more months of postproduction. One saw the same material times without number as it evolved, beginning with the freshness of a first rushes' viewing, and going from familiarity to overfamiliarity, then from overfamiliarity to screaming tedium and inner revolt. The film became an enclosing world that we inhabited night and day. The dialogue became so familiar that one could even repeat some of it backwards. One character who yelled "Molly!" would seem to answer himself by calling back "Yeah?" when the Moviola went in reverse.

Beyond this colonization of the mind came, rather astonishingly, an indefinable oasis of largeness and acquiescence. Expecting to go insane, one instead discovered new facets and connections in the story, new aspects to characters, and new depths of ungreased emotion. This was especially true when we layered in sound effects and music. Postproduction turned out to be an object lesson in Zen acceptance, demonstrating what I later found true for other art forms—that the creative process is a labyrinth in which only the imprisoned can grow.

After three years, I was forced to leave for "national service" in the military. There I packed parachutes for the Royal Air Farce (as we called it). Returning two years later I found the film industry in decline. The American money on which it had subsisted throughout the 1950s and early 1960s had migrated to less regulated pastures in Spain, Italy, and Yugoslavia. I began working with Bill Lewthwaite, who in later life became chief editing teacher at the London International Film School. A generous friend and an excellent teacher, he encouraged me to covertly assemble the puerile comedy we were working on. I was horrified one day when the producer called up to say that he and the director would see the film tomorrow. When I breathlessly reported this to Bill, all he said was, "I'll be there. It'll all go fine." Convinced we would both be fired, I sat numbly through the showing, registering every body movement and intake of breath by the higher-ups. When the lights came on, they had requests and criticisms but not the cries of scandalized disbelief I had anticipated. I had survived! This experience—of opportunity followed by an excruciating ordeal—is really the paradigm for each advancement.

That Christmas I strayed temporarily (as I thought) into television. Soon I was editing full time. It was nonfiction material—first for children's television, then current affairs for German TV, then documentaries for Granada TV in Manchester and the

BBC in London. I was shaken at the outset to discover that, even after years of assisting and assembly-editing, I still had almost everything to learn. Having creative control over a film for kids about the training of a seeing-eye dog was novel, heady, and very threatening. Day by day I had to reinvent film language for myself, to find my own way toward creating a believable stream of cinematic consciousness. Each problem cut or difficult sequence became a test bed for my ideas about perception.

Again, it was the prolonged and agonizing immersion to the humdrum that goaded me into recognizing how film language, for example, was predicated on the way one reacted inwardly to a stream of reality in everyday life, and how so many anomalies and contradictions lie at the heart of representing reality. Unavoidably, documentary used what I had previously assumed were fictional techniques. By successfully orchestrating reality materials, even on a very modest scale, I could make myself (and anyone else present) experience the same surge of emotions at every viewing. Though it was relatively easy to impart factual information in an orderly and logical way, making one's audience feel something was more difficult and more satisfying.

Now, thirty years later, it's hard to be sure if I knew that I was working to trigger processes of emotional recognition, but somewhere along the line I must have realized that an audience hardly discriminates between fiction or "reality" films except in the early moments of viewing when it decides how to suspend disbelief. Ultimately we compare screen truth with what we know viscerally from life, no matter whether real people or actors depict it. And when we feel changed by what we see, it is always because of strong feelings rather than new information. Film works best when it acts on the emotions, not just the intellect.

My break as a documentary director came without warning. Again I had to make things up as I went along, because my only knowledge of documentaries came from my five years of editing them. This ignorance of the traditions that nurtured us—both in fiction and documentary—was near universal among those in the film industry, for there were few gurus, and no film schools. Of course I tried reading Pudovkin and Reisz on editing, and Kracauer on film theory, but they were so removed from my pragmatic, craft-oriented world that it felt as though I were reading Urdu.

My first editing had been seat-of-the-pants, and my first directing was more so. Several of us new directors worked eagerly under our quiet and empathic producer Brian Lewis. I, of course, complicated matters for myself by directing my first film in Paris with a mixed crew who couldn't speak each others' languages. Directing a cameraman years older than myself, jealous because he wasn't the director, was another searing rite of passage. I knew what I needed, but not how to get it. Other directors with less craft foundation fared less well and in time disappeared.

During the next five years I planned and directed over twenty biographical, political, oral history, and arts documentaries, and loved every moment of it. We worked in a small earth manner, doing all our own preproduction with only one or two staff. Once the crew arrived, one shot as fast as one could. There was no time to seek guidance even when I grasped the nature of a particular problem. I had to make up methods where none seemed to exist, and learn by osmosis from teammates. We had no critical language for what we were doing, so problem solving was always through specifics using everyday language.

Each film had a similar trajectory: research for two or three weeks (and once as little as three days); form a shooting plan; and try to figure out my authorial intentions. Unconsciously I was casting a story, as though still at Pinewood, with each protagonist having partly known, partly unknown potential. My task was to reveal each character, to cover the story, and to catalyze any new developments as the time, resources, and ethical or formal limitations that I had set myself permitted.

Invariably I was underwhelmed during shooting and by the rushes. Certain I had failed, and sure I would never again direct, I would set to work with an editor to rescue something, anything from the ashes. Usually I uncovered aspects in the rushes that I had missed while shooting, so a slightly better film would emerge in the four to six weeks allowed. Then, after the film was transmitted, I would be astonished to hear from friends, or see in reviews, that some of my lost objectives were being named as something seen or felt. Like automatic writing, the process was always out of control and always delivered. Even more, it could covertly deliver meanings I was certain I'd failed to convey. How could this happen?

By the early 1970s the BBC was running out of money and cutting loose its freelancers—especially those, it seems, whose leftish sympathies were antagonizing conservative newspapers at a time of rightward national drift. Finding I was completely disposable, I was depressed and for the first time standing on an unemployment line.

My next job, intended to rescue my ruined finances and to last only a year, was at an upstart school bravely calling itself Columbia College Chicago. Three of us ex-industry types, hired to resuscitate a film department that had imploded, found ourselves in charge of some angry students, a few clockwork cameras on wobbly tripods, and several sheets of smudgily mimeographed instructions for an editing exercise. Having once taught 8mm filmmaking in a London night college, I took on the tech education. And so we began.

As always, the beginning was blind and fumbling, but instinct told me to teach in the way that I myself had learned—through setting hands-on work. I soon found that my students' expectations were unreal and their technical and cultural preparation inadequate. Then it dawned on me that maybe I, rather than they, was out of step. Perhaps I had made a much longer journey of discovery during the previous sixteen years than I'd known, and teaching it was a much larger job than I'd imagined.

For years to come, my quest and that of my cofounders Chap Freeman and Tony Loeb was simply for technical adequacy. I had thought our students' difficulties came from our being underequipped, but gradually a complex of educational and cultural impediments took shape. Writing, acting, and directing did not even become relevant until students could handle the basics of camera, exposure, sound, and editing. They did not, and could not, learn as I had learned because their lives and culture were different. I came from a handicraft-oriented family, and had learned everything from within the imperatives of actual production. They were paying to be taught, and like most young people in that more secure era, went about their work in the detached, speculative, and laid-back manner of...well, *students*. Though I wanted to impart all I knew, they slithered instinctively away from film's tedium, rigor, and drudgery. Why, they must have wondered, was I so earnest? It wasn't cool.

One day, putting together a short account of my life for a degree program, I stumbled on how truly insensible I had been. Writing that my films had no discernible common denominator, I was shocked to intuit that something entirely different was true. I broke out in goose bumps realizing that every film I had ever made dealt with the same theme, that of captivity and its corollary, finding ways to break out.

Why? As a child I had been the only middle class boy in a rural blue–collar village and had felt completely different from everyone else. But now, even as I set these words down, I see this theme even more deeply embedded. Having been a child in wartime when England was in a state of siege, my films would be likely to refract the anxieties about invasion and defeat that, invisible and unspoken, must have preoccupied the adults around me. Now, how on earth could I have made over twenty films without appreciating this? And further, wouldn't I have been a more focused and effective filmmaker if someone had helped me find the source of my own drives?

Twenty-five years have elapsed since I arrived at Columbia. With 1,400 undergraduate and graduate film students, we must now be one of the biggest film schools anywhere. As we grew, so my part in the operation could narrow down to teaching just my own professional specialties—editing, and making documentaries. Through the school's generosity I was able to start our Documentary Center in 1989. Around 1990 I started teaching workshops and seminars in other countries. There I discovered that other film teachers were also singlehandedly inventing the art of teaching film. There was (and still is) almost no teaching literature. Production texts and film theory are in abundance, though by some quirk the latter is always written by historians, philosophers, linguists, semioticians—everybody except filmmakers. Writing by experienced filmmakers is often useless to production students because it is the "war stories" of anecdote rather than the prescriptive help they need. So, after buying my first computer in the 1980s, I set out to fill a void by writing about the conceptual work of the director, aiming at the directness and clarity of Kris Malkiewicz's *Cinematography*. Between 1984 and 1989 I wrote the first editions of *Directing the Documentary* and its fiction counterpart *Directing: Film Techniques and Aesthetics*. Both are now in third editions and are widely used. When users say they like the writing, it is probably because I try to write not for "students" but for friends or colleagues learning the way I learned—by doing, by reinventing the product or process oneself.

And so I come full circle to revisit the boy lost in the coils of the factory process at Pinewood. It probably never occurred to him to wonder who controlled the process, or who gave a film its identity. We knew our films lacked distinction, but when the French New Wave burst on the scene, it was painfully obvious that their semi-improvised films, lacking big budgets and technical polish, had an authorial reach and lyricism that ours entirely lacked. Maybe "industry" films need stars because their oversize personalities compensate for the authorial voice that gets lost (or more accurately, never found) in the assembly line process.

From documentaries I grasped how elemental and subjective film language really is. As an editor, you are inside somebody's mind looking out through their eyes and hearing through their ears. When camera and sound work arrives through an integrated, questing intelligence, you merge into the pulse of reactions, feelings, and an authentic quest. Very little camera and directing work has this individuality, but I saw that editing could often make film work come alive by organizing it into what an audience would accept as a lively, authentic, and engaged stream of consciousness.

Whose consciousness, though? Mine? Well, partly. The director's or cameraman's? Well, yes, again partly. Really the film's stream of consciousness belonged to all of us and none of us. Editing made it universal so anyone could enter. And here's the bombshell which has a truly spiritual significance: Film is only possible unless we all have similar perceptual and emotional processes. We differ but only in temperament and history, not in how we interpret reality, or cinema could never be the universal culture it is. Maybe cinema is popular because its very existence affirms what we share, and what we can cocreate.

Directing for the BBC was a wonderful exercise in improvisation, but I was often overwhelmed and running on auto pilot. Keeping to a tight schedule left no time to contemplate what I was really doing. Too often this was constructing word-driven documentaries. I can make excuses: with maybe only four weeks to research and set up a forty-minute film on the Spanish Civil War, I had to devise schedules and methods that delivered results. But in so doing, I lost sight of what I learned in the cutting rooms. So I was seldom in control of the film's point of view when directing because I lacked experience of using a camera. I still only knew how to create point of view in the cutting room. Consumed by the helter-skelter acquisition of materials, I was repeating the manufacturing process used in features.

While teaching I became aware of what, in the learn-as-you-earn industry system, was so internalized that one never puts it into words. Teaching became *learning* in film school, as I unpacked and repacked my filmmaker's baggage, and watched over the filmmaking process from the contemplative and analytical vantage of an observer. In the 1980s when my school started a graduate track, we began to teach authorship itself, first in fiction and then because the students wanted it, in documentary. What had worked intermittently with the more mature undergrads could now be applied purposefully to a handpicked population.

To my mind the preeminent part of the film educator's job is to uncover what passion and quest the student brings, then to connect this with knowledge, experience, and influences that that student will speak authentically through the screen. This ideal often breaks down, either because schools have too many students doing too many things, or because faculty are mercilessly overworked. Then there's the reality that new students and older ones remain stratified, and pass around more rumor than useful knowledge. By definition, successful students leave, so proficiency is capped off at a certain level. Most often there simply isn't time or focus—except in the more circumscribed world of documentary production—to properly teach the auteur directing for which virtually all students enlist.

From what I have seen, film schools tend to concentrate on the movie manufacturing process (which students love) and at best leave the individual to make a final project in which to incorporate everything he or she has learned. But unless the would-be director arrives in school with a ready-made artistic identity, or manages to somehow develop one in the fray, he or she will be too busy and too distracted to undertake the hazardous inward journey which alone leads to originality. Most, understandably enough, want to win acceptance by their group, but this is fatally removed from exploring one's buried need to tell particular stories, or from stubbornly trying to make sense of particular forces in the world. A work of art, said Zola, is a corner of nature seen through a temperament. But the frenetic working rhythms of film school or the film industry puts any awareness of this on hold, leaving the inner person untouched. When the time comes to independently produce the film that will define them to the outside world, many students so depend on the impetus of classwork that they are disabled. The years after graduation often bring withdrawal pains, disillusion, and underemployment. And this does nothing to assist the creative process either.

What should happen? The usual learning priorities of film history, theory, and production craft are good and necessary for training crew members, whose job it is to interpret ideas. But for would-be writers and directors, who must generate story ideas, too much looking outwards instead of inwards is a misuse of precious and limited time. Striking and original films always come from those branded by strong experience who find story corollaries for their driving preoccupations. Living by the dictates of the artistic process, such individuals play out, interrogate, reorder aspects of their chosen world in order to make sense of it. Outstanding documentaries, like their fiction counterparts, dramatize out aspects of the human predicament in order to scrutinize what is unjust, unusual, or unanswerable. For the rare young director already capable of working at this level of consciousness, all of life is grist for the mill.

However, most young people enter production classes driven by uncomplicated enthusiasm for movies. Happily submerged in productive and enjoyable activity, they merge with the school's Zeitgeist and learn how to be normal, which is to say, average. Unless the school seeks, as ours does, to raise consciousness by exploring the artistic process itself, even the most thoughtful and receptive can pass through film school finding no focused sense of purpose. In the film industry worker likewise, it is the individual's quest—the very heart of his one and only life—that normally goes untouched. This is serious, for the film industry hardly needs more competent operatives. What it desperately needs in all major positions is individuals of developed inner resources who can act provocatively on audiences.

These resources are inner and cannot be taught, but as they exist as potential in everyone, something can always be liberated. Film schools need to go beyond the one-size-fits-all approach and to develop conservatory methods like those in schools of painting, acting, and music where the most promising students are educated in an individualistic manner. Graduate school is supposed to do this, but unless the school can wrench itself away from tradition by stressing collaboration instead of competition, students tend to burn up their energy in deadly competition for perquisites and faculty patronage. Good film teaching develops the strong and supportive group atmosphere that, in any collaborative art, encourages the individual to flower. Like all artists, the film director or writer *must take possession of a lived, examined, accepted body of emotional experience* in order to know "what is" and to truly feel its significance. In this soil a director's sense of truth takes root; from this a sense of vision can emerge, even from a body of personal experience that otherwise seems wholly negative.

The journey toward awareness should not be as slow and wastefully haphazard as mine. Awareness can be awakened, guided, and accelerated through astute teaching, or (particularly among working professionals) it can be developed within committed work or support groups.

Ever the optimist, I dream that digital shooting and postproduction will speed and simplify learning by slashing expense and busywork. This should allow more time and space for self-development. First, however, we must acknowledge that most novice authorship, compared with its fiction counterparts, is sadly wanting. In documentary it's in better shape, but mainly, I think, because it's easier to reflect an existing reality than create one fictionally.

Even when one's goal is fiction and not documentary at all, using the improvisation and spontaneity of documentary is an invaluable aid to discovering one's screen "voice." The pull in the other direction—toward accommodating conventional wisdom or the industry dynamic—is powerful, but the documentary used as an antidote can be more so. Try going out with one or two friends, try using a camcorder to capture the beauty and transience of the actual. It will be a fascinating journey in its own right, and a solid foundation for reflecting life's truths via fiction. Real people and real actors—both in front of and behind the camera—have an infinity of depth, and learning step by step to respond to them, from the mind and from the depths of the heart, is the direction of true expressive power. It does not come from studying film, but from becoming fully oneself and making films which serve what vision already exists.

Thus, ultimately, we are responsible for midwifing our own humanity. We manage the birth of ourselves, over and over again, and in so doing aspire to the full clarity and largeness of which, as human beings, we are capable. If there be any road to originality, this is it.

A SEARCH FOR THE FEELING OF BEING THERE

RICHARD LEACOCK

When I was eleven years old and a pupil at an English boarding school something extraordinary was done; we were shown a film, a silent 35mm full length film from the Soviet Union, *Turk-Sib*, about the building of the Trans-Siberian Railway. I was riveted, astounded; here was what I had been looking for and it was simple. All I needed was a movie camera and I could do it myself.

I had been raised on my father's plantation in The Canary Islands. We grew bananas, tomatoes, we made cement pipes and pumped irrigation water. Of the more than 200 men and women that worked there, I think about three could read and write. They worked with oxen and camels. There were no schools where we lived so I had a wonderful time until it was decided that I should go to school in England: cold, dark, and little boys in short pants with chapped knees and chilblains... Eventually I got used to it and in a perverse kind of way, enjoyed it. But how to explain to my schoolmates, where I came from and what life in my Garden of Eden was like?

Turk-Sib was the answer. So three years later with the help of Polly and Noel from school, armed with our detailed scenario, a 16mm Victor camera and an elegant Thailhamer Tripod, we shot a fourteen-minute black and white silent film, *Canary Bananas*, a film I am proud of, that can still tell you all you need to know about growing bananas, but it fell far short of giving you the feeling of being there. It informed you but it didn't involve you.

In 1938 at the ripe old age of seventeen, 1 went as photographer–filmmaker to the Galápagos Islands as a member of David Lack's expedition to learn more about Darwin's finches. We lived on a "desert island," isolated, not even a radio. I spent most of my time with the Angermayer brothers who had listened to Hitler and fled; it was a bit like Robinson Crusoe; I loved it. I did what I was supposed to do and filmed the birds and just about everything else that moved, but the result gave you no feeling whatever of "being there."

By 1941 we were shooting sync sound. Features had been "talkies" for a decade but it was easier for them; they created their own controlled world in the safe confines of vast studios and here we were making a documentary on American folk music in the hills of Virginia and Tennessee. Madness! No electricity there. So a truckload of lead storage batteries and a motor converter from 110 volts DC to 110 volts 60 cycle AC, powering a 35mm optical film recorder and a 35mm film camera. You turned them on and adjusted the DC to get the frequency of the AC up to 60 cycles and when the sound camera and the picture camera stopped hunting you yelled "speed" and then the clap-sticks and the director, Geza Karpathy, murmured "relax" to the petrified musicians. And it was a good two weeks before you got to hear the playback! It worked but not much spontaneity with that rigmarole to contend with.

This was professional filmmaking, the leading edge. Documentary couldn't go on avoiding the issue by laying music and narration on silent pictures. We were going into the "real world" and systematically destroying the very thing that we were looking for. Why not make our films in studios like the big boys do? Don't be silly! It wasn't just the technology, it was the attitude of a professionalized industry aping the world of the fiction film—it still is.

Today, when we have available superb portable sensitive mini-digital cameras and sound equipment, the impact of filming or video-recording is just as ridiculous and even more so because it is utterly uncalled for. I have been filmed by various television crews and invariably the routine is just as disruptive as ever. Four or five large men come busting into our tiny apartment with tripods, camera, microphones, booms, and light-stands. It is politely suggested that you sit there, no a bit to the left, now turn your head, do you mind it we move the painting on the wall, it's distracting and we can see a reflection of the soundman...Can you give us a level? Just say anything..." And you start to say what you are to say and the soundman says, "Cut! I'm picking up the refrigerator, can someone unplug it...thanks, now just take it from the head again..." And perhaps they want a shot of you talking on the street so you are expected to walk "casual-like" with cameraman, soundman, and assistant walking backward in front of you. At last it is over!

In the early sixties I thought we had solved these problems by a set of working rules designed to make it possible for us to get as near as we could to observing our subjects with minimal impact. No lights, no tripod, no microphone boom or pole, never wear headphones (they make you look silly and/or remote), never more than two people, never ask anyone to do anything, and most especially never ask anyone to repeat an action or a line. Allow lots of time, don't shoot all the time, and if you miss something, forget it in the hope that something like it will happen again. Get to know your subject if possible. In order to generate some kind of mutual respect, if not friendship.

OK these are rules, not laws, and rules can be broken. This means no interviews; fine I'm sick of interviews, but when I filmed Louis Brooks in her very private apartment in Rochester, New York, it was an interview and that was that! Why not ask someone to repeat an action that you missed? it is not a question of morality but just try It. I was filming the editor of the Aberdeen, South Dakota, newspaper; while I was reloading my camera, his secretary ran in and told him that Senator McGovern was calling from Washington. It was wonderful so I loaded up and asked her to do it again. Weeks later, I was screening rushes in New York and Joyce Chopra and I and some friends saw it! Horrors! It was ridiculous, like some third-rate TV soap!

In general, when you are making a film you are in a situation where something you find significant is going on. Usually the people you are filming want to help you get what they think you want to get, often as a way of getting rid of you. And this can be fatal because they are then second-guessing you and can end up destroying the possibility of achieving your aim. I remember Bob Drew and I coming into the lawyer's office when we were making *The Chair*. He asked what he could do for us; we said, "nothing," put our equipment in a corner, and went out for coffee. A little later we came back in and he was back at work doing what had to be done, having decided that we were nuts. We kept our distance and started filming as he picked up his phone.

What am I looking for? I hope to be able to create sequences that when run together will present aspects of my perception of what took place in the presence of my camera. To capture spontaneity it must exist and everything you do is liable to destroy it—beware!

Filming is searching for and capturing the ingredients with which to make sequences. You are not going to get "the whole thing," you are lucky to get fragments, but they must be captured in such a way that you can edit. If there is dialogue you know that editing is more restricted and you must find ways to deal with this problem without recourse to that dreadful concept—the "cutaway." If music is involved the problems are even more complex.

The making of sequences is, for me, at the heart of filmmaking. I had always assumed that you just got the bits of an action and put it together and, bingo, you have a sequence. But there are all kinds of things that you may want to convey with a sequence, and it was not until I worked as cameraman on Robert Flaherty's *Louisiana Story* that I started to learn from him the complexity of this process. We were a tiny crew, most unprofessional. We shot, day after day, for fourteen months more often than not, just the three of us (Mr. and Mrs. Flaherty, she with a Leica, he and I often with two Arreflex 35mm cameras, recently liberated from Hitler's

Wehrmacht) and sometimes an assistant. We shot and shot. If something appealed to us—never mind that it wasn't in the script—film it. A beautiful cloud, swallows wheeling through the sky preparing to migrate, a water lily pad with a drop of water on it in perfect light, a spider completing the building of its web. Often the cameras in motion or panning and tilting, no rules except look, look through the camera lens, search.

The first time I ever met Mr. Flaherty was in 1936 just after I had completed the banana film. He was visiting his daughters, Franny and Monica, at our school. He had a 16mm camera on a tripod and he was filming blond Brenda McDermot brushing her hair to dry it in the sunlight. Fine, but he went on and on and on. I decided he must be mad. What on earth could be so complicated about a young woman brushing her hair? In Louisiana I began to learn. Only began. After that job I went back to work with "professionals" and learned that I had better behave myself or look for another job!

After long days of filming, often starting as early as six in the morning and on, with a long break to avoid the midday light, till twilight, then cleaning cameras, developing test strips, shipping film to the lab…to a well-earned, well-watered drink before bed, Flaherty would sometimes talk about making sequences. Mostly he talked about the making of *Moana*, how every sequence is a new and different problem. The use of different focal length lenses, the function of the close-up, not so much to reveal detail as to withhold information from the viewers, of the surround—or, as he put it "the camera is like a horse with blinders; it can only see what is in front if its nose"—and thus increase the visual tension that requires the viewers to search for the resolution they are experiencing. *Moana*, since this experience, has become his masterpiece for me, and the version that his daughter Monica has made with sound is superb.

The next step in my de-professionalization was when Roger Tilton invited me to shoot *Jazz Dance* in 1954. Now he was clearly crazy! Bear in mind that the only sync sound film equipment of acceptable quality was massive. Magnetic recording tape was available; the Reeves 35mm recorder weighed about seventy pounds and was said to be "portable" because it had handles on it. The handiest camera was a Mitchell NC, OK in a noisy situation but still massive. Tilton wanted to make a short film to be shown in theaters (35mm) of an evening at a place on the lower Eastside in New York where young people were dancing to live jazz music. Everyone had told him that it had to be done with the standard equipment described above. Set-ups, rehearsals, clap-sticks, take one, take two… take 23… So we got two handheld spring-driven 35mm Eymos (the same as we used in combat in WW II), 100ft loads which run just over one minute each, and on these cameras the longest you can shoot without rewinding is about fifteen seconds. My friend Hugh Bell was constantly reloading while I shot, and Bob Campbell shot with another camera and a rudimentary sync system close to the musicians.

Me? I was all over the place having the time of my life, jumping, dancing, shooting right in the midst of everything. What a fabulous night. We shot slow music, fast music and medium, just like buying T–shirts—large, medium, small! I had nothing to do with the editing, but what a job. They used a slow, medium and fast selection, and they matched the action to the beat. Fantastic! This was more like it. Now, on a big screen in a theater, WOW! You were there, right in the midst of it and it looked like it was in sync—It was in sync! But you couldn't film a conversation this way. It gave us a taste, a goal. Tilton tells me that he was invited out to Hollywood by the biggies, but when he told them that they couldn't do it with their clumsy equipment they told him to get lost and didn't even pay his fare back!

Right after this wonderful experience I got a commission to film a traveling tent theater show in the Midwest, a Toby Show. It was the first film I had made where I had control since *Bananas*. I wrote, directed, filmed, and edited. We used the conventional equipment plus a handheld camera for wild shooting. I had a small and wonderful crew. We worked like dogs and the result may look a bit stilted by today's standards, but it achieved a feeling of being there rather than that of a conducted tour.

More and more frustration. All we were asking was to be free to move and to record image and sound of quality and not be dragging an anchor behind us. It wasn't just me. Morris Engel was making headway in shooting *Weddings and Babies* with Viveca Lindfors, a clumsy rig but it worked. The Canadian National Film Board had experiments going on. Look at the documentaries they made of the pianist Glen Gould. Remarkable. In New York Leo Hurwitz was shooting with heavy equipment in a hospital emergency room, a bit like trying to light a cigarette with a stick of dynamite, but whatever, headway was being made.

My final film before the breakthrough was a report on my friend from college days, Lenny Bernstein, on a conducting tour in Israel. Lenny, Felicia, a young friend of theirs, Jean Stein and I left for Israel on the day after *West Side Story* opened on Broadway. I knew I couldn't take the standard truck full of junk so I switched to something the industry looked down on, 16mm, a camera that was quiet (we knew we had to film concerts) that recorded sound on the film optically, therefore low quality, but in sync. We also took the latest 1/4 inch tape deck, about the size of an overnight suitcase, but not synchronous. Well, I still think it's a nice film that shows Lenny at his best, but we missed absolutely everything that I wanted to have in it. The night when Lenny and Felicia performed practically the whole of *West Side Story* for their friends, including Teddy Kolleck, in their hotel room. The camera was in a truck, and so it went, but it cleared my head. Now I knew exactly what we needed and the standards that must be met.

Many disasters later, it was with Bob Drew, an editor on *Life* magazine who, after a year at Harvard as a Nieman Fellow, was determined to rescue television journalism from the boondocks of the perpetual interview, the hallmark cigarette of Edward R. Murrow that dominated the medium. Drew had seen the Toby film and followed it up with a brief visit and a drink with me in New York. He saw other works and, from firsthand experience as a *Life* reporter, knew what could happen with a good still photographer working with their relatively minute equipment. He was determined and we were with him. We got equipment made to our specifications. We were part of the development. I contributed the idea of synchronizing with a new Bulova watch that was controlled by a tiny tuning fork (the transistor was already there but the crystal chips were still a long way off). Morris Engel had already used a bigger tuning fork but ours was a neater solution. D.A. Pennebaker was with us and radically modified the Auricon Camera that we were using (it was quiet!). Mitch Bogdonovitch engineered it all but like so many geniuses he could never do the same thing twice—always the step forward and then again, sometimes, the two steps backward.

With Bob Drew, we formed a nucleus gang—Al Maysles, McCartney–Fligate, then Shuker and Lipscomb—making films that in general adhered to the list of rules above. With the appearance of *Primary, Yank! No!, On The Pole, Crisis, Petie & Johnnie, Mooney vs Fowle,* and the rest, we, at least I, thought that we had solved the problems of documentary filmmaking. But the industry didn't give a damn. The French intellectual film buffs did for a while, but then came Jean-Luc Godard and other obscurantists with heavy Marxist hangovers.

It is now thirty years later and the TV industry and the film industry haven't really changed. The new equipment has made news gathering more facile and just as dumb. The big boys of Hollywood are happy with the Steady-Cam and, in my view, both are heading for a numbing form of number-crunching disaster called *entertaining the billions.*

How to get away from the industries and their demands? Is this a problem that can be solved in part by changing the technology? We, the filmmakers, depend upon the industry to be shown, TV or theaters. In rare instances we have cracked the theater walls. Pennebaker's *Don't Look Back* and *Monterey Pop* did this and it was wonderful fun and most satisfying. My little short film *Chiefs* rode in on Monterey's back. But these were propelled by star attractions and performance, not something that I want to depend on. Television is relatively easy to satisfy but they want to own what they show; if they give you money for production they want control. *Monterey Pop* was made for ABC TV and we thought we had a winner. When it was completed we invited the newly appointed president of ABC, Barry Diller, to screen it. He came and he sat, through it. There was a ponderous silence till he turned and said, "This film does not meet industry standards," to which I responded, "I didn't know you had any." End of conference. It was the best thing that ever happened to us.

Happy Mother's Day was rejected by its sponsor, Curtis Publications; so be it. Others went on the air and that is the biggest bummer of them all. You have worked and worked and made your masterpiece. It goes on the air and, as Kenneth Burke once said, "It's like dropping a feather into the Grand Canyon and waiting for the echo!" And that is it, that is the end of your masterpiece's life!

Having gone broke with Pennebaker I went to teach at MIT helping to create a new documentary film school with Ed Pincus. Research! Let's make a cheaper system that will enable us to make films without having to go begging from the industry. I was naive. We modified cheap Super-8 film cameras and built a rather sophisticated video system around it which sort of worked if you had infinite patience. As Jerry Wiesner, president of MIT, said to me, "Leacock, you have managed to replicate all the problems of 16mm in 8mm!" He was right.

Finally in the eighties, the CCD was invented and a new chapter began for video with vastly improved quality, and by last year the mini-digital camera and editing system was available. I am retired. I live mostly in France where I fell in love with a French lady, Valerie Lalonde, who never had anything to do with film or video. We live and work together. I find that my shooting is still inhibited by my professional background. Valerie's is not. This makes for a wonderful mix. She tends to play the obbligato, and I the continuo which can produce great harmony.

During the last ten years together we worked successfully in High-8 making our final edits on Beta-Digital, which was a very expensive final move. We made a video for French TV: a story without a subject, *Les Oeufs a la Coque de Richard Leacock*, which I think conveys a feeling of love for what is shown. Some of our films get shown on TV and others don't. Today we shoot and then edit at home on the new mini-digital equipment which can go any number of generations without loss. Soon we will probably be working on the "Radius" nonlinear system which is said to be affordable.

We have two cameras, two edit decks and ancillary equipment for about the price of a car in the $20K bracket. You design your movie to go on a DVD with up to about four hours of quality video and distribute like books to a relatively small, discerning audience of like-minded people who are waiting to escape the nightmare of TV, cable systems, and the massive garbage heap of the Web. But as usual someone will find a way to screw it up, and Valerie and I will go on making movies for the sheer fun of it and the love of each other's company.

Last night I completed a wonderful sequence. It all started over a year ago when Sarah Caldwell called me from Siberia to say that she was rehearsing a symphonic drama composed by Prokofiev, based on Pushkin's *Eugene Onegin* that had been banned by "the authorities" in 1937. She asked if I could "do something about it" so, armed with the latest mini-digital cameras and aided by my daughter Victoria, Natalia Tsarkova (a graduate student from MIT brought up in Russia), and my long-time friend and associate Vincent Blanchet and his superb sound equipment, we went!

We did all the things we were supposed to do and it may work out in the end, but it's a sticky mess. What I completed last night was something that had nothing to do with all the above. We arrived early at the symphony hall where the performance was to take place. It was barely lit; cleaning ladies with buckets and mops were at work, and a lady was playing the huge organ, Bach! I videoed the organ and organist; Victoria videoed one of the cleaning ladies who always had her young son with her; Natalia videoed the other with her mop and pail. Last night I finally got it right! Two minutes and thirty-six seconds of music and visual bliss, concocted from three separate perceptions of an event that had nothing to do with what we were there for.

Photo: Pieter Vandermeer

Valérie Lalonde and Ricky Leacock

THAT is what makes it all worthwhile!

And if only this book that you are reading came with a DVD, you could see and hear all the things that this book is trying to convey. Combine text and movies, with no artificial limits on how long or how short a work should be.

Are good books ever written to be read in one sitting? Must they be geared to an audience of millions—absurd!

PART II

THE "MOMENT"

Photo: Barbara Trent

Woman talking about her babies' death in the camp.

FRAMING THE WIND

Dyanna Taylor

INTRO

I wait and watch. The crew readies, seamlessly. The subjects nervous, shy. The camera, ready now, with film, battery, and the chosen lens. My camera assistant swings it up to my shoulder where it finds its customary place, steady but alive. It is all deeply familiar to me now: the posture my spine accepts to take the camera's weight, my right eye as it seeks the chamois covered eyepiece, the prismed glass through which is seen the world in a frame, and behind it all the mind as it measures distance, light and the countenance of the subject.

My thumb tumbles the rocker switch and we whir into the filmic dance, a union of mind/eye/mechanics and celluloid. The black leather barney jacket my camera wears, like a sultry Frenchman, dampens the sound of the pull down claw on its 24fps mission of recording what happens now in front of us, now to the side.

Soundman/woman. The dances we've done. A dance we've performed hundreds of times, its rhythm conformed to the scene in front of us in the collaboration that is the creation of a documentary. As I capture the essential pieces of image/light, the soundperson records word/sound and together we hold the wind in the landscape.

My right eye pressed to the eyepiece. My left eye open to the soundperson. They watch me and we signal and respond, now the close-up, now the wide, now a reaction. Choosing perspectives. How do I know what to frame, that which is inside the frame or just outside it? Which better tells the story? Off screen, who glances/listens there?

A partial list of remarkable documentary sound people who have shared my doc life: Eric Taylor, Peter Miller, John Haptas, Aerlyn Weissman.

Photo credit: Dyanna Taylor. Tanzania Grasslands. George T. Butler

ACTION/LIFE

> *A woman, her shoulder,*
> *Eyes, ears, watchful, listening.*
> *Camera.*
> *Lenses.*
> *Curvature.*
> *Precision (less precise is life).*
> *The crew, the synchronicity.*
> *Camera Assistant.*
> *Sound Mixer.*
> *Tape Recorder/Microphones.*
> *8 Decibels.*
> *Sound ("if picture is lost you've always got a radio show").*
>
> *Lives, their moments,*
> *Stories, for viewing.*
> *An action begins,*
> *The crew dances a response.*
> *Subjective/objective? (that unanswered question)*

Christmas Day. A middle-class house in White Plains, New York. The black family it contains, educated, hardworking, loving and funny, have gone all out for this holiday. After days of food preparations, shopping for presents, invitations to the numerous extended family members, the Natal Day, which began at 6:00 a.m., is drawing to a close. The exhausted parents, one facing piles of dishes, torn wrapping, strewn presents, and the other patiently chauffeuring relatives to their homes, pause to get their three overstimulated, overfed kids to bed. Ben, six; Matthew, four; and Avery, three, are waiting not so patiently for their father, who promised earlier after many pleas to set up the gleaming new train set. It was a big, pending promise.

Christmas Day. A film crew on the clock since 5:00 a.m. After days of preparations to familiarize a family with the machinations of filmmaking (complete strangers trying to behave like family, moving furniture, hunting for outlets, turning off the noisy appliances, creating an entirely new practical *lighting scheme), an intensive

*"Practicals" are lights which are normal household lights or any nonmovie theatrical-effect lighting which can be seen in the frame and can be operated by the subjects in the film. In our case we "boosted" the wattage of some of the family's existing light fixtures and added some additional fixtures to their home to illuminate more effectively areas which had little light. We added one brighter lamp and changed the lampshade of another in the living room. We increased wattage in the kitchen ceiling, over the stove, in the refrigerator, on the front door porch, and in the bathroom. We hung a "poker style" lamp from the ceiling in the blue kids' room, and hid warm colored fluorescent tubes between the beams in the family room.

day of cinéma vérité shooting is drawing to a close. The weary crew has filmed since 6:00 a.m. when the kids first bolted out of bed. Covering the party with twenty-five relatives, the excitement of the presents, and finally the vast mountains of food, they have begun to realize that Christmas Day is extending long into Christmas Night. Everyone's exhaustion is beginning to show. Time—11:30 p.m. The kids, cranky and waiting for Dad and the train set, are in the small blue bedroom whining. Documentary wisdom says to hang on a bit longer to see what will happen.

I stand in the narrow hallway, lit with a single overhead bright practical, outside the blue room. Camera on my shoulder, with an 8mm lens and a full magazine. Peter, just behind me, Nagra hung from his leather chest harness and boom pole extended leans heavily against a hall closet door. By now we have become invisible. The family drawing their day to a close no longer pays any attention to us as they attend to their going-to-bed business.

I roll the camera as Dad comes into the room and says it's time for bed. Peter, his sixth sense tuned to my thumb on the on/off switch, swings his long boom into the room, avoiding making shadows from the ceiling fixture. In a chain reaction, one imitating the other, the kids begin to wail because Dad insists it's time for bed. He has broken his promise to assemble the train set. They get wild, their disappointment escalating by the second. Angry, the two older boys jump up and down on the bed, tears streaming. In the tiny space of the room, I flatten up against one of the blue walls. The space seems to close in. The bright overhead light. The overheated winter house. The cacophony of three wailing kids hides the camera noise. No one seems to remember we are there.

We keep rolling. Taut, focused. Something is about to give. Then the least expected occurs. Young Ben's expression suddenly changes. Overwrought and still jumping on the bed, his eyes grow large and he turns in the direction of his pleading father and propels an arc of vomit. Matthew, bouncing next to him in perfect synchronicity, takes one glance at Ben and compelled by some imitative genetic response does the same. The room is hushed in a shocked pause. Instinctively I know something is happening outside the frame that informs in equal measure what is central to it. And there, as I pan down to my left, is little Avery, jumping on the floor and making gagging sounds in total imitation of her brothers. Suddenly, she too loses her dinner. The room is blue no longer. Quick, time for a mag change.

Everyone is stunned. The crying stops. The camera rolls again as the parents fly into action. The kids are stripped and tossed into the bathtub. The sheets flung from the bed. The mattress flipped. Fresh linens. Floor mopped. A wildly efficient parental team yields a transformation which finds the kids, minutes later, tucked in bed. Dad profoundly and delicately apologizes to them about breaking his promise. He guarantees that he will assemble the train set overnight. When they wake it will be running. Kisses. Lights out.

We knew we had gotten exactly what we instinctively waited for: a fabulous demonstration of how siblings of different ages mimic and respond to each other, and the bonus of a human moment in the story of a fine family. But where does the story end? Perhaps it is the morning's resolution that would neatly end the tale? I pull the camera off my aching shoulder. My vision is bleary. Peter unhooks the recorder from his harness, removes his headphones. A glance to the director tells us the answer. Real life stops not when the crew is tired or the camera turns off. At dawn the camera rolls for the unveiling of a train set and the fulfillment of a father's promise.

PBS SPECIAL SERIES:	**CHILDHOOD**
SERIES PRODUCER:	GEOFFREY HAINES STILES
SEGMENT DIRECTOR:	MARY BROWN
SEGMENT ASSOCIATE PRODUCER:	RUDY GASKIN
SEGMENT CREW:	DP-DYANNA TAYLOR
	SOUND-PETER MILLER
	AC-ULLI BONNEKAMP
	GAFFER-NED HALLICK
FAMILY:	THE GOULSTONS

ENTERING LIVES

Entering people's lives
Strangers
Their living rooms
The effort to become known, trusted, liked.
The effort to see life as it is.
Easing toward a moment
The moment when a tacit permission is granted
Being ready.
Becoming gentle.
Watching the eyes.
The invisible barrier between us.
They are over there.

We are over here.
Hoping for the truth of the human spirit.
Its revelation. Its barren honesty. Its path toward hope.

Waiting in the last hours of a hot Arizona day. The unused driveway of an eighty-year-old woman. The film equipment locked away in the van, a veritable oven. A second visit to a grandmother who holds some secrets to a young woman's story of pain and abuse, our subject's story: a tortured, torturing mother, the mother's sudden death, broken fragments of memory, dangerous memory. Back home in the cool editing room, the footage we've completed with our subject awaits its counterpoint.

In the stuffy living room, waiting for the grandmother to speak, we dance the dance of patience and gentle persuasion, of respect. The clock ticks. A mourning dove coos hypnotically, rhythmically. Worn crocheted pillows with bright orange accents. The old woman in a blue and purple muumuu lies on a grey recliner, her left amputated stump crossed over her other extended leg.

A synthetic knitted throw tossed on a couch covered in pale green and brown western scenes. Three stuffed animals grin facelessly from the couch's back. Our subject, a childlike forty-year-old woman with large brown eyes and straight bangs, sits close to one corner. She wears shorts and a teddy bear T–shirt. A large brace is on her foot, the one which she breaks repeatedly. On the other, a pink aerobic tennis shoe, dainty yet practical. Her expression changes only as she hears the memories her grandmother recounts. I watch as her face loses expression. Eyes flutter. Lips tighten. She recedes. She engages only to correct a fact, then fades again.

I sit in a dinette chair brought in from the kitchen, close enough to feel present, far enough not to intrude. Through the drone of the heavy metal fan I speak only to ask a carefully chosen question or to corroborate something the director has said. Mostly I nod, agree, and choose to be silent. A dog barks. The rapid tick of an old clock brings its chimes to six. Soon we will lose our light. If she agrees to speak on camera, we will have to work as quickly and discreetly as possible. Silently I design a simple lighting scheme. My eyes search out the electric outlets. I measure the distances for extension cords. I decide we'll put the light cases just outside the front door. I feel into the quality of light and choose which fixture to use to best capture the grandmother's mood. I ponder whether to leave her in silhouette. Waiting. My stomach grumbles. I try to remember when we last ate. I scan for more details. Warm breezes through the screened, metal-barred front door gently blow faded curtains. Day's last light through the blinds. Street lamp light. Somewhere ceramic wind chimes.

The older woman lights a cigarette. A flame in the gloaming. She reaches a trembling hand and pulls a chain on the lamp next to her. Shadeless, the garish light blazes the dusk and captures the swirls of smoke around her head. The American Standard Bible, the "Red Letter Edition," sits on the folding TV dinner tray within the woman's reach. The Bible brings salvation and denial. A last inch of diluted ice tea in a tall plastic glass. Framed family pictures of brave smiling faces. Haunted eyes. Hidden rage. The younger, innocent granddaughter among them. Her dead mother too. The discordant chimes strike seven.

Grandmother suddenly begins to talk. The long awaited moment precarious. Revelations. My heart trembles behind the mask of our professional patience. We dare not interrupt. The camera, its eye spared the scene, remains in the van hotbox outside.

The younger woman, motionless, fades into the velour. The older woman describes a night when she was sixty-five. Her husband, the meat inspector, left her. He took a young woman to see Sonny and Cher. She was sure her life was over. Too old to work. Too old to have a man again. She took one of his meat inspector knives and cut her wrists. Nearly dead, she was found by the brown-eyed granddaughter who, now, barely breathes on the corner of the couch.

Grandmothers can say no. She does. She refuses to speak in front of the camera. She refuses her granddaughter the whole truth and the witness of film. The screen door bangs behind us. The van door opens to a whoosh of damaging heat. We drive our quiet subject across town to her place, ask her if there is anything she needs and bid her goodnight. I ache with what I've learned of her life. Documented only in my mind's eye. We drive off into the night. A faceless hotel. Real life. Film life.

TITLE:	**THE SEARCH FOR DEADLY MEMORIES**
EXECUTIVE PRODUCER:	HBO & SHEILA NEVINS
SERIES:	AMERICA UNDERCOVER
PRODUCER, WRITER, DIRECTOR, SOUND:	MICHAEL MIERENDORF

WAITING/PATIENCE

The wilds.
Places without clocks.
Light rhythms.
Day/Night.
Wild creatures.
Few humans.
Travel of great distances.
Remote. Unfamiliar.
The lands of the wild.
Telling their story.
Wildness. Vast. Impressive.
Distances. 300mm, 600mm, aerials.
A camouflaged blind.
A silent waiting observer.

Tana River Delta Camp. Kenya. North of Malindi, South of Lamu. Our canvas tent camp huddles under scant foliage on the backside of huge Indian Ocean dunes. A perpetual breeze, balmy and moist, blowing through the fronds of palms creates the aural illusion of waves.

It is said, that in this virtually untouched river delta, herds of elephant used to cross up and over the dunes and cascade to the sea where they would bathe and romp, the tidal flats mirroring their shimmering, stupendous bodies. Trumpeting and spraying, the sea wind caught their ears. They left behind huge circular footprints. But we are not here to film elephants.

I am shooting a film about wildlife and men, about the arc of the twentieth century as seen through the eyes of Roosevelts, fathers and sons, ideals of conservation, and about the rationalizations of great white hunters as they hunt a huge old crocodile. We hid for weeks, behind a hunting blind on the edge of a river in Tanzania and the great croc eluded the hunters and my camera. Now we have traveled to the Tana's tributaries where we were told we could find a splendid lookalike, and finally fill the croc gaps in a sequence long since edited.

The tide rushes to the sea. A spring tide. Nine people and equipment crammed on a tiny open boat test that tide. The straining outboard motor sounds like a drowning bee. I perch on the bow with the camera in the blazing incisive light.

Over the years, an odd symbiotic relationship has developed between the camera and me. We work in concert to capture images. I feed it film and a steady diet of 16 volts, spare it dust and salt, and ship it in sleek expensive grey cases lined with deluxe dense foam. In return, this camera frames the world for me in ways I might never have seen. It has led me to symphony orchestras, the great barrier reef, the hut of a Masai woman, a psychiatric ward, a valley of ancient trees, the caldera of an active volcano, an eastern European city choked with pollution, the canoe of a Kayapo hunter, births, too much death, and a window on life's intricacies. As the camera rolls, I choose, through a practiced and instinctual knowing, what becomes celluloid memory, what is left unseen. My camera has shown me the world and brought me home.

The tide continues to drive the waters against us. Sweating, I hold my perch. My reaction time is too slow for the wily and wise crocs. They quickly slither off the banks and watch us, only their two eyes showing on the surface. It becomes too shallow to proceed and Rinaldo and Daren, our croc wranglers, are waist deep pushing us through the rapidly narrowing channels. Daren accidentally slips while climbing overboard to push. He'd had no intention to get wet above his waist, but the unfortunate slip dunked him, and to my astonishment he yells not for fear of his life but for someone to grab his "cigs" out of his tattered breast pocket before they drench through. Interesting priorities, this croc hunter.

My moods swing. The heat, the mud, horseflies, glorious birds, storks, the huge tawny dunes with furry green splotches of vegetation—all bring on a kind of overwhelming sensation. As we force our way up river, I escape into naps even in the most contorted of positions in the boat. In my lap lies the camera wrapped elegantly in a garbage bag, the standard but useless effort to keep it clear of moisture and dust.

We come to the site on the river where a "croc blind" has been built. Sited to match the other in Tanzania it is made of fronds and branches, with carefully placed viewing/lens holes. It sits on a muddy island across from a dramatic dead tree, whose huge white limbs arch over the water. The tree, depending on the tide, is either totally exposed or partially submerged. I shudder when the frightened waterbuck is sacrificed, its fate to be hung from one of the branches to bleed and lure a huge croc. I have no place to take my horror but deep in my belly. Hiding my emotions in a professional armor, I vow never again to shoot a film where animals are killed at the whim of man.

When I am on a shoot with complex intensities, I protect myself, become more private. It's as if I save myself for the requirements of physical effort, intense concentration, and the translation of moment into frame. I feel totally wrung out when I am through, barely articulate. I need sleep. I need to be alone.

We wait on our island of mud behind the blind in complete silence. Three days we've come here, had no croc luck, and returned to camp for the evening. We've begun to worry that like before we may come away empty-handed. Today began at 5:00 a.m. and after another boat trip against the tides we settled in for another endless string of hours sitting, watching, and fighting the drain of heat. An occasional flap on the water's surface jerks us to attention. Is it the croc, finally come to feed? No. Instead, a pride kingfisher, an ibis, a white-headed eagle. It is quite magical, the world on the other side of the blind. We have front row seats in the Tana River Theater of Life. Unconscious of our presence, the performance goes on with great fervor. Herons. Hippos. Bird songs. Sibilant insects. Bathing Masai. Massive clouds. Hot breezes.

As evening falls, we've been caught by the tide because of a mistake in judgment coupled with a zealousness to not give up on the croc. We face a long night marooned on an eight-by-eight-foot earth island surrounded by muddy shallows as the tide ebbs. These tides to which we are tied. The tides crocodiles use to hunt. The tides on which our boat travel depends. The tides of public opinion about hunting. The tides of my adrenaline as it ebbs and flows. The tides of my life. Ebb and flow. Travel/work vs. home/family.

A night silence full of sound. Flopping mud from the island's banks. Odd splashes. Cicadas. Mosquitoes taunting, torturing, and tempting malaria. I sit on a canvas folding seat trying to keep my eye glued to a surreal night scene lit by the critical beam of a battery-powered handheld head lamp. Staring for hours, afraid I might miss the action, my eye socket becomes sore from the pressure against the eyepiece. My back and arms ache from leaning into the shooting position, right hand on the tripod handle, left hand up on the lens. By habit I obsessively check and recheck the aperture, the focus, the action of the tripod head, and feel against my cheek the evening's moisture settling on the camera's textured black metal casing. I fiddle with my zoom's focal length to keep my eyes stimulated and awake. I float between dream and hallucination and instants of reality. The fish nibbling inside the waterbuck carcass make it bounce and flutter grotesquely. The protruding eye of the buck. The protruding eye of my lens.

The crew takes turns sleeping on the chilly, buggy ground in strange contorted positions. Daren paces, draws on his cigarette, a bright glow in the darkness, and curls in his cloth kikoi to sleep. Head still pressed against the camera, I slip in and out of consciousness, my viewing eye actually going black without its lid closing over it. I finally surrender to lying down for an hour. I wrap my head in plastic to avoid the mosquitoes, which bite through my trousers.

Roused by a splash and in complete darkness I lurch up to the camera. Sleepy, I can't see anything through the lens and fumble with the eyepiece shutter thinking it's closed. I realize our valiant battery light is dead. Suddenly the whole effort is pointless. No light, no image. Stuck with only mud flats around us, we wait for dawn and the rise of the tide.

First light. No crocodile. The tide's rise seems endless. By 9:00 a.m. we have been out for twenty-eight hours. Bleary, bitten, muddy, and hungry, we accept defeat and finally head back to camp. We wend our way back down the tributary to the sea. I am discouraged. Yet as dawn touches the Tana, I am reminded of the gifts of my journeys with the camera and the intimate ways I have explored the world. Now the exotic Tana has become familiar to me.

I hate leaving a job unfinished and frequently blame myself for whatever obstacles are left unsolved. I always ask whether I have pushed hard enough. But time and money, those finite enemies of the filmmaking process, are gone. Waiting is a virtue. Sometimes waiting is not enough. Sometimes waiting is over. Absence demands imagination.

FILM:	**IN THE BLOOD**
EXECUTIVE PRODUCERS:	WILLIAM E. SIMON & R.L. WILSON
CONCEIVED PRODUCED AND DIRECTED:	GEORGE BUTLERC
DIRECTOR OF PHOTOGRAPHY	DYANNA TAYLOR
EDIT0R:	JANET SWANSON
MUSIC:	MICHAEL CASE KISSEL
	BABATUNDE OLATUNJI

Photo: Ulli Bonnekamp

Dyanna Taylor

Dyanna Taylor was raised in San Francisco, CA. In her childhood she was exposed to music and photography. Her parents were classical musicians; her grandmother was the photographer Dorothea Lange. Handed a still camera at fourteen years old, she began photographing, processing, and printing her own work in an unsophisticated darkroom she assembled in her family's basement. At nineteen, after two years at the University of California, Santa Cruz, Dyanna became interested in cinema and codirected/edited and shot her first documentary film in partnership with Warren Franklin. Both self-taught, they formed Taylor/Franklin films and while continually teaching themselves about filmmaking, produced local documentaries, industrials, and commercials in the San Francisco Bay Area. At twenty-four, Dyanna decided to specialize in cinematography and began freelancing as a documentary cinematographer. In 1978, she was hired as codirector/cinematographer for the first American women's climbing expedition to the Himalayas. They climbed Annapurna I (the first Americans and the first women to do so) and the resulting film became an hour special for ABC Sports. In 1979, Dyanna moved to New York City, continued to freelance and traveled extensively on domestic and international assignments. In the late eighties her career expanded into dramatic and feature film work. In 1990 Dyanna moved to Santa Fe, New Mexico, where she now lives. Currently she is director/director of photography for *Sahara* a Super35mm nonfiction feature in the Sahara Desert and director/director of photography for *Vanished* a HDTV documentary on the last corners of "wilderness" in the Southwest's red rock canyons.

A partial list of mentors: Emiko Omori, Judy Irola, Jon Else, Paul Marbury, Al Maysles, Ron Partridge.

"WOODSTOCK" ---
FROM VISION TO SYMBOLIC REALITY

DALE BELL

How do you make a film when you have nothing more than vision?

Imagine...

Five of us in a car, heading north out of New York City on the thruway. The time? Early morning, Sunday, August 10, 1969. We are heading for a destination far distant, a tiny town called White Lake. As we speed along the Hudson River, then veer into the Catskills, none of us is aware at the time that this odyssey we are embarking upon will one day catapult all of us, for different reasons, into the record books of filmmaking. Truly, we are on a trip into the unknown, a synthesis between concept and technology. Or a potential catastrophe of huge proportions.

We are a raggle-taggle bunch: Larry Johnson, a world-class swimmer from Florida with an ear for sound and music, the very, very youngest of us all; Thelma Schoonmaker, a prematurely gray brilliant film editor from New Jersey who types at speeds in excess of 100 words per minute; John Binder, a rambling storyteller from York, Pennsylvania, and Michael Wadleigh's original partner and soundman;

Left-Right: Michael Wadleigh, Director; Bob Maurice, Producer; Dale Bell, Associate Producer. Max Yasgur's farm, the "Woodstock" site, White Lake, NY. Aug. 9, 1969. One week before the festival begins, we plot the big one.

Michael Wadleigh, a Columbia University medical student dropout from Ohio turned cameraman with eyes in the back of his head, ears to match, and stamina extraordinary; Ed Levy, a cameraman friend of Michael's whom I had scarcely met; and me, a public television producer, very short of hair, brought up in eastern establishment schools, sprinkled with itinerant trips to Wyoming and Paris, now living on the shores of the Hudson River in a grand old Victorian house with my wife and three young sons.

In another car were Bob Maurice, chief negotiator; Eric Blackstead, music and performer guru; and Jeanne Field and Sonya Polonsky, Michael's production assistants.

For months, we had loosely speculated that we might make this trip. In the city, led by Bob Maurice, a new soon-to-be-partner of Michael's, we had begun some negotiations with another group of people, the promoters, who were going to put on a music festival—the biggest of its kind, ever. Bigger even than Monterey Pop, they said; bigger than the most recent Atlanta raceway concert. They had rented a farm in Woodstock, New York, as a staging area, but local townspeople had objected so violently to the possible presence of a lot of longhaired hippy freaks that the promoters were forced, at the very last minute, to move their venue. Announcements on the radio were describing the new site, telling listeners that three days of peace and music, craft bazaars and swimming, were now going to take place at the destination for which we were now headed—White Lake. All for $18, they promised; tickets would be required for admission. Fences would surround the perimeter, the announcements warned.

But why us? Our negotiations with the promoters had broken off about a month ago, and a new group of filmmakers, Al and David Maysles, veteran *cinéma vérité* producers, had entered the fray. They had told the promoters that the $500,000 rights payment they were demanding as a hedge against ticket sales was unrealistic, but that they would film it, in the style of *Monterey Pop*, and share the proceeds with the promoters. The essence of a new deal.

Then something strange happened. The Maysles, in this very small town of Manhattan, called to ask us whether they and we could join forces on the making of the film. At first, we didn't quite know what to make of this request. After all, we knew how we wanted to go about making the film, even then. We were documentarians, after all, brought up in New York City in the sixties. No better cauldron existed for those of us concerned about social causes, the state of the world, the war on the other side of the globe. We were as Saint Exupery had described us in *Night Flight*—a camaraderie built on danger and the threat of imminent death. In New York City, one could aspire for no higher honor than that of filmmaker. Now was our time. If the Maysles couldn't get it together…

I am getting ahead of the story. Michael Wadleigh and his original partner, John Binder, had approached me in 1965, looking for work. I was then a producer at National Educational Television. Michael would shoot camera, John would take sound: a two-man team, they pitched. If we didn't like the dailies, they said, we wouldn't have to pay them! So I gave them their very first job: we were going to film the first reunion of the Communist Party USA in many years. And because we feared that we might not be granted easy access to the get-together, Michael had ingeniously designed a forerunner to the stedi-cam, a belted rig and two connected pipes extending the length of his back, which held the NPR by its handle comfortably over his right shoulder, leaving his hands entirely free. With a little bit of black tape over the red signal light, he could walk about with the lens wide open and film everything he faced, without appearing to do so. I was astonished at his aplomb and his ingenuity. Of course, the Communist folks stopped us, but not until we had succeeded in a walkabout which captured the B-Roll we needed for this upcoming NET documentary.

But as luck or, perhaps, politics would have it, NET then canceled the documentary. We had shot for two days, fused our personalities, were rejected by a higher Kafkaesque authority, but the three of us were united forever. All we needed was another project.

The Vanishing American Newspaper written by producer John O'Toole filled the void just a few weeks later and brought us together again. A commuter train which did not stop where it was supposed to almost killed all three of us on the first shoot day, but we survived to spend eight weeks on the road together. Bound by Michael's plug-into-the-cigarette-lighter ice-cream-maker, all four of us were diabolically linked.

I would leave film production sporadically at NET to produce live, interconnected events: Control room live television became my forte, and in 1967, I even applied it to film. My subject was the tobacco industry. "A day in the life of..." It was to be "live on film," later to be edited for all the inherent contrast we could muster. A precursor to *48 Hours*! I teamed Michael and David Myers, my mentor cameraman from Mill Valley, together in San Diego. Ironically, they had never met before. The resulting film, which intercut all the poignant paradoxes of the smoking controversy, set the industry and Congress on its ear, so to speak.

On one of his European jaunts, Michael discovered a German electronic designer who had created a flatbed editing table called the KEM. Playing 16mm and/or 35mm film on cores through viewfinders and sound playback amplifiers, it revolutionized traditional film editing technology and concepts. One six-plate machine would enable the editor to combine two sound tracks to one picture. A larger, more formidable eight plate permitted the editor to weave one track to three pictures, or two tracks to two pictures, or three tracks to one picture.

Each of us in our own way was searching for that elusive answer to how to display, or exhibit, that reality which the world generated daily. We had pursued different technologies toward the same end: how to find the truth about what we saw, and how to allow, nay encourage the cameras to tell the story without the intervention of an outside figure. *Immediacy* was one essential component. We had taken to heart that Lerner and Loewe adage: "Don't talk at all. Show me!" Let the person in front of the camera show it. In its humor, its poignancy, its diversity. For us, I think, it was somewhat akin to *pointillism*, where each little bit in and of itself was not truly significant, but when put together and juxtaposed with each other, a sense of reality became visible from the dots once you withdrew and created a little perspective.

The first KEM to visit the U.S. had arrived several weeks earlier and was available to assist Thelma ("T") in her test edit of two songs, the first of which was called "Respect," Michael and two other cameramen had filmed in Providence with Aretha Franklin. The Merv Griffin show received their single-image edited version of the shoot for which they had contracted, but Michael had double-printed the negative. He put the three strands in the hands of Thelma who proceeded to fashion the very first multiple image rendition of a motion picture sequence since Abel Gance had succeeded so well with the silent *Napoleon* in the 1920s. Just two weeks ago, then, if you came to our offices at 81st Street and Broadway on the second floor, and went into the shiny white-walled screening room, you were treated to a singularly memorable event.

First, you had to stand. No seats. And not simply one traditional projector in a booth. Behind you on pedestals were three Grafflex projectors, all plugged into a single multiple electrical box, which also received the cord from a MagnaTech playback machine. Four synchronous machines united by a common switch. When the lights were dimmed in the room, and the four-way switch was thrown, a single, traditional image popped onto the shiny wall at the other end of the room. The other two projectors were running black leader in sync, lingering behind the center projector until they played their role in this daring exhibition. Then, on a word from the very formidable Aretha on the wall, two images appeared side by side. And, of course, on a subsequent music change, three images overwhelmed the viewer by their dynamic presence. Music bounced from stereo speakers on the two far walls, all designed by Michael's peach-fuzzed sound wizard, Larry Johnson.

The impact in that darkened room was truly overwhelming. Though the songs only lasted for a few minutes, it seemed as though you were suspended in eternity, so powerful was the experience. Sensory overload! At the end of Aretha's "We Shall Overcome" a la Wads and Thelma, you were very sorry you were only white. Already we had a "pilot" and the Maysles, in asking us to join them in making the film—whatever it was going to be—had heard the rumors of the three-image film reverberating on the street, so to speak.

Now, here we were together again: Those who knew how to shoot events with multiple cameras, as though live on film, harnessed with others who had the ability to record and edit those resulting multiple images and sounds into one coherent overall film were now speeding northway on the thruway, aiming for Max Yasgur's bowl-like farm two hours' drive from the city, passing hitchhiking longhairs with backpacks and guitars.

Michael had just returned from Wyoming days earlier where he had been filming a 30-day survival course for young people in the wildly rugged Wind River Range. It would later be titled *Thirty Days to Survival*. Another film he had shot several months earlier high in the Himalayas was now being edited by Thelma, under the working title of *Once Before I Die*, a man's fulfillment of a life-long quest to climb to 19,000 feet. Without oxygen, Michael himself had carried his camera and sound gear to this altitude. Now off his ice-cream fix, no one questioned his toughness.

As we approached the farm, all of us began talking animatedly about what we might encounter, which groups might be performing, how to handle the shooting of the music and the recording of the sound on multiple tracks, how to get behind the music to film the people who would be arriving. Our Saint Exupery camaraderie was evolving. None of us had seen the site. We had no idea what we would encounter, for we had only the briefest of phone conversations with the promoters who were in New York City and who had not yet visited the site themselves! And one of us in that car was even asking: Who was The Who? or Sha-Na-Na, or Jimi Hendrix? (That was me, but I could hum Verdi!) What was this reality? How to grab it?

Understand the technology and, in our case, push it beyond where it had ever been. Long before computers, we were the walking software. In filmic sense, we were pioneers, heading where we knew not, but filled with the sense of the possible. We were not saying to ourselves: This is the kind of film we are going to make. Rather, we were saying that it might be possible to make it this way. We had no idea of what we were going to do once we had shot it. Postproduction was on the other side of the planet, far from our consideration.

But slow down, here is our exit off the thruway. Several miles away, we would set our eyes on the farm with its sloping bowl leading to the stage, or so we heard.

Boy, these roads were narrow! Barely two cars could squeeze by. What would happen when more cars arrived up here? Rumor had it that maybe 50,000 people would show up for the three days. No one knew. (I wondered whether the promoters were aware that a recent concert at a racetrack in Atlanta had attracted 100,000 people!!! Could that happen here??)

And then we were at the actual site, driving along a farm road, looking down a glen towards a mass of longhairs scurrying about, one on a motorcycle, bounding over hills and through tall fields of grasses. Long hair. With many curls. Could he be Mike Lang? Yes, someone said. Maybe 100 men and women were working on the construction of the stage, right at the base of this bowl. Plywood had been built around it to protect it from the audience. Chain-link fence was on its way up. Yes, it would surround the site, we were told, but we remained skeptical. This was the only link between the promoters and profit. If it went, so did the venture as an economic experiment.

We looked at their stage, listened to the carpenters and designers. Conferring with Michael, I asked that they extend a lip to the stage, with back to the audience, just at the right height so that a cameraman, standing on this extended platform, could place his bent elbow on the stage proper to use it for support. Beneath the stage, with layers of more plywood, I asked that they create a large, crude table where the assistants who would be changing magazines for the NPR's would be able to work inside their black changing bags. Plywood would be needed in some of the towers, too, so that tripods could be hoisted up and fixed for the longer shots of stage and audience. Our sleeping quarters, such as they might be, would be under the stage or the trucks, again on 4x8 plywood, on the dirt. We would bring sleeping bags, I said, lying through my teeth! Who had money for sleeping bags? Who had money?

We discussed the kinds of lights they would be using to illuminate the performers, the sound system, and how we could tie into it to make multiple track recordings. Where were the various activities going to be held? Where was the food, the toilets, the medical facilities? How many people were they expecting? How were they going to arrive? How about the performers—how were they going to get into the area, if the roads were clogged. There will be helicopters, John Morris said. Food and water, and performers would all come in with the choppers. Like Vietnam, someone muttered!

We must have sounded as though we could do it, even though we had no idea that it truly might be possible. Instinct was taking over, not practicality. All we did was ask questions and listen to responses.

But something was happening. The more we talked, gave advice, argued, probed with the promoters who, at first would have nothing to do with us, the more we began to realize that we were capable of pulling this off, if.

We looked around. It would take a massive effort. It would require untold amounts of gear, of people, of vehicles, of food, for the promoters were telling us that they would have their own hands full trying to supply their own people with enough food when the 50,000 people arrived. We needed an army.

It would require extraordinary coordination and cooperation among us as filmmakers. If the Maysles were thinking in terms of two "divisions," we reasoned, maybe we should, too. One group would be in charge of the concert filming, another of the non-concert, or documentary portions. Michael and Larry would deal with the picture and sound of the concert. Thelma would act as assistant director. John and I would deal with the documentary portions, and I would be responsible for getting the people and the gear.

In the grass overlooking the stage, where none of the promoters could overhear us, we began to plot, among the echoes of the hammering and the boom of the loud-speakers ordering the winches to build the towers. One critical question remained: Were the promoters going to get the site prepared well enough in advance so there would be something to film? They only had five days before the first music was to begin and there was lots to do. Or would the whole project be a bust?

But, we looked at each other, that meant that we, too, only had five days! I remember surveying the tiny roads one more time before I said that if we were going to do it at all, we would have to bring everyone up by Thursday afternoon at the very latest. We could not count on working at night for there wouldn't be any light except very close to the stage.

We first talked concert. It would take six cameras, six cameramen, six assistants to change magazines, six runners to take the loaded or unloaded magazines to the cameramen, and six notetakers, each keeping meticulous track of what their person was shooting, with which roll, at what time, with which type of rawstock. The assistants would work under the stage, standing on plywood, their hands never leaving their black changing bags. Their tables would be comprised of many pieces of 4x8 on sawhorses at a comfortable height. They would have to get a head start on the cameramen so that they could then keep up. An estimated total of twenty-four people to shoot the music, if they were only filming over eight to ten hour days. But what would happen when the music began at noon and ran until the next dawn??

If there were six cameramen, we would need six 110 volt synch motors and a couple of spares, so count eight at least. Where would we find them? Where would we find eight NPR's? Most cameramen would have one, but some might not. Everyone had to shoot with the same kind of equipment, at minimum.

How could we keep track of sync? If each cameraman started at different times, how would we ever know how to track it? I suggested that we find a digital clock, luminous, which we would mount on stage at the back. Each time a cameraman started to shoot, he would hit the clock first, then keep rolling. This would at least give us a starting point. Could we slate each cameraman? It would be the job of the assistants or the notetakers. They would have to prepare in advance a series of labels which would be color-coded to each DP. Each notetaker needed a color-coded clipboard with preprinted grids to fill in information. This would help us enormously. Where would be get the people? Who would we need? Only the best, we reasoned. Since I had given much NET (National Educational Television) work to many of the best DP's in New York and Los Angeles, we ran a list which included Richard Pearce, David Myers, Chuck Levy, Ted Churchill, Ed Levy, Fred Underhill, Don Lenzer, among others. Where would we find enough assistants, and then the other people?

How could we get them here between Monday and Thursday afternoon. Could we pay them? What? How many people would we need on the documentary side? John and I calculated three teams of camera-sound each, hopefully on motorcycles so they could get about in the crowds. After all, if there were going to be 50,000 people milling around, it was going to be very crowded on this little farm. Each of the teams would have to carry walkie-talkies, all on the same channels so that we, at home base central nearby the stage, could communicate with all of them at one time, as though we were live, again. We would establish some sort of communication with the promoters, keeping up with their activities so that we could route one documentary team to cover a "breaking story." How were we going to charge batteries? Where would our power come from? Would the promoters permit us to tap their lines even while they would not get us food??

How could we make the film if we didn't have footage of the building of the stage? Who were those Brits who had been shooting here for the last three weeks? Could we buy some of their footage and include it in our own film? We would have to leave someone here this Saturday to fulfill that adage that "possession is nine-tenths of the law." John would remain behind with Ed Levy. He was garrulous and not threatening. He could get on with the people while the rest of us tried to sort out how to go about pulling all of this off.

By the time we had finished calculating, it looked as though we needed about fifteen people with cameras, an equal number of bonafide assistant camerapeople, about ten people on sound, six of them to work with the promoters on the concert sound and another four to work on the documentary side. We would need about twenty other assistants who would help to keep track of what was going on. Some people would have to sleep while others worked. Maybe we really needed five more assistant camerapeople and another ten assistants? Thelma, Michael, and Larry would deal with the music, aided by Eric Blackstead who knew many of the musicians and managers. And perhaps more importantly, he knew the music: he knew how the performers played their sets, which piece came up first, which performer had the lead and when it was transferred to another player, and how long each piece would run. All of this was very valuable information for those of us trying to plot out how to cover the music. (Eric would later produce both records.)

A new, young feature director we knew in New York, Martin Scorsese, who had just completed *Who's That Knocking At My Door?* with Robert DeNiro and Harvey Keitel, would assistant-direct with Thelma on the concert stage. They would be connected by headsets to the camerapeople, finding out what each person was shooting, so they could coordinate shots as live television directors would do in a control room environment. Michael would always take the number one position, down front and in the center at 6 o'clock, picking up the lead performer. Dick Pearce (if we could find him and if he was available!) would be upstage at about 11 o'clock, Chuck Levy would be at four o'clock, and Fred Underhill at 8 o'clock. Stan Warnow would be in one of the towers and Hart Perry would be in another, providing us with wide shots of the stage and audience.

David Myers and Al Wertheimer would be the lead documentary people.

Again, what does it take? One young woman in the film *The Girl at the Information Booth* would say it was "faith." "Blind Faith," she said, a "very groovy group." Was it our group, looking over us?

After Bob Maurice and Sonya finished their session with the promoters on site, we left that evening to return to New York City where we would confer again. On the way back, we talked more about what we would have to do. Suddenly we determined we had not counted on one element—the rawstock. How much would we need? How much did we have on hand? What would it cost? Who had that much? We calculated again: there were going to be three days of peace and music, as advertised! How many cameramen would be shooting the concert? Six! How many songs would we shoot? How long were the songs? How many of the acts would appear in daylight? How many at night? What kind of night stock would we need? Kodak was selling two kinds. How much should we push the stock? We couldn't determine any of that without knowing how much light the promoters were going to give us on stage? And particularly, how much white light? For if all they had on hand were a lot of blue and red gels, we would never see a performer's face clearly, and the whole night shooting would be eliminated. If the rawstock could not register the talent, and the film could not be made except with daylight acts, then the promoters would not ever recoup any of the money the film might eventually make. So, we reasoned, there was a direct tie in: light with profit. We would be able to argue that point tomorrow, we thought.

But if there were going to be twenty-six groups, and we wanted to film one song from each of them, it would take twenty-six times one eleven-minute roll times the number of cameramen shooting at that time. And if we wanted to shoot more of, say, "*Pinball Wizard*," the section from The Who's *Tommy* opera, and that piece ran for twenty-five minutes, we just increased logarithmically the requirement for raw stock by 2.5 times!

Then, what about the documentary portions? Many of us thought the motivations of the people, the lifestyle, the individual stories, the lay of the land at the festival, and any other activities might be even more valuable than some of the music. What would happen if someone was killed? Or if someone gave birth? It was possible, after all, for there were going to be 50,000 people, we heard! According to the radio advertisements, this festival was to be a statement to the world about the Vietnam War and about drugs as well. Hundreds of acres, a craft show, places for children to play, swimming, an art fair. It was to be more than music. As true documentarians, we had to listen to what they were saying and try to incorporate it into the overall film. Our role was not to comment on the action, except perhaps through how we eventually structured the film to tell the story. Our job was to get the best coverage we could under the conditions, with the people we could amass in this short space of time. And money!

Already in our minds at least, we were calculating the postproduction and beginning to worry about it. We had talked of color-coding, of organizing so that the synching up would be made easier. How would we ever get these multiple images onto one screen? Michael, Thelma, and I were always searching for a new paradigm. *Live on film*, to the extent possible. *Simultaneity*. How could we convey to an audience the explosive variety of activities happening live and simultaneously without invoking multiple images as appropriate? We couldn't release the film with three projectors, or six, or could we? Those answers would have to wait.

Where were we going to get the money for something like this? How would we get the permission from the groups to be able to film them? Would we need releases from the people who would be gathered there, or would the fact that we were filming constitute a release in fact? Was there a precedent?

How would we get food in? From where? The raw stock, how much?? How much money did we have in the bank? How to rent the gear? If we told the rental houses what we were doing, they would never let us have it. If they asked for money up front, how could we triage the money we had? What was more important—the gear, the people, or the rawstock?

At 7 a.m. on the following Monday morning, now four days away from the moment we would have to start filming the concert, we met and made plans on the second floor of our offices at 81st Street and Broadway.

We had $10,000 in the bank. On Monday morning, Bob and I would try to get money in from Michael's last film in Wyoming. That might add another $10,000. Most would have to go for raw stock, for without it, the whole effort would be lost. We might have to save some for film supplies, like audio tape, gaffers tape, and so forth.

We drew up a final list of people, with alternates. They were scattered all over the country, but I had my trusty phone book connecting me to them. We would—I would—tell every cameraman that we would guarantee them a day's pay at $125, the then-going-rate. If the project went beyond that, their time would be on "spec"—they might get paid and they might not. Because I had done business with most of the people on other projects, and given them days and weeks filled with work, this could be construed as "give back" time for them. My word had to be trusted. Those of us in the room would work on "spec," with the prospect of rewards later if we were successful in finding more money.

I would also have to find the gear. Because I had been renting so much gear in the last five years from camera houses in New York City—Ferco, Camera Mart—my name was trusted there, too. Perhaps I could tell everyone that I was only renting for a one-day shoot, which was going to occur on Friday. I would have the gear back to them by Monday, I could assure them. I would also have to pick up the gear early, so that I could get it to White Lake early enough to be useful. But I couldn't tell them about the actual site for they would be fearful that their insurance might not cover loss or damage. They could hear the radio adverts just like everyone else! This was a strange form of trust in which I was basically telling a little white lie, for White Lake!! It bothered me, but I saw no way out of the dilemma. We would charge the gear, not pay cash, take the insurance coverage just in case something might happen to it, and then pray.

But how would David Myers get from San Francisco to New York. David would have to charge the plane fare on his own card. Preposterous! No one would ever agree to such terms, not even David.

By this time, we had determined that we probably needed an enormous amount of footage—enough to be able to shoot for 175 hours between now and next Sunday night when the festival would end, if they held to their schedule. One hundred and seventy-five hours translates into 375,000 feet of 16mm film or more than 900 individual rolls of film, some of which had to be accessible for daytime use, the remainder for night time. With thirty rolls to the case, we would need thirty cases, which also occupied a huge space, easily the inside area of a panel truck. How to get it to the stage? In only four days? Where to store it safe from other people and the elements?

When Michael returned on Monday, he would take the twenty-five rolls remaining in the ice-box from previous shoots. I would purchase some more from whatever sources I could uncover, including Kodak up on York Avenue. We decided we would not purchase the full amount until we saw how we were shooting on the site. Wednesday would probably be the final judgment day for purchasing. I would send the rawstock up with whoever was going on Tuesday, and so forth. Michael and I would confer by phone when he arrived on the site.

We had a plan. We would spend everything Michael had in the bank. Bob Maurice, who was also helping Michael maximize some of his films through distribution, would continue the negotiations with the promoters with Eric Blackstead's assistance. Bob would also try to find big money from studio financiers. I would remain in the office day and night until everyone was on the site on Thursday. Sonya Polonsky would help me. Thelma, Larry, and Marty would get to the site as quickly as I could find cars, other people, and gear.

We realized that no one had ever done this kind of film before. Less than twenty-four hours earlier, reality had been a figment of our imagination. Until we had scouted, we knew nothing and feared everything. But contact with the site, the people, and assessing what we anticipated would be the conditions, gave each of us a deeper sense of confidence which we then passed on to each other by our very energy. One step at a time. It was truly an extraordinary feeling we were building among us. We felt we could conquer anything. If only Bob could make a decent deal with the promoters and their producers on site, we might have a slightly easier time when we finally got settled.

I looked around the room. None of us were over thirty years old. Whoops, that's not exactly right. I was. I was thirty-one, married with three young boys, the oldest of whom wanted to come with me to the site if I went! But I was the only one in a "traditional" relationship. And oh yes, Michael was only a year younger than I was. But everyone else? Larry still had peach fuzz on his upper lip, didn't he? Was he twenty? Maybe Bob was my age, too. I didn't know him very well. He was very philosophical and always muttering under his long hair and bushy beard while he climbed the rafters like an Indian on a construction site.

We knew we did not want to produce "news coverage." Let the news teams do that! We wanted to produce something which would last, which would be different, and which would truly represent the seminal role that music and their lyrics played in the life of the generation of the sixties. What chaos! Assassinations. Malcolm X. JFK. MLK. RFK. Their names and initials reeled off as a litany of torment. Turbulent civil rights struggles. Beatings. Dogs. Water hoses. Fires on crosses. Open marriage concepts. The increasingly hostile generation gap. Drugs, beards, and longhairs. Killing and maiming in jungles half way around the globe, matched only by burnings and shootings in our own South. Political upheavals at home. Wars on poverty. Gender wars. Chicago riots and brutality. Ralph Nader taking on the monolithic multinational corporations in David-Goliath fashion. Huge gaps burgeoning between government and the people, gaps of faith and trust.

And yet we were politically active then. Anything was possible. Hadn't Neil Armstrong taken one small step for man less than a month ago? One person could make a difference. We were doing for our country just as we had been admonished to do on that cold, windy January morning on the Capitol steps at the beginning of our decade. What was its reality? Could this festival become our symbol?

Now, without being told what to do, we actually might be on the threshold of accomplishing something significant on our own. How could we mature with this film? How, we constantly asked ourselves, could we produce a film for a general audience—not simply for a music-infected group of longhaired hippie freaks? That would be preaching to the choir! Was it because all of us had already been brought up on "educational television" that we felt the need to appeal just as our own television programs had been doing? Was it because each of us, in our own personal way, had literally or symbolically "been shot at by sheriffs" in Mississippi while investigating what we perceived to be injustices with the food stamp programs? Was it because we had attempted in our previous work to try to uncover the truth, or the injustice, as we saw it, and to reveal that "people story" to millions in their living rooms?

Michael soon packed and left with his camera. Larry and Thelma would join him and, together, they would go back to White Lake to join John Binder and Ed Levy who were already there.

Bob got on the phone with the promoters and the potential financiers, probing, cajoling, fighting, selling, holding back. His extraordinary effort was to prove we were not foolish.

Sonya and I set up one office with two desks and three phones. For the next four days, I ate and slept in that office, getting only a very few hours of sleep as I assembled the people and the gear, handling the logistics of moving this little band into the Catskills, working the time zones.

David Myers did pay for his own ticket and was in White Lake from San Francisco by Tuesday night.

Dick Pearce had contracted to film with another producer that week, but when I located him in Hartford, I promised to find his producer another cameramen so that he, Dick, would be free to join us. I gave away one of the cameraman from the Maysles team who called me asking to work on our project. I told him I couldn't take him to White Lake but that I could get him this job in Hartford! He accepted, and Dick drove across Connecticut into the Catskills. He arrived aboard his motorcycle on Wednesday.

Don Lenzer drove up from New York City, but not before he recommended that I invite a friend of his, Richard Chew, to join us as cameraman.

Richard was getting married that weekend. Already he was in Seattle. But yes, he would postpone his wedding! Who would meet him at the airport?? He would pay his own way. Could we get him a camera?

Al Wertheimer would also drive from New York with his converted Auricon camera. Because he was not slated to shoot any of the concert, I approved his unique gear.

Jack Willis kindly declined my offer to be a soundman and always regretted it.

Other people who had been contacted by the Maysles called and I had to reject them for fear of muddying the waters.

Ferco and Camera Mart believed my story about the one-day gear rental which had to be picked up on Tuesday, Wednesday, or Thursday, as the case might be. And oh yes, it would be returned on Monday afternoon. No, I could not tell them where their gear was going. I had to scrounge to find 110 volt motors and four magazines for every NPR. Why did I need a 25-250mm lens? Why did I need three 5.9mm? What was this project I was filming?? Later, as the New York Times began reporting huge traffic jams on the way to the festival, I became fearful that my cover might be blown, but it was only on Tuesday, when all the gear was returned, that I divulged what had actually happened!

Joe Louw, who had taken those historic Life magazine pictures of three men on a motel balcony pointing to an adjacent building while they huddled over the slain MLK in Memphis, drove up to White Lake to do sound.

Marty Andrews, an engineering wizard, nephew to Buckminster Fuller, made it on one of the early treks, for he had to design and build all the electronics under Larry's tutelage.

My wife, Anne, was able to get her mother to stay with our kids, so she filled our VW bus with food, blankets, and other people—and not our oldest son, Jonathan, much to his dismay—and became one of the chief notetakers on the lip of the stage. She was joined by Jeanne Fields, helping Larry, and by Renee Wadleigh, helping Michael.

Marty Scorsese was in one of the early trucks, transporting gear and headsets. He traveled north with Ted Churchill, one of our marvelous cameramen.

Many others joined the team, some of whom I did not know until they walked through the door to the office with a recommendation from someone else. They were hired on the spot. For nothing. I'm not sure I ever put the phone down in those four days. Sonya kept dialing people and held onto them until I could talk.

And the *New York Times* kept writing, radio announcers kept talking: "The New York State Thruway is closed!" Television stations, hiring helicopters, kept sending images of very clogged exits from New York City as seemingly the whole of New York State converged on Max Yasgur's farm. Eventually, we were to learn that the 50,000 had failed to add a zero! It was staggering!

The rawstock? On Tuesday, Kodak said they had thirty cases of the assorted emulsion numbers we required. I told them a truck would pick it up on Wednesday morning. Yes, we knew we would have to pay cash. It would be just under $18,000. Fine. On Wednesday morning, the truck arrived at the York Avenue pickup station. They had three cases, not thirty! I screamed! They, too, had failed to add a zero! What to do now? No one had ever purchased *thirty* cases at one time before, they said! I was in a cold sweat. Everyone was in the process of finding their way to White Lake. Already, some twenty people were on site with twenty more to head up on Wednesday. Twenty would follow on Thursday morning, bringing our total to more than sixty, all of whom were willing to do this gig on "spec," mind you! And now, no rawstock!!!

Break it down into pieces, I said to myself. Don't panic. Take small steps. How much do you have in New York? I asked Kodak. They said they could find another ten cases by tomorrow. In Rochester, I asked? In Washington? In Chicago? In Los Angeles? They would call back. Meanwhile, I sent the truck with the three cases up to White Lake along with a couple of sleeping bags and snacks and drinks.

Between that Wednesday morning and Friday afternoon, I did nothing but scour all over the East Coast for rawstock. I bought from rental houses. Kodak found cases in Rochester and Chicago. Each case had to be shipped carefully to LaGuardia where my messenger service, also working on spec, would take it off the airplane and transport it to the Marine Air Terminal where it would board a small aircraft bound for Monticello, New York. Several cases actually took a wrong turn and ended up in Liberty, New York. I couldn't find them for hours!

They had to be shipped back to the Marine Terminal before the rawstock could be bicycled to Monticello. From Monticello, the rawstock would then have to be airlifted, case by case until Sunday morning, on those very same helicopters which were depositing the talent at the Woodstock stage. Remember the choppers in the background on the sound tracks? It may sound like Vietnam, but that's rawstock they're transporting! Not just food and talent.

At one point, Michael and the crew were down to their last case, and it was only Friday! Ding, he said to me, what are we going to do? The music was going to begin that afternoon! Wads, I said, we had proceeded on faith to this point. All the people who were coming to help us were flying on trust. We had to extend ourselves just a little bit more, and pray.

By Friday afternoon, the first helicopter shipment landed on the big hill behind the stage. The festival producers brought it down to the film team huddled on plywood under one of the trailers to the side of the stage. We had achieved a modicum of co-operation!

I was able to leave New York City late Friday afternoon, laden down with foodstuffs I had purchased on upper Broadway. My tiny VW beetle made it to White Lake by about nine at night. Walking another hour, I arrived on stage just as Joan Baez was singing "Swing Low, Sweet Chariot," haloed in a mild drizzle. It was appropriate. I found Anne and we all hugged.

Over the next two days, I monitored the progress of each case of the rawstock from its various starting points across the country. By Sunday, it had all arrived. And so had the rain, the mud, the B-12 shots, and finally, some juicy steaks from the festival producers. Bob must have made a deal!

It was no accident that in editing, we began with Ritchie Havens singing "Freedom" and ended with Jimi Hendrix performing his world-famous guitar rendition of "The Star Bangled Banner"—bookends which everyone could appreciate. We were trying again to represent the truth as we perceived it, structurally this time. We began with a single pristine image, a green overture which exploded into two dynamic night images, side by side, and ended on that awesome helicopter view, taken by David Myers after I had removed the last case of rawstock on Sunday. But in between, with documentary and concert footage, we tried to tell the triumphant story of those three days of peace and music so that the nation and the world would comprehend both its symbolism and its reality. We let the people tell the story. We simply became the humble facilitators of those historic three days.

In the course of postproduction, when our evening meals would be provided by Max's Kansas City, we would move twice; once across the street on Broadway when our landlords became too greedy, and finally, when we packed up one hundred and fifty large crates of film, negative and equipment to go to Hollywood for the finishing. One of the KEMs we transported had originally been destined for Francis Coppola's American Zoetrope, but we off-loaded it at JFK and rented it for six months, much to his consternation! We thus became the first aliens to bring flatbed editing equipment to the film capital of the world. Seventeen longhair members of the postproduction team moved with the gear and lived in communal rented houses during the four months it required to convert our multiple strands of 16mm to cinemascope.

And no, we did not have to install six projectors into the theaters to represent the multiple images. In Los Angeles, we were able to solve those problems and every other one after we had displayed our eight-hour rough cut in New York on December 3rd and 4th, 1969. Warner Brothers, who Bob Maurice finally got to finance the film, put untold pressure on us to make a single strand film that would be in movie theaters by Christmas. They wanted the Christmas market. Don't make it complicated. Don't make it expensive, they shouted. Just get it into the theaters, and fast! All that is yet another story!

But led by Bob's steadfastness, we all resisted, even to the point of retrieving our negative to put a stop to the matching process while Bob, and all of us, negotiated with Warner Brothers. When Sidney Kiewit, the former javelin thrower turned attorney for Warners, came to our offices to assess our progress, I can vividly remember arm-wrestling with him on a daily basis, just to see who would buy the donuts. Everything required perseverance if we were to establish a new paradigm.

In 1971, *Woodstock* won the Academy Award for Best Feature Documentary. Larry Johnson became the youngest person ever to be nominated, his nomination coming for Best Sound with Danny Wallin. Thelma Schoonmaker was also nominated for Best Editing. Alas, she did not win then, but did take the Oscar for *Raging Bull* directed by Marty Scorsese. Warners did not enter the movie for Best Visual Effects, even though we had created the longest optical in cinema history with our vibrant multiple panels of images cascading over the screen.

Today, *Woodstock* is an icon. For the 25th Anniversary salute in 1994, Warner Brothers financed the remixing and reprocessing of all the sound to digital, the re-cleansing of all the images from the original techniscope negative, and the reconstitution into this new "Director's Cut" of forty minutes from the original rough cut Warners had eliminated for the very first exhibition.

In the intervening years, *Woodstock* revolutionized the music business by clearly demonstrating the enormous power of music and lyrics to affect people of all ages, races, and creeds around the world. Performers became even greater cultural stars as a result of their inclusion in our film. Did we give birth to MTV?

But beyond that, *Woodstock* also changed how films were made. Many producers tried to copy us, but no one ever came close.

Look at our use of *technology*: the slow motion images summoned before our eyes by our KEM editing machines later became a standard editing technique. As Alvin Lee exclaimed when we showed him his sequence of "Ten Years After" in a darkened projection room, "If that wasn't me up there on the screen, I would bloody well want it to be me! Can we play it again, please?" And the beauty of his images came quite by accident: while shooting his "Goin' Home" song, every cameraman save one, Michael, had run out of film and we had to flip *his* image to continue the two-panel optical! Looking closely, you can see when the second cameraman reloads his magazine and continues to shoot! The mother of invention—*Take advantage of accidents.*

Immediacy. Multiple panels within the screen enabled us to tell more than one story simultaneously, live on film. The audience felt it was in the middle of all that was happening. It added impact.

Listen to the sound. We were the very first to put primary source material into the surround speakers, much to the consternation of our dubbing stage people at Warners. As the stage is finally being assembled on the first two panels, we use the surround track to constantly orient the audience to where the action is. They feel engulfed by the effects. All paved the way for THX 1138 sound design.

Not only did editing style change, but editing gear was totally redesigned so that, today, computerized nonlinear video editing most closely approximates what we were able to accomplish with our elaborate color-coding schemes on site and in the editing room.

To return to the original question of how does a documentarian convert image to reality, I think the answer is: It takes guts, stamina, and humility before the subject so as to allow the material to speak through you as a vessel. It also takes technology and passionate people as dedicated as you are to wrest the truth from the people whom you film and then from the structure the material dictates to you. It takes courage and the ability to listen to your subjects and to the people you gather around you to help you through this labyrinth of filmmaking. Had we for one minute faltered in our resoluteness, we would have been steamrolled by the marketplace dictates of our distributor, or by the press, which was clamoring for a glimpse from the moment it was clear to us that we had fulfilled our dream of creating a film which would represent both the reality and the symbolism of the sixties. Luckily, with the help of Bob and Sidney, we held on to our original vision and resisted that coercion.

Dale Bell's productions have received an Oscar (for the 1970 feature film documentary *Woodstock*), an Emmy (for the 1983 *Kennedy Center Tonight* special on Eubie Blake), five Emmy nominations (for the 1980 *Previn* and the *Pittsburgh* series, for the 1983 PBS *Kennedy Center Tonight* production of *Medea* with Zoe Caldwell and Dame Judith Anderson, for PBS's 1984 *Chemical People* series with Nancy Reagan and Michael Landon, for NBC's 1985 *OceanQuest* adventure series, and for the 1986 KOCE *A Night to Remember* special celebrating the opening of the Orange County Performing Arts Center), and a Peabody Award (for the 1982 PBS *Kennedy Center Tonight* production of the Dance Theatre of Harlem's rendering of Igor Stravinsky's *Firebird*). Mr. Bell has also won two Christopher Awards (one for *Here Come the Puppets!*, a one-hour documentary hosted by Shari Lewis and Jim Henson, a second for the *National Geographic Special* "The Tigris Expedition" with Thor Heyerdahl), and two Cine Golden Eagle Awards (for his PBS *National Geographic Specials* on "The Tigris Expedition" and "Voyage of the Hokule'a"). In addition, the dramatic book-based anthology PBS series, *Wonderworks*, won The Children's Act Award annually and other domestic and international awards of excellence during Mr. Bell's tenure as executive producer.

Mr. Bell's more than three decades in the visual and performing arts media have included work on three feature films (among them *The Groove Tube*, starring Chevy Chase and Richard Belzer, *The Italian Americans* and *Mean Streets*, both directed by Martin Scorsese), and on two of the major commercial networks in the U.S. He has also enjoyed extensive experience in international coproduction and distribution. From 1979 to 1984, Mr. Bell was vice president for production at Pittsburgh's WQED. Most recently, Mr. Bell has directed *Shangri-La: Ancient Mystery* and

California and the Dream Seekers for A&E, produced *Pirate Tales* for TBS, *Battleship!* for Discovery, and *Chariots of the Gods? The Mystery Continues* for ABC. In 1959, during his senior year at Princeton, and as head of the summer stock company, *The University Players*, Mr. Bell brought Sir John Gielgud to McCarter Theatre for a one-night benefit presentation of *The Ages of Man*. Mr. Bell now serves on the Advisory Board of The Shakespeare Guild, and is a member of the Directors Guild. He speaks French and Spanish, has studied Russian and is the father of four sons.

THE INTIMATE MOMENT:
THE ART OF INTERVIEWING

Bettina Gray

The prominent photographer Ruth Bernhard was a petite and intense eighty year old when we interviewed her for the public television documentary series "Creative Mind." Her eyes, as probing as a child's, devoured the room unself-consciously. Nothing escaped her attention. She had enough vitality to keep the entire film crew busy answering her inquisitive observations while the microphones were placed and lighting adjusted. I was aware she was summing me up in her mind at a voracious pace as well. From her remarkable alertness I found my cue for how to begin our conversation. We would talk about acute focus of perception. In this interview she told me, "If you can't find something worthy to photograph within forty feet from where you stand you are not seeing. . . . "I try to teach my students the difference between looking and seeing," she said. "You must look with eyes that are awake to the extraordinary within the ordinary. I want to capture in my photographs that singular moment of tenderness I see in life."

Ruth Bernhard waits all day to take one or two shots of her subjects. This is all she shoots, not rolls of film with hundreds of duplicate shots hoping for serendipity. Her photography is an art of focused attention, acute perception. It is an art that applies to many disciplines. To listen as well as hear, to attempt to distill and then portray everything perceptible of the moment and the person, this meditative precision of focused attention yields the intimate moment in documentary interviewing as well as photography. It is that moment of extraordinary human encounter and it captivates us all.

I have learned much more of value in my life from people than from books. Human accomplishment is measured in product and most often valued by the material manifestations, the work of art, the building, the book, the symphony, the accomplished act. But I find an artistry which transcends product in the art of personality integration. The unification of contrasts being one definition of high art, I see in certain people an exquisite mastery of living. I am as much interested in who they are as in what they have accomplished. I look to these others for a pattern to life, an inspiration for meaningful, scintillating integration of existence. It is often a vain hope—a pipe dream of wistful imagination—but there have been enough moments both on and off camera when probing questioning has

Bettina Gray with the Dalai Lama

been rewarded richly, not by barter but by blessing—a beneficent gift of love to another—and, by extension, to all others. I would characterize my encounter with His Holiness, the Dalai Lama of Tibet, in this fashion and sincerely hope that this was also the privileged experience of the audience who viewed that conversation.

It is these moments of reward that bring forth a unique and intimate learning, not so much of specific answers to specific questions as a blessing of engaged and heartfelt exchange, an art form of living, personality to personality. It is an education into the range and expanse of consciousness, the potentials of humanity, an education that must be passed on generation to generation and gleaned from something as illusive as a manner of being, a look, a stance, a gesture, a critical choice, a moment of tenderness, an essence of being.

This ephemeral quality of human interaction surrenders itself much more completely in the technical medium of film than in other idioms. It is interesting to note that the longest running television show in the history of television, "Meet the Press," which dates from 1947 to the present, is based on the interview. Television interviewing is a powerful communications medium. In a few cases, it is the extraordinary moment of filmed silence between guest and interviewer which has held the most poignant revelation. And only film could capture the nuance of such a moment. The drama of theater or opera is inherently fictionalized. The live interview offers a drama of realism, and the camera provides the flexibility of intimate visualizations unavailable to other artistic renderings. This is documentary realism, but it is also living art.

THE APPROACH

I approach a new person to explore the way some might approach a first ascent in mountain climbing, cautiously plotting a course into this mystery called personality. This unknown ascent fascinates me almost as an obsession. Who is this human in front of me? Picking through the random heap of experience, upon what have they chosen to build a life? What is significant? What has shaped their passions? What makes them weep or dance for joy? Is there a revelation they harbor, carefully refined in the molten moments of their soul? Does it shout, or sing, or rest quietly meditating, awaiting . . .? And what will it take of honesty, forthrightness, integrity, or courage from me in order to induce them to reveal their cherished insights.

In interviewing, there are the studied anticipations, the mapping of direction, moments of arduous encounter, planned retreat, impossible approaches, as well as sublime vistas of personality unfolding. Unsuspected, illusive, unplanned thrilling moments where two strangers are no longer strangers. There is the estimate, the surmise, drawn from developed skills and the actual approach, which often varies considerably. And there are those moments of suspension into the void, not knowing if or how, suspended by the safety rope of another—total trust.

In moments of hesitant introspection, I ask myself, what right have I to ask a lifetime's distillation to be laid before me, and hence the public? What makes me think we are deserving of these treasured innermost reflections earned over a lifetime of challenges? If they are displayed like so many wares in a bazaar, as we (nauseatingly) see on the exhibitionistic soap-chat talk shows, what are we doing to the mystery of intimacy and privacy anyway? It is a momentary pause. Curiosity drives me quickly back into the fray. And I remind myself that it is the documentary interview that restores integrity to television talk. Much of the conversational on television is commercially driven, a glitz-blitz of self-promotion and product promotion, human interaction used as an arena of barter. Stripped of promotional hype the documentary interview is a revival, a model for basic, direct, honest communication of the kind that has carried humanity through millennia, a vital link of generation to generation and future to past.

WHAT IT TAKES: INSATIABLE CURIOSITY

I remember my family following me around regularly making apologies for my inquisitive intrusions into the lives of strangers. This intense curiosity for humanity has driven me most of my life. It is incurable. Maybe genetic. My mother once lost me in a train station awaiting the next connection when I was six, midpoint in our journey from Kansas into the deep South. She was desperate. I was delighted, completely forgetting my mother or the train schedule. I had found an elderly black bathroom attendant who would talk to me. We must have talked for fifteen or twenty minutes before the parental desperation descended. My mother found me quizzing this wonderful woman about every aspect of her life. In those moments I was no longer six, no longer white, no longer limited by age and race and upbringing, I was exploring the life of someone who had lived and loved and understood. Forty years later, I still remember the person and what she conveyed to me.

LESSONS FROM GUESTS

"Such open generosity of person," I can remember thinking of Isabel Allende, the Chilean writer, as she surrendered herself in the interview process, without hiding or dissembling, knowing that what she was saying was public, on camera, for anyone to hear, and saying it with complete ease. With feminine dignity and intensity she talked of the rape of her country, the murder of the artists, of repression and exile, and of the new life and love she has found since. She told me she writes in order to invent her life! She calls it inventing memories. She says she reinvents herself into new experience. As we were talking, in a singular moment came a flash of personal realization (cameras rolling) that this is why I interview, to escape the boundaries of life.

PROFESSIONAL INTEGRITY

A recent survey reported that the U.S. public trusts one group even less than lawyers and that is journalists. Unfortunately, I am not surprised. I am dismayed at how often I see journalists and interviewers more dedicated to finding the story they planned rather than the story that emerges. I am repulsed by attack-interview questions for the sake of humiliation and intimidation. What is called fact-finding, I often feel is truth-betraying. Pretense, false promises, trickery and editing to alter the speaker's intent are not considered legitimate forms of social discourse within society, and it appalls me when these are modeled for the public in certain forms of interviewing. Respectful inquiry or hard questioning does not have to involve ridicule or broken promises. Such practices betray a fundamental assumption about the audience and its presumed crassness, dislocation, and insensitivity which I find insulting. Integrity and trust are vital, they show in the results, and they are even more required in a difficult examination of controversial issues. Freedom of speech is a responsibility as much as a right.

PREPARATION

It is sad also to note that publicity managers and media advisors who coach guests on being interviewed suggest that they come ready to supply the questions, since many interviewers are not prepared. Spontaneity does not equate with lack of preparation. In fact, spontaneity gains from intense preparation. Even jazz improvisation is built around a structure of highly developed pattern and skill.

Contrary to the common assumption that anyone who can talk on camera can interview, the art of capturing unique moments of human encounter is a highly challenging and developed skill. Voracious reading is a cue to good interviewing. To prepare for an extended profile interview of a half-hour or hour duration, I will try to read a good deal of what my guest has written, reviewing related subjects as well. It is not unusual to have stacks of books in several different locations in my house, ready for me to pick them up as I get a chance. (My family has forbidden me the bad habit of extending this to my car with a book on the front seat as I drive through downtown traffic picking it up at stoplights.) If I am completely unfamiliar with the experience references of a guest I will sample them if I can. This has led me to Sufi-dancing, snorkeling with a pod of dolphins, attempted ice-skating with an overweight maverick theater producer, Zen meditation, cooking for forty over an open hearth fire in a dirt floor shack, learning to play a few notes on a new instrument, trying gymnastics moves, yoga postures, and mountain climbing. During the interview the command of focus for both participants, regardless of the wildly distracting elements of cameras, set personnel, lighting, technical interruptions, retakes and guest nervousness rests completely on the host. Before I branched into television production I trained as a classical musician. Having experienced the exacting mental and emotional discipline of concert solo musical performance as well as hosting a series of extended profile documentary television interviews with challenging and substantial guests, I would have to say that probably the latter is more demanding.

SUBJECTIVITY OF THE INTERVIEW

I am convinced that interviewing is a necessarily subjective exercise. My producers and I were once denied a grant from the National Endowment for the Humanities for an exciting series of interviews (later produced as *A Parliament of Souls*) on the basis that the proposed interviews could not be scripted in advance. That is, we were denied funds because we refused to conduct interviews with some of the world's top spiritual and religious leaders in such a way that the specific questions and outcome could be provided in advance to the grant providers. It was my naive initiation to the shock that there are those in this supposedly free–press country that are unwilling to risk anything so unscriptable as a genuine, fresh, spontaneous conversation with social, political, or spiritual leadership. Interviewing is intimate, it is spontaneous, and it is intensely subjective. It is this kind of subjective, searching conversation, held either in private or in public via the media, which is vital to social and political freedoms. It is imperative that the audience continue to have available to them these kinds of conversations.

I want to know what my guest has to offer because it is personally important to me and to my guest. I do not want to be forced to frame questions in relation to the guessed values of some Nielson-probed, focus group-tested, market research–assured, sanitized projection of a hypothetical audience.

RELATIONS BETWEEN THE PRODUCER / DIRECTOR AND INTERVIEWER

I have met producers and funders who feel that when they look for on-camera talent to conduct an interview, they are looking for a visual prop, someone who will be a vehicle for their questions: "If I want you to have an opinion I'll give you one." A job of this kind is an equivalent role of newsreader, no insight or independent reasoning is expected or appreciated. All questions are provided, don't improvise. In effect, it is an acting job and an attempt at scripting spontaneity. The result is very unsatisfactory, varying from a superficial fluff piece where the audience picks up an underscore of complete insincerity (or genuine incompetence) on the part of the questioner, to a real derailing of insight which an articulate and outstanding guest might have offered in a once-only opportunity. Most blame the interviewer when such a production fails. However, even the most outstanding interviewer when reduced to a list of scripted questions over which he or she had little influence will obtain an unhappy result. Good interviews (as life) are not scripted. It is easy to vent production anxiousness in overcontrol, but the best way to exercise control is before the interview and not during it.

LEARNING FROM THE MISTAKES

A young Asian jazz pianist sat in front of me in a freezing cold, darkened set on a bleak February day. The aim had been to interview the musician in his performance element, a jazz house in downtown San Francisco. I had spoken to this guest in a preinterview to get a feeling of his personality and of any special clues to his interests. I sensed trouble immediately. He couldn't get through a sentence on the phone without stammering though after we talked awhile things seemed to go better. He was intensely nervous. After my phone chat with him, I went to the producers to warn them. I was not opposed to the concept they were looking for in inviting him, but in my opinion it was going to prove a very difficult interview and I personally knew several musicians who could better fill the programming slot. The producers were committed, we couldn't back out. I cautioned them to make the setting of the interview as intimately cozy and reassuring as possible. Instead what we had was a large, cold room on a set where nearby noises repeatedly interrupted.

The producer was calling retakes every few minutes. I could not ease my guest as I had previously on the phone. He was so tense he couldn't keep his train of thought on the retakes. The technicians were boiling from the intruding sound breaches—promised not to happen again. The producer and I were new to each other, this being only the second interview we had worked on together. Everyone was hoping that I could magically pull the musician out of the bag.

Sitting on the edge of my chair, doing everything I could think of to put my guest at ease by posture, voice intonation, and body language, as well as questions, we finally had some momentum going. He was relaxing, speaking in full sentences now. The interruptions from nearby offices had been quelled and things other than heads were beginning to roll. My guest was politically fixated as well as nervous. We had covered his political views but I was supposed to interview him as much for his art as for his politics and was trying to move the conversation in another direction. No go. So in desperation, departing from the preplanned questions, I asked him if he had ever fallen in love with a sound just for the sake of that sound, the purity and beauty of it. And, in the momentary flash between question—pause—answer, before he could give his response there came the booming sound of a *Toilet Being Flushed Overhead*! We all heard it. The room was acoustically over-live, an echo-chamber. Stop the set. Tempers flared. Did you hear that! (As many of us were breaking up!) Of course we heard it. Was it recorded? Yes. OK . Retake! Rolling. Repeat the question. "Have you ever (chuckle) fallen in love (te he) with a sound. . .?" The humor should have helped but it was lost. We never recovered. We went on but I could never get the interview off the ground. (In my opinion many of the politically obsessed lack humor.) The interview aired but I didn't have the heart to watch it. My guest told me afterward that he had never been interviewed on television before. I had assumed on a series of this magnitude they wouldn't try a completely inexperienced guest unless they had other assurances. They had wagered at least $150,000, which is probably what the production averaged per show, on that gamble. The next day the producer called a group review asking ME what had gone wrong. We finished the series amicably and quite a few really good interviews followed, but that one remains one of the lower moments in my career. Moral: check the bathrooms and tape them shut first!

THE RISKS

The risks are emotional: getting caught up in the stories of the guests. Some of the most personally embarrassing situations have happened on the occasion where I have finally achieved that moment of intimacy with a guest, when just the two of us are probing the mystery of life together, every fiber awake and listening—no cameras, they have ceased to exist—and at that moment a guest launches into a tale of some tragedy (as far too many in this world can tell) or tenderness they have lived through. It makes for wonderful moments of film. However I have been taken by surprise in these situations to find a welling up of empathetic emotions that can and do waylay. I once interviewed a guest who had lost his wife to Alzheimer's only a few weeks before our interview. He sat in front of me talking of their exemplary life together as public servants and international leaders, he having survived Nazi incarceration for his part in the French resistance. He was talking quietly of his feelings that she was still with him, helping him. Unexpectedly I was teary-eyed and not in control, moved by the nobility of spirit and the love and generosity of this politically prominent man to talk so candidly and sweetly of his lost wife. We had to stop the cameras and take a break in order to continue. Again it happened to me as a guest told the story of one ordinary Dutch Christian mother who risked her own children and her life in harboring and raising a young Jewish baby boy during World War II. The guest told me the story, speaking of the terror of both sets of parents as they sought to keep each other informed, the love these strangers had offered, the belief by the natural mother that her boy was dead (when communications had broken down), the sacrifice she made as the natural mother lied to her husband about the well-being of the child she believed dead, and the final reunion after the war to return the child to his parents unharmed. It was a story like many I had heard. We were on solid if sad ground. Then my guest revealed at the end that he was that child, now grown and involved in international humanitarian relief projects, a rabbi, saved by a Christian woman. It was obviously hard for him to tell this story, but he said he would continue to repeat it because it was a genuine living example of compassion that saved his life, the kind which is vital to any hope of our future. There I was, suddenly nailed again, unable to go on. Cut! Break time. Professionalism demands self–control, but God help me if I should ever become so accustomed to this as to stage it and remain unmoved. That will be how I know it is time to quit.

WOMEN IN TELEVISION

There will be a day when this last commentary is unnecessary. It is eagerly awaited. However, at present, even though women have broken many barriers in media over the last few decades, Martin Lee and Norman Soloman point out in their book, *Unreliable Sources: A Guide to Detecting Bias in News Media*, "We are told that [women's presence in the mass media] is improving--but usually without reference to how bad the situation remains." They go on to say that 94 percent of the top management positions in the U.S. news media are held by men. Fairleigh Dickinson University's dean of graduate studies, Barbara Kellerman, says, "Women are by and large still excluded from the select group that constructs our national reality. . .for a female to play the role of commentator, expert, or analyst—that is, to be the resident sage—is still disturbingly rare."

Lee and Soloman continue by quoting Marlene Sanders: "I think women are going to be a presence in broadcasting, but we've had a slowdown [at the networks] in the last eight years. . . The move for affirmative action has been played down. The pressure is off the people who hire. The women are there but at a quarter of staff." In a 1989 survey of the networks, researchers found that 22.2 percent of the stories on CBS were reported by women, 14.4 percent on NBC, and 10 percent on ABC. "There are fewer women on air at the networks now than there were in 1975 when I went to work at the networks," said Linda Ellerbee, "The reason you see us on TV is so you don't notice our absence in that room marked 'executive producer' or 'CEO' or 'network president'."

With a few notable exceptions, those who decide what we see and how we see it are male. This situation has many sociological and psychological historic roots and reasons. But I must say, I do not think I am from Mars OR Venus and I would like much more opportunity to see women as well as men in television relate to the world and to sexual roles with considerably more depth. When women are more a part of the media decision-making structure, when the media presentation of women allow the public to see women (and women to see other women) as intellectual, capable as much of logic as of emotionalism, capable of reason, authoritativeness, self–control and leadership without a loss of those qualities of femininity that gift the world with grace, we will all benefit richly.

PART III

VISIONS AND EXPEDITIONS

© 1988 Stuart Keene

"THE BIG WET"

Jeremy Hogarth

It is late in the evening on an early December day in 1991. I am standing on the fringes of the vast flood plain of the South Alligator River in the "Top End" of Australia's Northern Territory. There has been no rain for almost six months, the ground is parched and hard, the grasses withered. The river has long since ceased to flow with fresh water, and the only movement of the water now is tidal, even though the sea is some 50 kilometers away to the north. To the southeast the lightning dances through the clouds in a dramatic vista that is beyond the wildest dreams of the widest of wide screens.

With Mark Lamble, my friend and cameraman, I watch as the early wet season storm approaches, ushered in by a vanguard of black clouds, darker by far than the coming night, clouds that are seemingly lifted from the ground and supported by a column of rain. Continuous lightning is sheeting through the clouds, illuminating them from deep inside. Every now and again a bolt flashes and forks to the ground. Away to the east, the tinder dry grass crackles and flares, ignited by the lightning. The low glow, a red sheen against the black rim of the night, spreads, builds, and spreads again—a red sheen against the black of the night. Another fire, and then another is ignited by the leading edge of the storm. Steadily the distant fires join in a deep horizon-spanning red glow.

I am a maker of documentary films. I have been in the film and television world since I was sixteen when I started, as a mail boy, with an English television company. My entire background has been in film, first (after mail delivery!) in editing, and now for seventeen years as a director, a producer, and a writer. Since 1974 I have specialized almost entirely in my great love, Natural History films.

For me there is a tremendous appeal in taking something natural, whether it be an animal, an environment, or an event, and weaving it into a story replete with the drama, the twists and the turns that the natural world so often reveals. Documentary making is but one branch of filmmaking. It is storytelling and in that sense, at least, it is no different from the making of dramatic films. Natural

History filmmaking must plait together the three major elements—of natural drama, a strong story line, and the consistent truth of nature.

My particular passion is to make films that fit into a landscape, for we all belong to the land and we all live within the climate that shapes the land. I love to take a wide canvas and paint in the minutiae; those brief poignant moments of the struggle that life must endure between birth and death. I love both the drama of a seasonally changing landscape, and the challenge of combining all these diverse elements into a film and a narrative that people will watch and, I hope, enjoy.

Back in 1991 I had returned to the north of Australia to make a Natural History film about what happens to life during the wet season. My previous film in the region had been about the Kimberley district of the Northwest. It was to be the story of a landscape carved by time and by the winds and rains, and of a coastline dominated by some of the highest tides in the world.

The northern part of the Australian continent is ruled by two major seasons, first the "Dry" and then the "Wet." All European Australians who live in the North recognize these two main seasons, for this is not the temperate world of the south of Australia, or of the Northern Hemisphere, with its ponderous quartet of winter and spring, then summer followed by fall. The northern part of Australia belongs to the tropics. Here European Australians recognize a dry season, when the days are long and hot and virtually no rain falls at all from April to September, or October. A wet, or monsoon, season, lasting from December to March is also recognized. This is a period of intermittent storms, some lasting a few hours, others lasting for days. It is during the Wet that the north of Australia is ruled by the monsoon that sweeps down from Asia. It extends south as far as the 19th parallel, then retreats, leaving the North once again to the long curdling heat of the Dry.

But there is a third, briefer season that some also recognize—the "Build-Up." At some time in late September or early October—each year it is different—the air, long parched and dry, begins to absorb moisture. The humidity begins to rise at an increasingly uncomfortable rate. Out of nowhere thunderheads commence their ominous swelling and building. The promise of rain becomes ever-present, though rarely is it more than just a promise; seldom does the rain fall. The Build-Up has another name; Europeans, driven crazy by the relentless humidity, call it the "suicide season." Some Europeans also recognize a short interval between Wet and Dry. This is the briefest period of all, a time of "knock-em-downs," immensely violent, but mercifully short-lived storms. Strong "knock-em-down" winds bend and break the now 3 meter (9 feet) tall sorghum grasses which have grown at a phenomenal rate throughout the Wet. And just occasionally, adding insult to injury, a tropical cyclone roars in from the Arafura Sea, lashing the land with rain and sometimes bringing destruction and death.

But Europeans have, however, only lived in this part of the world for a little longer than a hundred and fifty years. For this country, and for those people who have lived here for a time measured in millenia, the concepts of "December" and of "April" are very recent, very recent indeed. December is the time of the European Build-Up, but it is a season that the Gagadju people call "Gunumeleng," one of the six seasons that they recognize.

The Gagadju are a clan of the Aboriginal people of Australia, and whilst on those flood plains of the South Alligator River I was standing on their land. This land, by common agreement, is leased back to the Australian people as a part of Kakadu National Park.

Australia is an ancient continent, a time-worn land. The continent has remained isolated for over 60 million years, since the last remnants of the supercontinent of Gondwana split asunder. What is today Antarctica slid southwards, began to freeze, and almost all of its life disappeared. Australia, however, drifted towards the north and the tropics, carrying with it its remnant Gondwanan fauna and the flora which has since continued to evolve and adapt in isolation. But even in its isolation Australia has been touched by the rest of the world, and has been influenced by the natural events that have shaped the planet we live on. Ice ages have been and gone; sea levels have risen and fallen over the millennia. Flying animals, birds and bats, arrived into Australia from Asia many millions of years ago, island-hopping along what is today the Indonesian archipelago. Other animals arrived too; small rodents drifted on flotsam and landed on the northern shores of the continent.

And much more recently people came.

Perhaps those people who first arrived on Australian shores were the human race's earliest seafarers, or perhaps they too drifted like so much flotsam across from the islands to the north, carried unwittingly by the winds and the currents. I like to think of them as seafarers; I think that those early settlers made journeys that were planned and deliberate. They were set to change the continent forever. I like to think that from their islands to the north, perhaps what is today Timor, they saw over the horizon the smoke from fires lit by the early lightning storms of

"Gunumeleng," the season of early lightning and humidity, the season of the last fires. For fire is as much a part of the natural Australian environment as are wind and rain.

On that early December night in 1991 Mark tried to film the storm. We had just flown up from the southern state of Victoria, and the financing of the film was still not fully in place. I was even still unsure of exactly what kind of film I was going to make. We had just enough money to produce a half-hour film, yet I really wanted to make the standard hour that suits the television channels of the world. An "hour" can be anything between 46 and 55 minutes, the "half hour" somewhere between 24 and 27. Though only measured in minutes, there is a quantum leap between the two, from the half hour to the longer film. I knew that to do the Wet Season any sort of justice it must be a film for the longer time slot, and that I would need two seasons for the filming.

Then, standing on the South Alligator flood plains, I just wanted to get as much as possible onto film and into the can. I knew that I was going to use the chronology of the Wet for the story structure, but I was quite literally shooting in the dark. I had one other great certainty in my mind, that this film, like my previous film in the Kimberley, would acknowledge the Aboriginal people who have lived continuously in these lands for longer than we have any certain knowledge.

It is still argued for just how long people have been in Australia. In 1996 newly found evidence from a rock-art site in the north of the continent would suggest that human beings may have been there for as long as one hundred and sixty five thousand years. Even in 1991 I already believed that the Aboriginal people have lived in their country for far longer than the fifty or sixty thousand years which is typically recognized by Western science. Regardless of the exact time frame, however, one thing is certain: they have lived in this part of their world for longer than any other members of the human race anywhere else on our planet. They have a unique affinity with the land. To try and make a Natural History film in the North and to ignore the aboriginality of the country seemed to me unthinkable. And so, as I watched the storm dance and play across the distant sky, and while I listened to the camera clicking off a frame at a time, I decided to fit the film's chronology to the Aboriginal understanding of a year and not to the European one. The Gagadju people recognize the shifting seasons in this part of Australia by subtle signs. No two years are ever the same. The seasons may last longer, or shorter, than the year before; they may start at different times and end earlier or later, and in some years they may simply never happen, vanishing into timelessness.

The seasons are all powerful, but how can one visualize, let alone characterize, a season? Just where are the characters and where is the drama? Who should be the star of the film? As I stood on the South Alligator flood plains I realized that the star of this film had to be the monsoon itself, and for reasons still unclear I knew that the monsoon was a "she." I had at last a female lead for my film, but she was still a star with no face or character. I would have to learn to understand her, to know her, to come to love her. I had to try and know her in an Aboriginal sense.

The first white settlements in northern Australia were English, military, and disastrous. Those European soldiers and their families came to the North and tried to live as they had in the southern, temperate part of the Australian continent, making no concessions to the climate.

The Gagadju tradition was both oral and written; their stories were painted with ochre onto ancient sandstone rocks. The Gagadju world was created by great Spirits and Beings that moved over the formless land. These great ancestors fought each other, they made love and hunted, and in so doing gave birth to the features of the land. For Aboriginal people their land is everything; it is a part of them and they remain part of it. The people grew with the land, and changed with it as it changed. Their understanding of their land and their total world was perfect and complete; an absolute comprehension of all that was connected to their own universe.

At this time of the year the winds shift around the compass. The early storms come from the east. Later, as the season changes, the winds shift to the west. The humidity builds, eventually to almost unbearable levels. It rises because a heat trough over the northern part of West Australia draws in a humid southwesterly airflow. This is a local feature of the Australian climate, not part of the broader-scale interhemispheric wind patterns. At this time of the year Australia still enjoys its isolation.

The Gagadju recognize that their year is subtly divided into six distinct seasons; their recognition is born of an ancient understanding. The season of Gunumeleng, which I was to experience first, consists more or less of the months of November and December. The winds blow randomly from all corners of the compass; storm clouds build, and in the afternoons there is often the distant rumble of thunder. At this time of the year, the ground is dry and suspension-rattlingly hard; the surface layer of cracked mud remains as just the merest reminder of the water that, at a different season, covered the flood plains and the billabongs. The humidity is stifling. It is like living inside a warm, damp sponge. Clothing remains constantly wet.

Mark and I had decided never to use air conditioning, either in the car or wherever we stayed. To fully understand the climate one must live in it, and anyway the change between the cool of the air conditioning and the heat and high humidity outside would play havoc with the lenses, generating condensation that would beggar belief.

Gunumeleng was the time when, in pre-European days, the Gagadju would leave the flood plains and move to the ancient sandstone escarpment to the south that looks down upon the plains. The sandstone of the Arnhem escarpment was deposited in a shallow sea some 2,000 million years ago and now at its highest point rises to little more than 500 metres (1,600 feet) above sea level. The last time that salt waves broke against those cliffs was many millions of years ago. Since then, they have seen the storms of countless Wet Seasons.

The image of "Namargon" is painted in this ancient sandstone fastness of the Gagadju world. Namargon is the creator of the storms that herald the coming of the monsoon, "the Wet"—the storms of Gunumeleng that will in their own time change to the season of "Gudjewg." I had already decided that I would not film the image of Namargon; somehow that would be too easy. The painted image of the Spirit has featured in too many films. I wanted more than the image; I wanted to capture the very essence of Namargon, the creator of the lightning and the storms which lead to Gudjewg, the monsoon season proper. Gudjewg approximates to the European calendar months of January to March. The winds from the northwest carry clouds laden with moisture sucked up from the oceans. In this season the isolation of Australia is lost, as the land is touched by the rains carried on the back of the wind from the world to the north.

To the north and to the west of Australia spread the great expanses of the Indian Ocean. This vast mass of warm water, combined with the tilting of the earth towards the sun for the southern summer, forms a veritable weather factory. The interplay of sea, land masses, and air creates a global climactic rhythm. During the Northern Hemisphere winter a high pressure system becomes established over Siberia. Blasts of cold air flow southwards from this system, reaching chilling fingers across the equator and towards northern Australia. As this cold Northern Hemispheric air travels over large expanses of warm tropical ocean, it warms, becomes moist and unstable. This stream of air, known as the northwest monsoon, converges with the southeast trade winds in a broad, low–pressure region called the monsoon trough.

Even during the Aboriginal season of "Gurrung," the hot dry months approximating to the period from July to September which precedes Gunumeleng, the factors that control the monsoon are already at work far from Australia's shores. The oceanic waters to the north and west are being heated by the sun, and moisture is drawn up into the atmosphere by evaporation. But land heats faster than water. Over land the hotter air rises and leaves a void which is replaced by the cooler, denser, and moist air from the ocean, sucked in towards the Australian land mass on winds that have now swung around to the northwest—the monsoon air flow. Once this moist air reaches the warm continent it rises rapidly. As the clouds tower and rise they pass from hot air into colder, the water molecules condense and fall—the monsoon rains thus begin.

A significant part of the problem I had been grappling with was that the drama of my film was to centre around the climate. The monsoon, when she arrived, was to be my star. Everything else had a minor part to play, some were to be just cameo roles. I had also decided I was going to follow the Gagadju seasons, commencing my film in Gurrung, the hot blistering days at the end of the European Dry, and ending it as "Yegge" began, as the monsoon season drew to a close and when the winds were once again blowing from the southeast across the vastness of the arid Australian continent.

But how does one film a season? How does one show the capriciousness of a shifting and uncertain six months? How does one film humidity? What are the scenes and where is the tension? What are the key aspects of the character of the leading lady? And more importantly, as no two monsoons have ever been the same since weather records were begun, I knew that I was to be pandering to the most temperamental of all possible stars.

She is fickle with her favours. She changes her mind at an instant. She teases, but gives nothing away, and then suddenly, with no warning at all, she overwhelms one with a tempest of delusion. Everything else in this patient country plays along to her capricious moods.

The other minor stars were to be tangible creatures: the Frill-Necked Lizards and Saltwater Crocodiles; the Magpie Geese that nest on the floodwaters of the plains; and the Agile Wallabies that must move from their Dry Season grazing grounds.

The cameo roles were to be played by Orange Horseshoe Bats, small rare rodents known as Calaby's Mice, marsupial Sugar Gliders, Green Tree Ants, and a unique red and blue grasshopper.

Ludwig Leichardt disappeared into this vast land in 1848, but not until after his name had been bestowed on the extraordinary grasshopper that lives there. The nymphal stages of Leichardt's grasshoppers are first seen even before Gunumeleng begins, but that is to jump ahead, for the last days in the adult form are at the start of the Dry, after the last violent storms of the Wet, during the brief season the Gagadju call "Bang-Gereng." To the Gagadju Leichardt's grasshoppers have long been known as "Aljure," the children of Namargon, for they appear as Namargon creates the storms which every year bring new life to the tropical vastness of northern Australia. The children of Namargon just had to feature in the story.

The lesser roles for the film were fairly easy to visualize. Humidity could be revealed by the movements of the Orange Horseshoe Bats within their dark and humid caves, and by the Frill-Necked Lizards that come down from their trees as the humidity builds.

The floods could be dramatized by the Saltwater Crocodiles which nest during the Wet. Tension would be supplied by the females, which must take a gamble on the placement of their nests—too low and the eggs will be swept away by the floods, too high and they will be too far from water and the hatchlings might not make it to the safety of the cooling and turbid flow. Magpie Geese could also be used to dramatize the coming floods, for they must wait for the water levels on the flood plains to stabilize, otherwise they risk losing their nests to the rising floodwaters.

But what of the monsoon herself? She marks her passage by the clouds that shift with the winds. They appear first slight and almost fluffy. Then the first thunderheads that herald Gunumeleng start to tower. The thunderheads are themselves dramatic. They grow rapidly towards the stratosphere, some reaching as high as 22 kilometers (75,000 feet) building at speeds of over 180 kilometers per hour (110 miles per hour). If a man were to ride one in a glider he would be carried aloft into the upper reaches of the earth's atmosphere! I knew that the clouds would be easy. And the clouds would easily lead to rain, another vital face of the multifaceted star.

But one more face of the monsoon posed very different problems, and that face was lightning. I stood with Mark on the South Alligator flood plain as the first storm swept towards us, and we both realized that lightning was to be the key to this film. It was lightning that would show the changing moods of the monsoon. And then came our problem. How were we to capture natural lightning on film? We were shooting film and not video tape, for film, with its better contrast range, more precisely controllable frame rates and shutter angles, is still the superior medium for these types of documentaries. But some years earlier Mark and I had tried filming lightning at night. That storm had been stupendous in its intensity and brilliance.

We filmed it as slowly as the camera would allow, at about eight frames of 16mm film per second, yet the results, black film with timid flashes of white, were pathetic. The film revealed no sense at all of the boiling clouds or of the lightning sheeting behind the cloud cover; it gave no hint of the ferocity of the lightning bolts as they linked the sky and the land in a blinding instant of power. Somehow we had to overcome these technical problems.

The early storms of the Wet are mainly electrical. Very little rain falls. These "pre–monsoon" Build-Up clouds are not the moisture-laden clouds that will eventually flow in from the north and west. The main airflow is still across the dry continental interior, occasionally mixed with some moisture from the seas to the north. The clouds look threatening, promising but rarely delivering rainfall. The hot humid air from the land pushes the clouds racing upwards through the colder air at sports car speeds. The moisture droplets in the clouds contain positive and negative charges and as the gap widens between them the charge builds until it is bridged by a bolt of several hundred million volts—lightning. Lightning was the key to the monsoon, and was to be the key to my film, yet I still had to work out how I was going to record it successfully.

If we got all the finance we needed, then I had scheduled two wet seasons to make the film, and so with the first storms Mark and I began to film lightning, and to record as many of the moods of the clouds as possible using a time-lapse camera. But as I have said, the clouds were easy—the lightning was the problem.

Mark and I filmed that first storm in December of 1991. It came towards us, then the winds changed and the storm died. Being only too aware of past failures, for the three weeks that we were in the north we filmed every storm we saw, but there were precious few. We filmed at the European television film standard of 25 frames per second when the storms were caught in daylight, but at normal speed the clouds were static. We filmed using slower camera speeds, we filmed using a hand–operated intervalometer, we even tried to superimpose lightning onto the lowering clouds using a Heath Robinson type of infield aerial image.

We viewed the dailies back in the temperate south of Australia in January 1992. Without fail, every single storm we had filmed was a complete failure. The lightning shoot was a total disaster.

Mark and I returned to the north in February 1992, once we had confirmed the necessary budget. The season had now swung to Gudjewg, or at least it should have. But that year the monsoon failed, the storms were few and far between. In fact we had seen only one decent rainstorm, and that was the one we had filmed back in December, but it had been a daytime storm and there had been no lightning. That storm had at least revealed another face of my star, and yet another problem. The face was rain, and the problem was how to film it, and have it appear natural. If the camera is under a shelter, an umbrella, or a roof, then the droplets falling from the edge are noticeable, even if one is filming through them on a telephoto lens. This film was to be about the Wet, and the audience had to be made to feel wet, they must feel as if they were actually in the rain. Mark and I filmed the one decent rain storm that came before Christmas 1991. We took the camera out into a field of grass, covered it with plastic bags and waited for the storm we had seen building. This was a rain storm, not a lightning storm. And hit us it did. Mark's eyepiece for the camera filled with water, but the body, cloaked in plastic bags, remained dry. But we could not point the lens into the wind and the rain, yet it was there that the drama lay. I watched as the rain lashed towards us, blown by the gusting wind that bent the grass stems this way and that. Somehow we had to be able to film directly into the rain for it to appear natural, yet with the camera under no other shelter than plastic bags. As the rain passed, we stood soaked to the skin and talked about the problem, and left the North with the germ of an idea of how to film facing into the wind and rain.

The idea was a simple one, based on the devices used at sea on the windows of the bridge, that enable the helmsman to see his way through the roughest of seas. We planned to use a "clear screen" of revolving Perspex in front of the lens. Mark built a proto-type over the Christmas break, and it worked a treat. He tried many different devices to cover the eyepiece of the viewfinder. Condoms were thought of, but the rubber proved too thick, clear plastic film was another possibility, but that too proved hopeless. We filmed in the rain and under waterfalls on many occasions during the making of the film, and each time all that we could do was to take the eyepiece apart immediately after filming and dry it with warm air from a hair drier. When filming in the rain we had to choose our shots with care so as not to run out of film, for to change a magazine meant having to strip the camera out of its covering bags, dry it, and clean it before reloading. Most of the rainstorms were filmed knowing that all we had was ten minutes of film in the magazine.

However, Gudjewg, the Wet of 1991/1992, was one of the least impressive on record. We were able to film many of the lesser roles, and some of the cameo appearances, but none of the drama. The Magpie Geese tie their nesting into the season; they nest mainly after the storms of Gudjewg, but that year there were no storms and only about 10 percent of the Magpie Geese were able to breed. It was a similar story for the Saltwater Crocodile. And as for the monsoon herself, my star didn't even deign to show her face. By early February 1992 there were a myriad of dragonflies over the still waters of the billabongs; for the Gagadju this was a sign that Gudjewg was shifting towards Yegge. Bang–Gereng delivered a couple of violent "knock-em-down" storms which blew the long sorghum grass violently back and forth before flattening it completely with the brief rains that lashed in from the east. Our first Wet Season passed with little lightning, and we caught none of it on film.

There was one brief twist that year; a cyclone loomed up out of the Arafura Sea. Torrential rain hit the Tiwi Islands of Bathurst and Melville. We called the cyclone watch in Darwin and noted the position of the storm and monitored its progress. The cyclone intensified into a force four, with winds gusting to over 220 kilometers per hour (135 miles per hour) in the centre. It headed toward Darwin. It paused, then moved again, then paused, then headed away. That was a relief for Darwin, for over Christmas 1974 a cyclone called Tracy had flattened the city, with the last wind blowing the needle off the scale. Darwin's relief was not ours; we had hoped for the winds and the rains for the pictures they might have given us, but they were not to be.

Mark and I drove the 3,800 kilometers (2,350 miles) back home over two and a half days in early April 1992. We looked through all the shots we had of storms, all the footage, and began licking our wounds. We had captured just one distant flash of forked lightning slashing through the rain, linking the ground with the swirling clouds. The monsoon had kept her face well hidden from the camera. I had no footage of my star, and she had already retired far away to the north.

Mark and I talked about lightning, the technical aspects of trying to catch the elusive flash. We talked about the problems of advancing the film when the shutter hid the negative, we talked about the different lenses and different film stocks that were available. We talked about the problems of trying to film the storms at night, for that is when they mostly happen. We talked about the storms that sometimes come to life at dusk, flickering in their host clouds as the light dims and fades, springing into violent life only at night, the storm clouds billowing up and up and the lightning streaking from cloud to cloud, from earth to sky and back again. We talked, but we were still not sure whether we could overcome the technical difficulties.

I returned to the North with a different cameraman in September 1993 to capture the last days of Gurrung, but that was just a period of heat and haze.

Mark and I returned together to the North for the Wet of 1993/1994. For the technically minded, in addition to the standard high speed 16 SR that has become the mainstay of most Natural History films, we carried an ancient 1960s vintage Arriflex 16 ST camera which Mark had modified. Mark had also built his own intervalometer so he could control the frame rate with some degree of accuracy. This time we had learnt a little more of the star; we knew a little more of her fickle nature.

This year there were more storms, yet still the early results were disappointing. But we kept changing our methods, adapting to the nature of the star; we kept trying. In the end we learnt.

"The climate rules—OK" was to be the guide. The storm itself dictated how it was to be shot. Every night we would drive to a spot some 60 kilometers (35 miles) from Darwin. It was flat, had permanent water and gave us a 360° view. As we drove we tuned in to an AM radio station, for we had learned that the greater the intensity of the static crackle, then the stronger the storm would be. Strange as it may seem, the final adjudicator of the storm was to be the contact lens in my right eye. If that eye began to tingle, then we learnt to trust that the storm would be good. I still have no idea of why that should be, perhaps something to do with the pH level of the solution, yet it was to prove an accurate indicator.

We would watch the storms grow and fade; watch them as they were blown this way and that by the winds. We watched as they would flicker with lightning, and then die. Sometimes they would build, and by watching we could tell which ones to film. In fact the greatest storm of all was too big to catch on film. One night a bank of cloud rolled towards us from the east; it stretched from horizon to horizon on a front that was well over 100 kilometers (60 miles) broad. As with many of the storms there was little or no thunder to be heard, and the lightning was too spread out along the width to be filmable. It came towards us as if it were some devouring beast spawned in hell that had come for retribution. Some ten minutes before that storm fell upon us the wind hit us and forced us to retreat into the car. We sat enthralled as our heavy four–wheel–drive Landcruiser was shaken and buffeted by the winds, and then within minutes the storm had passed us, and in its wake the stars were returned to the night sky. My star had shown her face, but it was a performance that was beyond our ability to film.

Always Mark would film with an open shutter. He would gauge the amount of light that had fallen onto each frame, he would allow in his mind for the exposure, he would gauge the swirling clouds, then advance the next frame, and continue his calculations.

By February 1993 our star had made her entrance; she had reached center stage and by now we knew her moods well enough. Also we now understood the technology of the camera and its little black box. The results were getting better, but there were still some odd occurrences. Some storms photographed cold, the sheet lightning lit the clouds in blue; others photographed warm, the clouds were lit red by the lightning. Perhaps it was the distance of the storms which altered the color temperature of the lightning, perhaps there were other factors at work which we didn't understand. I felt that the star was a warm, not a cold one, so in post-production we kept the color as a constant warm.

Then one night in March 1993 we experienced the ultimate drama. Some 300 kilometers (185 miles) away to the east a storm began to build over the Arnhem escarpment, the stone-country land of the Jarwon and the Gagadju. Mark and I were driving back to a place called Noonamah, some 30 kilometers (18 miles) south of Darwin, when we spotted the storm. We stopped the car, watched, then began to film. It took almost five hours for the storm to reach us. It built up, sweeping inexorably closer. The lightning was ferocious, the clouds were lit again and again from within, but unlike the wide storm that had previously escaped us, this one was contained. There was no thunder, no claps or crashes, just silence except for the constant whine of mosquitoes. With the storm still some two and a half hours away the frogs began to call; somehow the males knew that rain was coming and that the females would start to move to the ponds of water. Perhaps there was a change in the atmospheric pressure that we couldn't detect; perhaps their brains were stimulated into knowledge by the lightning as it closed upon us. This was yet another chance to mate, for the males compete by singing; the female chooses the male with the sweetest song—the song and not the singer.

Still the storm came closer. Mark was forever changing his exposure times, as the line of clouds blew in towards us. The lightning was now bringing brief flashes of daylight color to the night, the sorghum appearing green and the magnetic termite mounds standing out as stark silhouettes against the blackening clouds.

About ten minutes before the storm hit the wind began to gust, a cold wind bringing relief from the humidity and the heat of the night. We kept filming as the storm swept over us; then as the curtain of rain advanced we hid the camera in the car and closed the doors, for this camera would not take the clear screen device.

We stood in the midst of a water-born chaos, wind and rain lashed us, lightning split the darkness, and all around us the frogs sang to each other. Then she passed us by, streaking towards the west and the north and to Darwin, before she faded away into the night. The frogs ceased to call, the mosquitoes buzzed and bit and we stood soaked to the skin, in awe of the power and of the performance that we had witnessed.

In those five hours we filmed just six feet of film, a mere two hundred and forty frames in total. In postproduction I was able to slow the frame rate even further, then with the magic of digital mastering, I was able to average the frames and smooth the motion. The storm lost none of its intensity or drama, the power was still there, and the power was awesome in the true sense of the word.

The film that Mark and I made I called "The Big Wet" and the star was the monsoon; the lightning was the key to her character, which was at times fickle and capricious, at other times moody and sullen, then suddenly flickering to anger. I was able to structure the film to the Gagadju calendar, and to my great pleasure many of the Aboriginal people who finally saw the film were happy with the treatment. I bookended the film with fire, the last fires of the old season and the first of the new. Namargon had, I hoped, shown something of his face.

The resulting film, the story of an exceptional season, "The Big Wet," was aired on the Discovery Channel in the United States, and has since won many awards internationally. For those technically minded the lightning was filmed using exposures that varied from up to thirty seconds per frame to as low as half a second. The camera was a 1960s Arriflex 16 ST and we always used prime lenses. The film stock was the incomparable low speed and fine grain Kodak 7245.

The Gagadju calendar is as follows; the months are only approximate:

GUNUMELENG   (October to December) The European Build-Up.
GUDJEWG   (January to March) The European Monsoon, or the Wet.
BANG-GERENG   (April) The "Knock-em-Down" storms.
YEGGE   (May to June) The season of plenty, the start of the Dry.
WURRGENG   (June to July) A cool season, still the Dry for Europeans.
GURRUNG   (August to September) The hot season, still the Dry.

Jeremy Hogarth has been involved in the film and television business since he was sixteen. Born in England of Irish parents he has always been fiercely proud of his Celtic blood. His adopted country is Australia. His first job was with Granada Television in London as a mail boy. However, the day before he was to start work he was knocked down in a car accident in Piccadilly, was unable to walk very well, and was put into film dispatch. There it was discovered that he had a brain, and from film dispatch he was put into an office that handled writers' contracts. Jeremy lasted just over one year, and then decided to emigrate to Australia at the age of seventeen and a half. When he landed in Sydney in 1968 he did not know a single person on the continent.

He found a job as an assistant film editor, and worked on news and current affairs programmes, but always with a love of the documentary. In 1971 Jeremy spent nine months in Asia, and then attended the London Film School where he graduated with first class honors. He worked as an assistant film editor on short term contracts with the BBC, before once again returning to Australia. Once back in Melbourne in 1974 he worked as a film editor, and then began to edit Natural History programmes for the Australian Broadcasting Corporation and decided that he had found the niche he wished to concentrate on.

In 1981 Jeremy left the ABC to pursue an independent career as a producer/director and as a writer. He has filmed in many countries on every continent except Antarctica. He has lived and worked in five countries, including the United States. Jeremy is now living in New Zealand where he is the executive producer of TVNZ Natural History based in Dunedin. His love is to take a wide canvas of nature and paint in the detail. That style of filmmaking has now been combined with his love of Asia, and Jeremy is series–producing a ten-part exploration of the wildlife of Asia to be made as a coproduction between TVNZ Natural History and NHK of Japan.

A PASSION FOR TRUTH

NICHOLAS WEBSTER

I've spent most of my life making documentaries, but because I grew up in the studios of Hollywood, I've always retained an interest in theatrical directing, even while being a creative part of the 1960's Golden Age of Documentaries in New York. It was a time when lighter equipment, Arriflex cameras and portable Nagra sound systems, which could be carried about by hand, freed us from the tyranny of the tripod. I was producing such innovative programs as "Walk in My Shoes" and "I Remember."

During those years most of my assignments were with the ABC CLOSE UPI documentary unit, headed by John Secondari, where I faced a wide variety of challenges.

The first was to follow a former prisoner back to the concentration camps, in several of which he had spent time, including Dachau, the last one from which he had escaped. He had first been arrested with his parents in Holland and sent with them to Auschwitz, but had become separated and had never seen them again. Now he hoped to discover what had happened to them.

The program had to be shot and edited in five weeks to meet a deadline caused by the postponement of the trial of Adolf Eichman. There was no time to research or even write an outline. Three of us, Leo Swaim, a staff writer, Simon Gutter, the former prisoner, and I, were to pick up crews in Germany and Poland behind the Iron Curtain.

The urgency of the rush turned out to be to our advantage, as we followed and filmed Simon through the various prisons, and Leo wrote down his thoughts as Simon remembered the horrors he had witnessed.

But it was not as simple as that. We needed a cinematic theme to tie the sequences together. I found it by chance as we traveled on a German train and filmed Simon in the dining car at a table covered with immaculate linen and silver. A huge difference from when he had traveled that same route earlier, hungry and miserable, huddled together with other prisoners in a cattle car.

Now, as we looked out the window, by chance we passed some cattle cars on a siding. That, and the sight of railroad tracks we later found leading into Auschwitz, gave me our theme: the sights and sounds of railroad tracks and cattle cars carrying Simon from one camp to another.

We were allowed to film only one day in Auschwitz with a Polish crew. Unlike the camps in Germany, the Russians had left Auschwitz exactly as they had found it at the end of the war; pathetic personal belongings lying about, piles of battered suitcases, artificial limbs and even false teeth. The gas chambers were left untouched. Sadly, no trace of Simon's parents was ever found.

Later we re-created his escape from Dachau with the camera running wildly through the woods; the very woods through which Simon himself had scrambled, sixteen years before.

The problem for Simon was that we were filming behind the Iron Curtain; and, as we approached the border, he became more and more terrified that he would be arrested again. We tried to reassure him, but at the final checkpoint he became rigid, staring straight ahead. Only when we had shown our credentials and were safely passed across did he breathe freely.

When we eventually got back to New York and edited the film, we put together a narration using Simon's own words, which he then narrated himself. His hesitant, deeply involved delivery gave a reality few professional actors could have given us.

The whole experience was very traumatic for all of us. Simon said he had managed to get through the nightmare of his incarceration by swearing to himself that he would live to tell the world of the atrocities he had witnessed. We were caught up in his emotion and were glad to be the instrument through which he *could* tell his story.

Stopping off in London on the way home, I felt filthy and exhausted. I remember taking a room overnight in a very posh hotel and spending an hour coming back to sanity in a bathtub full of hot, sudsy water.

Once, covering a huge rally held by a new black leader, known as Malcolm X, I was startled at the depth of feeling of the thousands of Afro-Americans present. It was like a gathering of several hundred church congregations, and Malcolm X was their charismatic, forthright-speaking pastor.

If this was a sample of how the new blacks felt, we deemed it necessary to bring their story to the entire country.

It was immediately decided that it should be told completely in their own voices. No white host or narrator present. Those filmed were encouraged to speak out, to say whatever was on their minds.

When the program aired, it caused a sensation. In fact several southern stations that had previewed it refused to run it. One state announced they would no longer use the sponsor's (Bell and Howell) projectors in their schools. A northern state countered that they would, from then on, use *only* Bell and Howell equipment. The sensation was caused by the very frank statements from the Afro-Americans' own lips, words and thoughts white-America was hearing for the first time.

We presented the program, not in agreement nor in disagreement, but just to let the people of America know how one-seventh of the population felt.

A different kind of problem was presented when I directed *The Long Childhood of Timmy*, about the difficult, painful decision a New York family made in sending Timmy Laughlin, their nine-year-old boy afflicted with Down's syndrome, away to a Catholic school where he would have proper care in order to make the most of his limited life.

The family members were a mother and father, Timmy, a teenage sister and two brothers, one in college and the other in the sixth grade, who all lived in a small, New York apartment.

The problem was how to add our crew of a director, cameramen, assistant, electrician, and Susan Garfield, the coproducer and writer, all to the already crowded apartment, and film natural scenes of family activities without the feeling that a camera was present.

We sort of moved in with the Laughlin family for several afternoons and evenings without attempting to shoot. We were as unobtrusive as possible; we tried to become part of the family, helping with the dishes, etc. We used very fast Eastman Tri-X, black and white film, in order to use available light, aided by a few permanent soft lights placed around the apartment.

I even ran quiet drills, so that we could casually move to our equipment and start filming when anything significant was happening that was important to the family relationships with Timmy, or their feelings about the impending separation. After a while they were so used to us, we were able to get intimate scenes we needed.

We also filmed the trip to St. Colleta's school for children with special problems, in Boston, and the painful, but necessary, transfer of Timmy to the kindly nuns.

Apparently our careful planning worked. The reviewer for *The Philadelphia Enquirer* wrote, "The Laughlins and all others seemed utterly unaware they were being filmed." *The New York Times* said, "Scenes almost overwhelming in their poignancy brought something rare and beautiful to television."

From time to time in New York, I had opportunities to direct feature films and television projects. First the film *Gone Are the Days* with Ossie Davis, Ruby Dee, and Alan Alda, from Ossie's Broadway play *Purlie Victorius*; then the TV series *Eastside West-side* with George C. Scott and Cicely Tyson; but most of my thoughts and energies, at that time, were with the documentary.

When I eventually did return to Hollywood and was directing TV series such as "Bonanza," "The Waltons," and "Mannix," I soon discovered that I was right in the first place—the world of the documentary was much more satisfying and exciting.

As I had always subconsciously added a sense of reality to the dramas I filmed, and a sense of drama to the documentaries, I naturally gravitated into docudramas.

The best examples of these were those I produced and directed for David Wolper's *Appointment with Destiny* series for CBS, *The Last Days of John Dillinger* and *Showdown at OK Corral*.

These docudramas permitted no invention of scenes or dialogue. We did take the liberty in *OK Corral*, that television existed at that time, but whatever we filmed had to be based on fact.

Each of the several movies made of the Wyatt Earp-OK Corral story took wild liberties with the facts, staging long, cliché-ridden movie gun battles wherein the participants ran about setting fire to wagons, climbing stairways, falling off balconies, and using up enough ammunition to start a small war.

We felt that the true facts, of four men facing four others in the middle of a corral, firing at close range in a gun battle that lasted for about thirty seconds, and missing half the time, had a ring of reality that was more ridiculous and believable than all the standard gunfights of movie westerns.

To counter the fact that it happened so fast, I reshot it again in slow motion ("as it appeared in the memories of those who were present") so that we could show and analyze just what happened. It worked, and the audience could sense that, for the first time, they were seeing what really took place that day in Tombstone, Arizona.

Not to put down that wonderful, old John Ford western, *My Darling Clementine*; it just wasn't the way it happened (for example, Old Man Clanton, who figured strongly in that gun fight, had been dead for several years). It was pure fiction; ours was a different approach with, we felt, a virtue of its own.

By whichever form used, docu or docudrama, the documentarian has a great responsibility to present the truth. Audiences for a feature film know they are in a world of make-believe and can watch and accept the most outlandish scenes. They know it's all been made-up and the hero didn't really die, but when they watch a documentary they take what they see as the truth and hopefully form opinions and make decisions based on that truth. I'm not talking about propaganda films. I mean true documentaries about serious subjects that can have profound effects.

I have traveled the world for many years, filming documentaries and docudramas, always seeking those truths. It's been a satisfying and enlightening journey.

Growing up in Hollywood, working in the studios as a young man, I acquired a distorted sense of reality. The viewing of one documentary turned my life around. It was Robert Flaherty's epic, *Man of Aran*.

Thus began an odyssey that has taken me several times around the world, to the deserts of Afghanistan, the bat caves of Guatemala, the Nepalese Himalayas, and to London, Paris, Rome, Moscow, and eventually back to Hollywood, meeting and filming fascinating people: President John F. Kennedy, Indira Gandhi, Orson Welles, Walter Cronkite, Robert Flaherty, Simone deBeauvoir, Ossie Davis, Ruby Dee, David Wolper, the Maharajah of Jaipure, Elizabeth Taylor, and Pope John XXIII.

These true stories from his book, *How To Sleep On A Camel, The Adventures Of A Documentary Film Editor*, are dramatic, sometimes heart-warming, and often hilarious.

Nicholas Webster's films have received many Emmy nominations and have won international awards in Venice, Vienna, and Berlin. Critics have given his work high praise: "An overwhelming experience. Sixty high-tension minutes punctuated by glowing arcs of emotion." *Variety*. "A stunning accomplishment . . . a work of artistry, courage and power." *New York Times*. "Ranks high among the handful of memorable documentaries made for television. With this show, producer-director Nicholas Webster is established as one of the eminent talents in the documentary medium." *Variety*.

THE ICE CLIMB COMMITMENT

Bob Carmichael

For better or worse, I seem to have made a career out of hazardous filmmaking. I dislike the pigeonholing that comes with that handle but at least the specialization of my work helps it to stand out. With so many directors around these days at least it is clear what I do: create and capture action in potentially dangerous environments. How did I come to this esoteric job description?

I am definitely a Type T or thrill-seeking personality. I understand sports and athletes because I am an athlete. I played organized football from third grade

through college until an injury suddenly ended my career. With fourteen years invested in a sport that ended in one play, I was suddenly no longer part of a team. I was devastated and lacked clear vision of who I was. Fortunately I was introduced to rock climbing and as soon as I could walk again, I was roping up.

I fell in love with climbing. One of the major reasons I'd gone to the University of Colorado was my love of skiing and the mountains. My skills as an athlete translated very well into my new sport. There were major differences, however; climbing was a game with consequences far more dire than football. Also climbing had a poetic and metaphysical level that really appealed to me. I taught skiing in the winter and climbing in the spring and summer.

Climbing was almost mystical in its tales and drama, and for someone who had been climbing trees since he could walk it held all my attention. In those days many climbs had an aura of invincibility, and a free climbing revolution was sweeping the sport. The accent wasn't solely on athleticism as much as the idea of breaking through psychological barriers. There existed a reverence towards the rock. The climbs had a real totem back then. It was the early 1970s.

I was then a twenty-two year-old political science major fresh out of college trying to figure out a direction for my life. I had an interest in still photography, thanks to the movie *Blow-Up* and I had three summers of a training program at ABC Television behind me. I decided to put everything on the line and produce a film about climbing. I sold my truck and virtually everything of value I owned to pay for my first film. It simply had to be done. If nothing else I wanted my family to know what I was into.

We ended up making a short film that in many ways captured the time and place of Eldorado Canyon, Colorado, in the early seventies. The film captured the dance of climbing and the union of climber and nature. We hauled a 16mm camera up the one thousand foot vertical route the two men were climbing. The talent were a couple of great young climbers named Roger Briggs and Duncan Ferguson. It was scored by a brilliant local musician named Tommy Bolin who would later rocket to national prominence, then tragically die of an overdose of heroin. I literally hitch-hiked to New York City with my new film in a backpack. I promptly sold it to CBS Sports who had never seen a rock-climbing film before. I flew home to Colorado and my adventure film career was underway.

Twenty-four years later I was back in Colorado to make another in a line of thirty odd climbing projects going all the way back to that first *Naked Edge* film. This project was to film a 450 foot frozen waterfall known as Bridalveil Falls in Telluride, Colorado, for the *National Geographic Explorer* series. The previous year I'd done an eight-week shoot on big wave surfing in Hawaii's Oahu's North Shore for *Geographic*. The ice-climbing film would be a homecoming of sorts for me. I now live in Malibu, California, but I was going back to Boulder to make a film on extreme ice climbing. The person I was particularly interested in was Duncan Ferguson. When I arrived in Boulder on the scout to interview Duncan he came into the room and I looked carefully at him. He had the same lean build, but his hair was frosted with gray. He was just about twenty-four years older than the twenty-one year old climbing prodigy he'd been.

I was struck by the continuity Duncan had managed to maintain in his own life. He had stayed in Boulder, he had continued to climb, and to all I asked he was ice climbing as well as anyone in the world. When I shot him and Roger on the *Naked Edge* I'd gotten to know the purest in Duncan. He climbed like a dancer, he had a very Spartan diet, and he was prone to rappel on the most minimal of webbing. He reduced everything to its simplest form. Even as a twenty-one year old Duncan was all about style and control.

He and his wife Sue Billings were living up in James Town. Duncan was a product designer and tester for a number of prominent outdoor manufacturers. Both he and Sue had their offices at their home, and their children could walk to school. I was struck by how much control Duncan had taken over his life; he shaped it to fit his values and his love of the mountains. There was little compromise to the fast-paced world that I had bought into. His family clearly took precedence as to what was important. Both he and his wife were involved and devoted parents and it showed in their beautiful children. It was as if Duncan put up a sign that read, "World, I'm not buying into your beliefs; this is what I believe." It certainly made me take stock of the direction and accomplishments of my life.

I think it boils down to the fact that in everyday life as we know it there is little of what Duncan calls the "mirror of climbing" where climbing becomes almost a metaphor for life. Duncan sums it up and it makes sense to me: "Life is a lot of changes as climbing is, and all we can really do is to respond to those changes with grace and style. And I've taken climbing to be just that for me. Climbing throws things up in your face. It throws challenges up. It throws fear into your face. And if I can learn to respond to it with grace, with style and control, and learn from it, then hey I'm a happy man."

I was happy for what Duncan had achieved, for both his clarity of thought and his ability to express himself, but I was very curious to see him climb again. The first major climbing scene of the film was to be a free solo of the Rigid Designator, a 125-foot-high vertical icefall. In simple terms, he would forgo all the safety afforded to roped climbing. A slip-up would be fatal. Given all the climbing shooting I had done, I made it a point to turn down assignments to shoot soloists. The reason was very simple: I knew that the presence of a crew and camera altered the environment for the soloist. It only takes one mistake for me the camera operator to witness the climber plunging to his or her death. I had shot enough great climbers who just happened to accidentally slip or fall while we were shooting. Big name climbers. But with Duncan, I felt that because it was so much a part of what he'd always done that he had the focus and maturity to handle the added pressure of the camera crew.

It was a windy, blustery day up in Vail and some twenty-seven inches of snow had just fallen. The Rigid Designator was wild and spectacular. Duncan's climbing left me in awe. It was like seeing Nolan Ryan pitching in the last stages of his career. He was simply a master of his sport. Duncan was poised, confident, and each of his tool placements, sure and precise. I kept my communications to a minimum. I didn't want to interfere. David Breashears and I were on the route and we just let him climb by. One hundred and sixty feet off the deck with no rope, I knew that Duncan Ferguson was the perfect choice for my film. With a lifelong commitment to climbing behind him and being at the top of his ice-climbing career, he deserved to have this film made about him. I wanted to let people see him climb and hear his story.

Joining Duncan as the other member of the ice-climbing team was Nancy Pritchard. She was ten years younger than Duncan and a recent Ph.D. in history from the University of Colorado. I wanted a woman in the film and one that could express herself well and was good enough to lead on Bridalveil. It promised to be an interesting matchup. I liked the idea that Nancy through her then job at *Rock and Ice* magazine knew a lot about climbing and represented a different era than Duncan with his traditional climbing roots. Nancy represented a much more modern, more commercial side of climbing. It was obvious that she was something of a self-promoter; Duncan was at the opposite end of the spectrum with his climber as visionary roots. He had little written about him and he eschewed publicity. I thought the pairing would be interesting. I didn't realize it would be combustible.

For Nancy, going down to the San Juan's was taking on a very large challenge. Not only was she going down to climb the biggest, most notorious waterfall in the state but she was going up with a climbing legend who was intimidating in his own right. On top of it all, Bridalveil was a very difficult ice climb with an approach that was threatened by major avalanche activity. What would happen? How would these two people get along? It was going to be a difficult project.

Aside from the obvious tension between our talent, and the unsettling avalanche conditions, I was breaking in a new assistant director, a very good climber/rigger and former actor, Kevin Donald, but despite our long friendship, it soon became obvious that both of our styles were clashing. At first my inclination was to simply release him from the film. Instead, we sat down and talked it through. I was amazed to hear how similar his family background was to mine. I learned about his life and he learned about mine. We'd gone to college together and knew each other reasonably, well, but not until that night did we really talk intimately about our pasts or our feelings. We hadn't really ever opened up to one another before, and the result was a much better relationship than either of us ever felt the other capable of. We were forty-five-year-old men and we hugged each other at the end of the talk. It was a revelation of sorts for me.

Very coincidentally we both knew that, given the friction between Nancy and Duncan, the same understanding that Kevin and I arrived at was lacking in Duncan's and Nancy's relationship. We knew we were in a position to make a film that went beyond the conventional inane dialogue of adventure films and into a much more interesting dimension of two very different people struggling to find mutual ground and undertake a formidable task. It promised to be an intriguing journey. I thought of it as the first adult climbing film. We made a pact that communication between Duncan and Nancy take place on camera. When they were off camera we kept them apart.

Our first ice climb was slated to be Coronet Falls. Nancy was going to lead it. A great local climbing guide Charlie Fowler and Paul Sibly had rigged the falls for me to go up and shoot.

The documentary ethic we adopted for Nancy's climb was that we just rolled the film and recorded her climb. No interference. Every attempt would be to capture the events as they unfolded. No contrivances, no fiction. Coronet was dangerous. The top cone of the falls was only about two inches thick with a running torrent of water under it. It was virtually impossible to protect. On top of all that Nancy was under the gun to perform; it was the first time Duncan had seen her climb and she was nervous. Both Kevin and I watched as Nancy flailed up the climb. As the director and cameraman, I was seriously considering calling off the climb because Nancy was really close to falling off and taking what I figured could be a disastrous long fall.

There have only been a few times in my life that I have looked through the viewfinder and thought the subject was going to disappear if he or she fell, and this was one of them. It was serious but it was essentially Nancy's call and I kept my mouth shut. Kevin saved Nancy from a serious injury by quickly preplacing some protection for her because she was climbing so poorly. If he hadn't done it she undoubtedly would have peeled off the rock. She managed to get up it, but both Kevin and I knew that the objective of climbing Bridalveil with Nancy Pritchard leading looked like it was in serious jeopardy. It concerned Kevin and I that Nancy seemed to conveniently forget that Donald had played a major role in her getting up the climb. I really wondered what I'd gotten myself into. What we didn't know was Duncan's reaction to the entire drama as he belayed from below.

What had taken Nancy around one and a half hours to lead, Duncan walked up in five minutes. My idea of joining these two people for a serious climb was looking extremely ill conceived. What I didn't anticipate was Duncan's response.

It was agreed at the beginning of the film there would be no off-limits to the shooting. The talk they had on camera after that climb was as serious and personal as any I've ever filmed in my life. After being thrust into the position of climbing partners, Duncan wanted to clear the air because he felt that Nancy had misrepresented her climbing talent to him and the production.

As I rolled my camera using hushed tones to my soundman and assistant, we let the camera take it all in. In no uncertain terms, the usually mild-mannered Duncan let Nancy know that his climbing stemmed from a personnel rapport with his climbing partner, with mutual respect and honesty the cornerstones of that relationship. He didn't feel that Nancy was being honest about her reasons for wanting to do a big major icefall. Why was she so eager to do a notorious climb? He didn't think she was ready for such an endeavor. He felt that she was endangering both herself and a partner by going into a remote big climb. The bottom line was, Duncan didn't want anything to do with the project if she wasn't ready to step back, reevaluate her motivations, make some serious adjustments in her ice-climbing technique, and develop a more honest/open relationship with him-period, end of story.

Nancy was in tears. And it was all on film. This was a genuine crisis and I wasn't sure if the film was over, or what was going to happen. I did know that this clash of style, approach, and philosophy was potentially very interesting. A lot depended on how Nancy took Duncan's criticism. It was a very quiet walk out of the canyon that evening. My producer and I were wondering whether to give the money back or recast another woman climber.

After a night of soul searching Nancy emerged the next day ready to postpone the scheduled climb of Bridalveil and take Duncan up on his offer to go back to basics on the ice. I for one admired her decision to stick with the project. A lesser person might have walked but Nancy Pritchard, while she got off to a very shaky start, was just gearing up to show us all just how strong-willed and talented she was.

We took our crew down to Ourey to a beautiful narrow 150 foot deep box canyon that was flowing with azure blue ice on both sides. During a beautiful, heavy snow fall Duncan and Nancy got down to basics, and for Duncan that meant climbing with no hand tools. Nancy is an accomplished rock climber and this new gentler, or athletic, approach made an instant difference in her technique. She got tuned into the ice and started working with it. Almost overnight Nancy was a lot less dialogue and a lot more climbing. Duncan's talk certainly got rid of any pretenses in their relationship and they were communicating, actually enjoying each other and making a lot of progress. After a couple days on tool placements and footwork Nancy climbed a lot better and she was eager to get back to Bridalveil. Hanging off ropes right next to them I was able to get some great footage of them actually having fun together in a spectacular gorge of colorful ice.

Nancy was both articulate and very tough. Her ice climbing made a tremendous jump with just a few pointers and sharpened tools. She was extremely goal oriented. She had her sights set on doing Bridalveil and I learned that once she set a goal she had a long history of seeing that it got done. Nancy is something of a pioneer in ice climbing and as she said, "It makes great stories for family and friends. Whenever I go back to Oregon, you know the whole neighborhood, my Mom's school, everyone wants a slide show and they want to hear and vicariously experience these magnificent things that they either don't want to do or they can't do and I like that. I like to be able to be a storyteller and the only way you tell stories is to live them. And I'm a historian by profession; Michelet says in order to write history you have to make history. I solidly believe that."

The following day the two were going to ski in to start the climb on Bridalveil. It took about forty minutes to ride a snow cat up the switchbacks that lead to the base of the falls. All along the way, tortured and withered trees stood in testimony to the fierce avalanches that unpredictable avalanches that sweep the box canyon. We had arranged for a control blasting of the slopes above the cliffs in the canyon. Major avalanches shoots come from three directions. For the uninitiated it looks like 800 foot rock cliffs in a picturesque box canyon at the end of Telluride. But the frightening reality is that 1,200 foot snow slopes lie unsuspectingly above these walls. We wanted to bomb them to give ourselves the safest possible access to the falls.

I had my sound person next to me in our staging area and my camera turning while the helicopter dropped several canisters of plastic around the canyon. Nothing. One last drop and he was going to clear out. A few seconds later, Duncan yelled out "Oh my God." Knowing Duncan's penchant for understatement, I knew something big was happening. I went into a mode I try to attain while shooting serious stuff; for want of a better word it's maintaining grace under pressure. My camera was on their faces as Duncan made his remark and I slowly swung behind their heads to show what they were seeing. I was shocked to see two huge torrents of snow launching into space off the high cliffs. It scared me. As I lay down on the ground to shoot them full figure with the gathering massive snow plumes behind them, I ungracefully asked Charley Fowler if we should run for it. He said no. I trust Charlie. I kept shooting.

In a matter of moments a cloud of spin drift snow about 1,000 feet in the air pillowed across the entire one-half mile canyon. Sixty seconds later the thick churning cloud engulfed us. As my camera rolled both Nancy and Duncan were hit by 50mph wind blast and literally blanketed by snow. The brilliant blue sky was eclipsed to dark gray by the spin drift. What we witnessed could only be described as a nuclear event. The speed and volume of the snow clearly demonstrated to us the amount of power a big avalanche can produce. It was sobering and scary.

No one would have had a chance had we been in the path of that avalanche. Clearly conditions were not good. A couple days earlier seven cars had been buried in avalanches in Vail Pass. To climb Bridalveil we were required go up and down that two miles of switchbacks twice a day with our eyes peeled on canyon walls. We now clearly understood why the trees in the canyon had knurled twisted stumps.

This film wasn't proving easy for any of us. Our talent were learning that just getting along with each other was proving to be more difficult than the climb itself, and now the natural defenses of Bridalveil were showing us their force. Not only were the on-camera people wondering what they were getting into, but so was my crew.

© M. Tobias

After the avalanche, Nancy and Duncan and the crew retreated to the local coffeehouse and Nancy got her chance on camera to let Duncan know that while he may have been accurate about some of his accusations at the base of Coronet icefalls, she felt he was far too hasty in making decisions about her climbing after one climb. I really appreciated her side of the story. She hadn't been climbing for twenty years, she wasn't a Duncan Ferguson, but she was confident she had what it took to be a solid partner for the upcoming climb. I gained a great deal of respect for her as she handled Duncan in a completely graceful manner but still made a solid rebuttal for herself. Duncan and she came away from the discussion with the air clear and both their sights set on the Bridalveil.

It was nearing the end of three weeks of shooting. Shoot days start around 5:30 a.m. and end for Kevin Donald, my producer Doug Millington, and I when we do our production work and Apple-assisted storyboards for the upcoming day. Having a mobile office with the right software has made production a, lot more detailed and buttoned up for me and my staff who are all armed with powerbooks. By 11:30 p.m. we were generally ready for the sack. It is an intense experience. As the director you are always thinking of coverage and ways to bridge into new areas of interest in the film. We kept a five-by-five-foot post-it board in the room and we tacked each day's scenes to it. Next up was scene 33 and that was Bridalveil Falls.

While we were out in the lower climbs, head rigger Paul Sibly, Kyle Copeland, and Billy Westbay had been flown into the top of the falls and helicopter long-lined the serious hardware into the climb. These boys were busy installing the secret weapon of this shoot. In 1988 we'd taken a prefabricated platform with wheels on it 2,000 feet up El Capitan to shoot off the Bootflake for *Star Trek V*, and that was considered state of the art. Now we were ready to take a technological leap and actually install a winch-driven camera platform that would raise and lower myself and Kevin to virtually any spot we wanted to shoot from. The platform promised be a great creative tool. We called it the God platform.

After twenty years of working together, I implicitly trust Sibly as a rigger and designer, but this rig was a prototype and it was raising and lowering 500 feet. By the time we got to the climb it was ready to go and Paul had done the test piloting. It worked and he was excited. It wasn't your average elevator. Kevin and I had to climb up the ice cone at the base of the falls and traverse a fixed line into the rig. I will never forget looking up as I climbed out to the platform. Massive columns and stalactites of ice hung over our heads, and it was terrifying. It was like, turning a corner and facing a firing squad.

The truth is, the place literally made me whisper; as I told Kevin, I knew we were in the wrong place. We ordered Paul to slowly bring us above the most overhanging of the ice blocks and got down to the business of shooting Duncan climb the pitch. I marveled at the grace and calm and precision of Duncan as he wove his way up that labyrinth of dangerous ice. It reminded me of a house of cards, all ready to come crashing down with a single wrong move. But as usual, Duncan was unflappable. He was at home. After twenty-four years he was perfectly slotted in this world of fragile, overhanging ice. I thought it was the scariest place I've ever been. Sitting sometimes eight feet away from the cliff in thin air, Kevin summed it best when he observed that "if there ever was a separate reality this was it."

After we rappled off for the night both Kevin and I honestly discussed that if we could live through tomorrow's filming, the worst would be over. That night, I wrote my children a letter in case we were killed shooting the next day. Somehow, knowing Kevin was ready to go and recognizing my own commitment to shooting this film, I knew I would get on that platform the next morning and go to work. It was my film, and it was a very important statement to me. I wanted to capture what Duncan Ferguson was all about. To do so, I had to meet him on his ground. I didn't like it but I had to go. I had to fulfill that commitment, no matter what. I didn't get much sleep that night.

The next day we came down from the top to avoid that rotten cavity at the bottom. Dangling 500 feet above the talus was an eerie perspective but the platform offered a great perspective. In space hanging five feet from the wall. It was truly a God's view of the climbing. Duncan led the next pitch which was the crux of the climb. Both Kevin and I shot dry-mouthed as I covered Duncan doing the wildest stemming ice overhang I had ever witnessed. He kept telling Nancy to watch him, and while his voice didn't betray any anxiety, the mere fact he was saying anything had Kevin and me gripped as we whispered back and forth to one another.

It was another of those spots where you don't want to turn off the camera because you never know what will happen. It was as extreme as I ever want to shoot. A fall would have been unthinkable, due to all the fragile curtains of ice. Both climbers would have been torn from the ice if Duncan had fallen. My camera purred along as I watched Duncan spread-eagle out an inverted V notch with hollow, rotten ice all around him, somehow staying on the ice. After leading that pitch twice so we could cover him with two ground cameras and my on-climb camera, Duncan's climbing of Bridalveil was essentially complete.

On the upper 100 foot headwall of 100 degree ice he soared up with one perfect tool and foot placement after another. All that was holding him on the ice were the one-inch crampons on his feet and the ice picks in either hand. He climbed the entire final portion of the climb with only one screw placement. That meant he was essentially free-soloing again. It was a remarkable performance in a truly spectacular arena.

For her part Nancy stood for five hours, without a complaint, belaying Duncan up the second pitch during his two on-camera ascents. She also managed to get up that hideous crux after standing in the cold for so long. The final day when we came back to shoot her on the final pitch, she took the lead and was all business. All the wittiness and fast talk were gone and in their place was a very solid, woman athlete who climbed that very exposed pitch safely and without any faltering. In my mind she did a great job of climbing and was a perfect partner in this film for Duncan. They both had represented themselves extremely well and hadn't backed off the emotional issues that arose either. I was proud of them both.

As Nancy said, "Climbing Bridalveil for me was a real humbling lesson and a real empowering lesson in being a female in a man's world, being expected to be part of a team but realizing that I can only be myself. I'm a 110 lb. thirty-two-year-old woman who hasn't been ice climbing for twenty-five years and hasn't been swinging axes or hammers, things which help when you're a climber, an outdoor man; my experience was just fine, being myself, and I didn't have to be just like Duncan Ferguson or just like Joe Mountaineer. I could sort of stand up for being a female. It sounds a little odd but I still climbed the dang thing."

The film *Ice Climb* appears on *National Geographic Explorer* series. My crew of eighteen people came together and decided to give their all to an idea. In four weeks of work and 30,000 feet of film we accomplished some very ambitious goals. We all left the project with the satisfaction of having made a film that went beyond the well-known physical world of climbing into a much more intricate personal journey.

Bobby Carmichael

Academy Award nominated, Emmy Award winning filmmaker. Carmichael directs and shoots national commercials and feature 2nd Unit action sequences. His recent credits include a 70mm film on the Daytona Speedway and 2nd unit sequences for *First Wives Club*.

STRANGE BEDFELLOWS:
THE FEATURE DOCUMENTARY, TELEVISION,
AND ANTHROPOLOGY

ANDRÉ SINGER

In 1991, the BBC for the first time created a regular series to promote, commission, acquire, and coproduce auteur style feature documentanes. The series was called *Fine Cut* and the films to be shown on peak-time British television were to be international, reflecting the aspirations and dreams of the filmmakers rather than those of the broadcaster. Founding and running that series for its first three years was the most rewarding and creative process I have undertaken in twenty-five years of filmmaking experience despite the fact that I directed none of the thirty-three films broadcast under my aegis and that much of my time was spent battling corporate financial and administrative bureaucracy whilst avoiding what I would have loved to do most of all—interfere in the productions that came within my area of responsibility. But working with gifted, temperamental directors who were notoriously wary of the constraints laid on by television structures proved to be perversely rewarding, particularly when the results of the relationship led to inspirational films.

My primary ambition for the series was to enable talent. The series was not meant to have preferences for style or subject matter. Yet—and hence the title of this article—I found that the implicit, and sometimes explicit influence of anthropology was enormous. This could, I hear the skeptic mutter, be attributed to the fact that in the person running the series, the BBC had an anthropologist and anthropological filmmaker. But although this was clearly influential, *Fine Cut* was never regarded in the film world as an anthropological series. I was anxious to be balanced in my support for feature documentaries from as wide a variety of sources as possible; what I found were elements in both the genres of documentary and in anthropology that were essentially complementary.

When introducing the *Fine Cut* series in 1992, I wrote that of the many and different definitions given the documentary genre, the one that I liked best came from the pen of that most influential filmmaker of them all, John Grierson. Grierson wrote, over sixty years ago, that any significant documentary should have "the power of making drama from our daily events and poetry from our problems." He added that it was also a genre that "offered a contact with the life of the community deeper and more intimate than anything journalism and the other arts were giving us." The first part of his quote could not be said to be fundamental to anthropology, but the last part could not be more apposite.

In starting the series I was essentially searching for a platform to present a style and form of filmmaking that went beyond reportage; that provided an intimacy missing elsewhere; and, in this age of television imperialism, was finding increasing difficulties in attracting suitable funding or (and never believe the filmmaker who tells you that this is not important) an audience outlet. It also seemed important at the time, and continues to be so today, to find a platform for directors whose endeavours are geared away from televisions structured boundaries. Certainly, once the restrictions of time are removed and a narrative no longer has to be squeezed into a statutory broadcast hour, most filmmakers find that in common with a feature drama, longer is stronger.

It has been more than twenty-five years since Alan Rosenthal interviewed leading documentary filmmakers in the U.S., Canada, and the U.K. to provide us with his fascinating comparative case study. One of the most interesting features to emerge from his book was how the funding structures in the U.K. for documentaries between the 1950s and the 1970s had almost totally been monopolized by broadcasters—primarily the BBC and later the ITV network. Other sources of funding from educational foundations, endowments, or government were negligible. British documentary filmmakers increasingly worked for television where their creativity depended upon whimsical patronage, or they rapidly moved into features. In America the influence of television was far less marked. Directors such as the Maysles, Fred Wiseman and Richard Leacock were able to find their funding outside television from sources such as The National Endowments for the Arts and Humanities, the MacArthur Foundation, etc. As a result it was American filmmakers with an increasing number of French, Dutch and other non-British European filmmakers who dominated the Festival circuit up to the 1990s.

In Britain, an occasional Denis Mitchell, Ken Russell, Jack Gold or Norman Swallow were in the past enabled by television to create new and experimental documentary forms, with in the 1980's Channel Four Television providing a new source of support. But few had the freedoms enjoyed by their American counterparts. Yet it is the work of these documentary artists that both endures and has fashioned the rest of the genre. The access work of Bob Drew and Don Pennebaker in the

U.S. or Jean Rouch in France, the gentle observations of Denis Mitchell, the structured style of Joris Ivens, the romanticism of Robert Flaherty; these survive not merely as historical steppingstones but to quote Richard Griffiths, they "deaf with eternal things" and so survive the passage of time. Unfortunately, much of British documentary filmmaking has followed the pattern long established in the U.S. by TV dependent films. It has allowed (or been forced to accept) market forces and criteria of popularity to dictate funding for programmes. The public service remit of the PBS system in the U.S. is still (just) the prerogative of the BBC and Channel Four in the U.K. but advertising revenues and linked ratings increasingly dominate programme decision-making on other networks and in the U.K. those networks have proliferated from four terrestrial channels to fifty cable channels almost overnight, with hundreds of digital channels en route. In this maelstrom there is little scope for the feature documentary to survive, let alone thrive. And yet somehow it has. Below, I have listed the films shown under the *Fine Cut* banner between 1991 and 1993. 1 am delighted that Nicholas Fraser, who took over the series after that time has continued to protect the genre inside the BBC and scored some very notable successes with such productions as *Hoop Dreams* (Steve James), *When We Were Kings* (Leon Gast and Taylor Hackford), and *Little Dieter Needs to Fly* (Werner Herzog). But I am concentrating on this list because they are the films I know the best, and because they enable me to revert to my original observation of pointing up the fertile links between contemporary filmmaking and anthropology. Of the first ten films to be broadcast in the U.K. (numbers 1 to 10 below), only Robert Gardner and Jean-Pierre Gorin claimed to be directly working on anthropological themes. Both filmmakers had anthropologists as partners on the production (Akos Oster on *Forest of Bliss*, and Dan Marks on *My Crazy Life*) and the directors were clearly swayed by the specialist research and approach of their colleagues. Of the remainder, some of the links are more explicit than on others. Les Blank, for example, accepts an affinity towards the 'tribal' approach of anthropology, and his producer for Innocents Abroad, Vikram Jayanti, has a long association of working with visual anthropologists. Stephen Olsson and Scott Andrews both studied visual anthropology prior to Olsson's work with French anthropologist Maurice Godelier in New Guinea. Their joint film *Last Images of War* was able to draw upon those sensitivities when looking at the relationship between the Afghans and the journalists who died trying to understand and relay the story of the cruel war in Afghanistan in the 1980s. And I would regard the approaches of John T. Davis (Hobo) and Susan Meiselas, Richard Rogers, and Alfred Guzzetti (*Pictares From A Revolatzon*) as having the intimacy and "bounded" structure essential for an anthropological understanding of a community or cultural group. The late-lamented and wonderfully sensitive Peter Adair in his approach to HIV-positive individuals (*Absolutely Positive*) would also find anthropology familiar territory; after all, his father John is one of the most influential anthropological filmmakers in America. Only with Russ Karel's archive-based look at black cinema (*In Black and White*) and Otto Olejar's story of Czechoslovakian World War pilots (*The Forgotten Men*) is the association tenuous.

Later in the series, several filmmakers are perceived as coming directly from a tradition of anthropological filmmaking. These are Melissa Llewellyn-Davies, David MacDougall, and Jean Rouch. Not surprisingly, the subjects tackled by these three filmmakers were classically anthropological, although their approaches were highly idiosyncratic. Jean Rouch, in a hugely amusing and distinctly innovative film (*Madame L'Eau*), took characters from earlier films on a reconstructed journey from Amsterdam to Niger in an attempt to show how they could construct windmills on the banks of the river Niger. The film moves from drama-documentary fantasy to access documentary. Melissa Llewellyn-Davies (*Memories and Dreams*) revisited the Maasai of her earlier oeuvre and looked at the passage of time on both Maasai and her own perceptions; whilst David MacDougall (*Time of the Barmen*) followed a more traditional pattern in recounting the lives of Sardinian shepherds at a time of increasing change.

Were subject matter to be the criteria that determines whether these films are 'anthropological', several of the others are instantly identifiable. Mike Apted's

© 1988 Stuart Keene

Incident at Oglala deals with a miscarriage of justice against the Sioux; Nick Gifford (*Bitter Thorns*) tackles identity and home for Somalian refugees; Haile Gerima (*Imperfect Journey*) returns to Ethiopian society with Ryszard Kapuscinski; Gil Cardinal (*Our Home and Native Land*) also returns to his society to view the struggle of Native Americans within the Canadian political system; and Paolo Brunatto (*In Search of Buddha*) analyzes the relationship between the West and traditional Buddhism in Nepal during the making of Bertolucci's feature film *Little Buddha*. But it is far more pertinent to realize that anthropology is no longer about 'tribal' society, or even issues affecting the developing world. Rather, it is about how we view society, about the institutions that constitute society—any society; and about the methodology used to view and understand society. Anthropologists need to tackle their subjects from within, hence the importance of field study and participation by the scholar in the subjects of his or her study. Great filmmakers have the same ethos. You can only understand and project your subject when in possession of intimate and detailed knowledge about it. Perhaps the links between anthropology and film are as simple as realizing that good anthropology and good filmmaking (or at least the good filmmaking that particularly appeals to me) both rely on a deep and compassionate understanding of society.

The films that made up the *Fine Cut* scenes on BBC Television between 1992 and 1994 under the editorship of Andre Singer were:

1. HOBO — John T. Davis
2. ABSOLUTELY POSITIVE — Peter Adair
3. INNOCENTS ABROAD — Les Blank
4. LAST IMAGES OF WAR — Scott Andrews & Stephen Olsson
5. THE FORGOTTEN MEN — Otto Olejar
6. LESSONS OF DARKNESS — Werner Herzog
7. IN BLACK AND WHITE — Russ Karel
8. PICTURES FROM A REVOLUTION — Susan Meiselas /Richard Rogers/ Alfred Guzzetti
9. FOREST OF BLISS (a) — Robert Gardner
10. MY CRAZY LIFE — Jean-Pierre Gorin
11. IN THE LAND OF THE DEAF — Nicolas Philibert
12. MADAME L'EAU — Jean Rouch
13. MEMORIES AND DREAMS — Melissa LLewellyn-Davies
14. INCIDENT AT OGLALA (a) — Mike Apted
15. BITTER THORNS — Nick Gifford
16. THE TIME OF OUR LIVES — Mike Grigsby
17. TIME OF THE BARMEN — David MacDougall
18. THE WAR ROOM — Don Pennebaker/Chris Hegedus
19. I AM A SEX ADDICT — Vikram Jayanti/John Powers
20. ASPEN COLORADO — Fred Wiseman
21. TITICUT FOLLIES (a) — Fred Wiseman
22. HIGH SCHOOL 11 — Fred Wiseman
23. FALLEN CHAMP (a) — Barbara Koppel
24. IMPERFECT JOURNEY — Haile Gerima

25. MOVING THE MOUNTAIN   Mike Apted
26. OUR HOME AND NATIVE LAND   Gil Cardinal
27. IN SEARCH OF BUDDHA   Paolo Brunatto
28. RISE AND FALL OF A DYNASTY   Bob Drew
29. DREAM DECEIVERS (a)   David van Taylor
30. THE HUNT FOR THE JACKAL   David Munro
31. THE EXECUTION PROTOCOL   Stephen Trombley
32. THE TROUBLES WE'VE SEEN   Marcel Ophuls

Films marked with an (a) are acquisitions bought "off the shelf." The others, whether called coproductions, presales, or commissions, all had editorial participation from *Fine Cut*.

PART IV

THE POLITICS

AND POSSIBILITIES

OF ADVOCACY

© Robert Radin

FROM WALDEN TO WAO KELE O PUNA
TO WETLANDS

Sheila A. Laffey, Ph.D.

Ballona Wetlands

The heron hatchlings keep me going. Their home in the Ballona Wetlands is threatened by the proposed development of 1,800 condos, called Playa Vista, which would rise above and obliterate their habitat. This area is part of a megadevelopment so large the *Wall Street Journal* reported it is "touted as the biggest real estate development in America over the next decade."

Three weeks ago, these big ungainly babies could be seen poking their heads above the nest gulping down food flown in fresh by their parents accompanied by a wondrous squawking cacophony. Something soared inside me when I spied them through my binoculars, and I knew we had to capture them on film. At that moment I also knew there was no turning back; we had to keep the vision and complete our documentary in spite of having raised a fraction of our budget. Maybe the herons and other wildlife through the documentary could plead for their very existence.

I visited the hatchlings again with Bruce Robertson, who, by bonding with the herons, returned many times like an accepted family member to document their development on video. But the hatchlings' feeding also deserved to be covered on film. Their cozy domestic scene would contrast with the cold, concrete buildings and tacky signs which surround Ballona. Once I committed myself to sharing the wonders of the hatchlings with a large audience, things fell into place. A cinematographer friend, who had started with *National Geographic* and now worked on big features, volunteered his time and got a friend to donate film equipment for half a day.

The Ballona Wetlands issue shifted into high gear when the Hollywood studio, DreamWorks, announced at the end of 1995 that it was becoming a one-third developer in Playa Vista. DreamWorks' partners are Hollywood titans Steven Spielberg, Jeffrey Katzenberg, and David Geffen. With 95 percent of southern California's wetlands lost, the preservation of Ballona has become a messianic mission with many Davids struggling against Goliath. As of December, 1997, over eighty groups had joined a coalition to oppose the megadevelopment. The struggle was referred to by many as The Last Stand.

I figured someone must already be working on a documentary on this issue. What a story! A real-life drama starring citizens, environmentalists, Native Americans, scientists, developers, filmmakers, celebrities, politicians and, most importantly, endangered wildlife, all set against the backdrop of Hollywood. Who could resist covering a development venture fueled by corporate welfare with political connections which extend to Sacramento and the White House?

There was a handful of committed activists armed with camcorders, but I didn't see anyone producing an in-depth program for major broadcast. I met Marcia Hanscom of Wetlands Action Network, and we talked about doing a PSA. I read stacks of articles, watched news clips, and talked to players in the drama. More than one environmental group had received funding from the developers, directly or indirectly, and not joined the coalition. Others felt the land would inevitably be developed eventually and, since the developers describe the project as environmentally sensitive, it was best to support this venture. I wondered how sustainable a project could be when so much of the land would be altered. The issue was indeed complicated.

When moving from Hawaii to L.A., I swore I would no longer struggle to produce issue-oriented videos without funding up front and, with some relief, recycled piles of grant guidelines. After all, I have a Ph.D. in Cinema from NYU, taught film as an assistant professor, know a few people in the biz, and am a Type A personality. It was time to get real and make some money.

I had already devoted the last seven years to conservation. Maybe I could work on a feature film like *Free Willy*. Richard Donner had come to a party we gave in Maui ten years earlier. Maybe he'd remember. Maybe I could make a difference AND make some money! Or maybe I'd just go back to teaching. Someone else was bound to come along and document this issue.

I found myself sitting next to Joanne D'Antonio at a monthly lunch with other women in the film biz. She edited *Broken Rainbow*, a film about Native American women struggling against the mining of native lands. I had once shown this film, which won an Oscar for best documentary, so I was happy to meet her. She also told me she edited the ten-part *Voice of the Planet* series for Turner Broadcasting written, directed, and produced by Michael Tobias.

I'd heard about Michael's amazing body of work from our mutual distributor at The Video Project. Michael was excited to hear about a possible documentary on Ballona and volunteered his services as executive producer. The PSA had become a documentary!

I had always been curious about Ballona when my family shuttled me to and from the airport on visits to L.A. Whizzing by what appeared to be dry, yellow fields, I'd ask them what was happening to this vast open space. They gave me updates: it's being developed, it's not being developed. I had no idea what flora and fauna lived there until I moved to L.A., walked the land, and realized how truly alive it is. I discovered that "Ballona" is derived from the Spanish word for whale and that the area had functioned as a whale calving ground.

The heron hatchlings keep reappearing in my mind's eye. Bruce called to announce they are airborne. This update reignited my endless revising of proposals to foundations and possible coproduction entities, phoning, faxing and visiting celebrities, or more likely their assistants, e–mailing back and forth with Michael, and following up on leads, any leads.

One PBS station which had expressed interest over several months in a possible coproduction finally admitted they turned us down, in large part, because they sensed our program would be an advocacy one. It is disheartening that our society has reached the point where advocating for wildlife is considered unbalanced. We told the station we would make every effort to let the players tell their own story, but we also sensed there is more at stake in their rejection.

The file of foundation rejections grows larger than the pending and approved files. Fewer and fewer foundations fund media projects, particularly issue-related ones. And very few include southern California in their targeted areas. It seems some consider it hopeless. More than one grants officer advised us to focus on Hollywood donors, but it's difficult to find celebrity conservationists who have the courage to break the conspiracy of silence surrounding this issue. It's easier to support rainforests in remote areas.

In spite of the lack of funding, events cry out for documentation. We filmed migrating birds before they returned home and interviewed Jerry Rubin during his twenty-eight day hunger strike. We caught him as he watched the Food Channel, recalled his friendship with the "original" Jerry Rubin, and spoke movingly about Spielberg's *Schindler's List*. During our filming drama is heightened as the noon deadline for an agreement about a meeting with DreamWorks' principals approaches, and the studio's spokesperson calls.

The colorful four-day Earth-Water-Air-L.A. (EWALA) trek, which followed the path of the L.A. River, and culminated at Ballona Wetlands on Earth Day, also couldn't be missed. At the end of the thirty-eight-mile walk, participants and supporters sat in a circle sharing their experiences and we placed a microphone in the center. I was so affected by the insights expressed and sense of solidarity of the group that I joined hands with the participants. I couldn't help but remember other times I'd similarly shifted back and forth from documentarian recording events to activist engaged in some form of action.

We also recorded performances by FrogWorks, a street theater satire on the Ballona issue, and interviewed the pregnant woman who played the Frog and who had walked a good part of the trek.

Thank God for Todd Brunelle, a talented young director whom my Mom met while he was growing tomatoes next door. She said whoever was growing those tomatoes had to be a nice person. At first, I wondered if Todd was too creative. For the opening sequence of our demo tape he turned down the color knob on the TV and filmed right off the screen the black and white image of a screenwriter who had testified against the development. Tilting the hand-held camera back and forth, he moved in closer when the screenwriter's tears began to flow. It worked. He learned the technique at UCLA as a substitute for more expensive effects.

Spielberg's film, *The Lost World*, grossed $141 million during its first two week-ends. The developers of Playa Vista paid $158 million to purchase over 1,000 acres at Ballona. The irony strikes me when I realize I've been worrying about renting a camera for $100 for half a day or spending $25 an hour editing our demo tape. I remember Peter Kreitler's words: "We can entertain ourselves to extinction or educate ourselves to enlightenment." Tom Brokaw ended his "Nightly News" about the Playa Vista controversy saying that "no special effects can duplicate this," over the image of a snake wending its way through the grass at Ballona.

Everyone agrees that we have a hot story, but it seems that a media oligarchy holds sway. We keep running into political resistance. Hollywood artists concerned about the issue tell us they are hesitant to speak out; coproduction possibilities seem more limited. A cable network known for its docudramas returned our demo tape saying they don't do "reality programming," but suggested we send it to

Sundance when it's completed. A feature documentary had crossed my mind but if raising money for a TV program is so challenging, what about the much higher cost of transferring it to film?

I met a filmmaker from Germany who thinks this could be a big story in Europe. We edited a longer demo tape and sent it over with him to pitch. He said Germans like programs with a liberal slant and don't expect "balanced" programming about environmental issues as do the British and Americans. A production company is producing a segment on the Ballona issue for a public affairs show which airs on PBS, but they only offer $400 for ten minutes of footage. At that rate, we decide it best to retain what we have, so I put the researcher in touch with one of the activist videographers.

To help with the funding void we consider expanding the focus to include other wetlands soon to be designated as the Southern California Coastal Wetlands Complex. The title would change from *Hollywood's Dream* or *Nightmare at Ballona Wetlands* to *The Pacific Flyway: Cradle of Life in Peril*. A *Steven and Me* approach could also be effective, perfect for POV.

Sometimes small miracles come when you need them. We got a betacam camera for only $500 for five days, just in time to film the boycott of *The Lost World* and to interview actor Esai Morales. Esai says with a laugh that he worries about becoming a "hero addict," adding some levity to the program. He refers to Ballona as "the lost world right here in our own backyard."

In the spring, I checked out the wildflowers with a cinematographer in an area of the wetlands slated for a marina. We were amazed by the huge size of this area, the colorful flowers and the wildlife: a rabbit, hummingbird, several herons, many mockingbirds, and an array of exquisite swallows who glided around in a choreographed circle in front of us. My main thought was how to get all this on film, especially the wildflowers before they faded, when we had so little funding.

I've started work on a culture of violence and animals documentary, which actually has funding, and trust we can get the word out about Ballona before it is too late.

Paradise in the Pacific?

The wetlands documentary was not the first time I desperately sought funds to produce a program to help save the environment. It happened in Hawaii in 1990 with "Geothermal: A Risky Business in Hawaii's Wao Kele O Puna Rainforest." With a couple of broadcasts on PBS and over fifty on cable, many taxpayers were struck by the evidence against the development. Clips were screened for legislators. It may have been one of many factors which contributed to the developers' canceling of the project, citing public relations problems. It happened in 1995 while producing "Hawaii in Transition: Vision for a Sustainable Future." Maybe knowing these programs made a difference helps drive me now.

I teamed up with hazardous waste expert, Dr. Paul Conant, and Roger Bailey who interviewed W.S. Merwin, the Pulitzer Prize winning poet who lives on Maui and opposed the geothermal project. Months earlier I had interviewed Randy Hayes, head of Rainforest Action Network, at a large demonstration against the development in the Big Island rainforest. We heard that Jerry Garcia, who was in Kailua–Kona on a diving trip, was concerned about such issues, so, after a number of phone calls, we were able to set up an interview. But it was mostly native Hawaiians and other citizens, scientists, and energy experts, who cogently addressed the problems with the development in the documentary.

Viewers of the program told me how well done it was and how it had helped change some minds about the development. Though it was a low–budget

Photo: Sheila Laffey

production shot on a one chip hi 8 camera, their response suggests that content can be more important than form when it covers a heated issue.

Fortunately I didn't have to fund-raise for activist videos for five more years. In the interim I coproduced children's programs in Hawaii, and PSAs in American Samoa with actors outfitted in fish costumes to high-light marine problems. When it came time to docu-ment a number of exciting solutions to some of Hawaii's problems, "Hawaii in Transition: Vision for a Sustainable Future" was launched. This last produc-tion took three years to complete, including endless fund-raising, arranging screenings and broadcasts, and finding the right distributor. The PBS broad-casts actually cost me money since I sent out flyers to 200 PBS stations reminding them of the date and time of the program's uplink. I wonder when society's priorities will change and documentary filmmakers will receive the kind of support they do in England through the BBC.

We are now completing a related guide and bio-patrol game to accompany the video though grant moneys for my work have been delayed for four months. If I didn't meditate, I would have gone crazy years ago.

And yet life could not have been more full. I helped a friend in Hawaii, Naomi Sodetani, on her documentary, *Malama Halawa,* about the most expensive highway in the country which was being built through Halawa Valley and would pass through more than a hundred sacred sites. We rode in a van with members of the press on a tour into the valley by a Department of Transportation official who proudly displayed the engineering feats under way. Filming huge piles of displaced earth, pipes and girders and the mechanical intrusion of heavy equipment into this once peaceful valley, we lamented this raping of the land in the name of "progress."

I sat in a large circle with native Hawaiians and others who, one by one, shared their feelings about the cement trucks which would hurtle down the road the next morning for the opening of the tunnel into the valley. Some said they planned to be arrested; others said they would wait to be guided by a higher power.

Awa root was ceremoniously ground in a gourd, and a cup filled and passed to each person in the circle amidst chanting. We were asked that night to remember the spirits of the ancestors whose bones would be reinterred in the valley before dawn and to remember them with every step we took. We were also asked to mentally link the Hale o Papa and Luakini (male and female *heiau* or sacred sites) every hour on the hour after midnight when the conch shells were blown. The sites would be severed physically by the highway, but not spiritually. I often changed hats in Hawaii as well from observing documentarian to committed activist.

I am reminded of my early childhood connection with nature in New England where I spent hours exploring neighboring fields and the woods with my cousin, tracking animal prints in the snow, and accompanying my uncle as he fished and trapped.

At Tufts University I asked my literature professor if I could produce a film on Thoreau's *Walden* instead of writing yet another term paper. My boyfriend, Fred

Cardin, shot some exquisite footage on color reversal film with his 16mm bolex during the height of fall, often using three planes of focus of leaves, trees, and water. When we screened the film around Boston, we played a reel-to-reel tape of Fred reading appropriate passages from the book over music from the Brandenberg Concerto.

I eventually received a grant to record a poet reading the *Walden* passages, and Bruce Langhorne scored the film in Hollywood. First Run/Icarus Films still distributes *Walden* twenty-five years after it was filmed.

I somehow feel that the birds, trees, plants, and fish have called upon me to share their lives with others through the programs I have produced on the West Coast, the East Coast, and in the middle of the Pacific. Except for the fund-raising challenges, these adventures have not usually felt like work. They've been a way of life.

Sheila A. Laffey is President of Echo Mountain Productions, Inc. whose mission is programming that makes a difference. Award winning works include: *We All Need the Forest, In the Middle of the Sea*, and *Hawai'i in Transition: Vision for a Sustainable Future* which is distributed by The Video Project. She was a producer of *Geo-thermal: A Risky Business in Hawaii's Wao Kele O Puna Rainforest* and Associate Producer/writer for ARTV, a ten part art history series.

Having earned a Ph.D. in Cinema Studios from New York University she has been on the faculty of several universities. She also worked as a conservationist with the National Audubon Society and University of Hawaii, Sea Grant.

A MANIFEST ON THE SUBJECT OF DOCUMENTARIES

BY STEFAN JARL

Let's begin at the beginning.

What is a documentary film? Exactly what characterizes a documentary? There are three criteria:

1. Julia Roberts is not in it.
2. If you enter a movie theater and it is completely empty, then you can be sure that they are showing a documentary.
3. If there is one person in the audience and he or she isn't laughing, you can be equally certain that it is a documentary.

Joking aside, one generally associates documentaries with cinéma vérité. Cinéma vérité is defined as a movie that is both *objective* and *accurate*. What we see is the truth, filmed by the filmmaker in a certain sequence. The scenes flash before our eyes, objectively put together, as close to the actual sequence of events as possible. That is how filmmakers love to perceive the situation; they see the filmmaker as a so-called *True Witness*.

Nothing could be further from the truth. There is no such thing as an accurate and objective documentary. The filmmaker affects the situation when he or she enters a room with a camera. An immediate psychological transformation takes place. Someone objects to being filmed and someone else thinks, "Why didn't I wash my hair?" Another person is in the midst of planning his or her Hollywood career, just waiting to be discovered, and so forth. None of these things would have happened if the filmmaker and a camera had not been in the room at the time.

Stefan Jarl and his cameraman Per Källberg, (left)

The intelligent spectator is aware of all this. Movie scenes are never shown in the order they were filmed. They are always rearranged to suit the filmmaker's purpose. A filmmaker is a manipulator. He or she arranges the scenes in the manner thought best. That's why the audience is there in the first place. An audience is meant to be manipulated. The more manipulation the better. "I don't make objective and accurate documentaries, I make feature films," says American Robert Wiseman, who has probably been more closely associated with cinéma vérité than anyone else in modern times.

There is no difference between a documentary and a feature film. However, the nature of each is different. They both came into being so that filmmakers could express themselves. There is always a person behind the images on the *silver screen*, and the easier it is to discern that person the better.

The Swedish national television company rule book states that television documentaries must be objective and accurate. If they are not, the Swedish national television company will not broadcast them. I detest television and never watch it. I have never made a television film for one simple reason; I hate objectivity and *truth*. My movies are subjective; they express <u>my</u> truth. The world and how it is presented is directly related to how <u>I</u> experience it. Other people and their experiences have nothing to do with it. My perception consists of the things <u>I</u> see and what <u>I</u> consider important, not what other people see and think. Furthermore, I want to influence others using what I have seen.

What I have seen is important to see and what is more, my vision of what I have seen is more valid than the perceptions of others in this respect. To tell you the truth, I want everyone else to see things as I see them.

I make movies because I want to influence others.

The filmmaker who implies that he or she is making an objective and accurate movie, in other words the television filmmaker, is deceitful and two-faced. Such filmmakers want us to believe that they portray the only true image of reality. That is not true. They are, in fact, being untruthful. The truth is that they are *playing the client's game*. They do as they are told and cling to *objectivity* and *truth*. The worst thing of all is that the *orderer*, the state-owned Swedish television company, in actuality the Swedish government, holds all the power. The objective and truthful filmmaker carries out the will of the powers that be.

Who wants to watch movies that express the values and hierarchies of the powers that be? My movies are not part of a world of false suppositions and agreements. They belong to the proud European tradition of rebellion; my movies represent another way of looking at and perceiving *reality*. They are on the side of the common man. Not only that, they profess to be the voice of ordinary people, the people whose voices we seldom hear. That's why the man in the street is my protagonist.

A good documentary is only as good as the rapport between the people in front of the camera and the people behind it. Bad relationships make bad films. Every person has his or her own story that deserves to be made into a movie, but few movies touch on such matters.

In 1922, Flaherty's movie *Nanook* opened in Sweden. It was a big success. More than seventy-five years later I was fortunate to have a similar experience with my film *A Respectable Life*. It became one of the most successful films in the history of Swedish documentaries. Like *Nanook*, it deals with ordinary people and that is exactly why it is so unique. After his success, Flaherty received many offers to make more Nanook-type films. Someone told him about an island called Aran in the middle of the Atlantic Ocean. The people there were said to lead a harsh existence that was primarily dependent upon fishing. Flaherty went to the island to make a documentary about these poor but industrious people. When he got to the island, he realized that the things he had heard about the inhabitants were completely untrue. The people had put their narrow wooden boats on land and not used them for many years. He had been told tales of a bygone era. What should he do now? Should he return home? Flaherty shed a tear and went for a walk. He had come a long way and might as well make a movie after all. Although becoming leaky, the old boats were not yet completely rotted. He managed to find a couple of old fishermen at the retirement home who hadn't completely forgotten how to row the old boats. So, why not continue as planned? The old men out in the huge waves would make great footage! It would look as if they were endangering their lives to earn a living. Take it from me, it was a great documentary, full of action and breathtaking scenes. Eat your heart out, Arnold Schwarzenegger; *Man of Aran* has it all! There's nothing that Flaherty hasn't done. He is the father of the creative documentary, and I carry on in the same tradition.

I make my movies for the *silver screen* using 35-millimeter film and Dolby Stereo Sound. In my native country of Sweden, 85 percent of the movies are American in origin. I am fully aware of this fact and I know that I have to compete against such films for my audience. I have to be just as adept at captivating audiences as the American filmmakers are. I have nothing against competition; I've seen the beginning of *Jurassic Park* forty times.

I cannot deny that competing with American movies is hard, especially if you are outside the sphere of the commercial filmmaking business and the giant television monopolies. It's not easy to get production capital. You have to finance the movies you want to make with the money you can get your hands on, primarily from your audience. I call this my Robin Hood strategy. I take from the rich and give to the poor ones closest to my heart, namely me. My strategy works something like this: I court government agencies and similar bodies that control vast sums of money. I tell them that I want to make a movie about the activities of their government agency, showing their work in the best possible light. I offer my services to them as a commercial filmmaker and I convince them that I am the one who can portray their agency or similar body in an outstanding way. This is music to an agency director's ears. Later, I use the money I get to make movies of my own. For example, if I receive funds from the Swedish Environmental Protection Agency I use them to make a movie criticizing the Environmental Protection Agency in Sweden. Making a good film is very important. Otherwise, a government agency might turn the matter over to the police and claim that I swindled them. They could even send me to jail. However, if you make an outstanding movie that also happens to win a prize at a renowned international film festival, the authorities tend not to bother you. Everybody loves a *winner*, don't they? Robin Hood was not at all worried about being wanted by the government of his day, and neither am I.

This kind of strategy only works if you are your own producer, scriptwriter, director, distributor, and movie theater owner. I am all these things. I have been involved in establishing a noncommercial distribution company called Film-Centrum and a commercial chain of movie theaters known as Folkets Bio in my country. For example, *Misfits to Yuppies* is playing at one of our movie theaters in Stockholm at the time of writing. It's now in its third year. I received the European Academy Award for *Misfits to Yuppies* in 1993.

There are many more subtle problems in making documentaries today. One is that no one wants to be considered a documentary filmmaker. Everyone wants to be thought of as a creator of feature films. Nowadays, filmmakers make documentaries while they are waiting for a chance to make their first feature film. Film schools start with documentaries as *exercises* before students move onto the *real* thing, namely feature films. The Swedish government subsidizes feature films at a rate ten times greater than the amount allocated for documentary film productions. Documentaries are rarely reviewed on opening night, and a documentary may never be reviewed at all. Books on the subject of film history almost never mention documentary films. People tend to think of them as second-class films akin to the lumpenproletariat of the *art of film*.

The idea that the documentary belongs in the gutter is common among the elite in society, and it can drive the most insensitive person crazy. *Depicting reality is not fashionable.* Perhaps it's because we are so saturated with information nowadays that we

Stefan Jarl

are unable to absorb more reality. People are looking for relaxation, escapism, antireality and fiction. What happens to a society that is unwilling to see any longer?

In my opinion, it's a blessing that documentaries are in the gutter. That's where they belong; documentaries should be in places like dirty factories, retirement homes, Sarajevo, mining galleries, culverts, and hospital corridors. Documentaries should also be in the homes of the hungry and the unemployed, with vagrants and the outcasts, in the dark passages and neighborhoods, on the park benches, in prisons, with the downtrodden and the oppressed, the abused, the unjustly rewarded, and with those whom we have deprived of everything and alongside people without a voice—the unseen and the unheard. In short, documentaries should cover the backyard of society, the home of the guttersnipe.

This is the historical *mission* and *fate* of the documentary film. Such films cannot expect to captivate audiences at the finer movie theaters around town.

It is becoming harder for documentaries to survive at movie theaters. Television companies turn their backs on them more often than not. The same calls for entertainment and diversion are echoing throughout Europe.

A fear of being earnest and of speaking in real earnest too. We must not allow the documentary film to disappear. If it does, how can we protect ourselves against prejudice, misconceptions, myths and disinformation?

Stefan Jarl received a Silver Medallion at the Telluride Film Festival in 1993 for his work as a European documentarian. His credits include *Threat* (IDA Award, 1987; L.A. Critics Award, 1992); *Time Has No Name* and *Javana, Reindeer Herdsman in the Year 2000*, both IDA Award nominees; *A Respectable Life* (Silver Plaque), Chicago Film Festival; and *Misfits to Yuppies* (Felix Award, 1993).

AT RISK:
THE ANATOMY OF A DECISION

Barbara Trent

The purpose of my work in film and video has always been to find the truth and shed light upon it. Now, that's a pretty subjective mission and certainly everyone and everything has its own truth. So, I've narrowed my "truth" down to exposing to the world information, facts, testimonies, documents, visual images and analysis that have not been readily made available to the public about an issue or an event of significance.

Immediately we can agree that my films do not spend equal time illuminating all sides of an issue, but rather I spend the precious little time I'm allotted to illuminate sides of an issue that have not been seen and that provide necessary information which must be factored in prior to coming to a conclusion or an opinion. Basically, our films reveal what the major media suppresses.

Now, regarding objectivity: No one is objective. The cat and the mouse each have a different subjective perception of what is going on during any encounter. Likewise, the cat lover and the mouse lover will each have a different perception, opinion, judgment, and feeling watching that encounter. How we look at things is based upon our belief system. I believe in some basic personal truths. I believe that it is usually very easy to tell right from wrong, that honesty is essential, and that self-determination should be nurtured, and mitigated only by the most essential universal frameworks necessary to provide enough order in which to be free. I believe in lots of things, too numerous on which to fully elaborate. This set of beliefs forms my perception of what is true as well as what is important.

I began making films with David Kasper in 1983. I was inspired by watching Haskell Wexler and his team (of which David Kasper was a member) document an anti-nuclear caravan (of which I was a member) on its way from California to the United Nations' Second Special Session on Disarmament in 1982. It occurred to me that film and video could be powerful tools for change. As a community organizer since the sixties, I was acutely aware of the challenge of disseminating information to the public in a way that was honest, useful, and motivating. Film and video quickly became my new tool of choice.

David and I formed the Empowerment Project in 1983, produced a few videos to augment local organizing efforts in California, and quickly got swept into the world of U.S. foreign policy. Our first film was *Destination Nicaragua*, a look at the illegal CIA funded and directed contra war against the Sandinistas. Later, when the Iran-Contra affair broke in the news and it became apparent that the investigation by Congress would be in and of itself a cover-up, we decided to act. The result was *Coverup: Behind the Iran Contra Affair*, a seventy-six-minute feature film that we distributed to theaters in eighty cities across the country, a handful of courageous public TV affiliated stations, and countries around the world.

On December 20, 1989, David and I turned on our TV to watch the news over breakfast and there stood George Bush explaining to us and the rest of the American public that he had just sent 26,000 troops and the stealth fighter to arrest one man in a country virtually already under U.S. military occupation. Our response was instant. We could not sit by and let this one go unchallenged. We were furious. We knew that there would have to be enormous casualties on the ground as a result of the sheer force that was deployed. We also knew that there had to be another agenda. It does not take 26,000 U.S. trained and armed troops to arrest one man. Something else was going on and the public, as usual, was not in the information loop. After two years, many hardships, several crew deaths, emotional and financial devastation, we ultimately completed the film we set out to make that December morning. The Panama Deception went on to win the Academy Award in March 1993 for Best Feature Documentary of 1992, has been broadcast nationwide in over 25 countries, shown theatrically in the U.S. in over 80 cities, released to over 10,000 schools, libraries, organizations, and individuals on videotape, but as always was suppressed by U.S. TV with the exception of a handful of public affiliates, and eventually, Cinemax and The Independent Film Channel.

There are always lots of ethical considerations and decisions that have to be made both in the field as well as in the editing room when making movies like ours. None have ever been as difficult or unclear as the one I was forced to make over and over every second of the shoot at the Albrook Refugee Center in Panama.

We had come to Albrook to interview some of the 25,000 to 35,000 refugees whose homes had been destroyed during the invasion. Six months had passed since the bombing and the burning and thousands still languished in refugee camps. They had no money. Most of them had lost their jobs either to the bombing or to the civil and governmental restructuring carried out by the U.S. forces during and following the invasion. Many of them had lost family members. People died regularly in the camp as well. They called it dying from a broken heart, usually heart attacks presumably brought on by the stress of the situation. The day before we arrived, a child died of meningitis. A major outbreak was feared. There was an enormous volatile sense of hopelessness and frustration in the camp when we arrived.

The refugees, mostly black and mestizo, had no great love for Americans at this point. Even those who opposed Noriega were angry and traumatized by the brutality of the invasion. On top of that, unbeknownst to us, but understandably so, they also had a particular distaste for American journalists. American journalists had been there before and yet either nothing had been reported or nothing had been done. The refugees were people who no longer believed anyone wanted to hear their truth or their story. *Newsweek* had done an article; however, it mostly raved about the efficiency with which the U.S. AID office and the Panama Red Cross had constructed enough 10 by 10 foot cubicles divided only by sheets of black plastic to house 2,650 refugees in one airplane hangar at Albrook.

When we entered Albrook (a camera/sound man, a still photographer, and myself) we had to pass through a long corridor that had been built of barbed and razor wire with several U.S. soldiers and newly U.S. trained and directed Panamanian police stationed midway down the gauntlet.

Although they started to question us, I used my usual method of simply flashing our homemade press passes at them and moved quickly on past them and their guns. The key is to never slow down. Once they stop you, the status quo is in their favor. To subsequently initiate a forward momentum again can be perceived as an aggressive or belligerent action. Most of these young military personnel are no older than my son and are usually not quick to initiate a physical intervention with someone who has just spoken to them as if they hadn't yet cleaned their room. Of course, in the eyes of the military, they were not supposed to let us through. And once inside I knew that there was a chance that they would catch their breath, rethink what had happened, and then figure out a way to try to stop us. Meanwhile, we were inside and in motion.

We immediately asked the refugees who was in charge. They fetched several refugees who were part of The Refugee Committee—ten refugees who had been elected within the camp to help coordinate and run the place. Eventually, Ashton Bancroft, who was the president of The Committee, came forward and took us to a small office where the two administrative directors worked. Alejandro James, Jr., had flown up from the U.S. AID Disaster Relief Office in Costa Rica to coordinate the camp with one of Panama's Red Cross officials. We explained to them that we were doing a documentary exploring the reasons for the U.S. invasion, the events of the invasion itself, and the aftermath. We said that we wanted to know about the refugee camp, how it was run, and speak with some of the refugees as well as tour the camp. Both gentlemen were very cordial to us, agreed to submit to interviews, and assured us that we would have unsupervised access to the camp and the refugees for as long as we needed.

We set up our equipment, found a suitable spot, and began interviewing the two codirectors to give us an overview of the situation. In the middle of that first interview several U.S. MPs entered and informed us that we would not be able to proceed. This was a very interesting situation. There are three types of government/military jurisdiction in Panama—Panamanian jurisdiction, U.S. jurisdiction, and Joint jurisdiction. The camp was under Panamanian jurisdiction. U.S. military personnel were at the camp only to assist as needed and the Panamanian police didn't seem to care that we were there.

The interruption was of great interest to the two co-directors, because they had been accused by an Italian news team of not allowing access. Now it was apparent to the directors that teams not certified by the U.S. Southern Command and wearing Southern Command press credentials were not being allowed access. Since this area was not under U.S. jurisdiction and it was not a war zone, we, and I presume the Italians, would not register with or wear U.S. military press credentials.

I hastily pulled the lavalier mic off one of the directors and held it to the face of the

soldier attempting to stop the interview. We were able to catch some of the exchange on tape and provide them with visible warning that this incident was only just beginning in terms of future ramifications. Ultimately, we sat back down with the directors and continued the interview while the MPs went off to consult with their superiors. Upon completion of the interview, we moved over to another area to begin interviewing the refugees themselves. During the first or second interview U.S. military personnel entered again. This time there were more of them and they were not all in their twenties. They had brought in

Barbara Trent, with Refugee Camp directors, in confrontation with U.S. MP attempting to terminate the shoot. Panama, June 1990

Photo: Julio Cesar Guerra D.

people with more authority and of higher rank. But once again, I refused to honor their presumption of authority. They said they could not allow me to film. This time they got a little testier. They repeatedly disconnected camera and sound cables as Michael Dobo, the camera/sound man attempted to shoot the confrontation. Several times I urged him to continue shooting no matter what. When people tried to stop him he told them to talk to me. This situation began to escalate. A commotion was now officially in progress. The refugees and I were arguing with the U.S. soldiers and MPs. Levels of frustration and anger were rising. We all had an emboldened determination to prevail. Rising levels of adrenaline will do that and it can prove unpredictable and dangerous.

Now it was a standoff. It was clear to me that the refugees wanted these interviews to continue. They could already tell by the tone and content of our questions and the courage of our perseverance that we were truly interested in their personal stories. It

Photo: Julio Cesar Guerra D.

looked as if we were going to go the distance together. Ashton told the soldiers, "I don't think it's right. I think the world has the right to know the truth. Sir, please, we are the victims. We are the victims. We lose everything. We lose our family. Why is the world not supposed to know the truth?" The MPs repeated that they had been told to detain everyone from filming. I turned from the soldiers, walked back to the refugees waiting to be interviewed, picked up the

Barbara Trent continuing interview with Ashton Bancroft the Coordinator of the refugees.

microphone and informed the soldiers in no uncertain terms that "We're here under the authorization of a lot of people including congressmen. We're going to do this shoot. You can come in and arrest me, but we have the right to be here. We are shooting. We are on a Panamanian project and we have the right of the directors. I'm not stopping and we're not slowing down. So if you have to bring someone in to forceably do that, that's your business." As I proceeded to put the lavalier mic on the next refugee to be interviewed, Ashton picked up a bullhorn and started yelling to the growing crowd of refugees, "Señors, señoras, why do they want to throw out the reporters? They came to talk to us. They want to know the truth and they won't let them interview us. Why? Why?" Refugees came and lent their bodies to the forming circle around us, forcing the military to withdraw. It became apparent to me and to the soldiers that these refugees had been left to rot in this refugee camp. They had very little left to lose and were the soldiers to press on, violence would most certainly erupt. A bloodbath was possible. Despite all rules to the contrary, I later learned that there was a distinct possibility that some refugees were even armed.

Now I was starting to feel decidedly concerned about the blood levels of adrenaline and testosterone in both my newfound allies as well as my foes. I continued interviewing refugees. U.S. forces entered one more time and a middle-aged man approached only to be blocked by the refugees. He held a wallet up above his head and flipped it open to expose a badge, pronounced that he was from the CID (as if that meant anything to me—I later learned it is the Criminal Investigation Division) and that this interview was now terminated. I simply yelled, "You are acknowledged" and went back to my work. He left, but it had become unpleasantly apparent that the harassment was only beginning. They were not backing off and neither was I. The confrontation could only escalate. I finished a few more quick interviews and agreed with the refugee leaders as well as Michael Dobo that it was crucial to do a tour of the interior of the camp and record the conditions under which refugees were living before we lost the chance.

Touring the camp was much riskier than conducting the interviews. We did the interviews in the one open space that provided not only some daylight coming in the door, but a good 360° view of our situation. Touring the camp, we were corralled into long narrow hallways with cubicles lining both sides, interrupted only by a cross pathway every 20 or 30 cubicles. So, as we walked down the hall we were isolated from what was happening in the entrance and throughout the camp and had no idea what would meet us at the next intersecting hallway. Meanwhile the decibel level of the noise in this tin-roofed airplane hangar, home to 2,650 unhappy refugees, was rising at an alarming rate.

Michael Dobo and I led the tour. It was the only way to shoot—with us out in front. Of course we were backed up by unknown numbers of refugees and awkwardly flanked, when room permitted, by one of the refugee leaders. Nonetheless, if the military were waiting at the cross section, they could snatch us, our equipment, and the footage in a heartbeat. Because of the noise levels, we all thought something was afoot and that at the next intersection of halls, it would be over. The refugees begged us to give them the tapes we had already shot. Michael Dobo said, "The first rule of a good cameraman is never give up the footage." The refugees continued to implore me, guaranteeing their safe return anywhere, anytime. I took their advice, told Michael to hand me the tapes, had him replace the one in his camera, and, God help me, without even looking just handed them off to the men behind me who stuck them into their pants and melted back into the crowd, out the other side, and out of the camp.

Once having responded to fear, no matter how responsible the action is, the fear is exacerbated. It is, I suppose, a subconscious as well as conscious affirmation that you really are in trouble. We were preparing for the worst because we now believed the worst was going to happen.

The refugee leaders hurried us through the maze to a little room that had been set aside for them to use as their coordinating office. We stepped in. They locked the door. It had to be 120° and 100% humidity. Now, what to do.

Isolated inside the refugees' office, the shoot completed, and the tapes no longer my immediate responsibility, I settled into assessing the overall situation. I had a glass of water and sat down. I was up in a minute. I had two concerns. How would we ever get out and what was going on outside the walls of the office. To my surprise, the refugees had their own telephone in that office and it was not blocked for international calls. I called our office in Santa Monica and explained our situation. I asked them to contact Congressman Charles Rangel, Congressman Ronald Dellums, and Senator Alan Cranston as well as the Center For Constitutional Rights, the State Department, the U.S. Embassy, and the press. My message was simple: "We are very tired and hot but we are OK. The problem is we are trapped in here. We can't leave without being detained and having our equipment confiscated. We will sit tight and you see what you can do."

That accomplished, my attention turned to the events surrounding me. I became aware that the noise was still increasing outside the walls of the office. I told Kenneth Maxwell (one of the refugee leaders and the man who would later go on to work with us for the remaining three weeks of the shoot) and Ashton Bancroft I was concerned about what was going on in the camp outside the safe haven of this office. They explained that there was turmoil because many of the refugees held so much resentment for the media that they wanted to throw us to the wolves, but those that understood what we were doing desperately wanted us to stay. The elected Refugee Committee unanimously wanted us to stay and assured us that we must stay because that is how we could best serve all of those who were victims of the invasion. They said that they were out there spreading the word and that it just took time to get the word to 2,650 people. I was dumbstruck. We had only, until now, experienced support for our presence. Everyone who put themselves at risk, and when they work with us they do, had done so willingly. Now I realized for the first time that mothers and babies and elders and lots of different kinds of people were at risk as a result of our presence, and they had not been given a choice.

Many times over the next hour I argued that perhaps we should leave, that we had no right to put others at risk. Everyone must choose for themselves if they are to risk reprisal, injury, or death for a cause. We could not choose for them.

This has always been a basic premise under which we worked. I have flown across the country to meet with U.S. soldiers who got cold feet and changed their mind. I have been driven out to the countryside in foreign countries to interview witnesses who have gotten there and then gotten scared. When someone says they are scared, I don't say, "It will be OK," or "Everyone is scared". I say, "Hey, you are putting yourself at risk by doing this interview. If you are not sure you want to do this, it is completely OK. I support you in that decision 100%. What do you want to do?" If they say they want to go ahead, I ask them if they are sure. If they say they don't want to go forward, my role is to, as rapidly as possible, identify with them and my crew a way out for them and expedite that plan with all dispatch at my disposal. Anything less is not simply irresponsible and uncompassionate. It is morally criminal.

(In defense of my fallibility morally, I may have bent the rules when persuading John Hull—the CIA asset involved in so many deaths during the contra war against the Sandinistas in Nicaragua—to consent to an interview against the obvious wishes of his armed-to-the-teeth mercenary bodyguards. I believed we had to expose him to illuminate the issue. I also thought he was already a dead man. And to everyone's disgust, as the interview went on I began to feel a lot in common with him as a farmer and felt sorry for him as a man way over his head who would surely be killed by the contras, the Sandinistas, or the CIA. He didn't have a lot of friends left, and I too was about to betray him.)

The refugee organizers continued to slip in and out of the office, checking on the situation, bringing me back status reports, and reassuring me that this film must be made and that things would get worked out and that we must not submit ourselves to the military and allow the project to be killed. Meanwhile, the sheer weight of the bodies pressed up against the walls on the outside of the office caused the walls to sway in and out. I could not imagine the situation only several inches on the other side of those walls. They continued to ask me to trust them and I did.

Several hours later, Alejandro, the U.S. AID officer, sent a message to me through the refugee leadership. We agreed to meet with him. Things were calming down by then. The additional troops that had been brought in had pulled back from the perimeter of the camp, reducing the explosiveness of the situation. Alejandro delivered a message from Southern Command. It turns out he had taken the initiative to call his superiors in Costa Rica who called back to Panama to explain to the Southern Command that they were already in deep shit and that there really was no graceful way out. The damage was done. It would become public. We were the media. We were correct about our right to be conducting interviews in the camp since we had gotten the permission of the co-directors in authority, and that there was absolutely nothing left for Southern Command to do but to deal now with damage control and end the situation.

Alejandro presented to us a series of guarantees. We would be allowed to leave. We would take our equipment and our tape. No one from the military would talk to us or even approach us. We would not be hindered in our ability to return to our hotel. This unfortunate altercation was over. After checking several times to be sure that I had heard him correctly, I consulted again with the Refugee Committee. They were convinced of his sincerity and his access to those in charge. We gathered our things and headed for daylight. We got glasses of water and I went to the rest rooms, far removed from the parking lot, several times while we stalled to let those faceless men in the hallway jump on their bikes and head into the woods and nearby places to retrieve the tapes they had so efficiently hidden away. It took over a half hour for them to get back. I guess they had taken no chances.

Indeed there was quite an impressive contingency of Humvees and assorted armed and unarmed military vehicles that had gathered that afternoon to deal with us. They followed us as in a parade, but from a very polite distance all the way into Panama City. Perhaps they just wanted us to remember that they were there and next time there might not be a phone. Perhaps they wanted to be sure we got back safely. Lord knows they couldn't afford to be eating doughnuts while we were being hijacked and our equipment stolen at this point in the game. At any rate, although it had not been part of the plan, Southern Command now knew we were in the country and we would see them many more times before we completed our mission.

I will never know if I made the right decision. It is not a decision I am either proud or ashamed of. It scares me that I had to make a decision in a situation like that or that I may have to again some day. I know no one got hurt and things worked out brilliantly. We finished the film and it won the Oscar effectively increasing world attention on what really happened in Panama and why. The people who were on the ground when the bombs fell got a chance to tell their story.

Has all of this changed anything? Of course, but not nearly enough. Millions of people around the world are more aware of the deceptive practices used by the U.S. government and the major media to sell illegal and immoral foreign policies to citizens in the U.S. and to people and governments around the world. People who view *The Panama Deception* have a much clearer picture of what really happened in Panama during the invasion. Large numbers of people have taken action at a local and at an international level. Our footage has been used as evidence in some of the 300 cases being heard before the Inter-American Commission of The Organization Of American States (OAS). Concern and support for the refugees and all of the victims of the invasion has increased. Albrook is closed down now, although it took nearly two years. Some of the refugees are now living in housing built by the Panamanian government and funded in part by the U.S. to replace the invasion's destruction which left an estimated 25,000 to 35,000 people homeless. Some have moved in with relatives. Some are still homeless.

Was our decision to stay and shoot that day in Albrook right? You can only say yes if you think the end justifies the means. I don't believe that. I am simply grateful that the worst did not happen and that I don't have to live the rest of my life carrying the guilt of being the trigger of an explosion that would have maimed and killed innocent people already victimized by my country. That is really all I am sure of, nothing more. It's really not very comforting at all.

Barbara Trent is an Oscar winning filmmaker, former welfare mother, seasoned activist, and trail blazer for change. She has publicly exposed criminal activities in the White House, Pentagon and CIA; and has been the target of at least three FBI counter intelligence operations. Her personal story of courage, risk and achievement, starting in the 1960s has been an inspiration to many.

Trent appears regularly at colleges, universities, and special events speaking to diverse audiences regarding the forces controlling our media and exposing government covert operations, as well as addressing public inattention to these critical issues. Her films have been acclaimed, exhibited, and broadcast around the world.

Appointed as an Expert Senior Training Specialist for the VISTA program under Jimmy Carter, Trent has been decorated with the Gasper Octavio Hernandez Award by the Journalist's Union in Panama, and is a recipient of the American Humanist Association's Arts Award for her "courageous advocacy of progressive ideas." She, along with David Kasper, received the Videomaker of the Year award from *Videomaker* magazine in 1991. In 1993, they each received academy awards for Best Feature Documentary for *The Panama Deception*. Trent and Kasper co-founded and co-direct the Empowerment Project, a media resource center serving hundreds of progressive videographers each year.

Barbara will be featured in the book *Women Who Dare*, soon to be published by Turner Publishing, as well as the book *Globalization and Culture* published by Duke University Press.

SANITY LOST AND FOUND—
THE TRAVAILS OF A
SOUTH AFRICAN DOCUMENTARY FILMMAKER

Keyan G. Tomaselli

I travel to the USA a lot, mostly on lecture tours.

Americans, obsessed as they are with race, ethnicity, and origin, often ask me about my identity. I reply that I am a South African. This is met by awkward silence, and the further question, "Yes, but where were you born?" "South Africa," I reply. A confused frown. More interrogation: "But your name is Italian?" "Yes," I respond. "So you're not a South African, then? Where did you come from?" "Durban," I reply, increasingly enjoying the discomfort of my interlocutors. "Yes, but you're an immigrant," they tell me with assurance. "My Italian grandfather and European great-great-great-grandfather were the immigrants," I explain. "So most South Africans, black, white, Asian or indifferent are descendants of immigrants, like in the USA." With Nelson Mandela we like to think of ourselves as South Africans— Desmond Tutu calls us the "Rainbow Nation." In exasperation, one white Boston academic finally challenged, "So when are you going to emigrate?" "Why would I want to?" I asked? "Because you are not black," she irritatedly retorted. I responded, well, in that case, when was she going to return to Europe? Apartheid notwithstanding, colonization in South Africa had not had the genocidal consequence as had occurred in America. Our struggle had brought us together, not split us apart. Bewilderment. End of discussion. What typified the antiapartheid struggle was to create a new nonracial democratic South African society, not to pretend that part of us lives in another one, in a hyphenated identity across the seas, or the lands from whence our forefathers came centuries ago. That's old history.

Once Upon a Time

One period of my story as a filmmaker starts in late 1975. I had worked from Johannesburg as a professional documentary director-cameraman since January 1974. Now freelancing, I had just completed a safari film for Game Trackers in the Okavango Swamps, Botswana, Victoria Falls in Rhodesia, and another in the Tuli Block in Eastern Botswana. The war in Rhodesia had finally resulted in an eight-minute film covering the southward trek from the Falls to the Swamps being reduced to four minutes of the Swamps only. Land mines, guerrilla attacks, and the closure of the border between Rhodesia and Botswana had eliminated the northern leg of the safari.

Like most of my self-taught professional colleagues at the time, I knew nothing about film theory, criticism, or history. As with other technicians, I had learnt on the job by trial and error, there being no formal university courses in South Africa then offered on either production or theory. One learns fast when mistakes cost the equivalent of one's monthly salary!

I had cut my teeth on Super-8 antiapartheid protest and existential surfing and biker movies while a geography and sociology student at the University of Witwatersrand (Wits) in Johannesburg in the early 1970s. *Easy Rider* (without the drugs) and *Electra Glide in Blue* was one cinematic influence; John Grierson and Soviet montage theories (though I did not know it at the time) were others. At Wits while a student I had worked as a floor manager and studio cameraman at the then recently installed but obsolete monochrome TV studio, dumped on the South African market by a British company in 1972.

Books on film and TV were scarce in a country which had not yet introduced broadcast TV. In 1971, the government started gearing up for TV with a state-of-the-art complex in 1976. Working in the university TV studio was a frustrating experience—prevideotape editing meant that if anyone made a mistake, it was back to square one. I remember intervening in more fist fights between technicians and producers resulting from these frustrations than occur in the current World Wrestling Federation TV programs.

I recall reading Karel Reitz's *The Technique of Film Editing*, but having understood little of it. I had a vague idea that I had developed similar editing techniques. The book was sold to me by a sound engineer who understood it even less. However, *The Technique of Documentary Film Production* by Hugh Badderley seemed to me to part of the problem with documentary, especially with regard to the negative way that Africa was imaged on film. But at least I learned who Eisenstein was.

I knew that I was a talented filmmaker, and that my self-financed or sponsored movies were considered as art by students, professional colleagues, and festival audiences. My Super-8 films were screened as shorts prior to features in university lecture theaters, which substituted for the lack of TV, and at film festivals which took for granted their role in challenging censorship. I was in touch with my audience, who cheered, booed, wanted more, or walked out. They engaged me in hours of debate, or shouted abuse at me. The most politically compelling moments occurred when I screened the rushes of security police, uniformed police, and assorted thugs attacking protesting Wits students across the urban arterial which divided the campus from the city. In this way the silent Super-8 films I shot over a three-year period acted as the "news" of the day, and kept the student body informed of developments a few days earlier (it took Kodak three days to process the films.) The edited film was copied and sold to the Danish antiapartheid movement, and also shown in church halls, where I was sometimes accused of "setting up" the events. Where would a low budget Super 8 filmmaker get the funds to hire four to five thousand extras, police costumes, dogs, tear gas, guns, and police vans to hold up main road traffic for weeks on end, while shooting off 50 foot 8mm reels at a time? Such was the myopia of those who supported apartheid.

Eventually, in 1974, I shot one protest too many and found myself being interrogated by a security police general on the ninth floor of the Security Police Headquarters. Man, I didn't play around. Students and other photographers arrested were simply locked up by mere constables in the back of the black marias. I had four star comfort in a major's car. Detainees had previously "fallen" to their deaths from the tenth floor; others had met similarly mysterious "accidents" in this notorious building. The major phoned my father. He said to keep me there, he was off to play tennis. Perhaps I would finally learn my lesson. The police kept asking me if I had been "overseas." "Aah," they concluded, I had gotten my communist ideas from a visit to England!

A friend who came to bail me out was told by the ground floor police reception desk that "the ninth floor doesn't exist." My friend went outside and counted the floors. There were fourteen. He returned and contested the desk's ability to count. The police then told him that "nobody gets to the ninth floor." He checked the elevators. Indeed, the ninth and tenth floors were absent from the selector. He went back to his office in the city. Eventually, I managed to get released on my own recognizance, and gave him the fright of his life when I wafted through his door. And, believe it or not, I had managed to conceal the exposed films on my person. The only reel the police found was the one in my camera, which they confiscated; they later told me it was "jerky." But they did give me my camera back. They were impressed that my lawyer—my father's actually—was a soft-spoken conveyancer, not a brash, arrogant human rights lawyer with international contacts and a telephone number in Moscow. I went back to Wits and told a member of the Students Representative Council that I had been arrested. He offered me legal assistance which I declined. Many years later, he broke cover and turned out to have been a security police spy, who was involved in the 1980s in hit squad activities. So, too, were many of my film students at Rhodes University where I lectured between 1981 and 1984. I realized that the most dogmatic Marxist-Leninists in class were usually security police in conceptual drag.

The police still have the confiscated copy of my film.

Another Time

On becoming a professional, my commercial movies sold more paint, wildlife safaris, perfume, and guniting pumps than films made by some other producers. My style was generally considered innovative and refreshing by my colleagues. I worked on only two features and hated the experience. The first was a local Afrikaans movie—I was the fourth camera assistant to be hired and the fourth and last to be fired. In those days there was no union or control over working hours. We seemed to work all day, everyday, mostly because the director kept making basic continuity errors, which meant we had to reshoot on Sundays. My growing irritation with this led to my being "let go" and I returned to the making of corporate and sports documentaries, and later, vox pops which dramatized advertising research. Here again, disbelief occasionally met the accusations made by black consumers against rather haughty white-owned upmarket department stores which treated them with suspicion. The advertising agency, at the forefront of attempting to get clients to think about markets in terms of class rather than official apartheid racial categories, eventually fired the client. The store couldn't see that the world—and their consumer profile—was changing.

The other feature was a wildlife film for a French company, which was more competent in the sea than it was on land. They simply did not understand that wild animals can be taught to behave in terms of the scripts when trained properly. Fish apparently don't read scripts. I eventually passed them onto Game Trackers and left the production when my producer failed to come up with his finance. This producer was a dealmaker, who often lacked any sense of how to follow through. While working for him in a previous company, he kept telling our corporate clients that I could perform miracles, do the impossible, and work all night. Hallucination was part of the job, both his and mine, from a lack of sleep mostly. His boss, the owner of the company, made it a policy never to pay for facilities rented. So, periodically, my whole production operation would come to a halt. I would then prevail upon the boss to pay up so that I could finish what was in my editing table. When he did eventually pay up, usually on the steps of the Supreme Court, he inevitably took off 10 percent for cash, much to the irritation of the creditor. The first film I directed for his company was so good, he said, that he wanted to double the price to the client—mon dieu! He would open my mail, question my minuscule expenses, and spy on my crew to check that we had not gone on lunch hour five minutes early. That we might have worked all night with no overtime payment was irrelevant. Revenge was sweet when we persuaded a traffic cop to issue him parking tickets whenever he lurked in the loading zone from where he monitored minutes lost over lunch.

Discovering Africa

Armed with the professionally defective and incomplete arsenal of ideologically shaped techniques and production practices learned from my experience in the film industry, I set off in late 1976 as an independent to work for a producer in the Eastern Cape. We were to make a series of tourist documentaries on the Xhosa in the newly "independent" Transkei Bantustan.

In preproduction I asked the producer to employ an anthropologist to advise us. This was unnecessary, he told me, because, as he put it, "I understand the black mind. I've lived in the Eastern Cape all my life, you know." I soon learnt that this kind of tautologous rhetoric governed the extremely narrow world views of most Eastern Cape whites I met, confirmed some years later when I taught film and TV production and theory at Rhodes University, a small campus in a small town in that part of the country.

We nevertheless set off for rural Transkei with a white interpreter who was both a divinity student and a lieutenant in the citizen force of the South African army. With us was the producer's wife, his daughter and even his dog, to search for locations, witch doctors, war dancers, young maidens, chiefs, and kraals. I learned later when teaching at Rhodes that dogs are part of the Eastern Cape academic psyche. They go anywhere and everywhere, to conferences, to faculty meetings, to dinner parties, even to the local bug house. However, since the projectionist was usually drinking coffee somewhere else, and the picture was usually out of focus or jumping, the dogs provided a welcome distraction. These dogs would go nuts when their owners left them behind. The yowls of companionless inbred mutts haunts me even to this day. Even my eight-month-old son, Damien, learned to bark before he could speak, as he did one night when watching *Nanook of the*

North with my sullen students who were angry at having to watch a silly old black and white silent film (the projector sound was not working). Where was the colour, dialogue, and effects they demanded? When Nanook gets out of the kayak, followed by assorted family members (some of whom I later learned were Robert Flaherty's illegitimate children), followed finally by a husky, Damien started barking. The students were not amused. Two years later Damien sat with me and Alan Williams in the 16mm editing room for a month of Sundays while we researched *Myth, Race and Power: South Africans Imaged on Film and TV*. Then one day Damien ransacked the editing bin; he was not allowed back after that. Angry students again.

Back to the Transkei. The producer whizzed about making arrangements with a black trader, new to one of the rustic valleys in a beautiful part of the Transkei. The trader had been recently financed by the Xhosa Development Corporation (XDC). The producer bought copious quantities of Bantu beer from the trader and instructed him to deliver it to a particular settlement within twenty-four hours, as he wanted everyone in the right "spirit" for filming. Arrangements were made with headmen, or, if they could not be found, anyone who happened to be available. The date was made for the next day, Saturday, at 2 p.m..

Needless to say, when we returned, family and all (despite my objections), the location to which the beer had been delivered was deserted. The producer ranted and raved at the trader. The trader explained that he was little trusted by the locals due to his XDC affiliation which had financial ties to the central apartheid government. "Wasn't this typical of the black mind," complained the producer, "No sense of responsibility or time."

I then set off for the East London Library, and found some anthropology books I had last read in 1968 when I was enrolled for an anthropology course at Witwatersrand University. I learnt that a graduate psychology student from Rhodes University, whose research focused on indigenous healers, lived in the town. He agreed to assist as a consultant.

This time we set off for the Ciskei, another Bantustan, where the interpreter, had an uncle who owned a trading store. The uncle, well respected by the surrounding community, introduced us to the most senior sangoma (healer) in the area. We returned at the weekend to commence filming. All the way to the location the producer predicted, "They won't cooperate, I know these people." He was proved wrong. We had also on this trip, at my insistence, left his wife, daughter, and dog behind. Guided by the consultant we spent a very valuable few hours filming about twenty sangomas engaged in a dancing ceremony.

Then, a strange thing happened. A large motor car with mag wheels and an orange on the aerial filled with three heavyset shorthaired males and one female pulled up at the entrance to the settlement. These motoring accouterments were indicative of working class, rugby playing, beer-swilling whites, who were generally extremely right-wing. I became suspicious. The producer had been unable to obtain permits for us to be in the area legally. I thus assumed that these whites had come to arrest us. I had had one such experience, I did not want another. Reports prior to this trip had been increasingly filtering through on South Africa's military invasion of Angola despite vigorous denials by the government. I had been apprehensive for some time that I might be called up by the army. In the light of these unpleasant experiences, I was definitely not amenable to further disturbances from officialdom. I therefore took refuge behind the nearest bush I could find.

After about five minutes I realized that the twenty sangomas we had been filming had also disappeared and that a lot of chanting was emanating from behind the huts next to the road. I gingerly ventured out and was seen by our consultant, who hastily dragged me to where the sangomas were located. He was almost incoherent with impatience and told me to start filming immediately lest we miss the incredible event that was unfolding under the tree where the sangomas were treating one of the whites whom I had last seen in the approaching car.

Far from being the agents of apartheid come to arrest us, they were in fact a family of Afrikaners who had come to consult the senior sangoma. We later learned that this sangoma conducted a considerable practice amongst whites who lived in the arch-conservative Orange Free State province. After about another seven minutes the consultation was over, the illness diagnosed, the remedy prescribed, and the patient happy, but I was totally confused. So, for that matter, was our consultant. When we got the film back from the laboratory, he said we had better study it very carefully because there were forms of communication happening during the consultation that could not be explained scientifically. Local anthropologists, however, showed little interest in seeing the footage of the event I have just described. The production later sank under a welter of litigation as the financier sued the producer for misuse of funds.

My first experience in "ethnographic filmmaking" thus exposed me to treacherous ideological quicksands, questionable business practices, issues of ethics and crew-community relations, and, on virtually my first anthropological encounter, an unfathomable experience of cross-cultural divination. My book, *Appropriating Images*, can be partly traced back to the incident I have just described. It is also the result of my trying to understand this and subsequent filming experiences which often seemed to defy conventional logic and explanation. It took me nearly eighteen years to begin to comprehend some of my more extraordinary filming experiences and those related to me by others. But that's another story.

Fighting Communism

The South African public, of course, was the last to learn of the invasion of Angola, such was the totality of censorship at the time. Very soon it became clear that all white South Africans on the army reserve would be called up and shipped into battle. I had one year to complete on the reserve (ten years in total). I was certainly not going to kill Angolans (or anyone else) to protect apartheid or the government that so brutally enforced it.

Two immediate options were open to me: either I could dodge the draft and go into exile, or I could obtain exemption by registering as a full-time student. I chose the latter course. I registered as a Master of Arts student in the newly established School of Dramatic Art at the University of Witwatersrand, Johannesburg. Very soon I was teaching television and film production courses in the school, and making ethnographic films on indigenous healers in Soweto. This seemed to me to be a more satisfying activity than doing sound-effects tracks for the film sound company into which I had invested.

Inquiring about a topic for my M.A. dissertation, my advisor, John van Zyl, a key figure in introducing cinema studies into South Africa, uttered as if by command: "Semiotics!" I had no idea what semiotics was. I registered my title, rather boringly, as "The Semiotics of Film: An Investigation of Some Influences on the Language of Film." So began my travels and travails through film theory, though semiotics was still considered impenetrably mysterious by many academics, and utterly impenetrable by professional filmmakers other than Pier Pasolini, Jean-Luc Godard, and Sol Worth. Semiotics was the very epitome of the Ivory Tower.

The first books I was told to read were Christian Metz' *Language and Cinema* (1974a), *Film Language: A Semiotics of the Cinema* (1974b), and Peter Wollen's *Signs and Meaning in the Cinema* (1969). I soon realized that I would never make sense of Metz unless I also studied linguistics. A crash course in linguistics brought me back to Metz, and a variety of other semiologists besides, mostly within the disciplines of media, cinema, and performance studies.

On meeting visiting theater semiologists our uncomprehending film and drama students at Wits began to fear for the worst—semiology was not an aberrant concoction solely dreamed up by Metz, Van Zyl, and myself. Rigour, method, analysis, and theory were never quite like this in South African drama departments. Eventually I dumped the linguistic formalism of Metz and became a Marxist—not the kind that Americans think of, but one who used Marx's method (updated for the twentieth century) to make and study media.

I had been quite intrigued with Metz and what appeared to be the blanket adoption of his method not only by film semiologists in South Africa, but by film scholars in the entire English-speaking and French-speaking worlds. This adoption had occurred despite Metz's impossible prose and often seemingly bizarre and unpronounceable terminology.

My move from the film industry into drama, film and TV teaching and research in the late seventies also brought me into confrontation with archaic residues of a pre-Arnoldian literary tradition which had somehow merged with a technicist Arnoldian ("art is the best that is thought and done") position in English-language drama departments. Acting skills and voice training for high cultural production was their emphasis. Theory in this mishmash was anything its utterers wanted it to be, rarely approximating what philosophers or scientists understood by the term.

Readings such as Metz set for the film students were viewed with horror, trauma, and protestations by students and faculty alike. These works were discursively othered as being like linguistics, sociology, and philosophy—definitely not drama or film. Student actors and even those training to be film directors claimed that they did not need such conceptual complications in their lives. Neither did the professional technicians at the new broadcast quality Wits TV studio where I struggled against a repressive professional ethos to get access for my students. When students did get access, the technicians, who would only allow them to call the shots but not to use the camera or even touch the switching console, would on occasion deliberately overinterpret and subvert what they thought were the bizarre instructions being called out. Ironically, in today's postmodern world, these techniques—what they thought was then breaking the rule and therefore unprofessional—are now taken for granted. Academics can make a contribution after all.

Moving from geography (and brief spells as an urban researcher) into "drama" was for me something of a paradigm shock. I had been making films for seven years, so the "artistic" and technical dimensions were not the problem. The academic disciplinary emphasis on the technicalities of performance, voice projection, acting and stage direction had, however, removed any concern with how meanings are made, shifted, rearticulated, encoded and decoded. Some universal unstated meaning was held to be self–evident in the text, whether of dramatic, literary, cinematic, or televisual origin. The idea of drama having a "civilizing effect" on the campus as a whole rankled, for while apartheid remained, nothing could claim to be "civilized" or "civilizing." I did not then know from whence this elitist discourse derived, nor why our university principal, a surgeon, would so naively reproduce this Arnoldian discourse when asked in 1980 what he thought the school's mission was.

Semiology seemed to offer ways of making sense of cinema and drama not previously found in South African drama and film courses. Yes, we had read all the earlier pre-semiotic theorists of cinema, but their work seemed to apply to specific historical periods and specific kinds of expressions only. How to analyze films across historical periods, genres, styles and contexts in more general and much more systematic terms was the problem that Metz helped us to resolve. Similarly, studies on ethnographic filmmaking, like Karl Heider's *Ethnographic Film*, advised on how to approach representation of people who are the subjects of documentaries. My extensive work in 1980 for the Wits Psychology Department on sangoma rituals in Soweto benefited from the principles offered, and resulted in research footage unencumbered by large and noisy generator trucks, cables, intrusive TV film crews with their lights, reflectors, and notebooks, uncomprehending professional attitudes and sullen responses to unscripted and unpredictable situations. It's a pity that so many of my white students became nauseous on viewing these rituals in which sacrifices are the norm.

It was between 1976 and 1981 that I also became highly involved in the South African Film and TV Technicians Association (SAFTTA), which was set up to represent the interests of technicians, and to bring about some regulation to the insane hours worked by so many technicians, under appalling conditions, without any insurance or overtime. I later became its chairman and here is where I ran afoul of some members, who wanted trade union-derived benefits, but who saw unionism as some sort of communist plot. "It's my right to be exploited" was a plaintive cry. But SAFTTA also did some good work. This included taking on the producer of the *Big Valley* TV series, whose divisive tactics on a feature being shot in South Africa were causing all sorts of problems for the South African crew component. At the four-hour meeting we whittled away the grievances while he tried to intimidate us—the big–shot Hollywood producer yelling and goading me and my executive council about all the "greats" with whom he had worked. We were just "punks," "nobodies" who worked on Super-8 and 16mm amateur formats. He picked on us one by one until he got to Lionel Selwyn, a British editor, at the end of the table. When challenged with whom he had worked, Lionel replied with a dismissive dry humour, "Oh, just a few folks you wouldn't have heard of: John Ford, Roman Polanski, and Walt Disney." The producer shut his mouth after that, acceded to all our demands, and later offered our lawyer a job. But he did yell that had he known that there was a union in South Africa, he would never have come here. I replied that "Wherever producers like you have been, you leave a trade union behind even if there wasn't one when you arrived." The next week I marched on to an Italian producer, and the red carpet awaited my arrival. Word from the *Big Valley* had gotten out. We won that one for a while. Canon Films, however, broke the association's influence by hiring amateurs, fringe technicians, and paying them very little. They complained, of course, but did not join SAFTTA. In turn, the association discouraged its members from working on Canon film sets.

My experiences with the industry are related in my book, *The Cinema of Apartheid: Race and Class in South African Cinema*. This study was my attempt to theorize my professional experiences and the contradictions, behavior, and ideology of the South African film industry during the 1970s.

This book followed my earlier studies of the history, theory, and criticism of cinema, and, I am told, even by those in the industry who were extremely apprehensive of my story, has obtained wide acceptance. Even the local film lab imported copies. I think this must be for two reasons: because my publisher in New York nearly drove me nuts in making me revise every sentence to make it readable; and because I am one of the few film scholars who actually has direct experience of working in the industry itself. This is the dilemma of being an academic—how to get enough sabbatical to immerse oneself in the topic being studied. It also helped that at the time I did not have the theoretical tools to really understand how the industry operated. I simply saw the contradictions, learned the clichés, and questioned the assumptions; and then later found the explanatory framework through which to explain them.

It was from the above intellectual and practical bases that my subsequent filmmaking career developed. Using theory to make antiapartheid movies, which could not be (mis)appropriated by the state's security apparatuses as evidence against those whose struggles they imaged, became my prime concern. This quest brought me back to the ethical dimensions offered by the rapidly growing field of ethnographic film, as well as historical materialist postulates on cinema which emerged from the revolutionary climate found in France in the late 1960s. The notion of "reflexivity" was a prime influence on my own thinking and video making; while participatory scripting and production practices was the other. Reflexivity was an anathema to professional filmmakers, though it has been now subverted into an advertising tool. Think of the 1990 Mastercard TV advert where the chimps-eye-view substitutes for the zoo spectators after one of them drops his camera into the cage. Reflexivity is really a method of imaging, one which explains the assumptions and methods used by the filmmaker in a production. The idea is to alert the audience to the fact that what is on the screen is a social construction, not reality, or even a tracing of reality, as Andre Bazin would argue. This, we thought, would be successfully arguable in treason trials, courts of law, and commissions of inquiry, thus protecting those imaged in the videos. The other tactic was to discuss with our subjects—who often had asked us to make the video—the implications of transgressing a growing phalanx of censorship laws.

The consequences ranged from being chased away to treason trials. Once agreement was reached on the degree of risk to be tested, we got on with the job irrespective of the potential consequences. Some of my colleagues died in "action"; others lived to see the onset of democracy; gardening became a pastime for the burned-out. Some, however, thought they would get rich quick making antiapartheid films. One skeptical Canadian TV theorist took me to task for discussing these traumatic events in terms of "transmission" models of communication. Oh well, one can't please everyone, especially under fire. The security police must have been bemused.

One of the films in which reflexivity was applied was *I am Clifford Abrahams. This is Grahamstown*, directed by Graham Hayman of Rhodes University. I was the cameraman; for three months we followed Cliffie, a raconteur, an alcoholic, dope smoking, coloured down-and-out, but whose personality and ability to waft through any kind of social space as if he owned it was the presenter. It was his job to teach the crew and audiences about poverty. How could we the crew know about this condition?

We were all, even the coloured sound man, from the middle class. In the process, the video reveals the invisible structural forces which made Cliffie what he was;

which made the crew what they were; and which made all the characters, ordinary and bizarre, what they were. While Cliffie got all the royalties and star status, he never really understood what the video was about.

One man who did understand how to mobilize video was an illiterate, coloured peasant farmer, who had never seen TV, who lived in the Ciskei Bantustan. He and his 200-year-old farming community were about to be dispossessed by the apartheid government so that the land could be handed to the Ciskei. The video's director, a historian, had been working with the community for five years, and wanted a video to function as a public memory of a long-viable community. We found old Piet Draghoender up a mountain. We asked him a few questions about his land and its history. Piet immediately recited a spontaneous Lament, in an Afrikaans dialect. However, this kind of astonishing performance has rarely been documented anywhere else by anyone at any time. We knew something extraordinary was happening. The boom swinger had diarrhea; I was in the wrong position; but we kept recording until we ran out of tape. We cut the Lament's length in the final video because audiences were so emotionally overcome that they often failed to see out the end of the screening. We subjected the tape to literary, linguistic, and historical analysis. But like an archaeologist, no matter how deep we delved into the Lament, we always knew that there was more beneath the textual surfaces already excavated by these scholars.

Eventually, a scholar of orality cracked the code; this isolated, illiterate Afrikaans-speaking man's grammatical structure was almost identical to that of twelfth century European peasants experiencing similar traumas of dispossession. For him, the Lament was a confirmation of anthropos, an original state of language and being. Heady stuff. The video captured an unrepeatable moment for academia; but a few weeks later Draghoender had sold up; he was no longer the lord of his mountain; but his Lament lives on in print in English, Afrikaans, dialect Afrikaans and French, for whatever this is worth.

Since the mid-1980s I have worked mainly as a script consultant and professor. The scripts I have worked on include *Call for Freedom*, a German ZDF production on South African cinema of the 1980s; and *Indaba Ye Grievance*, directed by Kevin Harris. The former film reveals the depth of South African critical feature cinema even as the hostile press critics were claiming that there was no such industry. Some Germans visited me in Durban after seeing the film. In *Indaba* we were asked to make a movie which persuaded illiterate migrant Zulu-speaking construction workers to accept grievance procedures rather than just leaving the job in the event of a dispute. We succeeded. Problem: the bosses (and sponsor) disagreed. They saw the revolutionary gestures, songs, and aesthetic developed through the vignettes based on actual case studies by the workers themselves, as "subversive." Management declared the film a failure. I had to write a counter-argument which explained to the film's sponsors that the research results were accurate. If we had made a film that satisfied management, it would not have appealed to the workers. Management's world view was not everyone's world view. I think the sponsors paid up eventually, but they shelved the film.

The Future

My work as both a producer and especially as an academic resulted in my being invited to work on some major projects during the transition from apartheid to democracy and thereafter, between 1991 and 1996. One concerned a two-year industry-sponsored research project into the future of public service broadcasting. The others were consulting for the film subcommittee of the Arts and Culture Task Group, and the writing of the government White Paper on Film, assisted by my cowriter and a reference group of top industry professionals. The White Paper on which I worked made an impact in Zimbabwe, which is adapting it for their industry. My critical academic study of the South African media was being studied in African university communication departments; a Zimbabwean cabinet minister even contacted me and once the academic boycott was lifted, I was made external examiner by two African universities' communication departments, and co-opted onto international media training bodies working in Africa.

Being able to move from resistance to reconstruction, from opposition to policy making, from the clandestine to the open, from the parochial to the pan-African, has been a most exhilarating experience indeed. Our insanity under apartheid has become a sane democracy. This "miracle," as the popular media have dubbed the outcome, was really the result of very hard work, supreme sacrifices on the part of many, and an obstinate belief that oppression could be beaten. Rainbows, however, are optical illusions. We must not forget that miracles are related to hard collective work. And they have to be sustained.

So, who am I? "I am," as ubuntu philosophy puts it, because "we are."

References

Baddeley, W.H. 1970: *The Technique of Documentary Film Production*. New York: Focal Press.

Heider, K. 1972: *Ethnographic Film*. Austin: University of Texas Press.

Reitz, K., and Millar, G. 19**: *The Technique of Film Editing*. New York: Focal Press.

Tomaselli, K.G. 1996: *Appropriating Images: The Semiotics of Visual Representation*. Hojbjerg, Denmark: Intervention Press.

Tomaselli, K.G. 1988: *The Cinema of Apartheid: Race and Class in South African Film*. New York: Smyrna Press.

Tomaselli, K.G., and Smith, G. 1990: "Sign Wars: The Battlegrounds of Semiotics of Cinema in Anglo Saxiona." Degres, No. 64, cc-26.

Tomaselli, K.G., Williams, A., Steenveld, L., and Tomaselli, R.E. 1986: *Myth, Race and Power: South Africans Images on Film and TV*. Bellville: Anthropos.

Keyan G Tomaselli is Director and Professor of the Centre for Cultural and Media Studies, University of Natal, Durban, South Africa. He was the cowriter of the draft legislation on film for the first democratic government and received a KWANZAA Award for his book, *The Cinema of Apartheid*. Tomaselli serves on the Training in Developing Countries Board of the International Association of Film and TV Schools, and was a Smithsonian Research Associate in its Department of Anthropology (1995-1997). He was a Fulbright researcher in the African Studies Center at Michigan State University in 1990-91.

THE SEARCH FOR REALITY

MICHAEL TOBIAS

The shock of getting closer to the kernel of something in myself, whose origins were mirrored beyond anything I had ever experienced, has been a persistent motive in my life for orienting a camera towards a subject. The technology has always been subsidiary to this personal quest, a means of reconciling my ephemeral inward-dwelling eye with an overwhelming exterior.

The ideals and images born of that deliberate caress, or haphazard collision, are the nurturance of every art form. Yet, the documentary occupies a peculiar and strangely naked niche amongst all other human expressions. Perhaps, because the camera itself is so unblinking, regardless of the light which lends it the sole rationale for being part of the enterprise, so eager to embrace whatever highlight suggests itself. The camera is a tyrant of randomness until that moment of human impulse guides it—and then it will savor, ravish, celebrate, obscure, remark upon, investigate, challenge, fondle, and any number of other transitive or intransitive verbs, in the service of exclamation.

When I first started directing films, these bursts of punctuation—shots of seemingly equal importance and urgency—hurled towards me like meteorite showers shorn of nuance or subtlety. Everything declared its adamantine moment of aesthetic temptation. The subject exponentially crescendoed and these explosions of visual possibility seemed sufficient in themselves to say something. Audacious color, blurred images against startlingly blown-up details, and gradients of the silhouette all became ends, or at least did so for as long as the camera upheld the trance. In essence, the camera seemed to be the story during those moments, the "medium the message."

But as the images became unwieldy—too many sunsets, gloamings, some beginning to appear less spectacular than others—of course the whole genesis of storyline, editorial sentience and restraint began to dictate new terms along the way towards capturing the idea which had propelled the film to begin with. The image, like the lens, lost power to the argument, the web of ideas and facts. Only experience could meld these elements, could indoctrinate me in the necessary, rarefied balance between image and content.

In the case of a PBS biography of Nikos Kazantzakis, I had initially scripted a theatrical approach to the artist's life, but countless false starts led to a modest half-hour haiku. For five weeks our small crew moved efficiently across Greece, revisiting the monasteries, churches, tavernas and other haunts of the great poet, sage, novelist. Very quickly, the camera lost its importance for me and became, nearly, an encumbrance, incapable of keeping up with the swirling pace of ideas that began to demand, at least, equal time with the images. Images whose proliferation argued for a tight narration to reign them in.

All of Greece gave visual fodder to Kazantzakis' story and I recall feeling a fantastic elation at the recognition that old faces, sculptures, pedestrian traffic, cityscapes, old-world semblances and remnants, all summoned forth relevant elements of illustrative evocation. The union of image and narration, dialogues and interviews was the perfect alchemy for conveying this particular story, at that time in my career. Not until I had spent weeks, then months in the editing room did I feel the pangs of elusiveness: Kazantzakis would not yield up his vast universe so readily or simplistically.

Indeed, the real work began in that editing room, surrounded by a 40-to-1 ratio of material that could only hope to glimpse the myriad surfaces of a man who had died nearly twenty-five years before. Fortunately, Kazantzakis' wife, Eleni, and his close friend and translator, Kimon Friar, as well as Anthony Quinn, Melina Mercouri, and Ghika all added enormous feeling to their respective recollections of the artist.

Still, the footage looked not nearly so exotic as it had appeared on our little monitor those late nights after shooting, when the crew would huddle together in one hotel room or another examining the day's work. In fact, by the time I was back in the editing room, the 40-to-1 was feeling rather lean. In some cases, thirty minutes of footage—original on 3/4" tape, shot with a three tube camera—was worth, perhaps, thirty seconds of usable material. This was all a learning experience for me. What was crucial were the interviews, not the B-roll. And the lesson in that concerns the truth, unmanipulated, laid out in its own time, its own words, at its own pace. There was no disputing the excitement when someone actually had something to say, and said it with verve and personality. And, I believe, *everyone* in the world has something to say.

I was working out what it was that mattered to me most about my subject. Certain prime connections erupted, and they were undeniably crucial to the film. I knew it as they were being spoken. As when Mrs. Kazantzakis detailed the extent of Nazi persecutions and then relayed how Nikos had wisely filled an old jug on their back porch in Aegina with edible oil. As a famine swept the island, it was a ration of one tablespoon of oil per day which kept the couple alive. Too weak to get out of bed, in six weeks Kazantzakis completed his first novel, *Zorba the Greek*. It was his imagination, fueled by that oil, which kept him alive. We had the bed, and the corroded jug overlooking the sea. We had Mrs. Kazantzakis' description of the times, and the necessary ingredients to render an effective segue to the character of Zorba, as played by Anthony Quinn. This was a pivotal point in Kazantzakis' life, and in the film. The method of portrayal came easily, once the logic was in place: the slow, tense, handheld moves from the oil jug to a slow dissolve into a still image of Kazantzakis, to a soft cut to a group of wild Cretan musicians performing on a cliff over the sea, as a dancer among them executed a ragged Hasapiko, his fingers snapping, the live image merging with a still of the real George Zorba superimposed on the Anthony Quinn rendition from a movie poster. The rhythms, the snapping fingers, all transcended the Nazi madness. That was Zorba's divine gift, and a key to unlocking Kazantzakis.

When it all came together, forty seconds of film time, a half-dozen edits and images, I could well believe that the spirit of that great novel, and the circumstances surrounding it, had been faithfully intimated. I had not interfered or distorted, as far as I could determine, but had midwived an approach to the material which felt authentic. This one instance was the first of a cumulative impression, a groping. When the film debuted, the subject was no longer the point, or not for me; but, to paraphrase the poet Cavafy, the journey to *reach* Kazantzakis. That's what mattered most.

Since that time, I have had the good fortune to direct films in dozens of countries and hundreds of places, where the same fabulist iconography of surface details always exerts a similar syndrome: the temptation to fall swoon before the color and pageantry of other cultures and settings, no matter what the reason for being there. This is what I love about the nonfiction realm. Free of excess paraphernalia, moving lightly through a crowd, or across a desert, the subject—if it is powerful— incites a whole other unexpected awakening, a geyser of glints shedding light on myself. The process of giving inevitably begets. To love is to learn; to embrace, to be somehow embraced. Or, as the poets have long understood, the soul awakens when it is touched.

In another sense, a visual plane imprints the optic nerves. But the process of conceptually and kinetically exploring subjects that are not puppets, who have not been told what to say, how to act, what to do, engenders rare dynamics that tell as much about the filmmaker as the subject. One is forever learning about the world, growing as a person. But these truisms pale before the rush of inarticulate sensations, as fleeting and at times astonishing as light itself. Because the documentary aspires after what is, or has been, it cannot help but reflect the filmmakers involved. There is no objectivity in this world, neither in the supposedly tranquil minds encompassing the Supreme Court or in the furiously focused brain of a hummingbird. We are all out there making sense of images, making sense of ourselves. The "reality" of the image—the ceaseless play of photons on the machinery of the eye and brain—is built of the cosmic surreality of physics and biology, momentarily coalescing, enshrined in the ongoing physical dimensions in which we have been shaped by yet other evolutionary forces. We are always being born and dying at the same instant and this we call reality. It is not reality, it is experience that is translated, passions that are personal, visions that can never obey the artificial theorems and parameters of a preordained realism. This is not to deny that so called "reality-based" programming, the brain-numbing routines and formulas of daytime talk shows and recreations, has not tried very hard to emulate a kind of nightly news of truth, born of predictable provocations and a fanfare of confessions and allegations. These are genres, the daily foodstuffs of culture, the white noise of shopping malls, and hundreds–of–thousands of hours of video lines of resolution. Resolution of what? Of unresolvable reality. As information, or pure entertainment, such programs fulfill a deep need in the social psyche for highlights, sports commentary, thirty–second titillations, single-breath summaries, salacious scandal sheets, or plain daily facts. Personalities teem and tremble on every network, spewing their guts.

The documentary form I am referring to, however, concerns a very different reconstruction of "reality"; one expressly growing out of the filmmaker's own private coming-of-age. With *Kazantzakis* it was the homage, on the occasion of the 100th anniversary of an artist's birth, a poet that had hugely influenced my own life. In the case of my PBS film *Sand & Lightning* the motivation was my long-time obsession with Japanese aesthetics, as spelled out in a 500-year-old, 38-centimeter-high needle juniper—Tosho—and twenty-two species of moss gracing the hilly enclaves of Ginkaku-ji, the former estate in Kyoto of the late fifteenth century tea celebrant, Ashikaga Shogun Yoshimasa. I was very lucky: for the first time in history Japanese Buddhism had gone on strike. Our crew enjoyed total access to the inside of the Shogun's tearoom. I sat at his table, traversed his floors, lit whole rooms that would otherwise have been unfilmable. The entire mansion had been abandoned. Barefooted, we wandered at our ease throughout the interior confines, filming for the entire day.

A similar passion was consummated in Ireland, when the prime minister's son piloted me around in their private helicopter for twenty-four hours, dropping down on beaches, in meadows, atop buildings, all over the country, in order to get me from one crew to another as part of a marathon effort entitled *A Day in the Life of Ireland*. My wife, Jane Morrison, was directing a crew in the far west of the country, braving rain-soaked seas to find a certain dolphin; while my close friend and associate, Robert Radin, was up in Belfast and Derby coordinating a portrait of nonviolent protest. Between us—and with the dedicated efforts of nine Irish film crews—the production slipped into place like a subtle wine washing down a fantastic feast, which, of course, is the Irish way of life, its buoyancy, humor, and brilliance. Between serious time-outs in one pub or another, the production made me dizzy with my Irish upbringing. If poet Percy Shelley insisted that all the world was Greek, then my other mentor, Joyce, was equally right in reminding us of our universally Irish heritage. This film was a homecoming, a compassionate embrace, a love letter. My filmmaking has been one ongoing series of such letters.

My feature film for the national Indian network, *Doordarshan*, *A Day in the Life of India* (also known as *India 24 Hours*) was a tribute to a woman I have loved. And twenty-five years of returning to my roots. We employed 150 members of twelve Indian crews to fan out across the country for one week and capture the fleeting perfection of the Indian psyche. But it was the twelve journeys themselves that made it into the film; journeys tempered by the abundance of Indian culture, humor, and sobriety.

With *Cloudwalker* (Channel 4, U.K.) the film reflected my lifelong pursuit of granite walls and glacial backcountry. A mountaineering attempt on an impossible 5,000 foot cliff, the Moose's Tooth, with three film teams dangling over the icy escarpments with the climbers for over a month. Near death experiences could never have been told in any other medium.

Later, Alaska cried out to me in another way, when the Valdez disaster made headlines and hundreds of miles of coastline were tainted with oil. I waited for six months before embarking on the film, after the rush of news crews had died down, and the real story started to sink in. I have always believed that a documentary should only be made if it is the one and only way to tell a story. The motivation must be that specific and powerful; otherwise, it is a sheer waste of time, money, and effort. In the case of my Discovery Channel special, *Black Tide* I could think of no better way to viscerally convey the tragedy of an environmental shipwreck than by showing the dead cormorants, the oil–infested otters shivering and suffocating, the seals and eagles begging for their lives, and the surrounding melodrama of conflicting opinions by "experts." The crew happened to be on the North Slope just after another oil company had unleashed a 20,000 gallon spill on the vulnerable tundra. Had we not filmed the incident, the public might never have known, a fact which underscores the avalanche of oil and chemical spills through the world which go unreported. Not too long after the airing of *Black Tide*, and a screening for Congress at the Smithsonian, the president by executive order signed the double-hull tanker legislation, one of the key recommendations of the film.

Many of my documentaries have attempted to capture the dark shades of something that has happened, and is happening. Aside from an ecological background academically, this penchant stems from my own shame of wantonness as a human being; my conspiratorial situation as one member of a particular species which continues to wreak havoc on a miraculous planet of life. The goal of exposing our transgressions has always absorbed me and it is through the documentary medium that I have found the most efficient and effective means for communicating those feelings.

Voice of the Planet, a $4 million, ten-hour Turner Broadcasting epic, starring William Shatner and Faye Dunaway, was shot in over twenty countries and sought to fashion a new kind of docudrama—a ten-hour *My Dinner With Andre* filmed not at a dinner table, but throughout the world. Shatner (the character of William Hope Planter) played a cynical professor of ecology in dialogue with Mother Earth (Gaia) represented by the voice of Dunaway and projected via the convenient means of a funky computer whose energy was powered hydroelectrically by the waters of Sagarmatha (Mount Everest). In truth, her power was coming from Mount Everest, which was a few miles above our basecamp for filming at Thyangboche Monastery in Nepal. The electricity had begun flowing just three days before our crew arrived at the 14,000 foot high monastery, thanks to the ingenious and dedicated efforts of alternative energy experts and Sherpa aficionados, Brought Coburn and Dee Dee Thunder, our local liaisons.

Voice of the Planet was docudrama by dint of a very rarified technique, much like a drop of drama in a glass of pure documentary. The two principal characters had a precise script, 600 pages of dialogue which I had adapted from my novel by the same title. We filmed William (Shatner) in a studio at Maryland Public

Broadcasting, having matched a Buddhist monastery interior which Jane Morrison had carefully photographed in Kathmandu during a previous scouting trip. To the alchemical chamber I added a very funky fifth generation talking computer and an extraordinary Buddhist terrarium designed by a Baltimore landscape architect, which was stocked with marvelous live creatures lent the production by the Smithsonian Institution. We shot all of Shatner's interior work with three studio cameras over a period of three weeks, then set off around the world for fifty-two days with him. Meanwhile, two other crews were filming A and B-roll sequences for five months in Australia, Iceland, China, Bangladesh, the Soviet Union, Turkey, India, France, Switzerland, Brazil, Venezuela, and a dozen other countries and thirty-five U.S. states. There were extraordinary moments throughout: samurai who refused to pee in the bushes outside the teahut (as was customary 500 years ago); the Italian one-armed chemist speaking of disasters whilst standing in the largest wastedump in Europe; the re–creation of fire among the Walpiri people of Central Australia; our discovery that cheetahs love cream cheese; the sheer scope of the series.

Back in Burbank, California, several editorial teams wrestled with nearly 700 hours of footage, round–the–clock for fifteen months, while a separate research team scoured global archive sources for rare stock footage needed to fill in the blanks, including the rarest of the rare—lemming migration footage. After eight months of searching, then negotiating, the never-before-seen footage arrived in a package one morning. When I opened it, I discovered not lemming, but lambing footage. The two words sounded the same over the phone to Oslo. (Eventually, we did find rare lemming migration footage.)

Shatner and Dunaway then came into the studio for ten days each to record voice-over. The ten one-hour-long films focused on the emotional aspects of biochemistry (*The Thinking Earth*), the nature of life (*Sex and Death*), water pollution (*The Sacred and Profane*), population dynamics (*The Numbers Game*), alternative energy and the ecology and psychic impact of fire (*Fire in the Mind*), sustainable agriculture and indigenous ethics, as well as reincarnation (*The Transformation of Sarah*), chemical pollution (*A Plague on This House*), a rational alternative to extinction (*Paradise*), and finally, the folly of believing that humans could solve all of their problems here on Earth by terra-forming Mars (*Starstruck*).

The miniseries could not have been a more personal essay. Unfortunately (and ironically, given its comprehensive nonviolent message) the series premiered as five two-hour movies back-to-back the same week Western forces invaded Iraq.

TBS's Gaia could not easily compete for ratings with CNN's fireworks show in the skies over Baghdad. The series was repeated each night, for one week at prime-time, then promptly disappeared, with no video release. That was seven years of work, two of those years full-time. And it drove home for me the truth of my earlier assertion that the most important and rewarding aspect of the documentary is the opening up of one's own feelings, the journey taken by the filmmaker. In the case of *Voice of the Planet* I made several wonderful new friends, and was able to explore much of this Earth with an intensity I would never forget, or lose.

I had for years been a practitioner of Jainism, one of the oldest spiritual traditions in the world and the first and only ecological religion ever embraced in ancient history by millions of people whose descendants still practiced its tenets today. Ahimsa—meaning nonviolence and compassion in as pure and absolute a manner as the imagination, in daily concert with human pragmatism, can conceive—is the basis of Jainism, a vegetarian religion. Three years of inroads into the Jain community resulted—with the production help of the Denver PBS affiliate, KRMA (principally the former heads, Don Johnson and Ron Salak)—in the first mainstream film ever made for Western audiences about this remarkable community of nearly 10 million people. Shot beautifully in over 100 locations throughout India by Stuart Keene, lovingly edited by Bruce Neale, and narrated by Lindsay Wagner, the one-hour special premiered nationwide on Christmas Day. Remarkably, there were numerous scenes of naked monks wandering through towns, at temples, and being hand-fed by community leaders; even a scene of a naked man sitting surrounded by dozens of children, delivering a sermon. Lifelong nudity is one of the characteristics of the male Digambara Jain monks or munis, a profound sign that they have renounced all material possessions. In Christian tradition, St. John the Baptist and St. Francis exemplified the same spirit. Despite the deep neuroses and hypocrisy of American audiences with respect to nakedness, there was not even a murmur of protest regarding frontal male nudity on Christmas day over PBS.

I'll never forget the final shot before credits of the film, for it reflects the most exquisite natural timing I have ever witnessed in documentary filmmaking. Quite by luck, a Digambara monk at the temple of Taranga happened to be standing atop a sculptured platform with his only possession, a pinchi or broom fashioned from naturally shed peacock feathers, and used by the monks to gently brush any hapless insects out of their path. As the monk walked to camera left, his broom sweeping back and forth, a languor monkey, her tail also swinging back and forth, moved to camera right, directly below the monk. The two naked, perfect beings were spectacularly choreographed in a spiritual interdependency that is the essence of Jainism, its reverence for nature. That deep reflection could only have happened in "reality." To have shaped it in a drama could never have worked the same effect. Indeed, we had no idea when we first arrived at Taranga that there were two Digambara monks staying there a few days. The monks spend their entire lives out on the roads of India, naked, walking from village to village speaking of non-violence. When we ran into them, they were most agreeable to our filming them, acknowledging that a TV documentary was a powerful tool for extending the message of peace.

Similar moments where the truth proved more perplexing and fantastic than any dramatic re-creation could ever be certainly occur in patiently waited-on, well-planned natural history films. When our cameras recorded an Argentine helicopter pilot deliberately terrifying an Adelie penguin rookery with his low-flying chopper, scattering the birds down icy hillsides into the sea at Base Esperanza on Antarctica's Western Peninsula, adults crushing eggs in their panic, the persistent problem of reckless base operations endemic to the scientific, political, and touristic presence on the last continent was made abundantly clear. Base personnel still eat penguins, and used to throw live ones into the furnaces on board their ships for fuel. It is alleged that U.S. base personnel were once seen playing football with live penguins; and French soldiers deliberately blew up a penguin rookery while building a runway on the ice "in order to see penguins fly." MacMurdo Sound is more polluted than Chesapeake Bay. Garbage is tossed overboard by offshore science vessels. Open pit burning, tourists stepping on delicate moss forests, taunting the wildlife, the accumulation of huge garbage dumps adjoining rookeries—all of these horror stories, and many more, were conveyed in *Antarctica—The Last Continent* for PBS. The White House Science Office responded to the visual allegations and vowed to look into problems at all U.S. base operations. It was a beginning.

In China, while filming *World War III* for PBS, reality once again proved stronger than anything I might have scripted. We happened to be on the Nanking Road bridge in Shanghai on a holiday where there was more pedestrian traffic directly below us than on any other street in any city in the world. The seething crowds said it all in a film about global human overpopulation and the impact of Homo sapiens on the biosphere. Later, also in China, we encountered the horrible torture of two pigs. I filmed the sequence. It is in the opening title shots and leaves the viewer absolutely heartsick and suspended, providing the appropriate pall of horror for the duration of the documentary. Only at the end, just before the credit roll, does the viewer gain relief, and hence some hope, as I buy the two pigs from the tormentor, surrounded by curious (I should say incredulous) Chinese villagers, and release them into the fields. What I also bought, with the "official" aid of the camera crew who were recording this ad hoc transaction, was a guarantee that these two pigs would be left alone. Money was paid, the cameras were rolling, and a "covenant" hastily written out was signed by the owner before fifty witnesses. With our U.N. van, a government liaison officer from the State Family Planning Commission, and the signed document—all for international TV—the fellow who had been riding his bike to the butcher with the two live pigs lashed to the back and dangling upside down, in agony and screaming, was himself now terrified. At the time, though aware of the cameras, I was lost in my anger, emotions, and pain, focused on only one thing—not directing, but saving those animals. The power of the documentary to remind me and all other viewers of the possibilities for redemption and positive change, that the individual *can* and *must* make a difference, was overpowering.

This is why I make documentaries. Nearly every network I've made films for has demanded certain editorial deletions, invariably of shots or scenes their programmers or lawyers deemed of concern—too strong, or legally indefensible, even if only in a gray area of uncertainty. This, of course, is always frustrating, though input should always be welcomed. Gatekeepers, advertisers, sponsors, and government censors are fearful of reality. To have to fight for every second of reality in such embroiled instances renews my faith, time and again, in the power and importance of nonfiction filmmaking.

Most of my films are very personal essays, private expositions which are not, by definition, for mass appeal. Between the easy flaws of self-indulgence and the equally fatal panderings to public ovation, there is plenty of private elbow room for conveying one's vision or story in a manner that is not entirely inaccessible, and that can be acceptable by broadcasters. Nearly all my films have been in that uneasy category. If there is a public sector, even the smallest coterie (for example, the new generation of "target audiences") that takes notice of such a film, so much the better. The point is to communicate, unfettered by any expectation of ratings; to reach out as befits the work without compromise. There is no other reason to go to the expense of mounting a film unless it can reasonably be expected to reach at least some audience, however modest. This is the key to social advocacy in film-making, and it is imperative that artists involved in the craft take responsibility for the potential power of their medium. Social advocacy is just another expression for subjectivity, and it is essential, I think, to good documentary filmmaking.

With the new broadcast quality chip cameras, digital high-8, and the ease of "hauteur" productions, one-stop-shops, and one person crews, the temptation to engage in the essay form should increase and the public stands to gain immeasurably. Many years ago, filmmaker Kevin Duffy wrote, directed, produced, executive-produced, shot and edited a marvelous film on the pygmies of the rainforest. The film, as I experienced it, was the author's own love letter to a people he knew intimately. NOVA eventually aired the film, which had been, again, the creation of one man and those who participated in it. He did not, I suspect, set out to make a film that would garner awards or money, or even a large audience. He did it from love.

I assumed when our company, JMT Productions, produced *A Parliament of Souls* (twenty-six half-hour interviews hosted by my talented colleague, the San Francisco-based producer/interviewer, Ms. Bettina Gray) that the audience would be limited. This thirteen-hour series was made for under $20,000 cash. PBS-San Jose—thanks to Executive Producer Danny McGuire—threw in all of post-production and served as the umbrella station for the eventual release over the PBS interregional Pacific Mountain Network, where it has been seen in about eighty markets. The Vision Cable Network out of Toronto contributed a crew and gear in exchange for Canadian rights. And the Presbyterian Church of America also donated a crew and gear. The Blackstone Hotel in Chicago donated their exquisite presidential suite for nine days of shooting. And Saito Antiques of Chicago gave us whatever authentic pieces we wanted for set-dressing. Sir John Templeton provided some funds, and VISN Cable network in New York pre-bought nonexclusive domestic cable rights. Pacific Mountain Network agreed to sharing the broadcast window, which made the deal possible. Robert Radin donated his time as official photographer of the production. Later on, KQED (the PBS affiliate in San Francisco) published the book tie–in which Jane Morrison, Bettina Gray, and I edited, with Radin's still images. KQED also released our two-hour cut down version of the home video series. The series has now aired repeatedly. The book sold out. Quite unexpectedly, millions of people have seen a series of twenty-six half-hour films, very serious in-depth portraits chronicling great spiritual leaders from a dozen countries; their views on virtue, community, God, the fate of the Earth. All of this with virtually no money going in. Tie-ins, nonexclusive presales, broadcast window sharing, coproductions, foundation grants, and a team of friends who agreed out of love of their subject to come together without restraint—this was the essence of *A Parliament of Souls*, a method that worked for our purposes and shows what can be done with little. There are myriad avenues available to nonfiction filmmakers who are keyed into the wants of what turns out to be a rather large, if often hidden audience. Even the most passionately private of documentarians are likely to be surprised.

If the production insists on integrity, which it must, then the truth can yield up images and handholds, and it is powerful. "Insist on yourself," said Henry David Thoreau. It is the courage of the subjective, the "indwelling" (to borrow G.M.Hopkin's expression) that marks the approach; the journey, without pretense or expectation. "Reality" is each person's vision, embedded in the senses, fashioned from fleeting reflections, made of uncertain substance which, in even the most durable, replicable digital domain, will vanish, sooner or later. There is no more thrilling adventure than the many metaphors which the process of documentary filmmaking can elicit in the telling of that passing flame. Kazantzakis took it a step further in his thinking when he said, "It is not the human being who interests me. But the flame that consumes the human being."

The mirror image of reality is the coming out of the filmmaker. Each film begins there, at the moment of risk and vulnerability and conviction, with no other reason or money and only the flame of an ideal to guide one. Those personal ideals, I believe, are the key to documentaries.

PART V

THE CHANGING

TECHNOLOGY

OF NON-FICTION

Photo: NASA.

THE FAMILY FILMED

ROBERT W. WAGNER

Recent academic interest in family films has been directed to interpretations of their sociological, psychological, or aesthetic aspects and the "reality" or the mythology of these early cinematic artifacts.

The entire Summer-Fall, 1986, number of the *Journal of Film* and *Video* was devoted to homemovies and amateur filmmaking. Their commercial uses have been exploited by television in the homemovies of Desi and Lucy, John and Jacqueline, and even Adolph and Eva, not to mention the backyard antics of garden-variety Americans.

Theoretical and commercial considerations aside, the original motive of the typical American pioneer snapshooter and home moviemaker was simply to preserve a moment, person, place, or an event. As Andre Bazin, referring to the human impulse sometimes known as "the mummy complex" commented in *What Is Cinema?*: "If the plastic arts were put under psychoanalysis, the practice of embalming the dead might turn out to be a fundamental factor in their creation." The impulse to preserve personal and family identity through photography was instantly implemented by George Eastman's 1888 Kodak camera placed in the hands of amateurs with the simple instruction: "You press the button, we do the rest"—a directive which proved applicable to people using any of the technologies in the twentieth century and beyond.

In 1923, with the introduction of the Cine-Kodak Model A camera and projector the home moviemaking period began in America. Fortunately, because the film was 16mm black-and-white reversal on an acetate ("safety" or noninflammable) base, much of it is still preserved. If the first home moving images had been on videotape, little if anything would be left. The Model A was an exciting new toy and, like the family's first Model T, or the first son's first electric train, it was typically operated by the father whose judgment was usually dominant at the dinner table and featured on the home movie screen as well. The camera was at his eyelevel and he was the one who turned it on and off. The writer's case for the importance of home movies as a significant chapter in the history of the American documentary film is based on the inspection of many collections of family films;

on recent experience in the making of motion picture and video productions using footage from such collections; and on more than sixty years of experience with the home movies of his own family.

My father was a professional photographer whose career began in the early dry-plate era of the twentieth century when prints were still being made by sunlight and interiors were illuminated with flash-powder. The first home movies in our family were made on short-ends of 35mm negative in a camera about the size of a steamer trunk. My father would bring it home after making photographs and motion pictures of coal-mining activities in southern Ohio for a mining machine manufacturing company where he was on the staff of the art department. He would have my brother and me dress up in our cowboy and Indian outfits and give us a brief verbal scenario accompanied by shouts such as: "More action! This is a MOVIE!" He was the C.B. DeMille of home movie production and also the Arthur Mayer of its exhibition.

He had printed titles made for his production and showed them on a hand-cranked 35mm Keystone (which still works) to sometimes understandably disinterested relatives and friends, using one of mother's best white tablecloths with the wrinkles carefully ironed out as a screen. Sometimes he would cut in a snippit from a feature he got from an exhibitor friend who either deliberately clipped out a shot from a silent Tom Mix or Greta Garbo film or retrieved it from the floor of the projection room after a break in a reel.

Among the one-minute films documenting various events such as the arrival of a train and workers leaving a factory, the Lumiere brothers of France as early as 1895 included perhaps the first films with the "home-movie look." *Le Repas de Bebe* was an exterior scene of a small child being spoon-fed. *L'Arroseur Arrosee*, showing a gardener watering a garden being hosed by a small boy, might have been the prototype of the tv show, *Funniest Home Videos*. Both episodes were contrived as home movies and are still staged today.

The Wagner family films are much the same as those found in other such collections of the period. Generally they document rites of passage - weddings, birthdays, vacations, pets, Christmases, the new car, the new house, the new baby, and visiting relatives and friends whose names and connections have been forgotten since Aunt Flora or another elderly family historian passed on. The record is one of active rather than passive moments; of beginnings rather than endings. The firstborn is most filmed. The siblings that follow generally receive fewer and fewer top billings. Adolescents often resist being filmed at all. On one memorable occasion in the 1960s the writer's three longhaired offspring threatened to call the Child Abuse Center if he carried out his innocent intention to film them during some backyard family event or other. The very old and the dying seldom appear, and then generally without their knowledge or consent—undoubtedly because as the once-debonair David Niven in the latter days of his romantic career ruefully observed: "The trouble with getting old is that everything begins to sag!"

As with the pioneer photographers, the first home moviemakers were inventive, educated, often well traveled, and able to afford the equipment, film, and processing. Even during the dark days of the Depression large collections of home movies of upper-middle-class and affluent families are found intact, often including footage made on the first color film available to the 16mm amateur. This was Eastman's Kodacolor—a lenticular, black-and-white reversal film shot and projected through a filter composed of sections of red, green, and blue glass onto a small screen of high reflective quality.

The amateur learned to make movies first because of the meticulous care taken by the Eastman Kodak Company to educate users of their products through publications like *How To Make Good Movies*, and *Kodakery*. Specific instructions were found on each yellow box of film and the correct aperture settings were also often engraved on the camera itself, including little graphics symbolizing "sunlight," "snow–and–beach," "cloudy-bright," and "dull-overcast" conditions. The film had a lot of latitude and the short focal length lenses in 16mm cameras, and especially in the later 8mm versions, had great depth of field thus improving chances for acceptable sharpness of the images and better definition of the reality being filmed.

Interviews with pioneer home moviemakers reveal few specifics on how they learned to improve their pictures, but they certainly quickly found out by watching their own films and especially from the candid comments of family and friends. Shots that were blurred, too short, too shaky, too far away, or too unflattering would chasten the amateur producer as a bad audience reaction sobers a Hollywood director at a sneak preview. The home moviemaker, of course, was also influenced by the theatrical films of the time. There is no hard evidence of this but anyone watching a western knew what a close-up of a hand on a six–shooter portended, and that by moving the camera vertically or laterally more of the landscape could be shown and the action could be followed. Amateur films gradually reflect changes in technique. Takes are longer; the use of a tripod is more evident; pans and tilts are slower; titles are often inserted; trick effects appear; shots are edited chronologically, and in some cases creatively. Although these were images of "reality," the model was the theatrical film, since few Americans had ever seen a "documentary"—a term invented by British filmmaker John Grierson who used it to describe Robert Flaherty's film, *Nanook of the North*.

The Amateur Photo League founded in 1926 included advanced amateurs as well as novices and its publication *Movie Makers* described its interest in "...films made for family records, travel movies, experiments in scenic pictures made with artistic intent, tentative and sometimes fully-fledged photoplays, studies of athletic form and records of games—all these of extremely personal character in the non-theatrical film category."

By 1935, Kodachrome popularized the use of color as a major contribution to "realism" in photography and motion pictures, but the credibility if not the reality of the early home movie still seemed to be associated with images in black and white. Scratches, shaky camera, and jump cuts which characterized the work of the amateur were later transferred to the theatrical screen as in *Citizen Kane* (1941), which included simulated black and white newsreel clips. Scorsese's *Raging Bull* (1980) and Woody Allen's *Zelig* (1983), the latter with some "amateur" shots carefully abraded with sandpaper, demonstrate how the home movie influenced the makers of theatrical films as Hollywood influenced the home moviemaker. The same sense of "reality" and "authenticity" is exploited in television commercials and political ads.

In the 1960s the home movie look emerged in the avant-garde attack on traditional narrative film form and content. Brakhage was producing his "dailiness film" in which, he said, "those commonplace daily activities which my wife and child and I share in some form or other with almost every family on earth are visually explored to the fullest extent of their universal meaning." Bruce Bailie was making creative use of overexposure. Defocused shots, intentionally blurred in Broughton's *This Is It: a "home movie,"* featured his naked son playing with a large red ball in the backyard. The "film diary" appeared in Jonas Mekas's *Diaries, Notes, and Sketches* and Jim McBride's fictionalized "documentary," *David Holzman's Diary* (1968). Saul Levine's obvious 8mm splices were not just a home-movie technological mistake but an aesthetic decision. Jump cuts, run-offs, perforations, flash-frames, and eccentric camera movements punctuated these personal visions and accelerated the demystification of the medium itself—a process to which the amateur home moviemaker unwittingly contributed. In 1975, a production by Ernst Edward Star and Steve Zeitlin based on home movies was featured in the

Smithsonian Institution's Festival of American Folk Art, thus elevating this form of amateur moviemaking to another level of significance.

By 1960, sound became available to the home moviemaker and spring-driven cameras were replaced with battery-driven models. Electric motor–driven cameras encouraged longer takes which became even longer as the home moviemaker traded his mechanical Super-8mm motion picture film camera for an automated, electronic camcorder. A new kind of videotaped family was in the making. The father was no longer the sole head of the home production studio. Mother had access to a fully automatic electronic camera and playback equipment and the children considered their own camcorders as just another one of their toys, another way to explore their world.

The writer, invited to discuss photography and moviemaking with his granddaughter's fifth-grade class, found that nearly all of the students owned or had access to their own camcorders. Groping for a subject they might find interesting, he suggested "getting to know your parents better by documenting aspects of their daily home life you may not have noticed before." This innocent comment was followed by a chorus of muffled titters and whispers.

Mystified, he later asked the teacher what the class found amusing about such a worthy, "family–value–oriented" idea. "They just had their sex education unit yesterday," she explained.

The history of the home movie may be referred to as either "B.Z." or "A.Z."— before Zapruder or after amateur Abraham Zapruder, whose 8mm record of the assassination of President John F. Kennedy reached television and motion picture screens from 1963 to the present, including its incorporation in Oliver Stone's fact-fict-film *J.F.K.* In the period A.Z. the importance of the amateur image-maker as a documentarian would never be questioned again.

George Bernard Shaw once wryly observed: "The amateur photographer is like the cod who lays a million eggs to get one fish." But that single fish may be a big one like that caught by Zapruder, or by the amateur who, using his brand-new camcorder for the first time, documented the beating of Rodney King. On December 10, 1996, the F.B.I. offered a half million dollars for amateur videotapes or snapshots made by visitors to the Olympics in Atlanta which could establish the identity of the Centennial Park bomber. Evidential uses of home videotapes are increasing, including surveillance cameras to monitor illegal entrants and negligent baby-sitters. A home video camera mounted in a Cessna aircraft for the purpose of recording a pleasure flight over the Continental Divide documented instead its crash in a wooded area where it was not found until three years later. The tape was intact, picturing the horror resulting from pilot error. The tape is now used in flight instruction.

Earlier it was mentioned that most home movies are records of beginnings without endings, marriages without divorces, birthdays without funerals, smiles without tears. These are the treasured moments in the family film. All the world's a stage and although most of us are merely bit-players, we wish to be documented and remembered at our very best. Family films, like the decisive moments of our life, are simply samples of our existence and, as every documentary purist knows, what is left out of the frame or edited out or simply not recorded is often more important than what is left in.

The camera documents us in our many Protean forms, but is there really a "true" picture of any of us? Can there ever be a document of anything that remains valid beyond the moment of its recording? The instant it is captured it is part of the past. As with the Heisenberg Principle of Uncertainty, the original reality of any artifact is gone forever once it has been recorded.

In 1997 a fifteen-minute videotape made from home movies taken by a father was exhibited before a jury deciding whether Timothy McVeigh, convicted of the bombing of the Oklahoma Federal Building, would receive the death penalty. It showed Tim as a happy child, climbing up on the lap of Santa Claus, playing with a toy train, and riding a tractor. "It's the Tim I remember most of my life!" the father and filmmaker said of these treasured images of his son's past.

Brian Lewis, chair of the Department of Communication at Simon-Fraser University, British Columbia, who researched the home movie in the United States and Canada, inherited two suitcases full of little yellow boxes of films made by his father and his grandfather, making it possible for him "...to meet a generation of relatives he had never known." My past," he said, "a past which preceded my birth, opened up like a magic box." Another friend whose twenty years of 16mm family films the writer transferred to tape reflected: "In company with various family members, I've looked at the VHS duplicates at least four times. It leaves me with strange feelings to look again at all those scenes and persons, most of the latter long gone; so many images out of what was certainly a very different and, in some respects, a vanished world."

Never vanished, but certainly different, because new audiences find new meanings in these homemade images and contemporary producers find new uses for them. As with all history, artifacts and arts are reproduced and reinterpreted with time and change. What makes them seem "real," or at least "believable" as documents of a single family or as a sample of a society, is our own inevitably partly fictionalized, partly factual perceptions of the way we thought we were.

Divorce, the death of a loved one, or a family feud prompt the editing out of certain faces, times, and places or instigate their digital replacement. This growing volume of family film documentation has become part of our memory system, making it difficult for children to distinguish what they recall as their own experience from what they have experienced through their family films and tapes.

Whatever their future form or content all images, professional and amateur, are "documents"—palingenesistic records revealing that we are what we are because we were as we were and maybe if we look closely enough, what we may become. They will, however, always be incomplete samples of moments both wonderful and tragic; always composites of artifact, artifice, and art. The day of the classic home movie once referred to as cinema-naivete seems to be over. Or maybe not. Children are making little videotape stories with cameras which still seem to be candid, and some independent producers still have the old documentary impulse.

One of the writer's recent short productions, celebrating the small town in which he lives, is titled *Portrait of an American Town: A Home Movie*.

Robert Wagner, consultant on a documentary titled A LAND LOOKING WEST, produced by John Izzard for Channel 9, Perth, Australia.

INTRODUCTION

GODFREY REGGIO

Poem as inspiration for film, word as path to image. What follows under the title ALL TOGETHER•ALL AT ONCE are trigger lines, projectiles of association. In these words is a beginning step to realize a wordless IMAX compilation film, a millennium piece, as yet only an intention unmanifested in celluloid: IMAX, for the power of immersion in the image; compilation/archival for a lexicon of iconographic history. For those who might not know the IMAX medium let me explain in this way: at a regular movie you look at the image on the screen; in the IMAX film you enter the image, the screen disappears, all referent points vanish. (IMAX film is ten times the size of the 35mm negative!) The impact of radical scale, of quantum, qualitatively differentiates this experience from the movies. It is precisely this <u>entering of the image</u> that interests me, as both the subject matter of the film and the medium of production become one.

I am at once overwhelmed and challenged by the feeling that humans are in a singular moment of untellable transformation; that the very ground upon which we stand as a species is giving way; that the human center of gravity seems not to be holding. Is it possible that we are witnessing the physical and metaphysical collapse of our firmament without knowing? Is it conceivable that our words are losing their power to describe this world? Is metaphor giving way to a metamorphosis of unimaginable consequence? In the globalized world, if the image is well on its way to becoming our new realityscape, then the IMAX experience prefigures this phenomenon in an extraordinary way. As emerging technologies have us "interfacing" with the medium, this notion itself is sliding into antiquity, as the interface gives way to entrance into the virtual. A clarity begins to emerge: the higher the technology, the greater the disembodiment, the closer we approach the zone of no return.

For ALL TOGETHER•ALL AT ONCE known images of our world are transformed through the viewfinder of the scenario, the poem. To resee the chaos of our times in the monstrous unity of the global world is the perspective of our lens. The story sets a grand stage as it risks the audacity of an epic drama of the now two faces of our existence: *Homo Sapiens*, at a turning point or vanishing point; *massman*, on-line and transfixed. Extremes of promise, spectacle, utterance, fragility, tragedy, and startling hope reveal this story, this <u>history</u>, in a dramatic representation of and for our times. The scenario conjures a vision of a world engulfed in the shadow of the mass, entering the awesome domain of the digital— a world of new definition, new classes, new functions, new needs, a world in shock. My intention is to create <u>a new mediums cinematic concert for the 21st century</u>, where the story and its form of presentation portend a vision of a new world coming, a story structured in the language of image and voiced in orchestral multi-media narration.

As we all have heard, a picture is worth a thousand words. For love of the word, I try to take a thousand pictures and give them the power of one word. Contradiction is embraced in this film to be, where narration is the medium, the subject is the process, the image is the word, and the poetry is to behold.

ALL TOGETHER • ALL AT ONCE

THE ROCKETSHIP
20TH CENTURY

GODFREY REGGIO

1.

SINGULAR
ALLURING
ACCESSIBLE
EXTREME
REMOTE
TOUCHING
UNFORGETTABLE
    COMPILATIONS, INDELIBLE FRAMES
    CONJURING THE MEMORY
    AN EVENT APPROACHING THE MILLENNIUM
BEYOND THE INTERFACE
ENTERING THE MEDIUM
IMMERSION IN THE IMAGE
IMAX, METAPHOR FOR THE 21ST CENTURY
    IN ALCHEMIC CELLULOID
    A DIGITAL GENESIS
MACRO TO MICRO
MIGHTY TO HUMBLE
INSECT TO STAR
VILLAGE TO BLUE PLANET
LASER TO FETUS
ONE TO TEN
GROUND ZERO TO VOID
    ENTERING THE IMAGE CALLED BEYOND

2.

IN THE MACHINE'S EYE
ON MOUNTS OF MOBILE STEEL
KALEIDOSCOPIC APPARITIONS OF NATURE, ROLLING
MOUNTAINS FLYING
LAVA FLOWING
OCEANS MOVING
JUNGLES BREATHING
THE FIELDS OF SAND AND ICE
THE PLAY OF THE AURORA BOREALIS
VAST HORIZONS
SUNDRENCHED MEADOWS
MOONLIT SWAMPS
CLOUDS ABOVE
SUN BELOW
COSMIC SEA
VASTNESS OF THE VOID
COMETS IN THE NIGHT
    THE ARK OF THE ANIMALS
    THE BABEL OF HUMANS
MODERNITY TO ANTIQUITY
MYSTERY TO KNOWLEDGE
GOD TO COMPUTER
ARCHANGEL TO ASTRONAUT
PANTHEON TO MICROCHIP
    SYNTHETIC INCARNATIONS
    G-FORCE RIDERS
AS ABOVE, SO BELOW
24 DAYS AN HOUR
OLD WORLD, NEW WORLD
FRACTAL LANGUAGE
ACCESS CODE
SECURITY ZONE
DIGITAL SYSTEM
OMNIPRESENT NETWORK

TECHNO GURU, MUMBO JUMBO
POST NATURAL, SYNTHETIC
POST MODERN, DECONSTRUCTED
POST HUMAN, UNSAYABLE
NOSTALGIA, THE NEWSREEL
ANCIENT MODERNITY, 1900
A THOUSAND YEARS AGO, FOREVER YESTERDAY
    FRAGILITY OF THE ONE
    SPECTACLE OF THE MASS
    ALL TOGETHER • ALL AT ONCE
YOU AND ME

3.

IMAGESCAPES OF WONDERLAND
HANDMADE CREATIONS OF THE SOUTH
FORBIDDEN CITY
REFUGEE NATIONS
ROLLER COASTERS, LIFTOFFS, SPACESCAPES
ART, ARTIFACTS, ADVERTISEMENTS, LAWYERS, CLERICS
THE GARDEN OF EDEN
THE SUPERBOWL
THE DOW JONES
   THE REAL THING, JUST DO IT, JUST SAY NO
BUNNIES, SMILING POLITICIANS, RAVING EVANGELISTS,
MP'S, MR. PRESIDENT, JOHN DOE, CEO'S
THE ROLLING STONES
THE AMERICAN PEOPLE
THE MONA LISA
WORLD PEACE
FALSE EVIDENCE
NOBEL PEACE PRIZE
FLYING POPE
RICH AND FAMOUS
GOD THE FATHER
EVOLUTION
   DIAMONDS ARE FOREVER
RELIGION, NATION STATE, INTEGRATED CIRCUIT, FORMULA,
INVENTION, GENOME, RITUAL, PERCEPTION, IDEOLOGY,
CRITICAL MASS
   THE SPIN
   THE EPOCH
THE RENAISSANCE, THE ENLIGHTENMENT, THE REVOLUTION
THE MARKET, THE FOUNDING FATHERS, THE EXXON
CHRISTOPHER COLUMBUS
AMERICAN EXPRESS
PARIAH NATIONS
UNITED NATIONS
WIRED WORLD, GLOBALIZATION

THE GREATEST STORY EVER TOLD
SCIENCE, INDUSTRY, MOTHER TONGUE, POPULATION,
STANDING ARMY, INFRASTRUCTURE
THIRD WORLD, SECOND WORLD, FIRST WORLD
ATOMIC SPLITTER, SUPER POWER
LIVE TECH, DEAD TECH
TEST TUBE BABIES
CRYPT MUMMIES
MICKEY MOUSE
PLASTIC HEARTS
SYNTHETIC PARTS
BIG MACS
SATELLITE CIRCLING
CHILDREN PLAYING
OIL PUMPING
MONEY FLOWING
NUMBERS CRUNCHING
PLANES FLYING
ATOMS SMASHING
CROWDS CHEERING
PEOPLE MARCHING
SOULS PRAYING
HEARTS THUMPING
CARS RACING
NET SURFING
LIGHTS BEAMING
PHONES RINGING
MACHINES HUMMING
MUZAK PLAYING
SCIENCE FICTION, USER FRIENDLY
    SPELLS AND INCANTATIONS
    THE GLOW OF THE CATHODE RAY
    ELECTRONIC ENLIGHTENMENT
    THE MANY, THE ONE
    ALL TOGETHER • ALL AT ONCE
MAINLINING THE DREAM

4.

AWESOME POWERS OF THE ELEMENTS, UNTAMED
EARTH, WIND, WATER, FIRE, MONEY
ATOMS FOR PEACE
ELECTIONS, ACCIDENTS, AND ALL
ALIENS ON OUR MINDS
TELEVISIONS IN OUR EYES
SIXTY CYCLES IN THE AIR
    MACHINE LULLABIES
    NO WONDER
ARENAS OF SPORT
MONASTERIES OF OLYMPIAN SPECTATORS
LABORERS OF THE WAGE
TIME CLOCKS, THE MASSES
EVERY SECOND, EVERYWHERE
ENCLOSED, ELECTRIFIED
MOBILE, CONSUMING
TRANSFIXED, TRANSFORMED
ONLINE, DIRECT FEED
CNN, BE CK, M-TV
TEMPLES, BARS, CONGRESSES, SUPERMARKETS, PRISONS,
INSTITUTIONS, SUBWAYS, THEATRES, ARCADES, REAL ESTATE
    PUBLIC PLACES, PRIVATE CHAMBERS
    THE PLACES WE CALL HOME
UNTELLABLE ZONES OF MORTAL COMBAT
WORLD WARS TO WORLD FAIRS
ISMS, DEMENTED CREEDS, WASTED LIVES, IN GOD WE TRUST
SACRIFICE LAND
BODY OF SUFFERING
FACE OF TRAGEDY
JOY OF LIVING
BEAUTY OF GIVING
THE GOOD, THE ONE, THE BAD
CONTRADICTION, PARADOX, ENIGMA
    THE POWERFUL, THE MAD
ELECTRONIC BATTLEFIELD, SMART WEAPONS
NINTENDO, SEGA, PAC MAN, ICEMAN

HANDS ON, FAST FORWARD
MIDNIGHT BAGHDAD, FALLEN ANGEL
APPROACHING TWILIGHT, ARMAGEDDON
    RED, WHITE, AND BLUE
STATESMEN, LAUREATES, SHOWMEN
ENCYCLOPEDIC SALESMEN, SELLERS OF THE TRUTH
ALL FOR ONE, ONE FOR ALL, THREE FOR $2.50
    THE DEAL, THE STORY
MYTH, HISTORY, COMIC BOOK, PC, CD-ROM, INTERNET
ALL IN THE FAMILY, BELIEVE IT OR NOT
NORTH, SOUTH, EAST WEST
    THE WEB, THE WAY
VIRUS IN ETHER
WASTE IN THE OZONE
MILLENNIUM EXTREMES OF PROMISE
    WORLD WITHOUT LIMIT
    MOVING WITHOUT MOTION
    TOUCHING WITHOUT FEELING
    BEING WITHOUT PLACE
    LANGUAGE WITHOUT WORDS
    PEOPLE WITHOUT BODIES
    ZONES OF NO RETURN
LOS ANGELIZATION, INTENSIVE CAR
DOS SPOKEN, EVERYWHERE
MIRACLE DRUGS, LIVING TOOLS
MICRO SAGES, INFORMATICS
    NATURE UNDER GLASS
BIRTH RATE, DEATH RATE
THE CHRONICLE OF TEARS
EXIT VELOCITY, SUDDEN COLLAPSE
RUNNING OUT OF GEARS
    THE PRIMACY OF NUMBERS
    THE ALCHEMY OF FATE
    THE MYSTERY OF LIFE
    TESTING, TESTING, TESTING
    ALL TOGETHER • ALL AT ONCE
A BREATH AWAY

5.

SPERM TO EGG
WOMB TO TOMB
SKYSCRAPER TO PYRAMID
MONUMENT TO SHOPPING MALL
MUSEUM TO MAUSOLEUM
RWANDA TO DISNEYLAND
    OLD JERUSALEM
    NEW JERUSALEM
MYSTERY TO FLESH
WOMAN TO MAN
GATHERER TO GROWER
VOICE TO PRINT
WORD TO IMAGE
REAL TO VIRTUAL
EMBODIMENT TO DISEMBODIMENT
TRIUMPH TO CATASTROPHE
TURNING POINT OR VANISHING POINT
    PACE OF TWO FEET WALKING
    VOICE OF PEOPLE TALKING
    BREATHING IN THE AIR
UNIVERSE OF THE NANOSECOND
OCEANS OF SILICON
SUPERSONIC MEMORIES
SHADOWS OF THE MASS
SIRENS OF A MILLION JETS
FREIGHT TRAINS IN THE SKY
SYMPHONY OF MENDELBROT
    ENOUGH TO MAKE YOU CRY
THE STARS ARE FALLING
THE ANIMALS ARE RUNNING
    ALL TOGETHER • ALL AT ONCE
    A STRUCTURE CRACKING TO A NUMBERED CODE

6.

CLOSE UP TO WIDE SHOT
LONG STARE TO QUICK CUT
ZOOM TO FIXED
MOVING TO STILL
LONG LENS TO WIDE ANGLE
SLOW MOTION TO PIXILATION
FADE TO DISSOLVE
BLACK TO WHITE
RIGHT TO LEFT
HUES OF COLOR
NEGATIVES OF REVERSAL
MICROSCOPIC TO INDOSCOPIC
FILM TO VIDEO
ANALOGUE TO DIGITAL
MUSIC TO SOUND
MAKE BELIEVE TO HYPER REAL
   VOID OF NOISE, DISCOVERED
   SIX DISCRETE CHANNELS, GIVEN
   UNIVERSE OF THE IMAGE, ENTERED
   REFERENCE POINTS, ENVELOPED
   SCALE TO FEEL THE STORY
   BRILLIANCE OF LIGHT
ALL TOGETHER • ALL AT ONCE
IMAX TO THE MAX

7.

THE ROCKETSHIP 20TH CENTURY, IMPLODING
ONTOLOGICAL EARTHQUAKE
DIGITAL TIDAL WAVE
SIGNS IN THE HEAVENS
BLUE PLANET
NEW ARK
NO HORIZONS
    THE VIVID UNKNOWN
    ITS TOMORROW, A MILLION YEARS FROM NOW
    ITS TRUTH, THE TRUTH
FUTURE IS THE PRESENT
BEGINNING IS THE END
KNOWLEDGE IS THE LIMIT
CONSCIOUSNESS THE FALL
GOING OUT OF ORBIT
THE MYSTERY OF IT ALL
    REAL SPACE, CYBER SPACE, INNER SPACE,
    OUTER SPACE, NO SPACE
EVERYWHERE, NOWHERE
PAST, PRESENT, FUTURE
ONE GIANT STEP
INTO THE VOID
    IN THE TWILIGHT OF THE REAL
    ALL TOGETHER • ALL AT ONCE
    ON THE ROCKETSHIP 20TH CENTURY.

Godfrey Reggio

1940—b. New Orleans

1954—Entered the monks, died to the world, lived in the Middle Ages

1961-72—Possessed by idealism/teacher, lecturer, organizer, worked with street gangs, developed community health clinic/excloistrated, monks left me

1972-98—IRE Collective, a way out of wage labor; authorship/subsistence way of living

1982, 1988, 1992—Wrote, directed, released three films: *Kyoaanisqatsi*, *Powaqqatsi*, and *Anima Mundi*

1993-95—First Director, Fabrica (school to "smell the future") in Italy

1996-98—Seeking metaphoric Holy Grail/Authorship Project-Naqoyqatsi/media weather

FOUR ARGUMENTS FOR
THE PRESERVATION OF TELEVISION

James Brundige

Like it or not, documentary film production is largely about television. Except for a small number of theatrically released films, the vast majority of docs are created and distributed through the television medium. The perceived success of a piece is often connected to its broadcast profile, so I think it's appropriate to include an examination of the medium itself in a collection of work about documentary production.

In 1977, Jerry Mander (yes, that's his real name) penned a book entitled *Four Arguments For The Elimination of Television*. Mr. Mander had made a fortune in the advertising business, but a conversion of conscience inspired this controversial and insightful tome. To his credit, his San Francisco-based agency had made genuine attempts at responsible advertising for political and environmental causes, but ultimately Mr. Mander decided that the medium itself was fatally flawed. The book examined the effects of television on the cultures and individuals who inhabit this increasingly media-centric world, and presented four reasons to pitch the whole industry.

A great deal has changed since that day, especially in the acquisition and distribution of television images. I'd like to examine how those changes may have transformed the positive possibilities for documentary production. Mr. Mander presents some compelling points about the evils of television, and, if I could not come up with an adequate counterargument, I would feel obliged to find another career. I cling to the notion that, against the mind-numbing excesses of some commercial television, there remains an avenue for documentary producers to make a positive difference. My arguments are not exactly four in number, but sometimes one has to stretch things a little to come up with a catchy title.

One dramatic change since 1977 has been the introduction of very low–cost camera and editing systems. Formerly, the sheer cost of film and video equipment concentrated production and broadcast in the hands of those with large pools of money. More than anything else, this has transformed the potential of television. It was not the beating of Rodney King that rocked Los Angeles. It was the broadcast of a VHS tape of the event that shocked the country and plunged L.A. into a cycle of violent upheaval.

These cheap cameras have created opportunities for a wide range of people, from amateurs to veteran documentary producers. In certain cases, the proliferation of cameras has allowed cameramen, posing as tourists, to acquire images never possible with the older generation of equipment. A colleague shot a large portion of an important political piece for PBS's *Frontline* in this manner.

In Britain, a producer has specialized in documenting political protests with these cameras. In addition to gathering some stunning footage, these protesters have defended themselves from prosecution with these images. Instances of police brutality have been recorded and perhaps curtailed because of the presence of the video-graphers. It has always been clear that the behavior of the police is modified when there is a news crew present. One no longer needs three people and a hundred thousand dollars of equipment (a film-era news crew) to keep the authorities on their toes. I wonder if the behavior of the Los Angeles Police Department is different now that they understand that there may be video cameras lurking in every window.

Who can forget the image of the Chinese protester blocking the advancing tank in Tiananmen Square? The presence of the camera did not prevent the ensuing slaughter, but those pictures did certainly raise the level of international awareness of the incident. The immediate reaction of the Chinese military has been renewed efforts to control the possession of cameras, but that becomes increasingly difficult as the equipment becomes cheaper and smaller.

Another example of the impact of these new systems comes from the Amazon jungle. The Yanomami Indians became used to the cameras that were carried by the anthropologists who visited. As the Yanomami struggled to retain control of their land, they started recognizing the utility of these cameras. They asked the anthropologists for the video equipment, and started taking the cameras with them to meetings with the Venezuelan and Brazilian authorities. The discussions and agreements reached at these meetings were recorded in an irrefutable fashion. Here is a culture with no written language entering the video age.

The greatest goal of a documentary producer is to actually make a difference. These examples of the beneficial use of television technology may not outweigh the millions of viewers glued to "Wheel of Fortune," but they do demonstrate that the potential for a positive influence may be expanding.

The dramatically lower cost of the new generation of equipment has opened up opportunities for more people to create films, but what has happened to our abilities to distribute them?

One of Mr. Mander's biggest problems with the television industry was the very powerful centralized control inherent in the network system. An exceptionally small number of executives could virtually dictate the content of what the entire viewing audience could see. With the advent of sixty-channel cable systems, that has clearly changed. There are channels entirely dedicated to documentary film, and the demand (at least in broadcast minutes per week) for documentary work has increased dramatically. With cable access, the distribution system has theoretically been democratized. Groups less connected to the white power structure may have more of a voice.

This situation is very much in flux. New cable networks appear almost every month. Multiplexing is vastly expanding the carrying capacity of cable, and direct satellite broadcast can offer something on the order of five hundred channels. In this transition from the big three (networks, that is) to the smaller five hundred, we frequently end up with the situation lamented in a popular song— "Fifty channels and nothing on." Maybe this will change as the industry sorts out the new landscape. Perhaps programming decisions will be driven by audience demand.

I've worked on a number of pieces that ended up on National Geographic or the Discovery channel. I'm pleased with the number of people who tell me, "That's all we watch—we're really sick of network sitcoms." If this is the case, maybe we can hope for "The Important Cutting Edge Documentary Channel."

Cable systems have not displaced the networks as the largest provider of information to the American audience, but high bandwidth satellite systems may make that possible. On the other hand, the high initial cost of satellite broadcast transceivers make keep distribution in the hands of media conglomerates with deep pockets. As much as I like the improved picture quality (and filmic aspect ratio) of HDTV, the huge expense of this equipment may accomplish the same thing. What cheap digital cameras give to the documentary community, High Definition Television make take away.

What will surely change the possibilities for distribution is the Internet. As telephone and cable technologies mature and merge, it will become possible to deliver programming on demand. Right now we are limited to surfing the Web for interesting reading material, but it will certainly be possible to send full band-width video and sound over the next generation of this system. One will be able to edit a show in one's computer and post it on a Web server for any interested party to download and view. This may be the real democratization of television.

In conclusion, Mr. Mander, instead of ditching the technology of television, we may just need to use it better. Time will tell.

James Brundige specializes in working in remote settings and extreme conditions. He has played important roles in a number of adventure and environmental documentaries. Shoots in the last year have taken him from the Amazon rainforest to Antarctica and again to Mt. Everest. Credits include BBC's *Mystery of the Brahmaputra*, PBS's *Taller than Everest*, and *Karakoram* for the ABC/ESPN series *Expedition Earth*. He worked on *The Native Americans* and *Wildlife Adventures* for TBS and has shot for NBC "Dateline," ABC "20/20" and "Good Morning America." He has filmed *Secrets of the Inca Mummy* and *Avalanche!* for National Geographic Television, *The Rocky Mountain Adventure Games* for CBS Sports, and *Antarctic Icecap Research* for PBS NOVA. James also worked on *Odyssey: The Art of Photography at National Geographic* (PBS), *Antarctica: A Presence on the Ice* (PBS/WMPB), EVEREST: *The Mystery of Mallory and Irvine* (BBC), and *Red Flag Over Tibet* for PBS "Frontline."

PART VI

COMMUNICATING

WITH A PUBLIC

Michael Tobias and friends.

© R. Radin

THE DOCUMENTARY—THE NEAR PERFECT VEHICLE

Robert Radin

Man has ever sought form and substance for his artistic expression, the telling of his story. His destiny up or down has never been without this vital life force, this inherent desire, this need to bring forth his feelings of creation.

Throughout history, in days of glory and in nights of despair, whether in crude rock structure or in elegant filigree, he sings his song from handprints on a cave wall to the treasures of the Louvre.

Over millennium he developed ever more intricate tools to more completely accomplish this task. At no time in history have these tools reached the persuasiveness of today's cameras and audio systems to convey feelings and spark the imagination, whether seen or only believed.

The capacity to inspire vast audiences, and the moment-by-moment wherewithal to engender vast worlds of thought and imagery, represents a veritable shift in history: our ability to reflect on ourselves in public, and for the public, like never before. But as with so much revelatory breakthrough in our past, this technology of mass audience appeal ignites other, less numinous fallouts: the all too habit-forming requirements of sex and violence and tawdry exploitation of the senses.

At this point in time, the documentary and the feature film diverge, however. The theatrical approach succumbs to entrapment, is dominated and confined. Whereas the documentary soars toward a rarified freedom, the pure confines of non-fiction, where it will enjoy a paucity of encumbrance and liberate itself from obstacles in its journey towards the truest of all destinations, reality.

Of all the adventures that constitute my life to date—from inventions when head of American Plastic Company in the late forties to CEO of several textile companies, to heading Kiowa Ltd. in Osaka, Japan—never have I found the form of expression that I have found in unending quantity and variety as is offered up in the production of a documentary.

From the moment that the concept gels—the story, either conceptualized or brought in by others—I know that I am in love, though my lover has yet to arrive, but arrive she will. As the story develops, the location plotted, the crew contracted, the liaisons drafted, you know the voyage has started and we shall not return until our destination has been visited and our story has been recorded.

The limits of subject are the limits of consciousness. The limits of the production are the limit of our ability to communicate with each other: From the sweet, warm, innocent story of the Jains of India, where one finds man at his most delicate and gracious self, totally nonviolent, harming none, in harmony with nature and his fellow man, his greatest protection, his simple dignity and pride; to the violence and ineptitude of *World War III*, where man strove and fought, worked to the devil's own capacity, for his own discomfort, against his own best interest. In *Voice of the Planet*, Michael Tobias's story of earth crying out for protection and offering protection for man in return, there is nature's plan to light man's path, but man is too confused to listen or to see.

The list is vast both of our productions and the production of others, but the one vivid and everlasting thread in common is the ability of the documentary to span from the depths of the sea to the heights of the eagle's path. From the scenes of Dachau and Auschwitz where man found his most bankrupt moment in history, to the gentle and heart–warming stories of devotion and sacrifice, that ever bright flame of the human spirit spoken and shown has never been conveyed in greater splendor, in more texture, in more detail than in the documentary.

Never has more or better equipment and technology been available to so completely fill the human need to explore. Limitless vantage points are all available; few inaccessible, some less friendly, but few downright inhospitable. From the first feel of the story, from the first concept of the subject, I know of few technical or conceptual restrictions. The monetary obligations are minimal in composing the documentary.

The food for nourishment upon which the documentaries are born, grow, and convey their messages not only contains a type of purity and vision for the sake of the production, but also carries an alliance and respect of the subject. Little or no profit here. Financial reward is not the motivation; the payback is the message, the vision of the subject the only true goal.

I am at the late stage of my life, yet of all of my life's great adventures, none have brought more deep-felt satisfaction, that inner feeling of time and creative energy best spent, than in the sharing of my feelings, my interpretations, my vision in a production.

All humanity has stories to tell. Humanity itself is the greatest story. Every man is a storyteller; to listen, to understand, to interpret, to record and then distribute is the task of the documentary film producer, handcrafted by few for the many.

A COMPARATIVE STUDY OF EASTERN AND WESTERN DOCUMENTARIES

PROFESSOR REN YUAN OF THE BEIJING BROADCASTING INSTITUTE

The 1980s awakened China's TV workers to a general fact: documentaries carry a great weight in elevating the cultural ethos of TV programs, and the level of documentary-making represents a TV institution's quality of programming. The making of TV documentaries in China, to a great extent, is an important approach to facilitating cultural exchanges between China and other countries. As a result, TV workers in China have brought their efforts into full play and managed to produce batch after batch of documentaries. In the past ten years or so, and especially in the past four to five years, TV documentary production in China has experienced an unprecedented prosperity. At China Central Television (CCTV) alone, for example, more than 1,000 documentaries per year are produced and broadcast.

The forms of expression have also diversified recently. For the past two years, documentary programs have been set up by local TV stations in Beijing, Shanghai, Zhejiang, Shanxi, Jiangsu, Tianjin, Guangdong, Sichuan, Liaoning, Ningxia, and other cities, provinces, or autonomous regions. These productions, which adopted a magazine format, became part of TV's regular programming, and thus contributed to the maturation of documentary-making in China. Chinese TV documentaries play a very important role in explaining important political decisions, illuminating historical events, and promoting international understanding, cooperation, and mutual development.

In 1986, CCTV extended its live broadcasts to overseas viewers. In July 1991, CCTV set up the Overseas Broadcasting Department, which undertook a joint effort with local TV stations to promote further international exchange. CCTV has established program-supplying relationships with Los Angeles's Panda Station and North America Satellite TV and maintains close ties with other overseas Chinese–language TV stations. CCTV has successfully secured access to the geostationary satellite, Asian No. 1, which is located at lat. 96°5' E, and is capable of broadcasting to such countries as Russia, Australia, Indonesia, Southeast Asia, the Middle East, East Africa, Eastern Europe, and other countries and regions.

Since 1992, CCTV has managed to make its Chinese and English programs available to viewers in North America through Chicago's New Century TV Station over K-band and C-band satellites.

In the past five years, China has conducted an annual appraisal of the programs for overseas viewers. The purpose of the activity is to summarize the work, to formulate policies, to improve production, to develop different creative styles, and to make TV programs more inviting to overseas viewers. From 1991 to 1994, many documentaries from both central and local TV stations won various national and international awards and prizes. Among them were *The Sand and the Sea*, *The Northern Tibetan Family*, *At the Crossroads*, *The Last Mountain God*, *My Faraway Home in Beijing*, and *The Maoyan River*, among others. Many other documentaries such as *The Changjiang River* (The Yangtze River), *The Huanghe River* (The Yellow River), *Looking Over the Great Wall*, *The Silk Road*, *A Trip to Guangdong*, *Mao Zedong*, *Mt. Lu*, *The Door of China*, *The Sword of China*, *China Mothers*, and *Ordinary Families of Beijing*, though winning no international awards for various reasons, have evoked even more wide-ranging responses. All these works taken as a whole show that China's TV documentary production has reached its maturation and that it bears the following striking features:

1) Documentary has won sound recognition, and its realistic approach has been affirmed. Most documentary makers follow the fundamental method of interviewing, recording real people and real events in real time and space while avoiding fabrication, reconstruction, or drama-tization, thus integrating production with reproduction and fact–finding with preconceived stereotyping.

2) Documentary-makers have greatly improved their skills in narration, relying upon an effective creation of screen images while verbal commentary and captions are regarded as secondary. Screen images include not only visual images but also synchronous sound. The realistic use of screen images has become part of the measurement of the merit of a documentary. At the same time, a strong dependence on verbal commentary and captions for instruction is regarded as too didactic and contrary to the nature of documentary.

3) More attention is given to details in narration. A preconceived conclusion is carefully avoided so as not to dictate to viewers' imagination and judgments; hence the principle of "saving conclusions for reflections" is followed.

TV documentary, just like the mass medium of TV, was a product of Western civilization. However, Chinese documentaries do possess qualities intrinsic and unique to the Chinese cultural context. To accommodate the need to communicate across cultural borders, documentary makers and their films acknowledge and explore differences in the practices of daily life—practices ranging from customs and clothing to emotions and their expression. The documentaries are a study in how different cultural roots have brought forth different flowers—that is, different ways of thinking and living. These differences are also reflected in the stylistic approach of the documentary itself. It is by recognizing differences that we can develop our strengths and avoid our weaknesses, thus winning a favorable position for Chinese documentaries.

Generally speaking, there are four major differences in Eastern and Western understandings of documentary production: differences in definition, in values and handling of the subject matter, mentality and method of narration, and TV language.

Differences in Definition

In the West, especially in Britain and the U.S., TV documentary grew out of documentary film. It has been some 100 years since the first film came into being. The Western tradition of filmmaking is deeply rooted in the hearts of the public. The history of filmmaking began with documentary-making, and it can be argued that the history of filmmaking is that of documentary-making. Ontology (in the creation of images) in filmmaking plays a leading role in the ideas guiding Western TV documentary-making. British and American filmmakers are good at image–creation and narrative development, which have become the basic tools of TV documentary producers.

In contrast, Japan's TV documentary originated in the radio special news reports. Its main task is to show "the actuality of Japan." TV documentary production in Japan is believed not to belong in the artistic domain for the simple reason that documentaries are made through the employment of picture-recording technology developed by the Japanese themselves. It is therefore understandable that unlike in Great Britain and the U.S., in Japan more heed is paid to "factual recording" than to "skillful shooting and editing."

The TV documentary in China is another case. China's TV documentary production grew out of filmmaking, but underwent an arduous and tortuous development. It was once much influenced by the Soviet Union's mode of "political stereotyping." As a result, early documentaries in China were monotonous in content, drab in language, and fixed in form so that they were simply "political and moral generalities."

In the first half of 1993, the NHK Broadcast Research Institute of Japan conducted an investigation into the documentary film theory and practice of seven Western countries. A questionnaire was sent to documentary film and video-makers, editors, and directors. Twenty-three of them from the U.S., Great Britain, Canada, Germany, Italy, and Australia supplied their answers. The investigation showed different definitions of documentary-making. But in light of the leading ideas guiding documentary-making, documentary–makers, editors, and directors may be divided into actuality—recording and news-reporting groups. The former upholds objective and impartial recording of facts as well as attention to balancing majority and minority views, and is opposed to "making content" via reenactment or dramatization. The latter stresses the conveyance of information, favoring the addition of personal explanations and comments by the makers.

The year 1994 saw the publication of the book *Definitions of TV Programs in China*. The definition of the TV documentary (the author of this paper did the actual writing) reads: "[It is] a systematic and complete factual report of political, economic, military, cultural, and/or historical events through video or film recording, containing an aesthetic appeal. It records the real people and real events of real life without any fabrication, reconstruction or dramatization. Its way of recording is videotaping or filming direct interviews for both general and detailed facts. Facts and fact finding are the lifeline of a TV documentary." This definition is perhaps not exactly flawless, but it has combined the qualities intrinsic in documentary-making with Western ontological practice: "A documentary is not political propaganda...and political quality is but one of the qualities of a documentary...Documentary-making is the art of discovery, the art of interviewing, and the art of editing." (For this quotation, see my paper "TV Documentary: Definition and Creation" in the *Journal of China Radio and TV*, 1995.)

In short, a documentary should be factual, while avoiding naturalism, stressing both its informational and artistic nature. Documentary-making should be the art of information, persuasion, and elevation.

Difference in Values and Handling of Subject Matter

The Renaissance of the fourteenth to sixteenth century in Europe exerted a far-reaching influence upon the development of Western literature and arts. Its very significance consists of the development of humanism. Human beings, rather than gods, came to be the subject matter of literary and artistic creation. Exploration into human thoughts and feelings became the aim of literature and the fine arts. All this has made documentary making in the West concentrate its attention on human activities and people's relations to nature and society. North American filmmaker Robert Flaherty's *Nanook of the North* enables us to step into the real life of the Inuit; his *Moana* allows us to live among the natives in a small island of the South Seas; his Louisiana Story shows us the bitter experiences of American Southerners. From Britain, John Grierson's *Drifters* (dealing with the daily life of whalers) and Harry Watt and Basil Wright's *Night Mail* successfully bring us a kind of life experience and enrich our perception of the world.

In World War II, this tradition of fact–finding and fact–recording underwent great development, and documentaries of this period provided the viewers with an unprecedented wealth of information about the lives of both soldiers at the front and civilians in the rear. In view of all this, Bela Balazs, the famous Spanish film producer, affirms "the great mission [of a documentary] is to record human history in frames."

Industrial development in the West has changed the relationship between material and life, which resulted in materialism in literary and artistic activities. "Returning to material reality" has been regarded as the functional equivalent to documentary–making.

In China, the long-standing aesthetic standards well observed by men of letters and artists are "literature carries reason," "poetry expresses the spirit," and "emotions are engendered in the heart and overflow into art." Actually, almost every form of Chinese literary and artistic creation has taken these principles as guidelines. The same is true of documentary-making. On the one hand, political and moral instruction are stressed, and on the other hand, inferences and imagination are advocated. In other words, documentary-making should "strive for the expression of [the filmmaker's] feeling through images. The creation of images is to facilitate the [audience's] imagination. When reality (or nature) is communicated in this way, a harmony between the filmmaker's individuality and nature's universality is reached." (Pu Zhenyan, *On the Artistic Conception of Chinese Arts*, Beijing University Press: 1995, p. 79.)

The typical example of this description is the documentary *Appeal of Tibet*, produced by Qinghai TV Station in 1988. "Tibet per se," Liu Lang, the producer, said in the postscript, "is an artistic conception." Even the documentaries that have won international awards, such as *The Sand and the Sea*, *Families of Northern Tibet*, and *The Last Mountain God*, have all, without any exception, managed to reach the high goal of interlocking appearance and essence, containing what is concrete and what is abstract, with the former being graphic images and symbols and the latter being the imagination formed through image-creation.

The idea of "yijing," or "artistic conception," an essential element of Chinese documentary, is implicit and indirect, and therefore different from Western "modeling" (a reproduction of the physical image of an object) because they are based on different philosophical and aesthetic contexts:

1) "Modeling" is mimetic while "yijing" is metaphysical;
2) "Modeling" is image-creation while "yijing" is appreciation;
3) "Modeling" is external, concrete, and explicit while "yijing" is internal (subjective), and cosmic.

These two theories are not equivalent in aesthetic psychology.

I firmly urge producers of Chinese documentaries to combine the two theories, thus reaching the realm of "being concrete in expressing tangible events, and implicit, free and unrestricted in conveying feelings (yijing)." In this way "objective description" and "subjective description" are joined together, striving for perfect balance.

Difference in Mentality and Method of Narration

In the literary history of China, the happy ending has been the long–standing practice in storytelling. In documentary–making, the ending or conclusion of the event is often clearly and completely given to the viewers. This is the enclosed narrative construction. After Western society was transformed by industrialization, they saw a great change in narrative construction, as the enclosed construction now turned into an open type of construction. In Western narratives, the viewers are no longer mere passive consumers but also producers of spiritual products. In this way, the ending or conclusion is not given by the writer himself or herself, but reached, developed, and supplied by the viewers themselves.

Western documentary-making is more skillful and flexible in this field. What a documentary offers is the facts, and facts are multiple in meaning. The viewers can well understand the multilayered meanings of the facts in their own way. But it does not follow that the makers take no part in the selection of the facts. The emphasis on certain facts and the use of seemingly objective methods conceal their social inclination.

I also believe that it is necessary for the Chinese to learn from Western methods of narration. In China, we value "penetrating perception." Wang Guo Wei, for instance, said, " The works of the masters are very penetrating when they convey feelings; they widen readers' vision when they describe natural setting." I think those who can express their thoughts explicitly and convey their feelings implicitly can equally reach this realm.

Similarities and Differences in TV Language

Owing to the influence of classical Chinese culture, the TV documentary in China places much stress on implication, suggestion, and offscreen meaning, most of the time with a serene frame to show that it is poetical and philosophical. But the flaw lies in the fact that it lacks the beauty of movement. Thanks to the long history of film and television, Westerners are better and more flexible than we are in China in dealing with movement and mise-en-scène. It is understandable that, in Western documentaries, there is more and better employment of continuous and background panoramic shots. Movement and activity are more emphasized; their settings are conveniently designed but rich in beauty. Their objective description is always attained by "forgetting the maker" in order to express manifold meaning.

Today, documentary–makers of China are learning from their counterparts in the West, recording with their cameras at the beginning of events so as to follow their development and record factual happenings. At the same time, they are taking advantage of the fine points of the "yijing theory," harmoniously integrating objective and subjective description. The documentaries that have won international awards, such as *The Last Mountain God*, *The Appeal of Tibet*, *The Maoan River*, and *The Sand and the Sea*, are very good examples. Even Western viewers do not feel estranged in their presentation of facts and feelings.

In closing, I would like to avail myself of the opportunity to invite fellow documentary-makers, both national and international, to tackle the issue of documentary script writing. Take the example of Chinese documentaries: we have a history of didacticism and overdone commentary. Although by now much of this problem is resolved, I urge documentary filmmakers to work hard to further refine their achievements.

Professor Ren Yuan of the Beijing Broadcasting Institute has trained many award-winning documentarians working in Chinese television as well as around the world. Professor Ren was a board member of the China Television Artist Association and a member of the China TV Art Commission, and has served as a judge at the Golden Panda International TV Festival. He has lectured in Berlin, and in Chicago as the Guest of Honor of the 1997 Windy City International Documentary Festival. Early in his career, Ren directed over thirty documentaries for Chinese TV, and he has published over two-hundred papers and fourteen books on TV production theory. One of his films won first prize in the National TV Program Competition.

INTERCULTURAL DOCUMENTARY AND
THE AMERICAN AUDIENCE

Martha M. Foster

Abstract

Since *Nanook of the North* swept the nation in 1922, filmmakers have documented cultures other than their own, or their own for audiences from other cultures. The potential for these films to reach a wide audience has never been fully realized, due in part to the lack of storytelling skills on the part of filmmakers, and partly due to lack of vision by programmers. Polarities of science and sensationalism hampered the tradition of intercultural documentary in America. With a little thought and effort, these films can fill a great need for innovative, quality programming for television and theater. Part of the answer for documentary filmmakers is in developing the skill of speaking from the heart and mind simultaneously.

Text

It set the pace for the century, for intercultural documentary. In 1922, Robert Flaherty had been turned away by major U.S. studios, finally releasing *Nanook of the North* through French distributor Pathé Frérés. Following the film's "unexpected" smashing success—distributors then, as now, were sometimes sorely out of touch with their audiences—the door was opened wide for Flaherty's ongoing work. None of his subsequent films—*Moana*, *Man of Aran*, etc.—have come close, in my eyes, to matching the fullness of heart that made Nanook an enduring and world-changing film.

I have spent the last twenty years pondering the fate of Flaherty's spiritual, scientific, and artistic children, who have rarely found the level of success that Flaherty himself finally achieved. With my background in visual anthropology, and as director of the Windy City International Documentary Festival, I have had many opportunities to see what's working and what's not in contemporary intercultural documentaries—that is, films and videos that are made by, for, and about at least two distinct cultures. The festival has received entries from over thirty countries, many of them coproductions with a U.S. resident. The Festival places a great emphasis on intercultural documentaries: In 1997, we had the privilege of hosting a visiting Chinese professor of documentary, Professor Ren Yuan of the Beijing Broadcasting Institute and China Central Television (whose paper appears elsewhere in this volume), and premiering English-language screenings of several Chinese television documentaries, such as *The Passing of the Mountain God* and *Boatmen of Baili Gorge*. The following essay draws heavily on my experience as festival director, as well as my experience teaching the history and production of documentary.

Some of the obstacles to documentary exhibition in the U.S. are historically based. Cinema itself started out with documentary, as the Lumiere brothers sent film crews worldwide to capture the mundane events of life, and ordinary people at work, home, and play in the waning years of the nineteenth century. At first these events fascinated audiences, for whom the miracle of moving pictures held immense power. After a short time, in a seemingly inevitable sequence of events, motion pictures became the domain of the rich, famous, powerful or dramatic—monarchs and dignitaries, public events, and disasters—the forerunner of contemporary television journalism. The small domestic documents of baby's breakfast, the train entering the station, and the workers leaving the factory receded into the background, as the more flashy and "important" events muscled their way into the spotlight in European cinema. This turn of events led directly to newsreels and then to today's television journalism, both news and analysis.

Across the Atlantic, when Flaherty searched for a U.S. distributor for *Nanook*, the mainstream American cinema had long since turned to narrative, a development due in large part to the cumbersome stationary camera developed by Edison. American cinema had already hardened into the mold that has yet to be broken: Who would want to see real people, especially strange ones like the Eskimos, reasoned the studio executives, when they can watch the brilliant silent dramas and comedies being cranked out—literally—by a prolific American film industry? This prejudice still lingers in television programming, where "entertainment"— i.e., fiction—still outpaces reality-based programming.

It is easy enough to blame the exhibitors, particularly network and cable programmers, for the underrepresentation of intercultural documentaries on TV today. Dozens of outstanding English-language films are made each year, simply because the filmmakers have to make them, often with small hope of making a dime or reaching a large audience. It is my firm belief that there is an audience out there, restlessly awaiting the "something completely different" these films can offer, and that we are still only one or two insightful and risk-taking programming executives away from a recognition of a rich and broad body of work ready-made for that audience.

However, as we've all learned by now from our various gurus, we can only change ourselves and what we are doing. How can filmmakers working internationally optimize the chances of selling their work? There is an enormous demand reported for (inexpensive) programming as channels proliferate. Why hasn't the connection happened between intercultural filmmakers and programmers? I believe there's still a lot to be learned from Flaherty and *Nanook*, and the evolution of the intercultural documentary.

You Can Get There from Here!

The elements of Flaherty's success have not changed. What was true for *Nanook* is true for contemporary intercultural (and other) documentaries. Even more so than narrative films, documentaries draw from and try to bridge three different arenas: art, science, and business. This is no simple task, and it is the rare individual who can handle all three with the necessary skill. Flaherty, unlike most of us, was very adept at all three. He knew the Inuit (Eskimo) people well from many years of living in close proximity, and was clearly fascinated with the historic lifestyle from which they had so recently moved on; he made impressive advances in storytelling through editing; and he had the persistence and confidence to continue to pursue distribution long after many of us would have given up. And above all, he cared deeply about his subject, and his film reflects his great understanding and admiration, even through the filter of romanticism that colors the film. So, easy as it is to blame distributors for lack of vision, it is also very important to acknowledge the difficulty of making films that are as deserving of an audience as *Nanook*.

So where have many filmmakers gone wrong? Again, a glance at the evolution of documentary in this country offers some clues. Browsing through the archives of intercultural documentary, a schism within the genre of nonfiction films appears very early in the century, and still exists today, hampering the popular success of documentary work. As early as the 1920s, American anthropologist Margaret Mead and a few others had begun to use film as a tool of scientific research on human societies, exploring shared qualities of humanity as well as cultural differences; meanwhile explorers and adventurers Martin and Osa Johnson and their "artistic" kin told thrilling tales of the great white masters, as they saw themselves, among the ignorant and laughable—to them—"savages" of Africa and elsewhere. Mead treated her subjects with respect and felt the fascination Flaherty shared, but with no intention of reaching a popular audience; the Johnsons used indigenous people viciously to "prove" how superior Western man and culture were to the "savages" they exploited, with a primary aim of entertaining their audience and promoting their colonial philosophy.

While it may be obvious (!) that my sympathies lie with Mead, there are lessons to be learned from both sides of this schism. Mead was a scientist and a humanist, not an entertainer, although her written work enjoyed great popularity; and the Johnsons and their esthetic kin were entertainers and anything but scientists. Because of these unfortunate associations with entertainment from this early era, it has become almost politically incorrect among serious filmmakers who pursue documentary to entertain. And nothing kills a potentially good, solid social documentary as quickly as a self-righteous filmmaker who refuses to "stoop" to entertain.

There are films out there that fall on every point of the continuum between these two extremes, and even some that manage to go to both extremes simultaneously. Over the years, there have been many approaches to depicting other cultures for an American audience. Many of these have been intended solely for academic use, but some have been directed at a more general audience. Through these many individual films and series, filmmakers have explored the issues of science, art, and business as they apply to intercultural film.

In the area of "scientific" intercultural film, i.e., ethnographic film, solid familiarity with the film's subject is the most important element to most filmmakers. Ethnographic films can be didactic and overly burdened with verbal information, as it seems difficult for anthropologists to understand the basic nature of film as a visual medium. Ethnographic films, traditionally made by members of the technologically and politically dominant culture about members of a less "advanced" one, are on the wane, as indigenous people take over control of their own media technology and images to be seen by the "outside world." The field of visual anthropology has increasingly concerned itself with visual research and developing teaching materials, rather than communicating with a wider audience via television.

Indigenous video is currently almost entirely politically motivated (as, it could be argued, were ethnographic films, but with a more subtle agenda). Ethnic minorities and indigenous populations are rapidly acquiring the skills and technology to manage their own images as presented in popular media, and to put forth arguments on political issues directly affecting them. In doing so, groups are gaining power never before accessible to them by appealing directly to members of the politically dominant cultures. Fascinating as this trend is, it is somewhat peripheral to the category of films discussed here. These films usually have a much more specific purpose than others, but are also a general learning opportunity for American audiences as well as an education about a specific issue. There are, however, fascinating developments on the horizon; for example, the series of Mexican television documentaries produced by various indigenous groups.

On the opposite pole, that of sensationalism, a familiar historic example is *Mondo Cane*, which caused a major stir among audiences at the time of its release. It is nothing more than a catalog of bizarre practices around the world (the most bizarre of which, to my mind, oddly enough, takes place in New York City among the sixties equivalent of the Yuppies): fashionable people dining on fine china plates featuring ants, grasshoppers and other insect delectables. Perhaps even the makers of *Mondo Cane* felt some sense of the equality of all the world's people— although the opinion was not a high one.

I have also seen, as a juror for various festivals, numerous films depicting "primitive" cultures as a palette with which to paint an unintentionally revealing portrait of the "artist." In these films (which never made it into a festival where I was a juror), visually exotic people are used as scenery, and a foil against which the artist ruminates on some pseudo-soulful (read:shallow) concern. "Art" used in this way is often an excuse for self-indulgence and intellectual laziness. This type of film perpetuates stereotypes and obsession with surface appearance, undermining the possibility of cross-cultural understanding. A few anthropologists, such as Robert Gardner (*Rivers of Sand*, etc.), have managed to combine science and sensationalism by focusing on the most exotic aspect of the cultures depicted, the ritualized behavior most easily misunderstood and least easily explained. This approach belies the individuality of "primitive" people, and distances the viewer rather than revealing common humanity. While these films may reach more viewers than most ethnographic films, due to the sensationalism, they do little towards promoting human understanding across cultures.

In Search of a Middle Ground

More towards the center of the continuum, but still falling short, in my book, are most National Geographic-style depictions of "primitive" peoples. The occasional depiction of exotic cultures in a series mainly concerned with wildlife immediately casts doubts on the cultural politics of the producers. Such films are often tainted by the wildlife formula, despite the extensive use of scientific consultants in the field of anthropology of the productions. Of course this is far more subtle, and quite differently motivated, than the early travelogues of the Johnsons'; but despite the apparent respect and appreciation of the "natives" in these films, there remains a resistance to depicting people as individuals, and therefore as real people who are in many basic ways very much like members of the dominant culture depicting them. The Discovery Channel, initially (and still) a promising venture in popularizing documentary, has also resorted to presenting sensational brief glimpses (many from Thames Television) at other cultures, despite an initial commitment to including more sophisticated social and intercultural documentary as a major component of programming.

There are reasons for the National Geographic/Discovery syndrome relating to both supply of "product" and audience preferences; but a slow but certain shift towards less sensationalistic and more sensitive and informative films could benefit both audiences and filmmakers. The finest intercultural films delicately and successfully balance sound research with artful and entertaining presentation of their material. The films bring their subjects to life, in a manner both thoughtful and highly engaging and entertaining. And the audience that is drawn to these films is a thoughtful advertiser's dream for upscale products: numerically smaller than the "mass" audience, this group is highly educated and holds economic power far beyond the average consumer.

One of the most successful and longest-running film series of all time in Britain, and one which strikes a delicate balance between science, art, and entertainment, has been Granada Television's *Disappearing World*. In this series, filmmakers explore and represent cultures around the world for a British audience. Documentary's positive reputation with the British public both accounts for and results from the success of this series. In the rapidly changing world, many of these films are already outdated, but at least they prove it can be done.

The New Millennium in Intercultural Documentary

The current trend in intercultural filmmaking is much more towards films made by a member of one culture about their own experience, for an audience of another culture. By downplaying both science and sensationalism, filmmakers speak much more from the heart, with both deep understanding and compassion, and often with an excellent sense of entertainment as well. Most interesting is the trend of filmmakers whose personal experience is in both the "subject" and "target" cultures. Contemporary examples would include films by ethnic Americans exploring their personal cultural identity, such as the film *Viet Kieu*, shown at the 1997 Windy City International Documentary Festival. We could also include the film *Snow White*, an intimate look into the world of the female drug addict in the Netherlands, which was shown at the 1996 Windy City Festival. This film was made by a woman who successfully made the transition from being a member of that particular subculture back to middle class society; and her film speaks as eloquently and passionately to an American audience as it must to a Dutch audience. A film on Jerusalem made by an Arab and Israeli team, *You, Me, Jerusalem* (honorable mention at the 1997 festival), also bravely explores new territory in the realm of the individual as cultural representative. *In Whose Honor* (1997 honorable mention at Windy City Festival, not screened due to contract with PBS's POV where it was scheduled for a July screening) compassionately and entertainingly documents the Native American crusade against Indian mascots for sporting teams, originating with a Native American woman graduate student at the University of Illinois at Urbana, whose children were disturbed by the Chief Illiniwek mascot. *One Hundred Eggs a Minute* is a beautifully photographed black and white portrait of a Chinese American woman's story of growing up working in her family's fortune cookie factory in San Francisco. These films offer a strikingly diverse view of the personal experiences of people between cultures, pointing up not only common humanity but the stunning variety and richness of our cultural traditions and their effects in our lives.

In short, intercultural documentary has gone through a very positive shift—oddly enough, one that nearly takes us back to Robert Flaherty, with the exception that this time around, *Nanook* is telling his own story—or even Mrs. Nanook, hers! No longer does a sterile scientific or pseudo-scientific pontificating appeal to a sophisticated audience; and hopefully, with some sensitive programming, exploitative sensationalism is also dying. The noble savage and the ignorant savage alike are disappearing from the screen in favor of articulate and thoughtful filmmakers telling their own complex and compelling stories, both positive and negative. Which is, in fact, just fine for the sophisticated and educated audience they can reach. What audiences deserve is a steady supply of fascinating, compassionate and factually sound films that truly show us what it is like to be a particular person in a particular cultural setting different from our own.

And finally, I see many other shifts taking place as well. Focus of some films is moving back to the small domestic matters of the earliest documentaries—raising families, making a living, coming to terms with families of origin, dealing with crises in health. What have been considered "feminine" concerns are taking their place alongside the "masculine" issues of politics, ritual, and public life. Many intercultural films are returning to visual storytelling, like *Seed and Earth*, co-Best of Festival in the 1996 Windy City International Documentary Festival, and *Kumbharwada, Bombay: Potter's Colony*, part of the 1997 Images of Asian showcase at the Windy City Festival. Fewer films are illustrated soundtracks or solely talking heads. And in a final leg of the journey back to Flaherty's wisdom in the creation of *Nanook*, audiences are being allowed to participate in films, treated as the equals of subject and filmmaker, allowed to discover rather than being told what to think. The experience of watching intercultural documentaries is becoming once again a rich and enthralling experience—much like that audiences must have had in 1922, when despite all obstacles, Robert Flaherty brought *Nanook* to the American screen. At a time when we can no longer afford to think of the world as a place inhabited by fundamentally different races or cultures, intercultural films create the promise of new communication and new human understanding across cultural lines.

THE ELUSIVE ART OF EUROPEAN COPRODUCTION

Jens Meurer

When I was a teenager, messing around with my Super 8mm camera, I had a clear idea of what it meant to be a filmmaker: I was sure that filmmakers got up at lunchtime, dressed in black turtleneck sweaters and met their fellow turtlenecked colleagues at bohemian downtown cafés, where they would sit for hours, smoking Gauloises or other French cigarettes. Thus, they would spend their days smoking, drinking black coffee, talking, and thinking about nothing but films!

What a rude awakening life had in store for me! I now make films myself, and every day I have to get up early in the morning, go to an office, and stare at a cold and grey computer. The object I think about all day is money!

Why am I telling you this? I was asked to contribute to this book dealing with everything from "nonlinear editing" to "truth." As I am still a fairly young filmmaker, at the beginning of a lifelong learning curve, I feel like I should reserve my reflections on *vérité* for later editions of this tome.

But what I can tell you about are the pros and cons of getting started and surviving in documentaries. By "documentary" I mean a very old–fashioned definition of documentary filmmaking—long, narrative pieces of film, not infotainment or talk shows. "Documentary" as in long films, point of view, time to wait for light, high shooting ratios, personal interpretation, cinema. In other words, a seemingly dying profession by the time I came around to it.

Legendary ZDF commissioning editor Eckart Stein once told a story of how one got documentary films made in the old days. One would have a late lunch with a commissioning editor, talk about this and that, and then have a good idea for a film that simply had to get made. This idea would then be scribbled onto one of the rumpled serviettes lying on the table and that was it, the commission for a new film. Probably one that involved sitting on a remote hill somewhere for weeks, waiting for the perfect cloud formation.

Unfortunately, I was born too late for this scenario.

It is becoming increasingly difficult to finance ambitious, unusual documentaries within one territory. In spite of the much heralded boom of documentaries, the market for creative films—not nature shows, animals, World War II planes, classic cars, or prostitution in the former Soviet Union—is becoming smaller and smaller. Only very cheap and very big films will survive.

The way out is straightforward: combine several territories and one can once again arrive at a budget and the editorial freedom that allows creative ambition and serious filmmaking with only an average level of self-exploitation.

The result of this logic is the much heralded European coproduction—in reality an ambiguous, elusive beast that is more than likely to cause terrible frustration and a severe co-financing headache. But it *can* provide a way out when your home market rejects or cannot sustain your ideas.

My solution, by conviction as much as by necessity, has been to invent myself as a European producer of documentaries, rather than the classical filmmaker of the imaginary café above.

Of course, there have always been European productions and collaborations, and between some broadcasters, certain producers and filmmakers, whenever a particular topic made it possible or inevitable. However, over the last seven years—since the launch of the EU's MEDIA programme—these rare and one-off coproductions have grown into a more systematic, regular and potent culture of European filmmaking. And although producer-directors are nothing new to documentaries, the emphasis is now on the catch word of the day: "European Producers."

Certain events such as the FORUM, coinciding with the Amsterdam Documentary Festival, or the Sunny Side of the Docs Festival/Market in Marseille have established a regular contact between professionals from all fields of documentary filmmaking that is beginning to forge a genuine new era of European collaboration. Certainly there is now a growing number of relationships between filmmakers, producers, distributors, and broadcasters across borders that opens up new avenues to get your film made when the old ones at home are blocked or have been wiped out. There is an exchange of ideas and experience that will slowly but surely fortify our genre and change it into something new, possibly something even better.

It was the now defunct Documentary programme of the European Union that got me started. This institution of the EU-MEDIA programme provided an opportunity in the form of small project development loans, intended to foster European coproduction. More important than the money, however, was the opportunity to meet filmmakers outside Germany at small coproduction seminars such as the one held for a few years at the Lussas Documentary Festival in France. Documentary's work is now being continued by EMDA, Brussel's Media Development Agency, and EDN, the "European Documentary Network."

To many this is nothing but *Euro-trash*. All the talk of co-this and co-that sounds unworkable, unthinkable, if not outright horrific. The resistance level is high. Why bother dealing with more bureaucrats, Eurocrats, and other hangers-on to the Brussels gravy train? Certainly, this new development serves to multiply the potential for misunderstandings, rejections, disappointments, paperwork, and awkward Euro-puddings. The new hodgepodge of funding institutions, broadcasters, EU-programmes, quotas, rules and regulations often seems insane and counterproductive.

But what is the alternative? The serviette days are gone and we can't all go off and make cheap DVC reportage with one-person crews. I believe in the European dimension. Europe has been my escape hatch to avoid being swept under by commercial television and to keep believing in the art of documentary filmmaking. I also consider it a positive challenge to document a European view of my world and age, rather than a merely German one. Why shouldn't I learn to consider an audience that is greater than my obvious one at home?

Germany is an ambiguous home for documentarists. It is one of the most important film nations in the world, the second largest market in terms of box office, with a strong film history and huge in the number of films put out every year. Nowhere are there more documentaries (of all descriptions) being produced than in Germany—a result of the staggering number of public broadcasters and film funds active here. Yet how many German documentaries have caught your eyes last year?

Germany is also an immensely isolated territory, for decades content with itself and considered "difficult" by our neighbours.

Granted.

I found this a stifling environment, one I wanted to break out of. Not to negate my German roots, but to expand on them.

Here are some of the programmes and places I found useful and motivating in helping me do this: Central is the "Amsterdam Forum for the Co-Financing of Documentaries," a frantic, four-day pitching session where filmmakers and broadcasters present their projects before an audience of seventy commissioning editors and 350 producers. Something in between a horse market and a boxing match, it is as useful and fun as it is intimidating. Similar pitching sessions are being held everywhere (Marseilles, Hot Docs, etc.), but the FORUM is the big one.

Then there are the training schemes, such as EAVE, which is a year-long programme split into three sessions, where all the aspects of producing films are studied with the help of a totally international support team of industry people. It literally unites youngish producers and filmmakers from all over Europe into a growing and increasingly effective network of European-oriented professionals.

At first, this was an overwhelming experience in a muddle of languages. Inevitably I would find myself sitting around a table with filmmakers from Bulgaria to Portugal, conversing in a pidgin-English that was no one's native tongue. Ridiculous! And everyone else seemed so much more experienced, best friend of a hundred commissioning editors, and with a bag full of prize-winning masterpieces. Not so, of course.

In fact, I found like-minded people from all over Europe, with similar aspirations, ideas, dreams and—especially—problems. This was a motivating experience. I was not as alone as I had imagined in pursuing my profession against the odds of a shrinking market.

Of course, everyone undergoes such a process in filmschool, through festivals, etc. But there was a difference here—the realization that by taking our projects abroad we could dramatically increase the possibilities for getting them made at a time when "difficult," small, quality documentaries really were being ploughed under. And that this doesn't require nondescript Euro-pudding ideas but simply strong stories where a clear cultural or regional connotation is an advantage and not the other way around. For myself, these excursions have resulted in a number of strong international relationships and a few actual coproductions. I have also brought back some foreign films to my home territory of Germany.

One should not expect any miracles, but with time such programmes do establish real relationships between filmmakers. For example, I became a founding member in the creation of the *d.net.work* with six like-minded producers from six different countries—a permanent, staffed support group for all our filmmaking activities, including marketing, distribution, and development. And friendship.

This has to be stressed because I consider friendship the main benefit of all these Euro-activities. The coproductions themselves are frequently burdened with a multiplication of the problems one expects to experience with a film: Suddenly one is dealing with not just one distributor or broadcaster, but a multitude—all equally headstrong, flaky, or plain unreliable. Not just one financing source to suddenly change their mind, but many. Not just one producer but a selection, all with their own opinions, egos and agendas.

To this add an assortment of treatments, contracts, budgets, and financing plans in an ever-changing variety of translations, and you face the typical European coproduction nightmare. It takes a lot of patience and relationship building over a number of years to work.

But it can work: My first feature-length documentary (*Egoli-My South African Home Movie*) was a film shot in South Africa by a half-European, half-African crew in two languages for partners in eight countries, broadcasting eight individual versions! Before it was finally completed, financing for the film fell apart at least three times when one of the partners dropped out for a variety of reasons, driving me as the producer/director to distraction and into serious depression.

But if the film is worth it, it will work: Peter Brosens, one of my partners in the *d.net.work*, is making his next film (*State of Dogs*), a highly unusual and ambitious documentary project, with no less than twenty (!) coproducers, broadcasters, and film funds from all over Europe.

If this sounds like madness to you, you're probably right. But it is our survival route. And it is, in fact, quite a good one: The constant exchange with film people all over Europe is constant motivation and inspiration that I feel lifts me out of the somewhat more claustrophobic confines of my home base. Working with Russians, Brits, French, Finns, and others is creating a new vision of our age which is exciting because it is more than national introspection.

There should be no illusions about (co-)producing in Europe. It's a bitch. But it's also an opportunity to chart the changes of our age from a nonnational point of view. To create a genuinely new vision of this place at a time when Europe itself is busily, awkwardly redefining itself.

In 1995 Jens Meurer was awarded the FELIX film award as "European Documentary Filmmaker of the Year."

Jens Meurer is a graduate of the 1995 EAVE programme for young producers in Europe. The same year, Egoli Films became a founding member of d.net.work, an association of seven European producers who pool information, share resources, and exchange ideas. The members have joined forces to strengthen their activities in the areas of marketing, distribution, and project development as well as to form a set of binding relationships which will foster co-productions between its members. The first joint project of d.net.work is the Theme Evening "Saturday Night," which is currently in development with ARTE.

Egoli Films is a German-based production company which Jens Meurer founded in 1993, initially as an independent launching pad for his own projects as a director. Since then, the company has come to produce both Jens's and other directors' films all over the world—in Russia, South Africa, Israel, and the U.S. With a staff of five, it is a partner in numerous international coproductions, and its office cooordinates the activities of the European producers' group, d.net.work.

Although Egoli Films works closely with commissioning editors and distributors in Germany, the company's outlook and attitude is distinctly international. Among our coproduction partners are the French companies Archipel 33 (Denis Freyd) and Gaumont in France as well as Mentorn-Barraclough-Carey and Filmit Ltd. in the U.K. Egoli Films also has an exclusive coproduction agreement with the St. Petersburg Hermitage Museum.

Egoli Films productions have been commissioned by the following networks: Channel Four, Bayerischer Rundfunk, ARTE, Saarlaendischer Rundfunk, Ostdeutscher Rundfunk, DR Danish TV, SVT Sweden, NRK Norway, YLE Finland, RTBF Belgium, and ORF Austrian TV.

While the company's mainstay is the personal, creative documentary, Egoli Films has also moved into drama production. Currently, the company is working with Oscar-nominated director Nana Djordjadze.

Most Egoli productions are made for theatrical release. To bring them to cinema and festival audiences, we are working with distributors such as Edition Salzgeber, Berlin; MFA Muenchener Film Agentur and Yildiz Film (both Munich), as well as London-based Jane Balfour Films Ltd.

In 1996/97 Egoli Films successfully worked with ARTE. The multi–European coproduction *My South African Home Movie* recently aired on the "Grand Format" strand; Jeckes and the compilation film *Made in Germany* are both coproductions with the Bayrischer Rundfunk and ARTE and are soon to be released in German cinemas.

Other productions currently under way include *Off The Pigs*, a coproduction with Archipel 33 (France) and a documentary on Europe's *Far Right* for the BBC strand "Fine Cut."

Egoli, by the way, refers to Jens's time in South Africa. It is a Zulu word and means "the place of gold and happiness," not unlike the Spanish "Eldorado." It is also used to refer to the city of Johannesburg, and there is speculation that Johannesburg might soon be renamed "Egoli."

THE AUDIENCE REPRESENTATIVE

Joanne D'Antonio

Why use an editor? The basic instinct of a documentary filmmaker often is: "It's my idea... I know what I shot... I want to make a film out of it so I will sit down and edit myself (besides, it's cheaper!)."

All of this is well taken of course, and some filmmakers successfully edit their own material. They can tear themselves away from what it took to film something and be the mercenary that leaves that bit out if it doesn't fit in. There are, of course, tricks of editing that come with experience, which they may possess; but even beyond skill in manipulating images and sound, it can often take longer to get to a clear story when the editor is too close to the material.

I remember when I studied aesthetics, we explored the concept of "distance." When the distance is "close" between the artistic material and the member of the audience, the art is highly appreciated because it strikes a chord with the perceiver. A story about poverty will easily ring true for a person who lived through the Depression. For someone who has known only wealth, it will take more communication to break the distance barrier with the same material. The challenge for the artist is to "get through" to everybody despite their background and make a universal statement.

When I was considered for the job of taking over the editing of *Broken Rainbow*, I was shown a two-hour cut. After the screening I confessed that I came into the meeting with no knowledge of the Hopi-Navajo land issues, and I could not follow the film at all. The story had not come across. Both the original editor and the filmmakers were so closely connected to the Native American peoples and their struggles that they could not distance himself enough to communicate to the uninitiated. They did not see the assumptions they were making, and a very complicated, yet very powerful, story was not coming across. They had captured the spirit in the footage, but it was not communicated in the structure, in the writing, and in the editing. Their knowledge and enthusiasm for the subject actually hampered bringing the material close to a viewer who was new to the story.

I offered to interview the filmmakers about the story they wanted to tell and create a structure for them over a three–day period. Then they could decide whether to work together with me. It was a powerful yet complicated story. By being an editor who could represent the most distanced audience, who knew nothing about what they had to say, I was able to help avoid assumptions and thereby communicate their story with clarity. They remained strong creative forces throughout, but adding an objective pair of eyes and ears completed the process.

This is actually a role the editor plays in every project. Directors like to think they want a mind reader, but if we just try to second–guess the filmmaker, it won't be enough—in reality he or she wants someone to bounce ideas off, as well as be a creative contributor. Motion pictures are by definition a collaborative medium. A filmmaker can be a captain, but the crew is not contributing robotically.

Voice of the Planet was a docudrama series with the structure of Socratic dialogues. Our team of editors was weaving imagery for the words as well as making sure the logic of the arguments presented was working for the audience. When appropriate visuals did not exist for the thoughts, we all put on our thinking caps. We brainstormed with Michael Tobias to either rework the ideas for the material or come up with alternative ideas for shots that would work.

Even on a more conventionally structured documentary such as *Black Tide*, we had a similar process. Michael Tobias wrote a script, and material was shot and stock footage ordered with that script in mind. This does not mean that there were necessarily visuals for each line of narration. As a starting point I made a temp recording of his narration script and made an assembly, putting in the sync sound bites and the narration with no visuals. I started to fill in the pictures and pace the temp narration, and in doing this process the writing changed. We found sentences that were not connectable to pictures, and repetitions to eliminate. We saw new relationships, new points to make, and to utilize images we wanted to incorporate we wrote "something for these pictures that says this." Many documentaries do not start with a prewritten script, but it helps if the filmmaker has a story in mind while shooting. The choices of what and how to film will serve the idea—what is the point of the piece? This is often an evolving process that changes during the shoot. The important thing is to continually be thinking about the story and keeping that focus as much as possible while shooting. This will make life easier in the cutting room since footage needs to "belong" to the story. Editing has always been the last rewrite, even in fiction films. The difference in nonfiction films is that if there is a narration track, a good writer needs to work through the postproduction process.

A vérité documentary does not have a writer, so an editor is important to keep the story on track and clear—is the message getting through to the audience? Is there a beginning, a middle and an end. *Reno's Kids* documents a high school teacher who conducts a "classroom of last resort" for dropouts. This film enables the audience to see the real-life drama of actual wayward teenagers finding their way back by learning responsibility, inspired by a teacher who dedicates himself to his students 100 percent. Whitney Blake, the filmmaker, knew the story she wanted to tell, but her dilemma in shooting was which kids to film. It was impossible to follow them all, but she needed to make choices that would serve her in the editing process and she needed the setup early in the material for the kids who would turn out to be the most interesting. As the editor, I came on just before shooting wrapped. I reviewed the footage and made a couple suggestions for shots that would be useful. When we edited, the story revealed itself to me easily, and we finished the film in two-thirds of the scheduled time.

Good documentaries follow the same structural guidelines as narrative films! They can be frosted with humor, flashy cutting, whatever, but the cake underneath has to hold up and tell a story to the audience. In nonfiction the bonus is that the story is real life, not make-believe, so it should be easier to make people interested. The trick is getting it on film in the first place—to successfully capture the right pieces; and secondly, to find the presentation, the communication that tells the story. This is where the editor functions as the audience representative.

A last note on the new technology. As with video games we are lured into wanting to play with the new gadgets. The reality is that the computers are simply a wonderful tool, but it is still a human who edits the film. It takes talent, skill, empathy with the filmmaker, a story sense, and enough distance to represent the audience.

Joanne D'Antonio has a broad spectrum of editing experience including documentaries, narrative features, television movies and series, and magazine shows and pilots. She was an editor on *Broken Rainbow*, an Academy-Award winning feature documentary that sheds light on the emotional Hopi-Navajo land crisis. Other major documentary credits include the Emmy-nominated *Black Tide*, an emotional evaluation of the destruction caused by the Exxon Valdez oil spill, made for Discovery Channel. She was the senior editor on the ecology series *Voice of the Planet* for Turner and edited the feature *Reno's Kids*, which covered a semester with teacher Reno Tahini who rescues dropouts in his "classroom of last resort." She is currently working on *Let's Talk*, the story of a group of activist mothers in the sixties who led the Women's Strike for Peace.

PART VII

THE BUSINESS

OF DOCUMENTARIES

© 1988 Stuart Keene

TEN GOLDEN RULES

ARNOLD SHAPIRO

INTRODUCTION

When asked to write a chapter for this book, I decided to contribute a "Top Ten List" which I believe contains important information for nonfiction producers.

This is a subjective list based upon my experiences, insights, and philosophy over a thirty-four-year active career as a nonfiction television producer working in Hollywood. Other professionals might have a completely different list or totally disagree with my list. That's fine. My hope is that you might derive some useful information, reality-checks, and inspiration from what follows.

#10: KNOW YOUR GOALS AND YOURSELF

It's crucial that you know why you want to make nonfiction films before you embark upon this very difficult, all-consuming endeavor. Knowing your motives will help you determine the types of films you make and how much of your life you devote to this pursuit.

There are no good reasons or bad reasons for becoming a filmmaker. There are only your reasons. Here is a list of legitimate reasons, all of which have applied to filmmakers I've known.

A. Making money
B. Achieving fame
C. Receiving awards, praise, accolades
D. Exposing and correcting injustices and inequities
E. Improving your community, country, planet
F. Entertaining audiences
G. Having an exciting, diverse life
H. Getting paid for learning about new topics

Certainly there are more reasons than this short list, and for most people there is more than one reason for choosing filmmaking as a career.

Knowing who you are and what you want out of this career will help you focus, be more successful and fulfilled. It means knowing your physical and psychological strengths and weaknesses so you don't embark upon a career that doesn't suit you. Here's another list of personal characteristics that need to be factored into your decision to pursue this field or continue working in it.

A. Physical health and stamina
B. Your ability to withstand rejection and unfairness
C. Patience and tact
D. Creativity and resourcefulness
E. Drive, ambition, assertiveness
F. Working collaboratively and with many different people
G. Curiosity about everything
H. Available time to devote to your pursuits

The happiest filmmakers I know are those women and men whose personal characteristics dovetail with the types of films they make, the schedule on which they do it, and the rewards they derive. The most frustrated filmmakers I know are those people who can't achieve their goals (often unrealistic aspirations for them), and who don't derive the satisfaction they hoped for because they and their goals are mismatched (ie., someone who makes public service documentaries for a local TV station, but who desperately wants to be a rich and famous filmmaker).

Being a filmmaker is very time-consuming. It's not a part-time job, not an avocation, and not work with regular or sane hours. It's an enveloping, energy–draining, difficult, full-time career requiring, in most instances, that you either sit at the edge of the pool and watch or jump into the deep end and prepare for the most arduous swim of your life.

#9: THERE ARE NO RULES AND THERE IS NO FAIRNESS

There are no rules in this profession, and there certainly is no fairness. If you require rules, predictability, structure and certainty, I suggest a career in civil service. If you are especially sensitive and are devastated by unfair, unjust and unpredictable things happening to you, then I suggest staying away from filmmaking and the entertainment industry.

The worlds of filmmaking, motion pictures, and television certainly have procedures that are followed in the process of creating, selling, producing, and distributing or airing programs. But, unlike many professions, there are not rules that everyone plays by. Shows get sold in arranged meetings in executive suites; and shows get spontaneously sold on golf courses and in saunas. Directors get hired in all the traditional ways; and directors get hired because they have "connections" or because someone owes someone else a favor.

"Show business" is so unpredictable that you can't rely on any rules, on strategies that worked previously, on other people's experience, on common sense or logic. And you certainly can't rely on something happening because it's right or fair. There are talented producers, directors, writers, and editors who slave away at low-paying, obscure assignments learning their craft, awaiting their "big break," but they never get it. And there are people right out of high school who make one "student film" and get hired to direct a feature film without "paying any dues." Anything you can imagine has happened at least once.

Think of a dangerous mountain that a hundred people start to climb. Some people will fall and have to start over, get tired and give up, become injured or disabled. Others will get lucky and make it to the top in record time, others will cheat and get to the top without climbing. My point is that advancing in your show business career is like climbing that mountain. It's that unpredictable and uncertain.

If you need a safe, orderly world, take my advice and choose another career. But if you have the temperament for uncertainty, setbacks, making your own rules, surviving by your own ingenuity and resourcefulness; and if you like a life of psychological adventure, then filmmaking might be for you.

There are no rules, there is no fairness. If you etch this harsh reality in your mind, you won't be quite as devastated when the inevitable rejections and cruel twists of fate occur. Fortunately or unfortunately, luck, "karma," good timing, chance, charisma, and coincidence (if there is such a thing) have as much to do with success as talent and good ideas. As Walter Cronkite used to say: "That's the way it is."

#8: SELLING IS EVERYTHING

To make a film, you are selling every step of the way from start to finish. When you create or find an idea for a documentary, you have to sell or convince someone with money to finance it (a studio, network, TV station, production company, foundation, private investor, etc.). Your ability to convince that funding source to provide the money is crucial in whether you can make the film.

Once you have funding, you are selling your idea to others you want to hire— writer, director, director of photography, actors, etc. Perhaps you don't have enough money to pay these people what they want. You must sell them or persuade them that working on this film has other benefits, that they should lower their rate for this project. Perhaps you need free services or products (film, equipment, locations, editing equipment). Again, you are selling your request using logic, convincing, begging—whatever it takes.

Finally, when your film is completed, you will need a method of distribution or airing, if you don't already have one. Now you are selling the merits of your finished film.

Selling—or whatever synonym you wish to use—is present throughout the entire process of filmmaking and producing. You need to be good at it, or find a colleague who can do it with you or for you if you're too shy or unskilled in this arena.

Selling as an integral part of producing a film or program takes two forms: verbal and written.

I believe that if you can't write down your idea in a concise, clear manner, then you haven't thought it through clearly or thoroughly enough. No idea is too big or complex or amorphous to commit to paper in a few pages—the shorter the better. There is a certain skill to writing sales presentations/proposals, or grant proposals. Besides reading books and articles on how to do it, the best way is to read the proposals written by other producers. Read ideas for comedies, dramas, documentaries; series, specials, movies. Soon, you'll see the ingredients, the styles, the mix of content with selling points (hype). More often than not, you will need a written description of your idea (together with a budget, production schedule, and your résumé). If you cannot write well, either improve your skills or hire a good writer.

Verbal selling - or "pitching" is equally essential. Throughout the process, you will always be trying to convince someone to do something important in getting your film made. Do you have good powers of persuasion? Do you have charisma? Do you come across as sincere, honest, and genuine? Can you clearly and concisely communicate your requests and selling points without confusing or boring the listener? Are you friendly and likeable? Do you appear knowledgeable and credible? Are you a really good listener, and can you remember what you heard in a meeting? Do you make a good visual impression (your demeanor, manners, dress, eye contact, confidence, credibility, attitude)?

Of course, not everyone can be charming, eloquent, dynamic, and charismatic. But everyone can work to improve his/her verbal selling skills and demeanor. Your verbal selling skills will be used every day that you are in the process of making and publicizing a film.

#7: ATTITUDE IS EVERYTHING

Your attitude during the creating, selling, producing, and marketing of a film or program is an essential ingredient for success. A positive attitude won't always result in success, but I believe a negative attitude increases the chance for failure.

My mentor, television producer Al Burton, believes that to be a realist is to be a pessimist because most ideas don't get produced, and most programs and films are not successful. In short, the odds are against you. So if you focus on the cold, hard reality of what you're trying to achieve, you will quickly become a pessimist. Al believes that to succeed (and he has for fifty years), you must be an optimist. To Al, the glass isn't half full, it's always overflowing. His enthusiasm and positive energy are contagious. Even when Al experiences setbacks, he seems happy. His positive attitude, optimism, and genuine excitement about each of his projects greatly contributes to his success.

The challenges of making a living as a nonfiction filmmaker are so numerous and difficult that if you don't have a positive attitude, I don't think it's possible to survive for very long. If, by nature, you are a pessimist, then you are adding lots of extra weight to your backpack as you hike up the steep and treacherous mountain.

For me, it's essential that I am excited about each of my ideas; that I genuinely believe I can sell each idea I pitch; that I communicate my enthusiasm for the idea I'm presenting; and that I never think failure or rejection. If I do fail, it will be apparent. Anticipating it doesn't help me or the project at all.

Can you learn to be an optimist? I don't know. But there's a useful saying that is applicable here: "Fake it until you make it." If you can imitate or emulate a positive, upbeat attitude about a project, eventually it might become genuine. It's worth a try. Turning yourself from a realist (pessimist) into an optimist might take a long time, and might only be partially successful, but I highly recommend you try it. You have nothing to lose and everything to gain.

Buyers have told me over and over how important commitment, enthusiasm, and passion are to convincing them to take a chance with you and your idea.

I don't always feel as confident about certain ideas as I appear in pitch meetings. Even after thirty-plus years of selling programs, I sometimes have to "fake it until I make it." If you can't be genuinely optimistic, at least learn to appear that way when you need to.

With a positive "can-do" attitude, anything is possible. Negative thinking and behavior are to creativity and success what an anchor is to a ship. It's as important to have a positive attitude as it is to have talent and good communication skills. You have a better chance at success if you expect success. A positive attitude is power.

#6: THE IDEA ISN'T EVERYTHING

I'm not underrating the importance of the idea, topic, or story. Without an idea, there's nothing. It's the first step in the process of filmmaking. But many people believe that given a good idea, a good film should automatically follow. If only it were that simple and straightforward!

First, a good media idea means a commercially viable idea. Good means saleable. Good means profitable. Good does not always mean top–quality. It usually refers to top-grossing. So your definition of a good idea and the buyer's idea might be different.

In addition to an idea that sounds like it can be profitable and attract large audiences, there are other essential ingredients that accompany most sales.

Together with the "good" idea is the ability and reputation of the filmmaker or producer. The same idea presented by an unknown talented producer and a known talented producer will usually be sold by the known producer. Buyers financing a film want as much assurance as possible that their investment is going to result in profits. If you are a first-time producer or unknown, you might want to partner with a filmmaker who can get the film sold, but who will allow you to actively participate in the production in some meaningful capacity. Then, the second time around, you can probably sell on your own.

Another factor that spells the difference between the success and failure of launching a project is matching the idea with the right buyer. Every cable network in the U.S. is striving for a unique identity; so are the broadcast networks to a lesser degree. Matching your TV idea to the most appropriate buyer is crucial in making a sale.

Timing is another important factor. Certain ideas are saleable one year but not the next. Some ideas are associated with holidays or seasons. Some projects have only regional or local appeal and should not be sold to a national network. Some ideas are only right for PBS and not commercial TV.

If you don't have an agent who can advise you on what various buyers are looking for or receptive to, then it's important that you watch the networks or channels you think are viable candidates for your ideas. Make sure they haven't already produced what you're trying to sell. If something similar has been aired, see how you can make your idea different enough to be viable ("new wine in an old bottle" is the way one network president described successful shows; a familiar theme or plot with a new twist).

Don't give up on an idea if you can't sell it now. Virtually no idea is dead until you are. Sometimes you have to wait for a better opportunity, a better climate for that particular idea or genre, or a different buyer at that network (executives change so often that you usually won't have very long to wait).

#5: MAKING A FILM IS LIKE FIGHTING A WAR

While filmmaking has it's rewards and times of fun and fulfillment, the process is more difficult and frustrating than anyone could imagine.

In Francois Truffaut's classic 1973 film, *Day for Night*, the "director" of the film within the film makes the truest statement I've ever heard about filmmaking: "Before beginning to shoot a film, I want above all to make a movie that will be beautiful. As soon as the first storms appear on the horizon, I lower my sights.

I hope, simply, to be able to finish the film, period... Shooting a film is exactly like crossing the old West in a stagecoach. At first you hope to have a good trip. But very soon, you start wondering if you'll even reach your destination."

While maintaining a positive attitude and being as prepared as possible, be aware that before you complete the film, you will have been on a journey that was rougher, tougher, and filled with mishaps that you would not have thought possible when you began.

Of the fifty or more documentaries I have produced, I can't think of one that went smoothly and was as problem-free as it should have been. Unpredictable things always happen. And the problems are usually different with each film, so whatever problems you are ready for, different problems arise that you're not ready for. Sometimes it feels like there's a mischievous spirit or entity assigned to make a producer's life "hell on earth." But with each project, we go into battle, we fight, and however great the sacrifices, we usually win—and after a bit of rest are ready to fight another day.

#4: DOCUMENTARIES NO LONGER HAVE CREATIVE LIMITS

A dictionary definition of a documentary no longer applies to all documentaries. Of course, most nonfiction films still utilize the classic ingredients: interviews, cinéma vérité original shooting, archival footage, music, and narration.

In recent years, other ingredients have become accepted techniques for the documentarian, with only some academic purists objecting. These newer ingredients include: recreations of events using either the actual people or actors; shooting and editing styles inspired by MTV and music videos; mixing fictional elements (sometimes without telling the audience); storytelling without narration. And more.

As the creative horizons expand and documentarians have the opportunity to try new techniques and new forms of storytelling and communicating information, it's important to remember that style is no substitute for substance and clarity. I admire filmmakers who are experimental, innovative, daring, and different—but only if the end result works, meaning that viewers have to understand what they are seeing; and they have to be motivated to watch the film until the end.

Conversely, there's nothing wrong with making documentaries in the classic tradition without gimmicks. If a "talking head" is saying something riveting, that image is more powerful than any other visual imagery you could use over someone talking. My documentary *Scared Straight!* is compelling and mesmerizing. But 90 percent of the film consists of talking heads. It's just that these talking heads are saying things that most people haven't heard before (or hadn't when it premiered in 1978). The film was bold and daring when it was made, but the ingredients and style were traditional.

Because of the latitude that's permitted for today's filmmakers, it's more interesting and fun to be producing documentaries now than in the past. You can make compelling films today using classic ingredients and styles; or you can be as avant-garde and innovative as your imagination allows.

#3: BE RESPONSIBLE

I do not believe in censorship of films by the government or citizens groups. However, I do believe in self-regulation by filmmakers and documentarians. When developing documentary ideas, I always factor into the process this question: "Is this idea/content going to enrich or educate viewers, or does it contain material that is dangerous, destructive, or 'mind-polluting'?" Although a given idea might be highly commercial, lucrative, and attention-getting, if it's also not in the best interest of our society; if it could negatively influence children; further cement racial or ethnic stereotypes; or possibly trigger dangerous behavior in some viewers, I won't pursue the project no matter how successful the film could be.

As filmmakers, I feel we have a responsibility to society to do good, or at least, not to do harm. But I believe this "censorship" should only come from within—"ethical and/or moral responsibility and self-regulation." I also believe that most documentarians are caring and responsible people in spite of pressures from the commercial marketplace toward sensationalism and exploitation to achieve higher ratings.

Nonfiction films must also be as accurate and factual as they are creative. In the competitive world of television, we now have "tabloid" journalism and reality programs. Some of these shows place shock-value, rumor, innuendo, etc., over accurate reporting and responsible journalism. Some of the tabloid TV stories are irresponsible and inaccurate.

When people watch nonfiction—news, reality shows, interview shows, and documentaries—they assume that what they are hearing and seeing is the truth. And that's what they should expect. When filmmakers use creative editing to change the meaning or content of what's being said, re-creations that aren't accurate, and inaccurate narration that misleads the viewers, that is, in my opinion, unethical and irresponsible.

If you are making what I call an "advocacy" or point-of-view film that is one-sided and has a singular message, that's fine as long as you tell the viewers that's what you're doing. Don't present propaganda as objective reporting. Of course, some creative license can and must occur, but the audience must not be duped or misled regarding important content: crucial facts, the film's message, the point an interviewee was trying to make, and so forth.

Just as doctors have oaths and guidelines they are obligated to follow, nonfiction producers should maintain the highest standards of accuracy and factual storytelling. We owe that to our audience because when they watch our films they are being educated, forming opinions, and being influenced by what we present. We owe our audience accuracy, honesty, and truthfulness.

#2: MARKETING IS VITALLY IMPORTANT

Marketing is the process by which your film is advertised, publicized, promoted, and otherwise exploited (videos, merchandising, and more). The bigger the campaign, the better chance that more people will be drawn to your film. The way your film is marketed is as important as the film itself.

In most cases, the filmmaker doesn't have much input or control into how his/her film is marketed. Sometimes there's no money for a marketing campaign and you have to be creative and innovative in devising ways to get the word out about your film.

To the extent that you can have access to those publicizing, promoting, and advertising your film, utilize the opportunity. Suggest visual and verbal ideas for ads, TV and radio promos, ways to utilize the celebrity host/narrator (if you have one). Try to have input into press releases and any written material about your film.

Remember that more people will see a ten-second or twenty-second TV promo about your film than will see the film itself because the promos run repeatedly at various times, so a large number of people are exposed to them. Therefore, these short advertisements must be compelling.

People whose job it is to prepare on-air promos, print ads, press releases, arrange interviews, and distribute review copies of your film are professionals. Some of them welcome input, ideas, and help from the filmmaker. Others resent the intrusion into their specialty. But it's vitally important that you actively participate in the marketing of your film, if you possibly can. This final step in the producing process often means the difference between success and failure. If your film is great but no one sees it, what have you accomplished? I can't place enough importance on the marketing phase of filmmaking.

#1: THE GOLDEN RULE

With the completion of each documentary, you look back on the entire process from the creation of the idea to the premiere screening or airing, and you are left with your "battle scars" and your memories.

I believe it's important throughout the process that you not do things or say things that you will later regret. For some producers, "getting the shot" is so important that they will lie, cheat, deceive, or do whatever else they have to do to "get the shot." That's not my philosophy. I believe that you should try everything you can to get the shot as long as you are being honest and ethical in the process. If you have a conscience, if you care about the way others feel, then you might regret the dishonest, disrespectful, or cruel way you treated others in the process of getting your film made.

In the end, it's not worth it. Being true to yourself, maintaining your integrity, your self-respect, and your reputation are what's really important. I have found that treating colleagues and those I'm filming with kindness, compassion, respect, and honesty is the only way to behave and not have regrets later on.

Taking the high road in the way we filmmakers treat others is as important as making a good film, in my view. Making a film is no excuse to put aside The Golden Rule. "Do unto others as you would have others do unto you." In the end, that's as important as accolades, awards, good reviews, and good filmmaking. But they're not mutually exclusive. I believe that you can have it all.

ARNOLD SHAPIRO

I have been creating and producing American television series, specials, movies and documentaries since 1963. I have been fortunate to receive an Academy Award, 13 Emmys, a Peabody, and more than 100 other awards. All of these awards have been for my documentaries. Of all the different types of programs I've produced, documentaries are my favorite. They are what enriches my soul.

I have numerous accounts and testimonials showing how various documentaries of mine have actually changed certain people's lives for the better. My Oscar and Emmy Award-winning documentary, "Scared Straight!," actually turned many kids away from a life of crime. My CBS series, "Rescue 911" which ran for seven seasons is credited with saving the lives of at least 350 viewers based upon testimonials from those viewers. "Scared Silent: Exposing and Ending Child Abuse," hosted by Oprah Winfrey, aired simultaneously on CBS, NBC, and PBS - followed by ABC. It has the distinction of being the most watched documentary special ever broadcast on American TV. Countless incidents of physical and sexual child abuse were stopped and prevented as a result of this powerful documentary of mine. For a producer, what could be more rewarding and fulfilling than saving lives and changing lives for the better?

ART OF DOCUMENTARY

MIKE FOX

For the last thirty years in Britain, television has provided nonfiction filmmakers with their only real outlet. At this time the country has four terrestrial television channels, BBC 1 and 2 which are publicly funded and ITV and Channel Four which rely on advertising revenues. Government gave commercial television the green light during the 1950s. The nation was divided into areas, and companies interested in applying for a license to operate were obliged to support the principles of public service broadcasting. That meant giving an undertaking to provide a reasonable number of hours per year for serious/factual programming. Further licenses to continue broadcasting, renewable every five years, depended on that commitment. Factual programming became a major part of television's output and resulted in documentary steadily growing as a truer reflection of British culture than the one mirrored in British feature films. Television was a growth industry and, in absorbing many unable to survive in our own contracting film Industry, harnessed the talent, ideas, and energy present in the film industries of other countries.

The 1980s and 1990s have seen an inexorable slide towards privatization in Britain, a process that swallowed up industry and public utilities as well as television. Setting aside the much publicized advantages of such a policy, the role of television, as expressed recently by Jeremy Isaacs, the first head of Channel Four, *to provide for minority as well as majority audiences*, has buckled to market forces. For commercial television, the present deregulated climate has resulted in advertising revenues being spread between more operators. Performance safeguards have been relaxed in tandem with reduced funding, making popular television production and bought-in programming attractive. The BBC, as ever in competition for audience share, is gradually following suit. In one stroke the will and availability of funds necessary to produce documentary have all but evaporated, bringing to an end a renaissance period enjoyed for nearly fifty years by serious nonfiction filmmakers in Britain. Caught up in that equation are hundreds of independent film companies, established professionals, and a steady flow of young filmmakers emerging from Britain's National Film School and other colleges in the country. As an individual witnessing this period of change and having enjoyed twenty years fulfilling experience as a cinematographer, I feel compelled to take a long hard look at where we are going and where we've come from.

From an early age I was certain of my ambition to work in film, but when old enough faced the same problems as others wishing to embark on such a career. The film industry was in theory a closed profession; scaling the ramparts or finding a breach in the wall was going to be difficult, and with no official film school one had to explore many options. To my parents' consternation, I enrolled for an uncertain future via an arbitrary apprenticeship. I was determined if rather muddled. My enthusiasm was for cinematography, but the dead-man's-shoes route to that plateau seemed to offer little more than a future diet of commercials, and if very lucky, not very inspiring feature films. Also it seemed that the best of British film only really existed because the American majors supported it. Whilst Pinewood churned out *Carry On* films and smaller independents explored life near the kitchen sink, it was they who were busy backing David Lean, or exploring the fertile ground of English and Scottish history, and of course, *swinging London*.

Documentary had traditionally been sponsored usually by government or industry. The Central Office of Information, Shell Oil, The National Coal Board, and British Transport were amongst organizations that produced many fine films, in the process launching the careers of filmmakers like John Schlesinger, Tony Richardson, and Lindsay Anderson. Lack of space on British cinema screens had been compensated for by television offering documentary a niche, where once established it thrived. Its influence was enormous, changing forever a situation where an interpretation of the world around us was only available to those who read or traveled. Television filmmakers brought the world beyond the home and place of work into living rooms. Social, political, historical, and anthropological issues provided them with their subheadings.

Having initially made an error of judgment by becoming a cinema projectionist in the belief that projectionist to filmmaker was a matter of course, I rapidly made other arrangements. A two-year stint in a film laboratory was the answer. Recognized as a back door into film production, it was worth working in the dark with a torch between my teeth just to eventually leave clutching a very necessary block of gold—a union card.

The Association of Cinematographic and Television Technicians regulated most jobs within film production; it wasn't possible to work without being a member of it. The union had evolved during the bad old days of long hours, poor wages, and the infamous quota quickies. Prior to laboratory technicians joining it and the advent of commercial television, its membership consisted of an enormous army of casual workers for whom it represented an effective bastion against some of the shadier practices of the time. By the time I won my ticket things had changed. With such a large membership of casual employees, it was perhaps more difficult than in other sections of industry where a work force was present in one place for the union to bring its members together in order to vote on policy, establish working practices, and significantly in the case of ACTT, appoint its representatives. Once the union had control in the laboratories and commercial television all that changed. With the new channels being described as "A license to print money" by some of its first entrepreneurs, ACTT and the other entertainment unions steamed in. They had for the first time captive work forces eager to share in the fruits at the opposite end of the bargaining table from television executives for whom no demand was too unreasonable, if the cost was loss of advertising revenues as a result of industrial action. It developed into a bizarre situation where ACTT's politically motivated representatives within ITV oversaw a spiraling manifesto of restrictive practices that suited the pockets of their ITV members, for the most part happy to go along with bigger wage packets even if the industrial gladiators they'd elected had a more ambitious agenda. Casualisation as it existed in the rest of the industry was just about tolerated. The union needed a political voice and that voice was at the TUC. Membership of the Trades Union Congress, an important forum with close links to Britain's Labour Party, required that a union should have five thousand members, and the thousands of freelancers, so despised by the new leadership in ACTT, made up the numbers.

But in 1968 and standing on the high ground of newly acquired membership, my only concern was the business of persuading someone to give me a job at something—anything! I began serving a ramshackle apprenticeship juxtaposed with periods of time driving a taxi. Although in hindsight the whole experience was formative, at the time I did wonder whether the process would ever end. I was an assistant everything, through camera stores, cutting rooms, dubbing theatres, finally ending up as a film researcher on Thames Television's *World at War*, a series that for all involved in its production was a consummate experience. My own involvement left me feeling that television in Britain had real stature, a conviction that gave me a new goal—to work within it as a cinematographer. Besides, I'd already concluded that the chance of even getting to touch a camera before my fiftieth birthday by any other route was fairly remote. Documentary was not only important as a reflection of our culture but occupied a special place at the very heart of broadcasting in Britain. As I began to seek employment as an assistant cameraman, the networks' commitment to producing several hours per week of factual programming seemed to offer a real and worthwhile future.

Traditionally for documentarists a social conscience had always been well up the list, although often understated—after all there was usually a sponsor to consider. Whilst Robert Flaherty, John Grierson, and Humphrey Jennings had in their time never been too shy to comment on society and those that governed our lives, it was television that had opened the floodgates for a deluge of filmmakers, eager to peer into the darker corners of British life, and who in the 1960s, conscious of new ground being broken in America by Wiseman, Pennebaker, Leacock, and others, were to play their part in changing the film language. The opportunity for the most significant change came with the arrival of a new generation of 16mm handheld cameras, making possible a liberation from long established filmmaking methods.

For the new wave filmmakers in France, Cinéma Vérité, made possible by the availability of the Eclair or Cameflex, was at the heart of their approach to storytelling. Although vérité in French feature films was relatively short-lived, it wasn't so in Britain. Documentarists grabbed the new technology and ideas with vigor. It enabled them to combine a significantly lower profile with much greater fluidity. It was now unnecessary to make an Indian villager walk through his door eight times until he got it right. The paraphernalia of the profession gave way to ideas and undreamt-of access into people's lives and circumstances, warts and all, constituting a brief moment of innocence when subject and author were caught off guard and where there were no obstacles to seeing into each other. Politicians, rock stars, business people, Indian tribes, the homeless, the persecuted, and the vulnerable had an unhampered voice, whilst the camera, close, wide, unsteady, and erratic, explored them. The prepared statement, the scripted message gave way to a collage of off-guard moments. Camera and recorder had become tools of the mind and a new breed of filmmaker emerged to break the rules.

I trained with one of them, probably Britain's best documentary cameraman. Charles Stewart taught me many things but above all to listen, to lock into a scene and find its natural dynamic. Following dialogue and the reactions of others captured natural rhythms and was the key to being able to respond decisively to what was happening in front of the camera and anticipate what was about to. I'm sure Charles once told me that he was working as a neg cutter when the first batch of Eclair NPRs arrived in Britain. It's interesting that many first generation vérité cameramen didn't come from the ranks of those specifically trained as cinematographers. Such varied and often unrelated training resulted in a style of cinematography that straddled the line between perceived amateurishness and innovation. But without question liberation from long established procedures and disciplines left more space for perception and the capturing of real moments.

Whilst working with Charles I realized that becoming interested in people was as important as learning camera craft. Perception and anticipation with a camera depended on having acquired a human behavior reference bank usually readable whatever the language. I also developed an appreciation of the true importance of sound and the recordist's possible problems in obtaining it. Cameramen can develop selfish tendencies in an environment that all too often is obsessed by the image. The wisdom of that lesson is for me manifest in the fact that I have worked with the same recordist, Michael Lax, for some eighteen years.

We first met soon after I made the break as a cameraman. Six years older than me, he had been around and working when some of the most exciting new ideas were being brought to bear in television documentary. Mike too had once been a projectionist, and via a brief career as a deck steward on a cruise ship, carrying would-be émigrés to a new life in New Zealand, had drifted into sound. It had been very timely; he was young, interested in life, and it was the sixties. Britain's ten-year party was up and running, the traditional class barriers had relaxed, and for Mike and many others access was fun and exciting. I doubt whether our first day together can even have begun to equate with time he'd spent with the likes of Margot Fonteyn, The Beatles, and Cartier Bresson, as by then much had changed.

It's difficult to pin down the moment when the lights started to burn in rooms occupied by the establishment in Britain. Certainly Ken Loach, Tony Garnett, Roy Battersby and others had more than once rocked the boat. Some say that documentary coverage of the anti-Vietnam demonstration in Grosvenor Square was the moment. Such graphic footage was at the sharp end of a torrent of information that in a democracy clearly couldn't be stopped. Perhaps Shakespeare's remedy for reducing love's passion—*If music be the food of love, then play on that / may sicken and so die*—provided a precedent. Increasing the volume of information, trivial as well as serious, as a way of dulling the television audience makes things not matter as much. But certainly from then on a voice on the airwaves of Britain would never again be available to the wrong people. As the world knows Britain maintains a three-tier class system. The middle classes, tangible proof of a democratic and free society, were the most defensive of it. Generally well educated and aware, defending public morality on television, albeit with the benefits of a reasonable standard of living, was useful for our age and many many careers. Graduates from Oxbridge filled the vacancies left by the awkward squad when they departed from television, venturing into other fields or obscurity. Debate was a fundamental tool for the new generation in their maintenance of democratic principles. Thus slowly but surely documentary on television ceased to define rights and wrongs, but merely debate them. Over time most issues international, domestic, serious, and frivolous were molded to fit the format and policy of given programme strands. The establishment of presenters as factual television stars, and the selection of contributors as type, caused a steady erosion of the power of film documentary to imply real truths. Thus, paradoxically, drama with well–drawn characters began to say more about reality, and documentary very little to audiences increasingly unable to separate issues of public outrage from a rock star's new marriage or haircut.

So what happened to the great promise offered by vérité, where had its inherent perceptions gone? Going handheld had become regarded as a legitimate way of closing the gap between filmmaker and subject, rather than the cinematic effect of wobblyscope. The sync cable between camera and recorder had gone, cameras were quieter, more user friendly, and film stocks faster. The filmmaker's profile had never been lower, and access never more possible. Yet the language had become rigid and images relegated to the position of illustrating narratives driven by the spoken word.

I believe that the change was on several fronts. Firstly, to look at television itself, it had become a career for many and a more practical prize than the uncertain rewards offered by attempts to generate interest and funding for one off projects with no sure outlet. Not everyone with a guaranteed career making films for television was blessed with a storyteller's mind. No matter though, because in any case individual voices were losing ground to the voice of the broadcaster. Their strands and slots divided all subjects into music and arts, science, general features, etc. Documentary became institutionalized, placing most aspects of daily life into its appropriate compartment. Having leveled everything off, real people became an inexhaustible supply of players, potential witnesses to issues in life. Once driven by issue, programme makers could select contenders for talking head participation on the basis of type and suitability in order to propel the argument at the heart of any given programme. Implying a considered structure, juxtaposing talking heads with little glimpses of real life established a format that became an easy and effective way of producing *good television*. Curiously, many who have been able to sustain whole careers by producing such dull and uninspiring programmes weren't beyond waxing lyrical about a new and usually foreign film they'd recently seen. But praising innovation or avant garde style was separate, and few would translate the experience into their own projects. Meanwhile, below stairs the staff technician had replaced the would-be artisan. Unionized and one of many in a department, an individual's commitment was smothered by the roster, the greater need for a crew to facilitate a next job they were not always able to feel part of. Being on staff had advantages but for many meant partial involvement in lots of projects each year. In such circumstances mustering an emotional response to a single story must become more difficult, except of course when witness to the breakdown of a contributor. It wasn't long before all the best programmes had such moments; there was literally no film without tears—and make sure you're in close!

Mike Lax and I first worked together as a result of a telephone call made to Document Films, to which I was attached at the time, by a BBC film operations manager requesting a three-man crew for one day's participation on an ongoing programme. It seemed that all my aspirations to photograph documentaries had led to that reality where apart from corporate films, all I could reasonably expect were crumbs from the broadcaster's table, with the odd longer offer to stand in for staff holidays or film in dangerous locations. Document Films was one of many facilities companies operating at that time. During the 1960s it had been an independent production company producing Roger Graef's *In the name of Allah* before finally having its fingers burnt with an undistributed profile on racing driver Jackie Stewart, sadly beaten to the post by a similar film produced by Roman Polanski and released theatrically in the U.K. With bankruptcy looming and no guaranteed outlet for future productions, it had no option other than to join the ranks of servicing companies operating to provide cutting room space and freelance film crews as and when required by the broadcasters. By the time I made the jump to cameraman, broadcast work had reduced to a trickle odd days when a staff crew was unavailable. And so most of my earlier work was for corporate film producers who, although looked down upon by people in television, were actually very energetic and inventive with film. In any case I valued such work, given my half of the deal with Document, to make their camera equipment work as much as possible, in return for their support of myself and other freelancers. Sustained by such a diet, Mike and I were able to work together enough to discover that we enjoyed one another's company sufficiently to face whatever future as a team. Both of us interested in ordinary lives, we realized a professional relationship where much could remain unsaid to be an advantage in keeping technical considerations in the background. Ideas and the space to look and listen were more important than the filmmaking process for its own sake.

Channel Four commenced broadcasting in 1983. Conceived and lobbied for by those frustrated with institutionalised television, its government–backed remit was to cater for minority tastes, provide real alternatives, and commission from the independent sector. In honoring that remit, it fought some very tough battles against well-armed critics. The advertising industry, the film unions, commercial television bosses, and later government itself all had an axe to grind. Surviving the onslaught it went from strength to strength, providing a much needed shot in the arm to independent filmmakers, whose numbers swelled as more and more individuals left safe jobs in broadcasting to go freelance and make programmes for the new channel. It seemed that at long last many of us on the outside had reached the light at the end of the tunnel.

Working for a new broadcaster with an expressed commitment to film was a glittering prize indeed. I was invited to photograph two major series, *The Arabs* and *Heart of the Dragon*. The latter was a two-year project in China. I leapt at the opportunity to become involved in such a series with producers I'd long admired and explore a land and culture that to most Western people at the time, was completely enigmatic. To this day I value the experience as unique, more especially because I learnt many things, of which one was to do with outside perceptions of our way of doing things. A Chinese cameraman, employed by China News Bureau to accompany us, remarked after viewing a rough cut of one episode that the film was for him "a real window on life." He and audiences in China had been influenced by the Russian school of film making. He gave an example of how he had once turned up in a rural community equipped with an Arriflex, a set of legs, and six ties with which to smarten up the contributors. His perceptions of our film were gratifying and illuminating. *Correcting*, the film in question, had been shot vérité style. It followed the progress of a young married woman accused of stealing a neighbor's television. Peter Montagnon, the film's director, during the setting up of the series had expressed a desire to examine the process of law, and after much deliberation the relevant bureaucracy had given a green light for him to film any one of twelve cases due to be tried by Nanjing court during June 1983. To their surprise he had turned down the eleven cases ranging from murder to grand larceny in favor of judicial response to a relatively minor offense by Western standards. His reasons to us were that inspired, large-scale theft and murder were serious crimes wherever they occurred and inspired a similar response regardless of a prevailing system. To film such a trial would have been interesting, but in the end have said very little about the criteria of the society that would be passing judgment.

The young woman whose forthcoming trial Peter chose to film was married and had a baby daughter. The family lived in one of Nanjing's many apartment blocks in company with twenty other families. A compulsory social system that required that those twenty families coexist and share half the number of kitchens and bathrooms was under threat by the encroachment of newer Western ideas concerned with individual achievement and the subsequent need for privacy. The young woman's crime was a manifestation of all that a giant society timidly approaching a free market system most feared. Even in 1983 the huge street billboards that less than two years before had heralded the thoughts of Chairman Mao had been replaced by images of China's first consumer products, and her new age crime inspired by envy of a neighbor's household possessions was at that time a worst nightmare. The court would be the blunt instrument of official response and would undoubtably punish her according to law. But the real trial would be one of orchestrated shame and disgrace and would be promoted by her family members, her neighbours and workmates. Peter sensitized us all to the layers in the story—there were to be no interviews. This was to be a documentary in the traditional style driven by ongoing perceptions and regular discussion amongst ourselves in the evenings. I had always been intrigued by just how quickly the subjects in a film became used to us and got on with their lives, but with *Correcting*, that syndrome attained new heights. During nearly three weeks of filming I only sensed one brief moment of eye contact between the prisoner and us and most of the time we were within six feet of her. Allowing for the fact that she had a lot on her mind at the time, her resolute acceptance of our presence on the horizon was astonishing and only equaled by a similar lack of concern by the other players.

Most people who saw the finished film thought it to be quite extraordinary, but for me there was an important lesson. The reaction of our Chinese accomplices to the rough cut illustrated something fundamental to documentary as a truly perceptive form—that its effectiveness was dependent on newness of technique both to the filmmakers and the subjects of their films. The experience in Nanjing where all were new to the process, even ourselves, by then used to the more ordered and formatted approach of British television, gave a glimpse of how effective vérité could still be in circumstances that allowed it. I recently rewatched, *Don't look back*, made at a time when the techniques it employed were also new to all. Even now it successfully reflects the filmmakers insights. As a cameraman the instinct to try and capture, as they did, what goes on between protagonists is ever present. Sadly though, as I've already expressed, television narratives had changed, rarely allowing such scenes the screen time necessary for them to remain as illustrative, when invariably edited down to the status of wallpaper in the interests of preserving the bigger ideas, carried of course by interviews to camera. Paradoxically documentary, given so much by television, had in my view lost so much along the way. But I have to be honest and also examine personal prejudices. Past glories have a tendency to blind us all to the present and it's a contradiction to admire a past approach to filmmaking, and not realize that once any style becomes routine innocence is lost when all concerned become stale to the process.

For filmmakers, new ideas are always necessary to sharpen things up again. I have been guilty of being irrational about interview-led narratives; talking heads are clearly here to stay and have become an accepted part of film language. In taking the view that the main problem is in breaking the spell, the atmosphere of a film; and in happening to prefer voice-over, I recognize that they can if thought about be very effective. However, I will never share the view held by some filmmakers that unless something is being said directly into the camera, it remains unsaid. I also believe strongly in conceptualizing them. As an example, Thames Television produced a very fine series on Northern Ireland. *The Troubles* juxtaposed archive film with interviewees all shot against a black background. The uniformity of style was extremely effective in maintaining audience concentration to the overall narrative. A silver lining when having so often been disturbed when an ongoing idea is interrupted by a cut to a contributor sitting bolt upright against a high key background—bookshelves for academics, ornaments or rubber plants for most other people. I recently photographed a series for independent filmmaker, Brian Leith. The films were concerned with mankind's relationship to the wilderness—past, present, and future. Interviews were a fundamental part of Brian's narrative, and given the outdoor nature of the subject, we agreed on a suitable and uniform style for them. That was to photograph them all against exterior backgrounds but in each case use neutral density filters to significantly reduce the depth of field. The desired effect was to bring each contributor into sharp relief against a very diffused but unmistakably African backdrop. Not only did they marry better with other images from many different sources, but the flow of the central narrative was undisturbed.

It's not often that one has the need or chance to sit down and put into words a set of impressions gathered from a career. For the last twenty years I have been doing for a living something that were it not a job would have been a hobby. That makes me very lucky indeed, since most people are not blessed with such sheer good fortune. But in thinking at this moment in broader terms, it's important to express some less parochial thoughts. Becoming a documentary cameraman was the fulfillment of an ambition, and gave me a jack-of-all-trades education unavailable in the schools most people attend. But seeing more of the real world as I did also confronted me with many contradictions. I've had the boat rocked many times by the circumstances of people's lives, or a gradual awareness that other cultures I was led to believe were uncivilized or barbaric were really not so at all. Whilst those impressions fueled responsive energy, they were always to be buried when back home and required to give to my family what they needed. It's ironic that people not in the industry often ask those who are how they sustain relationships when apart from each other for as often and long as they are. Deborah, my wife, is involved in film as well, so I think we probably have a better ride than most, but we've both been less successfully married before and have little doubt that working in a profession as demanding as film played a big role in the demise of our previous relationships. I've had enough experience now at combining both things to really hope that I've learned how to survive in both camps. Certainly I know that being away can become less of a problem than being back, either because of not having been offered any work, causing insecurity and usually impossible behaviour, or because involvement in films that deal with some of the world's more serious problems can shake you up emotionally. In the past I know that having returned home from such trips, I've had enormous difficulty in immediately fitting back into a home environment that by comparison seemed unjustly comfortable and safe. I have been guilty of not understanding when a partner resists the idea of my going away yet again, and also of feeling insecure when they really don't seem to mind at all, and rightly have developed so many interests that I feel my return home to be disruptive. Cameramen I know, being one, do I'm afraid have a few other problems specific to their trade. Broadly speaking, a life constantly away from home, loved ones and real things to do with one's own life, and the indelible nature of their work are at the heart of things. Missing a shot, or messing up one you haven't missed can take on dimensions appropriate in normal people to the loss of a limb. It's very possible to become obsessional and see most of life though a square black hole, although I think I detect a slight improvement in my own obsessive tendencies since the introduction of 16 x 9. In documentary we become professional onlookers to other people's lives, bringing perceptions and understanding to bear that are dangerously spent when back in the company of loved ones.

Now comes the big one, the giant amongst paradoxes. In the pursuance of film truths and these days there is a proliferation of them, we have caused unreality with our sustained reality. We can make rain or cold glisten, the filthiest industrial plant look beautiful when the sun is in the right place, and turn off from the reality of human misery, seeing only a beautiful image. The risk of seeming to be a hopeless neurotic is, I guess, an inevitable by-product of a genuine attempt at honesty. To continue this cleansing purge I would ask: How often do we ask the audiences for their reaction to our moral crusades? Recently, whilst waiting by a roadside near Oxford in England to film a main character driving by in his car, two young boys walked up to us. "What's happened?" they asked. In their minds there could be no other reason for a camera crew setting up shop by a busy road. Another occasion was whilst filming a series examining all the parties concerned with the problem of cruelty to children. One of the characters under investigation by the National Society for the Prevention of Cruelty to Children had allowed us all into his home, and had separated the film's interest in him from the kudos to be gained in appearing on the same television screen as the many video heroes that he, his family, and immediate neighbours regularly watched. In the final analysis, filmmaking is a necessarily obsessional vocation but should never cease to be measured against real life—that is the one that most ordinary people have to live, and that we make films about. Without it, the dramatist or the documentarist would have no subjects for their essays, nothing to laugh or cry about , protest, celebrate, or dream about. I have always been excited by films' potential to encapsulate ideas, express emotion, and sway an audience, and have consistently occupied my mind with better ways of achieving those things on film, either by means of the tools at our disposal or periodic adjustments to the language. But the most important consideration of all is surely knowing our audience both before and after the films we all make; otherwise life on a ground glass even in documentary can never be real life.

The present criteria for awarding franchises to companies bidding for space on the commercial television network, successfully outbidding rivals, have left smaller companies strapped for cash with which to make programmes; and with advertising revenues spread more thinly between more operators, cheaper programming is the order of the day. Documentary, other than natural history, doesn't come into that category, so less of them are being made. The BBC under pressure to perform efficiently, their funding via compulsory licenses being in the long term unguaranteed, has also to compete more openly with commercial television for audience share, in readiness for the possibility that the license will be scrapped and the corporation placed in the position of having to sell its own air time. Channel Four, constantly accused of pandering to minorities, something it was legislated to do, has fought off accusations of representing "one-legged lesbians" to become well regarded by audiences and other broadcasters alike. At present though, its substantial profits are being eyed enviously by government and business interests as making it ripe for privatization. There are an awful lot of independents and individuals anxious to not see that happen. Aside from the fact that it has almost single-handedly breathed new life into Britain's feature film industry, its publishing house policy and commitment to innovative programming provides rival networks with an important role model. Ironically the perceived crisis in broadcasting has caused documentary filmmakers to start a long overdue dialogue with each other. Every year, Birmingham and Sheffield, and Bristol for natural history filmmakers, play host to major and well–attended conferences. The hope in the minds of all who attend is that new ways, methods, ideas, and outlets might be found to ensure the survival of documentary. Once again the changes are accompanied by new technologies. Whilst I was never fascinated by Betacam, as in my view it raised our operational profile and I would add caused programme makers to become steadily more undisciplined, I do feel a value in the DVC technology most recently introduced. It offers once again the opportunity for a low profile presence in the lives of people being filmed. So-called amateurs and professionals have become almost indistinguishable, and given that effective real life filmmaking is in part a question of public perceptions of the process and its aims, for the time being the barriers are down again. However, I recently sat watching a demonstration of the new results with a distinguished documentarist who made a very interesting comment in response to the *hit 'em in the eye* New York Casualty sequence being offered up. He saw and heard nothing beyond the single dimension coverage of a focus concerned only with immediacy and in that case shock value. Will the new technology cause the loss of that most valuable element of the filmmaker's art? Authored ideas and perceptions, relayed to an audience via many layers, are paint and canvas for the good film storyteller. If for reasons of economics and audience ratings, shock and voyeurism take precedence over considered and crafted narratives then we shall be doing very little more than echoing the entertainment policy of the Emperor Nero and arguably for much the same reasons.

At this time documentary still has its champions: Channel Four and BBC 2 in Britain and the new players, Arts and Entertainment, National Geographic, Discovery Channel in the U.S.A., Canal Plus, Arte and others in Europe. We are fortunate that in Britain there are many talented filmmakers who still use the film language in an inventive way, steadily shifting away from talking head narratives and fly-on-the-wall in favor of more considered essays. I look back on my last year and take heart from the experience of having photographed Paul Watson's *The Home*, a wonderfully sensitive film dealing with our society's treatment of the elderly. I remain optimistic, as for all those wanting to say something through the medium of film, there are still a lot of people in broadcasting willing to listen and provide the necessary platform. In line with Orson Welles's famous remark concerning the Swiss, when he pointed out that several hundred years of peace and stability had only produced the cuckoo clock, it is perhaps appropriate that it's taken a crisis to cause all concerned with documentary to examine what they are saying and how they are saying it. I suppose then it has to be three cheers for the crisis. Oh, and let's send a message up to Robert Flaherty, John Grierson, and many others: "Dear All, I think that things might be fine down here—perhaps you can lay back down again."

Mike Fox started his career as a theatrical projectionist in the U.K., then film lab technician, assistant optical printer and clapper loader, assistant film editor, assistant film cameraman, and eventually DP and director. His work on nearly seventy films all over the world includes directing such specials as *In the Wild - Lions* with Anthony Hopkins, the BBC *No Ordinary People*, and the Granada feature documentary, *Lost Children of the Empire*.

THE DOCUMENTARY:
ENTERTAIN AND INFORM, NOT JUST INFORM

DAVID L. WOLPER

When I was a kid I saw a film in class that I really enjoyed. I went home and told my dad and his reply was, "If you had fun you probably didn't learn anything." Boy, was he wrong! To try to make documentaries that were entertaining as well as informative became my motivation in later years.

"The creative interpretation of reality" is the definition of the documentary by John Grierson. Not just reality as a news documentary, with talking heads or ciné-ma vérité; a documentary, yes, but not the only way.

In making documentaries using stock footage to tell a story, filming reenactments or real events as they happen, I always try to tell a story dramatically with a beginning, middle and end, using all the tools at my command: music, narration, interviews, stock footage, stills, etc.

Get the information and make it entertaining. My motto has always been "inform and entertain," not just inform. Make documentaries to tell a story to people who don't know the information, not just a few people who already know and just want to confirm it.

Before television, documentaries were made for specific audiences. But with the advent of television, audiences for the documentary multiplied by the millions so now new television documentaries are made for much larger audiences and require a much more dramatic approach.

When I decided to do documentaries, educating a large amount of people was my goal. My first documentary, *The Race for Space*, was a news special on the race between the United States and the Soviet Union to get into space, with exclusive footage from the Soviet Union. It was a hard news documentary and in the fifties, sixties and seventies, and even today, the television networks in America were not prepared to put on independently produced, hard news documentaries. They could only be done by the news departments, in-house. In order to get my programs on the networks I had to create different forms of documentaries. I made associations with the National Geographic Society, allowing those documentaries to get on the networks. I also made an association with Jacques Cousteau, the Smithsonian Institution, and the *American Heritage* magazine. I was able to get those documentaries on the networks. We had to create new forms. Believe it or not, the first Hollywood documentary compilation film was produced by my company. And we did *Appointment with Destiny*, a predecessor to today's docudrama.

Nanook of the North, Robert Flaherty's epic documentary, was comprised of scenes as they happened and re-created scenes, a no-no to early network news departments. The art of the documentary was so restricted by CBS News in the 1950s and 1960s that music in a documentary was forbidden, and re-creations were a sin! Creative interpretation means just what it says. We documentarians interpret in any creative way we can conceive to tell a story. Truth as we see it; honesty our rule.

But not the U.S. major network news departments. They have had a negative effect on the creative aspects of the documentary filmmaker. The networks had their own ways of doing documentaries. Deciding how documentaries should be made, they made so many rules they put themselves in a box, creatively, and affected the art of documentaries for many years, even to today. I say let's open up. Let's break free and let's create many new ways to make the documentaries interesting and exciting.

I did a television series in the 1970s called *Appointment with Destiny*. We had actors re-create scenes from the past before there were cameras. We re-created as though cameras were actually available at the time. We interviewed people as though they were people on the street. We even did a documentary on the crucifixion of Christ. We made the film look old by putting a golden tone on the film. We called it our "religious gold." We did films on Cortez and Montezuma, Dillinger, Grant and Lee at Appomattox, etc.

One of the programs we did was *The Plot to Murder Hitler*. In order to tell our story, we re–created scenes with Hitler to fill in where film on Hitler didn't exist. Shot in black and white and with a few scratches on it, the scenes looked exactly like the real Hitler footage (our Hitler looked like the real Hitler). The *New York Times* reviewer said it was a dangerous film precedent. He couldn't tell the real Hitler scenes from the scenes that we had done. We considered it a great review. We had done our job so well he couldn't tell the difference.

While re–creations were looked upon negatively in the past, today most television networks use that method to tell stories when film footage is not available. It's about time!

As we reach the end of the twentieth century, many documentaries are going to be made, summing up different events, different aspects of the century. I myself, am in production on two: a ten-hour documentary on the *Great Events of the Twentieth Century*, and a ten–hour documentary on the *Great People of the Twentieth Century*. While we are going to review the events and the people of this century, entertainment again comes into my mind and the entertainment aspect of these two documentaries will be emotion. They won't just tell a story of incidents. We'll read letters and poems, use music of the period, and create every way we can to give the emotional, personal aspect to the story.

Emotion is just another word for entertaining. Television documentaries have to be emotional and entertaining to the large audiences they are reaching today.

While they may be entertaining, one thing has to be kept in mind—the honesty and integrity of the documentary filmmaker. In the creative interpretation, honesty and truth have to remain no matter how many elements of entertainment we add to it. Today the documentary is very much alive and flourishing, more so now than it has ever been since its inception. With cable, satellite, home video, computers, etc., there are so many outlets for our work compared to the past. How lucky we are today! Before the 1940s, there wasn't much prospect for the documentarian. Only small theaters, university classrooms, or specific conferences were the outlets for the documentary filmmakers. Today we have it all. So many more opportunities to create new and exciting ways to tell our story. The documentary is still one of the great ways of communicating in human society. And as we go into the twenty-first century the documentary will not only be a form of telling us what has happened in the past, but will interpret the reality of events in the future.

MAESTRO

Jillian Robinson

It was my first major production. I was living in London and my partner was a veteran producer with many award-winning shows under his belt. I had lived in Italy and become enchanted with Italian culture, so when my partner suggested a series tracing the history of music in Venice I agreed but wondered how we could make it accessible to an audience beyond existing local music fans—maybe those who wished to visit Venice and see it through a new lens or armchair travelers or prospective classical music fans. We could add a strong travel element, create a sense of place, and have the music inextricably tied to the vitality of the city. I had fallen in love with the "city of dreams" years before. Communicating the wonder of this place would become a passion—and a mission.

We began pitching the project to British broadcasters. One said they loved it— and then "thanks but no thanks" for no apparent reason. Another was intrigued but daunted by our budget. In the American market we found an enthusiastic executive at a PBS station who championed the project for a long time. But when we decided to lose one editorial comment we also lost him.

Then there was a bright light. A new commissioning editor for music had been appointed at London's Channel Four, reputedly a sharp woman with a lot of vision. Rather than waiting until her Channel Four desk was inundated with proposals from producers around the world, we sent our treatment to her at her old job. When she arrived at Channel Four, we were among the first meetings she requested.

Finally, an executive who shared our vision and fully embraced the new ground we wanted to tread. At the time, the majority of British classical music productions were done in halls and studios where acoustics had been tested and could be optimally controlled. We wanted to shake some of the formality. Of course, a five-hour series tracing the history of classical music in Venice had to have superior sound, but we also knew we could have fun with the shows: stage the music "busking" in St. Marks square, watch them play on the beautiful exterior staircase, *scala de bovilo*, hear them playing in an old brothel. We knew their sounds should be from the streets, canals, and courtyards of the city. People wished us luck but knew this would never get funded; it was a big budget, it was breaking new ground, and it was ambitious. But Channel Four's music editor was not daunted and agreed to fund a large part of the budget.

Then began the seemingly endless trips to Cannes—MIP, MIPCOM, Mifed—to secure the remainder of the funding. Breakfast with German broadcaster, lunch with the Japanese, coffee with the Scandinavians. We sparked a lot of interest but secured no funding. We began to realize we were facing another hurdle: there was a small, select group of producers and broadcasters who were producing the majority of classical music programming. My partner had produced numerous music specials but very little classical music, so we were not members of this club. Broadcasters were not quick to part with funds to producers new to this genre. This was not an insurmountable hurdle; just another barrier to entry. After numerous days of traipsing the halls of Cannes' Palais de Festival—sore feet, talked out, a few remaining sales brochures in hand—we finally secured another sizable part of the budget from the French cultural channel La Sept.

Now we only had the last part of the budget to raise. As the months dragged on, we faced the challenge of keeping our key talent enthused. One of the world's leading musicologists, H.C. Robbins-Landon had helped develop the series. Venice expert and author, Lord John Julius Norwich had agreed to host the series (even though he, too, would later confess that he thought it was a wonderful concept but imagined it would be impossible to raise the production money). They were both busy men and could not wait indefinitely for the green light on this project. We also began to worry that Channel Four's enthusiasm would flag, although it never did.

We were nearly there—and there was another bright prospect. A major record company was interested in our concept. The head buyer took us to lunch. British protocol I had been told, said you never talked business immediately. Wait until the second course, or even the "pudding." This was terribly difficult for me as a forthright American woman (especially when we were so close) But, knowing I was in a foreign land, I waited patiently until our host raised the subject over port and dessert. It was a brief conversation, reviewing concept and money. A quarter of a million pounds? Sure, he said, no problem. We were elated. Deal letters flowed, animated conversations and production planning followed. Our office was buzzing and the talent was ready to go. Our dream project was finally a "go."

But the check never came. The company had a policy change and were no longer investing in this type of project. When the dust settled, we felt like we were back at square one.

Another record company began to court us. They had the money to spend and loved the concept - but wanted to film all of the music in studios, preferably in Britain. We were tempted by the offer; the endless fund-raising had begun to seriously dampen our spirits. But we could not make that editorial compromise. We had come too far and knew too deeply that our approach was the right one. This was to be a series shot entirely on location in Venice, and the music and the city were to be inextricably entwined.

By now, we had other projects in the pipeline and were spending much of our time in L.A., trying to develop the American side of our business. But our music series, *Maestro*, was still on our minds. After long days of work, we would occasionally take walks on the Santa Monica beach and, while Channel Four and Cannes seemed very far away, *Maestro* was not. Our passion to make it had not faded in the least.

The final stages happened quickly and almost serendipitously. A gutsy distributor who saw the strong sales potential of the series projected how much she could make from the series and stood firmly behind her figures. She believed in us, she believed in our project, and knew she could sell it. We sold the proposition to a British bank (then a very rare deal in Britain). We ignored the thinking that no business gets done between Christmas and New Year's, flew back to Britain and signed final production contracts the day before Christmas.

After nearly three years of tireless fund-raising, it was now, *finally*, time to open the champagne. The pre-production was truly a joy. We had planned to have different directors for each of the five programs, and we secured the best music directors in Britain. We attracted outstanding cameramen and crew and found the additional talent were all falling into place. Everyone looked forward to being in Venice and pushing the envelope a bit.

The production had its challenges, like any other: transporting an uninsurable eighteenth-century organ across the lagoon in a raging storm; a crew member whose personal problems began to consume her so that she ultimately needed to be sent home; arguments in broken Italian with obstinate gondolier men who routinely insisted on taking their lunch when the crew was on tight deadlines to reach the next location; sparring crew members who were interested in the same woman; losing an outdoor venue twelve hours before a key talent was flying in from Milan for a one-time performance, and spending the night drinking coffee and numerous cognacs convincing the Italian navy to let us use their deck (and officers) as an alternate venue. But the challenges did not detract from our passion at all. We were delighted to be making the series and believed in what we were doing. Our enthusiasm and commitment were contagious. One of our interviewees (Erica Jong) said one night on location that this was the happiest crew she had ever worked with. We explained our hope and belief that the work of a positive production team manifests itself in the final product.

We would like to think it did. The series was a real success. We had a gala premier party with British royalty in attendance, Channel Four got excellent ratings when the series premiered; the press loved it (from *Opera* magazine, who lauded its artistic and musical integrity, to the daily tabloids who praised our approach and ability to broaden the audience); it was highly praised in France, the series has sold in over forty countries (apparently all of those meetings in Cannes paid off, and our distributor could hold her head high!); and we received numerous letters from American, British, and Canadian viewers, who commended us on our approach, saying they had not been classical music fans before but could become converted now!

We, too, prospered after this: Two American companies saw the series and swiftly commissioned new projects with us, Lord Norwich joined the board of our company, H.C. Robbins-Landon became one of my partner's dearest friends and long-term business associates, Erica Jong and I agreed to develop a new series together and corporate investors began to court us. (It was interesting--the investors consistently claimed they were attracted to our persistence and tenacity.)

And now? As I reflect on this many years later, sitting at my desk as a public television executive, I wonder how this experience has shaped me today. Certainly, it has shaped my personal producing style. When I executive-produce or produce a show, I suppose my personal "stamp" is that I like to create a strong "sense of place" in films, and celebrate a part of the world through this medium. I also like to think I am a more active listener. When a producer comes to me with a true passion project, a track record, and the unblighted determination to get the project made, I listen. I also remind myself of what success can be achieved when television is made by individuals, rather than by committees; when producers with a clear vision and talent are left to their own devices to deliver that vision. And, I remember that—ultimately—persistence pays.

Jillian Robinson is currently manager of Program Development & Production at KAET, the PBS affiliate in Phoenix. In addition to her responsibilities to develop and oversee the production of all new KAET specials and series, Robinson has executive-produced or produced such KAET programs as: *Barry Goldwater: Photographs & Memories*, an Emmy award-winning documentary, broadcast nationally on PBS; *Over Arizona*, an Emmy award-winning coproduction with KCTS/Seattle; *Arizona Memories*; and the "Best of the West" award-winning *Legends & Dreamers*, a partnership with the internationally distributed travel/culture magazine Arizona Highways. Prior to joining KAET, Robinson was president of London-based Robclif Productions for six years, where she produced such series as *Maestro* and *Unseen Treasures* for The Discovery Channel. Previously, she was a script consultant for ITC Entertainment/London and a producer for Tim Miller Productions.

WRITING FOR REAL

ALEXIS KRASILOVSKY

Resisting the Inner Voice

After my last grant and a national tour led to practically zero income, I swore I'd never make another documentary. Bailed out of near–bankruptcy, I promised that I'd never do anything that hinted of noncommerciality again. Just when documentaries were becoming fashionable, I was going to sell out—or try to, so help me God! Two weeks later the 1994 Northridge earthquake hit and twenty years of documentary and experimental films plummeted to the ground.

I am a professor at California State University Northridge: that was the epicenter. All those lectures on the Mythic Journey—I'd taken them seriously. I'd staked my life on listening to my characters dictate wild, unimaginable tales the likes of which Hollywood had never seen, but was gonna die for.

I am the same person who used to memorize impassioned speeches for Millennium, in lower Manhattan, on how film fit into the revolution, and how the reality

Filmmaker Alexis Krasilovsky

of a documentary could change the world. The lights dimmed, and out of the darkness my first documentary sputtered out of the 16mm projector, starring Andy Warhol, Bob Rauschenberg, and Michael Snow. The film culminated in an atom bomb, blowing up the New York art world, and a quote from the Black Panthers: "Don't talk anymore; put some theory into practice." Decades later, I'm still theorizing. As for the film, it's still in distribution, but with the combined offerings of an entire adulthood devoted to documentaries and experimental films, I could have raked in more as a welfare mother.

Middle-aged hypocrite that I am, and $30,000 in debt over my latest documentary, I'm even more passionate (that buzzword again!) about making the break into feature films. Perhaps because I can dare to say more about reality—which I profess to know a thing or two about—through collective dreaming.

But when you've lived your childhood in a state of art akin to religion, and you find the art world crumbling, you wake up. When you flee the phony worlds of New York and L.A. for the warmth of the "fly-over people" so derided by bi-coastalites, only to be floored by the blues down in rural Mississippi, you wake up, paying homage to soul-penetrating sounds through your sync-sound vision. Not only do the blues, social struggles, and urban life beckon and demand witness, but when the earth opens up and destroys the very classrooms where you've been lecturing on "Universal Structure," why, what else is there but to grab your camera from the bottom of the junk pile of student papers, scripts, and broken pieces of ceiling, and tell how you feel on film?

I never intended to write a script for *Epicenter U*. I would have preferred operating like Frederick Wiseman, filming hours and hours of a mental hospital or other institution, free-fall. But even after donations of film from Kodak, Agfa and Fuji, free Panavision cameras and the like—practically the entire industry was taking pity on film students and their professor at a university without classrooms or equipment—credit cards still limited us to barely 8,000 feet of film. We wanted to finish our film in time for "Earthquake Recovery Week" to maximize the possibility of our film helping our city to heal. When Amy Tompkins turned down a 35mm feature in favor of editing what we'd shot, it had to be structured, and fast.

Writing for Real: The Process

I had already spent the summer transcribing the hours of interviews and logging an endless collage of rubble, aerial shots, and broken buildings. Unlike some of my previous films, hiring trained anthropologists to provide research, our research was conducted on the spot, plus a little day-to-day newspaper digging. Our detailed lists were long enough to make a book.

What our editor needed was a two-column script: picture on the left, sound on the right, and double-spaced to allow room for such technical necessities as code numbers and footage counts. Easier said than done—my word processor refused to budge from the right column to the left in the middle of a creative fit. I spent what felt like hours fixing format, mainly because I hadn't committed the ten minutes or so to master two-column format in advance.

Nevertheless, writing *Epicenter U.* on a word processor was a major improvement over the way I used to work. On *Beale Street*, I had had to thumb through pages and pages of dog-eared, irregularly cut pieces of legal paper and/or index cards, looking for the perfect, missing quote from the witness of the riots which followed the last march of Martin Luther King. This time, all I had to do was hit "F10" and poof! Vice President Al Gore commenting on $8.6 billion of earthquake relief for Los Angeles.

The question of narration comes up every time I write a film. Should it be the factual "$300 million damage to the campus" variety? Do we really need to know that CSUN is the third largest university in California? *Epicenter U.* was incorporating footage shot by the students and their professor, as well as footage shot of them, comparing their layered hopes and dreams with the frustrations and sorrows of their reality. Since it was more our collective diary than a PBS special analyzing rock formations, I felt that narration was needed to provide a personal perspective. So other than the roar of the actual quake over the Richter scale, the film opens with:

> I've got a certain way of making movies. Well, my students—they're into this Hollywood glitz and glamour way of making movies. These students want two hours for one shot that you never would have gotten on film, because you can't do a Hollywood setup as reality's marching by you. I have to make my own earthquake documentary for them, with them, and hope that they will help me, because I can't make it on my own. I have to be able to be big enough not to be angry at them for the fact that mass media, especially television, has vacuumed the imagination out of their brains and substituted it with Hollywood images. They <u>do</u> have emotional lives crying out to be expressed—that's why they're taking film production. But the only way they can do it is in a glamorous, glitz, formula, genre, Hollywood way—and I have to pull that formula open if I'm going to make them see anything.

Erik Barnouw's *Documentary: A History of the Non-Fiction Film* discusses film poets such as Bert Haanstra—who wrote and produced a lifeless, sponsored film about a glass factory in order to obtain permission to film the much-loved "cine-poeme," *Glass* [1]—and "poet–documentarists" such as Standish D. Lawder, with whom I studied at Yale University in the early 1970s.[2]

In keeping with my training and background, most of my films contain poetry, although I have tried unsuccessfully to avoid the financial marginalization that poetry implies. For example, in *Exile*, my film on assimilation and the Holocaust, I hid a poem about spiritual death towards the end of the film, afraid that it might be too far-out for the PBS broadcast it ultimately received.

But for dozens of students involved in *Epicenter U.*, filming the aftermath of the Northridge Earthquake represented a chance for personal healing and growth. I felt that emotional statements could be expressed at both the forefront and the climax of the film, with the "facts" structured around them. The film would begin, I thought, with visuals cut MTV-style to the words of the poem, "The Earthquake Haggadah," which ends:

> If we heal from the earthquake
> but not our heartache,
> it might be enough.
>
> Heal from our heartache
> but not the wounds of childhood,
> never enough.
> Enough jobs, enough money,
> enough facts, sex, date rape, battery and rape,
> battered wives and children calling for mama.
> Mother Earth, come swallow us up
> in the giant cracks
> of your 6.8's
> and hug us with your molten arms
> of lava.[3]

A poem about the Northridge Meadows Apartments, where two students and fourteen others died when the second and third floors crushed the first floor, initially appeared on page 42 of the forty-four page script.[4]

While I don't believe that documentaries have plot points, exactly, each documentary strives for a unique balance between visual and audio; beginning, middle, and end; forcefulness of a given piece of information; and the beauty inherent in the images themselves. For example, my documentary short, *Just Between Me & God*, which appeared on The Learning Channel, was structured cyclically to follow the natural course of the seasons, in juxtaposition to the devastation of the natural beauty and wildlife of this spot along the Mississippi

River by the developers of a dune buggy drag race strip. I didn't start out that film with a script whose climax would portray bulldozing and murder: I had simply intended to make a pretty little nature flick to give myself a break from the heartache of the political truths we were uncovering in course of making our longer film about the death of Beale Street. Often, it is only in the course of a script-less production that the real truths of your subject are revealed, altering the focus, the structure, and even the very subject of that film.

In the case of *Epicenter U.*, it was mostly a case of creative error: the interviews with students were, in fact, disarming and compelling statements which had to appear a priori to establish the mood for which "The Earthquake Haggadah" was to provide catharsis. But since the script was written as part of the editing process, rather than as part of preproduction, the final change of structure never entered into the revisions.

The main function of the revised scripts for *Epicenter U.* was to delete over-statements such as "I thought the world had come to an end." The cutaways, which we were still shooting, more than exemplified the horror our campus felt: a roofless library, crumpled bookshelves, broken monitors, houses without chimneys or walls. Shortened, too, were official speeches, which quickly became tedious on film. We wanted to include a brief clip of President Clinton's compelling on-campus speech about the disaster, but it was delivered after the film premiered.

Some restructuring of the film occurred early on when it was discovered that one of our key interviews—a film student from India whose lifelong dream of working in Hollywood was shattered in the earthquake—was out of sync. We had structured the film to include a cross section of the multicultural community that is CSUN. Towards the end of the production, I felt that female and minority students were underrepresented on film, and arranged for additional interviews: one with T.C. Warner, a white television actress studying to become a film director; and one with Michael Young, an African-American student in the middle of directing his senior film.

Ultimately, what they had to say about the earthquake was what determined their significance and placement in the film, rather than sex or race. Before the Honorable Andrew Young's final statement of the film, addressing "the common good of humanity at a time of crisis," seemed the perfect place for Michael's upbeat statement:

If I had to tell my grandchildren about what I went through making the biggest film of my life during an earthquake, I would have to probably express to them the faith that I had. My faith was strong. I believed in the project we were doing, and the people I was working with, and no matter what technical difficulties that we were to have during the earthquake, by no means were we to shut down and stop. Even losing my house. My house was destroyed during the earthquake. And cash was looted that was supposed to go to postproduction...thousands of dollars.

Fortunately for us the Sundance Film Festival had been going on at that time, so without any notice... I was on the next plane to Utah. We had no reservations, we just got there, and decided we were going to make something happen. If you want to learn about the film biz, there is no other way.

A large part of the art and craft of writing a documentary script is the cutting and pasting of statements within an interview. It was my job as writer not only to get to the emotional underpinnings of his hour-long interview, but to delete all the merely accompanying statements, such as "The house itself is still standing, but unlivable," or "When the quake hit, my safe came away from the wall, and so someone came by and took the money that was in the safe," leaving their essence.

The other part of the process involves staying alive while you write. While one of my friends who writes nonfiction scripts for hire bought a new car and recently moved into an exclusive neighborhood, he is the exception. The day I started *Mr. Boogie Woogie* on a National Endowment for the Arts Folk Arts grant, Memphis Light Gas & Water turned off my electricity. When I got evicted midway through the making of *Beale Street*, I moved in with share-croppers (leading to yet another documentary). Lab bills are high: if you're not the one producing what you write, you may be in luck. You'll have extra time to write commercials on the side, or you can write for the Corporation for Public Broadcasting, while it still exists.

Singing the Documentary: A Swan Song

Just as, when you're cooking, the characters of a fictional screenplay will tell you what to write, you hope that the inner voice of the people you've inter-viewed, as well as the feelings mirrored in what your cinematographers have shot, will ultimately dictate the message of your documentary. Writing a documentary script prior to production, like the one Haanstra offered the glass manufacturer, or like some of the forty-five to sixty page scripts required by the National Endowment for the Humanities, might be a means to an end, but also the closest thing to death that a writer can face.[5]   But a documentary script that gives cohesion to many years or miles of film, that gives weight to the footage by careful research (without being bombastically informative), and that unearths great truths, can make a writer's life worth living. But for the majority of us, whether documentary writing carries any significant financial worth is another story.

So what is a single mother, $30,000 in debt on her last documentary, doing in a book like this? Hoping never to write another documentary, let alone a book chapter! Hoping that the real–life experiences, both in making many a film and in befriending her subjects—a sharecropping family, a community of homeless students, a hotbed of artists, a street of double-crossed souls—will fuel her fictional screenwriting. Hoping that her next script sells to Paramount for $500,000, and changes the lives of millions. Hoping to give her son more attention, plus a legacy of appreciating real life beyond the boob tube. But she will <u>never</u> write or direct another documentary.

(...barring another natural disaster, crisis, or war.)

Alexis Krasilovsky has written and directed numerous films and videos, including the documentaries *End of the Art World*, *Mr. Boogie Woogie*, *Exile* and *Epicenter U*. Her documentaries are distributed through ArtsAmerica, the Center for the Study of Southern Culture, Facets Video, New York Filmmakers Co–op, and Canyon Cinema. She is a Professor at California State University, Northridge, where she teaches screenwriting and film production. Her book, <u>Women Behind the Camera</u>, was recently published by Praeger.

NOTES:

[1] Barnouw, Erik, <u>Documentary: A History of the Non-Fiction Film</u>, Oxford University Press: London, 1981), pp 193-4.

[2] <u>Ibid</u>., pp 196-7.

[3] Krasilovsky, Alexis, "The Earthquake Haggadah," in the catalog, <u>Community Properties</u>, Dan R. Talley, ed., Huntington Beach Art Center, Huntington Beach, California, 1995, p. 48, and the film <u>Epicenter U</u>. , Alexis Krasilovsky, producer, Rafael Film, Los Angeles, California, 1995.

[4] Krasilovsky, Alexis, "The Three Pigs," in "Of Spinners and Screenplays: A Woman's Journey Into Adaptation," <u>Creative Screenwriting</u>, Vol. 1 No. 3, Fall 1994, pp. 67-68.

[5] Abrash, Barbara, "Independents and the NEH," in <u>The Independent</u>, Vol. 18, No. 4, May 1995, pp 32-33. "Connie [Field] praises the agency but calls the script requirements a 'creative waste.'"

NOTES FROM JAPAN

CHRISTOPHER FRYMAN

A tiny lady, Mrs. Chiba, ninety-one years of age, old in body but young in spirit, sits by her weaving looms chewing the stalks of a hemp plant. It is part of the preparation for her art. She is a linen weaver and dyer and she handles the complete process on her own with a little help from her daughter. She is a Living National Treasure, a designation and award the Japanese government gives to special craftspeople. She was the subject of my first major nonfiction assignment for a National Geographic Television Special. It was a glimpse of a traditional Japan that is rarely seen, an aspect of the country that has largely vanished. The disappearance of the nonfiction film is a similar story.

Log riding festival. Japan.

Since broaching the half-century mark I find myself more reflective about my life and my work and also about the progress and changes that have been happening in this world.

Having spent most of my working life in Japan gives me a certain perspective. When I arrived in Tokyo in 1973 I had already established myself elsewhere as a cinematographer. It was relatively easy to find work, though a few Japanese were surprised a foreigner would want to work here. "Has Japan become a respectable country?" asked a worker in an electronics factory I was filming in.

I found work with Dentsu, soon to be become the biggest ad agency in the world. My job was to direct and edit TV commercials for the second best selling cola. In reality my job was to liaise between the American executive and the Dentsu account people, but I did get to direct commercials, something I had never actually done before. Not that they were to know that. I simply answered yes to their questions about what I could do. They were nervous about dealing with Americans. I learned a lot. I obtained work in Japanese nonfiction films. Not for television but for organizations like the Japan National Tourist Organization, and some companies on their industrial films about how well they made steel or soap. They were made in 35mm, and they all looked beautiful. The company films were quite boring, but the tourist films were wonderful to work on. I filmed famous sites of Japan, traditional craftsmen, potters and paper-makers, and generally saw an old traditional side of Japan which has largely disappeared. I think to the sponsors it was all just a product, but inadvertently some of the most exquisitely photographed films were made about the country.

In the late seventies I was fortunate to make good contacts with National Geographic and the BBC. These were steps for me into what could be considered a better class of nonfiction film. Certainly the producers were keen to make something of value, something artistic.

Ruby mining in Thailand. "National Geographic"

I have been in the film and TV business for more than thirty-five years. Fifteen years into my career I found myself in Japan. What took me there was the shooting of a film, and what kept me there was my love for a beautiful Japanese woman. She was my guide and interpreter, and thereafter became my wife and the mother of our son. Together we formed a film production company in Tokyo. Twenty years later, I am still in Japan, and going through a change of professions.

When I began working in this business things were very different. In 1959 I joined the Canadian Broadcasting Corporation in Toronto as an assistant working in the television studios. All studio programs were broadcast live at the time. Videotape was yet to arrive. The feeling all of us had at the time was that we were participating in something like theater with a battery of black and white electronic tube cameras as audience. We rehearsed as one would for a drama in the theater. Rehearsals for many days. And then finally the live broadcast time. Nine p.m. and the countdown: Five, four, three, two, one, and off we went. It was very exciting for us in the studio, and it was an experience for the audience at home. If a mistake was made, that was just too bad. Sometimes a camera would break down in the middle of a show, and the remedy was often to give it a sharp slap on the side. Audible enough so the audience at home must have wondered what was going on.

In those days there was a kind of apprenticeship system. I started out as an assistant to a studio cameraman. My job was to keep the thick camera cable out from under his feet while he maneuvered the camera on the studio floor. There were no zoom lenses; just four lenses on a rotating turret. Camera movement was accomplished by moving the camera. I was kicked once by the cameraman for falling asleep sitting on the cable and he couldn't budge his camera. It was a shock but something I needed to wake me up and spur me to learn properly. We were doing an opera at the time, *Othello* in English. I remember Richard Cassilly was the tenor playing Othello. The two-inch Ampex videotape recorders had been purchased recently by the CBC and each act was performed in complete, directly to tape. Every scene was done live to tape except for a short prerecorded bit of music because the set was so big. It took up the whole studio and there was no way to get a boom mike in. The orchestra was a mile away in a radio studio and monitors were strung up all over the studio so the singers could see the conductor. It was an amazing achievement when I look back on it. There were many productions of this size. Macbeth was performed with a newcomer brought over from Scotland to play the main role. It was Sean Connery, but none of us at the time knew who he was, only that his performance was amazing. The great choreographer George Ballanchine took over our studios for one of his ballets. He was a guest artist invited, as they all were at the time, by the CBC, and he promptly dictated the height of the cameras, very low, and had the video engineers stretch the pictures vertically so his dancers would look even slimmer and taller than they really were. I was only nineteen at the time, innocent and unaware of the potential greatness of this television world.

The variety of programs was astounding; Shakespeare drama, modern plays, opera, symphonic and jazz bands, as well as "intelligent" talk and game shows. There were educational shows teaching the audience everything from cooking to how to fix your house or car, or learn a language. The whole culture range was covered. These have largely disappeared.

There were times when television was seen, by the powers in charge, as an art medium. Programs like the "Hallmark" drama series demonstrated this; possibly the finest example was the commissioning, by CBS TV, of Igor Stravinsky to create an opera especially for television.

When I think about nonfiction films I can wonder what my interest is. There is the chance to see firsthand many aspects of the world. I don't know whether I have really thought consciously about nonfiction films, but most of my work has been in that field. The range is from the northern cold climes of Canada to the hot steaming jungles of Papua New Guinea. In the North of Manitoba, Fort Churchill, I was an assistant film cameraman with Christopher Chapman, a great Canadian documentary filmmaker. The old abandoned military fort was extremely cold and we went there by helicopter. It is really quite far north and isolated. The helicopter left and was going to pick us up later.

The weather turned very bad and we thought we were going to be stuck there, in the open, and with nothing to eat but chocolate bars. I remember being not the least bit frightened, even though the hours went by and it got very dark and stormy. At the very moment we were beginning to feel apprehensive and not believing the helicopter could manage to come back, it suddenly appeared out of the darkness and rescued us. We got out of there with a great sense of relief, but when I look back on it (1968) I can only think that it is just a part of my going through life living everything as it comes along. I have never had a regular 9 to 5 job so I cannot imagine being not as free as I have always been. The film was for the Hudson's Bay Company, one of Canada's big department stores. The history, though, is really that of Canada. The great fur traders of bygone days is what the Hudson's Bay Company was originally. Is it a nonfiction film or a PR film? Modern stores were included in the film as a concession to the client, but despite this it was a brilliant film with some incredible scenes. One showed a beaver dissolving to a fur coat.

When I saw it during the first screening it made me shiver. This film, shot in 35mm, was never shown on TV, never shown in movie theaters; indeed I don't know where it was seen other than at a board meeting and anniversary celebration. What a waste. But it is nevertheless a nonfiction film about the history of Canada, an intention of the director, and probably not realized that much by the company people.

I was director of the Papua New Guinea Tourist Board Film Unit in 1972-73 (nonexistent now), and we supposedly made films to attract tourists to the country. It was run by a madman whose hero, secretly, was Hitler. In two years we made exactly two films. When I made the films I also made a special attempt to go to places that tourists could never get to. Are they tourist films? Are they nonfiction? When I was in PNG I was asked by the BBC to find the airplane that Admiral Yamamoto was shot down in. It was a kind of forerunner of the docudrama. I actually found the plane, with the help of others. It was in a jungle on Bougainville Island, where civil strife now exists, but in those days it was just a peaceful jungle. I have a picture of me standing on the plane. The program was *The Commanders*, stylized with images of Yamamoto playing the Japanese game of chess—not him really, just an actor with his back to the camera. Did it work? In a way yes. At least it was a stylized artistic impression created by the director, whose name I forget. It was interesting. And there were no interviews.

Papua New Guinea. Standing on Admiral Yamamoto's crashed plane.

There was a film years ago called *A Married Couple*, directed by Alan King (not the comedian). I think the cameraman was Richard Leiterman. Shamefully I don't remember the soundman, who is important because of the way this film was made. The camera team, that is the cameraman and the soundman, simply hung around all the time—in the couple's house, in all the rooms, yes, the bedroom too—wherever the couple was. The logistics were worked out so the team had their own key and just came and went whenever they wanted to. The director never attended the shoot. It took weeks of effort, lots of hanging around—more hanging around than actual filming. The couple became completely oblivious to the crew being there all the time. This effort to me represents something of value; the energies of all these people working hard to create something new. A look at a marriage in detail. And they worked out a way of doing it without trumpeting the method, simply showing the result.

Nowadays the method would be advertised; how a computer was used to make the images, or details of the special effects. The content is lost.

MY WORK IN JAPAN

Amongst the films I worked on in Japan was the National Geographic Special, the *Japanese Living Treasures*. Mrs. Chiba was my subject. I received my instructions by telex, describing the scene as it would be. In the end it was mostly different, but directing myself shooting this scene, I could concentrate on the atmosphere of the craftswoman. There were no interviews. The pictures had to tell the story. It is this creative challenge that makes something worthwhile and satisfying. It is a beguiling way to make nonfiction and accords with the aims of visual art.

Another film I worked on was *Notes On Craft* for Australian TV. It had no narration at all and no interviews. It showed potters and other craftspeople at work, interspersed with evocative scenes of Japan. The film itself was a work of art, an art that has gone from present day documentaries. There are a few exceptions, which usually only get shown at film festivals. It's a bit like preaching to the converted. Television won't allow anything out of the ordinary anymore. The Internet will allow anything, but there really is nothing to focus people's attention on what is outstanding. Anyone who clicks onto something and then finds it a bit slow going will instantly 'click' on to something else.

Television used to show an enormous variety of nonfiction films. Now it is all beginning to look the same. Everytime I see a program on the Discovery Channel, which is seldom really, it seems to me it looks the same as the one I saw before. Slick, lots of dissolves, in good taste, but bland. It is a good-looking formula that has settled in on itself as the way to be successful. There is no more adventure, and little exploration of new ideas.

I lament the decline of television. The media has succumbed to heavy commercial interests, and television has become something to fill empty spaces in people's lives, in their homes and public spaces. TV sets pervade the land, along with the Muzak and ever-present Bose speakers. People seem to dislike silence. If there were some way to turn these things off, I would be a happier person. I often turn off the tv sets in airports, but it is a fruitless activity which only incites anger in someone who comes along and turns them back on again, usually someone who works there.

Nowadays the norm is to have interviews in docos. I even had a recent conversation with a representative for the Discovery Channel when he said that they were interested in standard documentaries, you know "the kind with interviews in them." It made me sick to hear it. Nonfiction for TV is dictated by certain unwritten rules: the film must be a specified length, and it must have a narration (running through it continuously), and it must have interviews.

Formula construction is the norm. The stories are mostly predictable. Broadcasting is twenty-four hours a day or close to it, and the number of channels has increased to unbelievable numbers. More broadcasting time promising more variety has not come true. There is less money to make quality programs.

The technology moves ahead, with advances made almost daily. It is the content that is lacking. Digital television technology will allow numerous channels. It was announced in Japan that by the year 2006 there will be seven or eight hundred channels available. How is it possible to fill that amount of air time with quality material? Theoretically it sounds good, but I suspect the reality will be more pap, more lowest-common-denominator programs, more nonsense. More information overload.

The new technology includes the Internet, where a person's attention span is becoming as short as the length of time it takes to click a button. Is the Internet a worthwhile outlet for our work? The audience is huge but also anonymous. Anyone can publish and there is no arbiter of taste or quality. I prefer to think about making something for small live theaters where even a tiny group of people can directly experience the event together.

When I was a child, documentaries were shown in movies ahead of the feature. A return to this would be welcome.

There is a lack of places for film art to be seen, and I think that nonfiction films should allow for an element of art if the producer so desires. I'm not against the genres that exist, I am only against the idea that some genres are not allowed for whatever reasons there may be—economic, political correctness, or committees deciding what goes on, or... or... perhaps an unadventurous taste on the part of too many people.

The climate of nonfiction films is bleak because of the special interests of the people running projection venues. Television doesn't serve the public, it serves the owners of the companies. The best talents go into advertising. Theaters are losing out to the economy of property. Most big movie theaters are being torn down, so there goes more lost future experiences. The Internet is too anonymous. CD-ROMs are too fiddly. Video rental stores might be the best bet, though a compromise since we're still stuck with the small screen, but at least there is a good chance that the renter is actually watching.

The first films ever made were nonfiction, things like a train racing towards the camera. It scared hell out of the audience. They had never seen anything like it. It must have been quite an experience. I can imagine people leaving the theater excited and exclaiming to each other what a marvelous thing they just saw, even if it was something only a few seconds long. It was a shared experience. It is the experience which is missing from present day entertainment. Marshall McLuhan's idea of "TV as a cool medium," is something I agree with. There is not a shared experience with the 'box' sitting in a living room and/or the kitchen, bedroom; all over the place. Airport cafes show sports events on large screens, but it is just to fill in time for everybody while they wait for the rest of their lives to continue. I suppose that is nonfiction too, but it is not in the medium, it is in the event.

The new DV (digital) cameras are so good that anyone can make something on very little money. Professional budgets are getting smaller and even though the technical quality of the images may be good, the artistic qualities are losing out. The marketplace is confused. It is already becoming a difficult task for producers to determine who is good at their respective professions and who isn't. The death of the apprenticeship system means that newer people have to learn skills on their own. It's like reinventing the wheel every time. Hollywood has embraced computer image technology so much it is becoming boring. Television now uses virtual sets. The danger is that the perception of what is real or not will become distorted. Anything can now be made in the computer and the result is so realistic it will fool most people.

The new mini-disk MD is a case in point. These things cheapen or lower the quality of sound. Mini-disc uses a compression algorithm which takes out the frequencies that supposedly are not necessary for people to hear. I feel uncomfortable listening to them. I have this nagging suspicion my ears are missing something. Computer video authoring programs make images that are relatively low resolution in a small panel on a relatively small computer screen. This is a corruption of quality. Any artistic undertaking perhaps must take this into consideration, but I can't imagine Stravinksy writing music for the mini-disc. What instruments could he leave out of his orchestrations? Or how about Picasso painting for the small computer screen! No doubt they would do something interesting, but it would be limited by the technology.

I am not unwilling to tackle the new technologies. I have my own nonlinear editing system. I also have a multitrack recording system, and I use the computer as a tool for my music composition. I welcome these tools, but it comes back again and again to one's attitude toward these technologies and how one uses them.

Fortunately I am aware enough to let my knowledge and experience accumulate and lead me on to other pastures. Fade-out the cinematographer. Fade-in the composer. As I get older the act of creating something has become significant and more important to me.

Music composition and painting give me a creative freedom that costs me very little money.

Failure has turned into success for me on some occasions. The first was in 1959, when I was a late teenager. I failed high school and couldn't find a job. The CBC accepted me, whereas banks and insurance companies didn't. Work in television was not generally recognized. Nowadays universities and film schools are churning out media graduates, all competing for almost nonexistent jobs, all with dreams about the "glamorous" work it must be.

Elephant shoot in Thailand.
"National Geographic"

My career as a cinematographer is at a standstill. The work from National Geographic, Nova, Infinite Voyage, has dried up. Video has taken over most productions, and a cameraman's talent is not valued as much by the younger producers. The present way to do things is to shoot everything you see and figure it out later in the editing, at least that has been my experience, so I have given up on most video work. Film assignments are few and far between. It doesn't bother me in the least. I take it as a sign from the Gods for me to move on again and try something else.

The film industry in Japan has been going downhill ever since the great films of Kurosawa and his creative contemporaries. The Japanese generally have little interest in art, unless it makes money or is famous or trendy, while individual film-makers struggle. There isn't an active documentary scene, and only occasionally something is created by someone under stressful conditions with no funding or worthwhile distribution. The Japanese tend to work together in groups or not at all. Individuals are quite solitary and don't have much of a voice. You only have to look at Japanese television to see that the lowest common denominator holds sway. It is all for money. So now I am a bit of a recluse, hiding away making small films which rarely get seen, and nowadays concentrate mostly on composing music for other people's films, dance accompaniment, and live performance. I am lucky though to have many interests, among them painting and music. In the past few years I have turned my energies to music and I have done a few music scores, using the same producer contacts I have as a cinematographer.

What do I think about nonfiction films is the question? I have been thinking lately a lot about what life is about. Not in a philosophical sense, but more in a kind of simple way like if you know that you have twenty years to live what will you do

Christopher Fryman in helicopter.

with the time you have. Will you (and I mean me really) spend it going to meetings. If you are stuck in an airport waiting for a plane you will talk to a stranger, but otherwise not if you are really thinking about spending your time usefully. There is a creative desire to make something. On the one hand one wants to be famous, or at least recognized. This, I think, is a thought about desire that those of us who have some freedom have.

One of the problems is where documentaries can be shown. When I was a child documentaries were shown in movie theaters before the feature film. This situation doesn't exist now. In its place are commercials for the next films coming, and in Japan for local establishments advertising themselves, or tv commercials dubbed for the big screen, with terrible picture and sound quality.

The Mrs. Chibas of this world are disappearing. Remembering Papua New Guinea recalls to me how quiet much of the country was at the time. I spent a few weeks in the mountains where the people lived without any modern convenience, no electricity, no radio, no TV, nothing mechanical. Pure nature. It was an exceedingly silent place. It made me think of what it might have been like in Europe a few hundred years ago. All sound was natural or created on real musical instruments. The tones of a violin played well must have been an absolute joy to hear. People experienced life as they made it, whether it was a family event or a festival. Even a hundred years ago it must have been the same. An event where everyone gathers together bringing a certain energy to the scene, a collective energy so to speak. More recently film viewing was a true part of that feeling. In my own experience I have seen collective screening that in retrospect is exciting to consider. In Papua New Guinea, a country that resisted television for a very long time, movies were shown by a team that went from place to place setting up a screen and projector in the middle of each village. People came from miles around to attend this event which was as much of a party as a film screening. In China I saw a similar thing. Fifteen years ago I filmed in a Chinese factory that made nothing but portable 35mm film projectors. These were used throughout the whole country to show movies to people living in distant and remote places. One that I went to see was the complete coverage of a Peking opera. It lasted five hours. Another time I was with a huge military group watching a movie outdoors of a fictionalized account of a war in ancient Chinese history. The soldiers cheered loudly at every battle scene. I have witnessed boisterous viewing on the part of the Chinese in a movie theater. I Watched Chaplin's *Modern Times* with a Beijing audience which continuously talked, joking and laughing loudly throughout the film. They were especially jovial during the scene where Chaplin is fed by a machine. And of course up to the sixties (??) the American drive-in was a social center where people gathered to live life, not just to watch a movie.

Events! These are all events! People gathered together. These are the things that are disappearing from the earth. Nonfiction as part of that problem has suffered as well. Even television was not so bad in the early days. A great show was talked about. Modern shows are talked about as well but in a quite superficial way. A show like *Beverly Hills 90210* has fans in Japan who have an unbelievable passion for the details of the show's characters, the actors, and the most trivial information imaginable. There is very little awareness of what is going on in the "real" world and so there again documentaries take a very back seat.

My own films border on the artistic world. They are about the traditional world of Japan, what is left of it, the way bamboo umbrellas are made, the depiction of festivals hundreds of years old, and the manner in which these things are also vanishing. Where are you, Mrs. Chiba?

DOCUMENTARY PRODUCTION AND DISTRIBUTION: BEYOND THE YEAR 2000

MITCHELL W. BLOCK

I. A Distribution and Production Overview—Economics 101

"Bad money drives out good money" or "What happened to diners after fast food was invented?"

History can teach us many lessons, some of which we'd just as soon not know.

And, there's that famous quotation—"Those who ignore the past are condemned to repeating it"—which itself is often ignored.

What the history of documentary production and distribution can teach us is: 1) documentaries are not immune from the cycles of business development in the culture of capitalism; 2) the nature of documentary at any one time is intrinsically connected to the state of technological innovation in film and video production; and 3) the consumption of documentaries by audiences often predetermines the ideas explored—that is, the tail often wags the dog.

The earliest of documentaries were recordings of everyday life, projected within hours for audiences often including the very subjects of the films. As movies moved away from nickelodeons and open-air screenings and into theaters, the "everyday" nature of the documentary subject changed to the exotic, lands and people remote from the audiences who parted with their nickels and dimes to retreat into the darkness. Once production companies became studios and determined that ownership of theaters could control what audiences chose to view, documentaries were relegated to second on the bill, along with newsreels and cartoons, mere hors d'oeuvres for fiction and fantasy. With the appearance of television, the distinction between news and documentary began to blur: television news took its course from radio, while the documentary borrowed from the deposed theatrical newsreel. Today, the profusion of cable outlets and the explosion in home video, along with the rapid rise of the internet, are forcing major revisions in the role that documentaries can assume in the whole entertainment realm.

Of course, this century-long development is a bit more complicated than this brief summary. Some examples from this rich history:

First, funding—or, better phrased, sponsorship. The movement from the Lumière Brothers' sixty-second *vérité* moments at the turn of the century to Robert Flaherty's large-screen portraits of *Nanook* and *Moana* twenty-five years later was made by seeking capital beyond the risk-full matters of contemplated sale of the finished product and audience admission: sponsorship of films on a specific project, by companies with a vested interest in the subject matter's reaching a broad audience, moved the documentary from the common to the exotic.

The entry of the government—first in the Soviet Union and then in the U.S., in Nazi Germany, and in Britain—into this role as sponsor, allowed the exoticism of subject to focus on the contemporary social fabric, the problems and solutions, with the brilliant works of Pare Lorentz in Depression America, the propaganda of Leni Riefenstahl for the Third Reich, and John Grierson's Empire Marketing Board in the U.K. The fact that these films made their way into theaters as single-feature attractions was a surprise to almost everyone, the sponsors included. And the threat to the commercial industry whose screen time might be displaced by nonfiction successes destined to stagnate this development. Which, of course, it did.

The Second World War trumpeted a return to the theatrical documentary, for the purpose of mobilizing audiences behind the cause and educating them about the efforts, with funding coming from governmental agencies. The mobility of camera and recording devices was technology's response to the needs of combat photography, perfectly complementing the approaches of Frank Capra's films for the U.S. government (*Why We Fight*) and those wartime masterpieces from the British Documentary Movement under John Grierson (to be replicated with the astounding and continuing work of the National Film Board of Canada).

In the late 1950s, when Robert Drew got a contract from Time Inc. to produce 16mm film documentaries of events as they happened, the independent non-fiction/documentary movement as we know it today began in earnest. Hollywood studios and the television networks were never committed to the nonfiction film for obvious reasons—those having to do with money and profits. Hollywood had already determined that its newsreels could not compete with the immediacy of television and that star-driven dramas and other fictional works would never be replaced in wide audience appeal by documentary features. Television saw its opportunity for news on a national, regional, and local level, and the hosted and/or narrated newsreel form became the prevailing style. Sponsorship followed suit: local programs could be sold to local advertisers and could be produced locally, and they could be made cheaply. And the networks could build global newsgathering organizations and produce classy nonfiction shows for sponsors with a broader range than local interest. In news, covering the local scandal or murder would drive local advertising sales and make money; on a national level, occasional reports on broader topics could attract advertising and sponsorship at unheard-of levels. News, weather, and an occasional special report became the realm of documentary for television, with guaranteed sponsorship from institutions wanting time in people's homes.

Next, the technology. The networks, powered with the huge cash flow of advertising and the insatiable demand for *entertainment product*, could take a chance from time to time with the documentary form and the "special report." By the early 1960s, a new kind of documentary could appear that took advantage of faster film stocks and the lightweight sync-sound cameras and recorders. Working with small, nonunion crews, under the visionary leadership of Robert Drew, these early Drew Associates—D.A. Pennebaker, the Maysles brothers, seasoned veteran Ricky Leacock, and many others—left the fathership filled perhaps with an ideological furor and a desire to make personal and other works. As a group and as individuals, they spawned an entertainment genre that continues today, as American *cinéma vérité* or direct cinema complemented the European work of Jean Rouch and others, paving the way for Ken Burns on PBS and *When We Were Kings* in the theaters. Funding was never easy, and few of these individuals saw their tax brackets quickly rising; nevertheless, the thirst for product was there, and much later the money eventually could be found. As cable became a viable force in the 1980s, HBO and Cinemax Reel Life and the Discovery/A&E/Turner channels became the NBCs for independent documentary makers. By the 1990s, conditions simultaneously technological, economic, and cultural allowed for mass media production on a global basis, delivering a wide range of works for consumption via broadcast and cable, in theaters, for home video purchase, and in distribution to educational institutions and libraries.

Which brings up the consumption of documentaries, a matter intrinsically tied to the technological developments. In a renewed interest in education and training, starting with President John F. Kennedy's desire to get to the moon, a small industry was born. The film strip was replaced by moving image media, and in-studio production (without the cumbersome and expensive 35mm film work) was replaced by 16mm film. Educational media staffers in schools and businesses rushed to build film libraries. They grasped this technology of film as they would later embrace video, cable, satellite, computers, laserdiscs, CD-Roms, and now the internet. Billions of dollars became available for the technology race, and no one wanted to be left behind. No one questioned whether the old technology was better or if new software represented an improvement. Production costs had become so low that television entities could make works on a local level, while business and industry, education, and individual artists could enter film and video production without the burden of expensive and heavy 35mm equipment and large, skilled crews. The simplification of the technology created a new industry. And industries, of course, are founded on clearly determined markets.

From the late sixties onward, the burgeoning markets—first television, then education, soon home video, cable, and the internet—spurred the technology: the first Kem and Steenbeck editing tables showed up in New York and Los Angeles in the late sixties, and the speed of editing works increased dramatically; the Eclair, other cameras, and Nagra recorders quickly replaced sound–on–film cameras as the preferred mode of production. Single system works could be made ready in short order for the six o'clock evening news and third grade classrooms, audiences eagerly awaiting the latest product. "Shoot today—air today" became the approach for local television news, harkening back to the turn-of-the-century work of the Lumière Brothers in France, shooting workers leaving a factory at lunch, and screening their product for the same workers during dinner. This immediacy impacted also on independent documentarians, eager to get their work onto television screens.

Which brings us to the late 1970s. For a documentarian entering the field, there were lessons to be learned. The heritage of a prolonged and thoughtful production period was over: when funding had become available to Robert Drew a generation earlier, he could shoot (and shoot) on double–system equipment for airing whenever he felt ready; for filmmakers like Francis Coppola, John Cassavetes, Terry and Dennis Sanders, working on independent features and trying to break into Hollywood as college-trained or independent filmmakers, there was also Martin Scorsese's first student work being blown up to 35mm for theatrical showings; festivals like New York and San Francisco in the U.S., and Berlin, London, and Cannes abroad were showing independent work; and nonfiction filmmakers like David Wolper had garnered immense success with works for television. The new documentarian would need to survey the successes of the past and merge these with the realities of the future. Not at all an easy chore.

From the early 1960s until the 1980s, nonfiction filmmakers were able to generate sales and later ancillary income from their works by setting up limited theatrical distribution for feature–length works (in 16mm and 35mm film); clinching television sales and presales on a global basis (although opportunities were limited working with the state-owned television networks abroad); and making educational sales and rentals of 16mm prints of their works for education and/or entertainment. A few thousand "distributors" (with as little as one film to a collection numbering hundreds of titles) sold works on 16mm film for $300 to $500 per thirty-minutes, copies which cost about $2 a minute to manufacture. Nonfiction filmmakers could make a living. The manufacturers (i.e., the labs) required a capital investment of thousands of dollars and a technically proficient staff. Marketing consisted of making a few hundred to a few thousand 16mm print sales to a small customer base, numbering perhaps a few million customers with access to a 16mm projector. The home video revolution in the late 1980s turned this market upside down, in the same way that recorded music had devastated the sheet music world a half-century earlier. With what would become universal ownership of VHS format players, a market for home and educational video was born. Instead of being worth hundreds of millions of dollars, like the educational film and video business it replaced, it was worth *billions*. (By the year 2000, it's estimated that home video will be a $21 billion business—compared to television at $12 billion and theatrical distribution about $6 billion; see *Hollywood Reporter* 7-28-97.) With the VCR and home video availability, technology made it possible for people to look at films inexpensively and easily in their homes or at school, at the library or at work.

And the meaning of all of this for today's imagemaker?

Because the largest suppliers of moving image media used a strategy of making mass sales of cheap copies, most of the creators and sellers of non-mass market media were driven out of business. The multibillion dollar content side of home video was rapidly taken over by the Hollywood studios, putting out the call: "Wanted: Product People." The cost of making thirty-minute copies of media moved to less than fifty cents, or just a couple of pennies a minute. Videos of most works are practically "free": taped off of television or rented from a video store or a copy borrowed from a friend. The documentary filmmaker, producing work that ignored the entertainment concerns of the mass market, found no markets (beyond some television) to generate enough income to support the filmmaker or future work or even pay for the production costs of the work produced. The movie studios had let the Betamax decision stand, making it legal for people to tape off of free broadcast television for their own personal use. Twentieth

Century-Fox licensed many of its titles to a home video distributor, and the studios decided that it would be "ok" to let people rent video copies of their films. (The record companies had seen the writing on the wall and successfully lobbied Congress to make it illegal to rent records.)

In the midst of all this gloom and doom, the seventies and eighties found the support of Congress and a willing alliance of National Endowments and private foundations to deem nonfiction work as culturally worthwhile, fitting to fund for showings on PBS and, occasionally, on the networks. A coterie of "Ma and Pa" documentary entities joined a few "studio-type" operations at the television stations to make up this nonindustry supplier. PBS and other nonprofits (National Geographic, religious groups, etc.) flourished, along with the network nonnews documentary studios. Here and there nonfiction filmmakers were able to produce interesting works by receiving grants, sponsorships, and occasional funding from investors. Students were trained at a few of the film schools to make these works and moved into the field, while other students were trained in journalism and liberal arts programs to produce nonfiction (broadcast news) programs. There was always crossover for these individuals, but the product production costs were generally mediated by the proposed market and use. And the amounts available for funding were usually barely able to meet the costs of production.

The democracy made possible by the technology and access realized by the shift in distribution control spread benefits from one group to another: the consumer (who wanted cheap copies and did not mind paying a little more to get nonfiction work), the broadcasters (with the breakup of traditional broadcast television monopolies to multiple cable channels), the distributor (who was selling high price copies on film), and the film producer (who was handmaking the works). And in all of this movement, the position in this game for the small independent player had not changed! The new technology of distribution gave the impression that making films as a business was possible; yet, without changes in distribution methods or either the growth of paying audiences or the price of access, filmmakers would never obtain the freedom to make works on less–than–obvious topics since funding would remain conditioned by marketing and distribution deals.

Consider the careers of filmmakers honored at Sundance in the documentary and dramatic categories: the success of an independent documentary feature has not rewarded the filmmaker with easy access to the next funder, unless the filmmaker wanted to shift to fiction films. Only HBO and PBS have made serious financial commitments to nonfiction. Turner, Hearst/ABC's A&E, Discovery, Lifetime, and the other cable entities would never have enough funding to produce serious nonfiction works unless they partnered with entities such as the BBC. Lip service is paid to making "quality" works by all of the broadcasters, and yet if one uses CableAce, Emmy, and Oscar awards as measures, it is clear that most broad-casters/cable entities are not funding high-end programs.

And why should they? There was a time when "high-end" meant the precision and quality control of (at least) 16mm film. But, technology in short order has made obsolete the distribution of 16mm film, a fact making production in 16 certainly uninviting. With the consumer having the option to make, copy, and time-shift moving images, along with the growth of *direct* television (multichannels of television other than "free" broadcast television, including cable, satellite, etc.), the demise of film distribution (other than in "theatrical venues") was predicated by the growth of low–priced, non-film media production technology, with cameras and editing programs remarkably "user-friendly." This shift from the chemical-based medium of film to the digital-based medium of tape was completed by the mid-1990s. Now, practically anyone—*anyone*—can produce a "film," distribute it, and even manufacture copies: first-time filmmakers can win an Oscar or fill local community access channels with programming; the "training" is widely available (the Alternate Media Center at New York University, for example, started training people back in 1968!). It is not a welcoming field for the aspiring documentarian committed to films of quality.

Those documentary works that are found on the "best" lists of film and television critics almost always cost hundreds of thousands of dollars per hour to produce and, in many cases, take years to create (*Harlan County, Common Threads, Hoop Dreams*, etc.); these are works that pay tribute to the successes in the tradition of documentary. But the works that are showing up in the mass media are, for the most part, produced at low cost for consumption in all media by large, corporately owned television entities. The slowly made (read "expensive"), handcrafted "film" by the independent has being driven out of the market for the same reasons the distributors of these works were defeated: competition. Even public sector producers/broadcasters (PBS, PBS stations, Children's Television Workshop, Cousteau, etc.)—in an era of decreased public funding and under pressure to make money—have decided to try to control the air time available to them and to capture the Barneys and the Burns in distribution. PBS, using production funds to tie up works for distribution, has been able to bury these costs into their Byzantine accounting systems, meaning there is no need to account for their failures or their paying "advances" without regard for any business reality. PBS executives openly invite independent filmmakers to submit work and, at the same time, advise them that it is the filmmakers' responsibility to raise funds to cover the costs of showing (including promotion). If this is not the bitterest pill to swallow, they add the requirement of signing over the educational and home video rights!

II.   The Present: "Whose air is it?" The Future: "The tag belongs to us."

"The only major difference between butter and cream is the location of the fat and the water."

A Lot of Small Things That End Up Hurting Independent Filmmakers:

Have I painted too bleak a picture of the future? Not necessarily, although this portrait of where things stand bodes less than enthusiasm. While an independent filmmaker might voice reaction to someone like PBS, of "Just whose air is it, anyway?" the response for the future from such bureaucrats is, "The tag belongs to us," signaling that any economic benefit to a program's showing resides with the broadcaster, and not with the producer. There are clearly some less than promising sentiments at hand that discourage the independent.

For the broadcaster, here's the view: the producer writes the show, sets up the shots, says "action," sometimes asks the questions, and supervises the editing. So, what do we need a director for? With weak guild contracts, television entities such as PBS, A&E, Discovery, and most other producers of nonfiction work can use *producers* to make films. These producers get none of the back-end income these works generate. Other than occasional Writers Guild contract productions, most work is not done by filmmakers with collective bargaining agreements. Without strong labor agreements—playing off one hungry producer against another—costs go down and quality receives no measurable improvement. Technology allows for one-person crews and not very many people notice that freedoms are being lost: the new economics of production does not provide for healthy filmmakers. Put another way, the doctors are getting fat while the patients are starving to death.

Prompted perhaps by penurious governmental funding during the latter half of the nineties, PBS's position is that if the service (or a PBS station) puts any funding at all into a program, they want in return the off-air tag to sell the video (or the book, the record, etc.). The producer's royalty is based on the net selling price. With a 50 percent plus discount, PBS cuts the producer's share of the distributors' gross at least in half! Quasi nonprofits like National Geographic, American Masters,

Frontline, American Experience, Wonder Works, CTW, and others push for the same kind of control and slightly higher budgets than the for-profit networks (Turner, Fox, HBO, A&E, The Learning Channel, Microsoft, etc.) The idea that works can or will make money in the future has not been lost on these funders. Like the sharecroppers of America's past and some of the small farmers who rent land today, most filmmakers are working for other people who control access or funding or both. They are unable to accumulate the capital to make their own films or even to make much money from the productions they're hired to complete. As employees for-hire or as small company owners, they are at the end of the money chain and they can survive only by making more and more works more efficiently. As Tennessee Ernie Ford once said, they owe their souls to the company store.

The current system, then, is designed to produce great amounts of nonfiction product at the lowest possible cost. If a moving image costs too much to use, then a pan

or a still or a freeze frame instead becomes the style. Programs are produced to become parts of unrelated content and then are sold as parts of a series. Portraits become "Biographies," history becomes "Experience," and controversy becomes another "POV"—cookie–cutter works for cookie–cutter channels. Take a look at the video boxes (see illustrations): Academy Award–nominated works are "copied" and look-alike works fill the catalogues and video stores. The only way the Academy Award-nominated films by Ken Burns on the Brooklyn Bridge and The Statue of Liberty can compete with the look-alike video programs by A&E is to be priced at $14.95 instead of $19.95! (Again, see the illustration.) The consumer cannot tell which production is which from a quick look at the video box. Commercial mass market series such as Cops are ripe for copying. Even an independent work like Road Construction Ahead, nonfiction for children, has been copied with a similar program and then distributed by a large company. In all of this madness, what happens to the independent?

The following chart shows how the technological changes of the last forty years have changed the shape of the nonfiction media world.

"A" is the cost of stock per minute: since 1960, this factor has dropped from about $10 or so per minute to fractions of a penny in video. (In reality, the cost of 16mm filmstock, processing, work print, etc., has gone up more than 500 percent!)

"B" is the cost of labor: this factor has gone up on an individual labor unit basis but has actually *dropped* as the number of people needed to shoot films has been cut from crews of four or five (or more) to a crew of one or just a few people. These economies are also evident in postproduction. The AVID-type nonlinear editing machines make it possible to never return to negative cutting or going on-line. What you see is what you get, and you can digitally edit a work in days. The process in film takes weeks and involves complicated and expensive postproduction, requiring a dozen or more people.

"C" represents "change in productivity" which is the other side of the labor equation ("B"). Fewer people can accomplish more in less time. (How many people does an Avid replace? How much faster can one go from transfer elements to on-air using this tool?) The speed of a production tool like the Avid is of some consequence: a thoughtful, six month schedule to edit is simply too expensive. A director working with an editor and an assistant editor costs even more. And these are dollars that could be spent making more (and cheaper) productions to occupy that production time. The new lightweight digital cameras can provide reasonably high quality at relatively low costs. Does the network need expensive union-protected camerapeople with these new cameras? One needs only to look at the business practices in employment over the last few years: the reliance on part-time workers (free of the expense for benefits) and "outsizing" tasks hitherto done in–house—these are practices not lost on television units. (Consider the marvelous institution of the ATM, that automatically available dispenser of your own money for which you pay a per-use charge: how many bank tellers were put out of work by this fabulous convenience?) Independent contractors have replaced staffers at station after station and the same holds true for shooters of many documentary series. A one-person director-producer-cameraman-soundman-grip-gaffer replaces a truckload of people and equipment. (The question arises: Does the public appreciate quality, that ingredient that can come with time and thought and care and diligence, complemented by the expertise of many skilled artisans adding their specialties to the finished product? "Doubtful" is the answer, since there seems no relationship between ratings and Oscars or Emmys in the nonfiction world:

one broadcast/cable executive producer of many Oscar–nominated nonfiction works recently opined: "Our network would not make those films today."

"D" represents the cost of the production. In 1960 dollars, productions today are cheaper—more for less. On the lower budgets, with faster schedules and small crews, it is more difficult for producers to make larger fees. The Discovery (1997) $500 million dollar deal with the BBC provides a lot of money on its face until one realizes that this fee is paid over five years for over 1,000 hours of programming a year, or about $100,000 an hour!

The very technological changes that have made it possible for anyone to make videos are the same changes that are making it so difficult for the independent filmmaker to survive. Rather than spend money to buy time for filmmakers to make thoughtful projects (with reasonable schedules), the buyers of nonfiction are for the most part using the gains in productivity to make more works for less money per work, using smaller numbers of filmmakers and tighter schedules. History repeats itself. The technological changes that made possible three decades of high–end personal documentaries become responsible for making such quality works obsolete.

ADD "A" and "B" and "C" and "D" BELOW WHERE APPROPRIATE

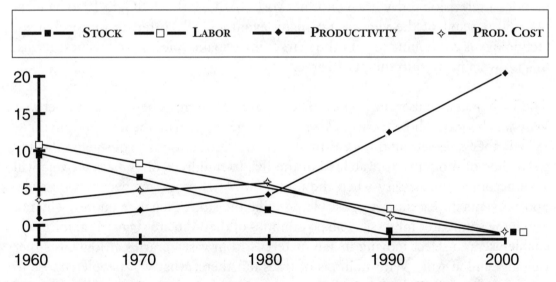

III. The Video Box—Broadcast Television to Broadcast Satellites to the Internet

"Just because one opens a good restaurant next to a McDonald's does not mean anyone will come for dinner."

"Once the Web can handle the real time distribution of moving image media, we can all be distributors. Just because we can make a work does not mean people will watch it or buy it."

There have to be some signs of relief in the offing, you might say. Perhaps. Then again, maybe not.

The current battle for control of cables and satellites and other broadcast media will be over as soon as the Web can handle full-motion media in real time. This does not mean that the world will be a better place or that filmmakers will have entered nonfiction film heaven—it only means that people will watch what they have always watched: high-end, commercially supported works from the networks. It also means that the cable companies (or the phone companies or someone) will be getting audience dollars for the wire (and switch) or signal that enters the home.

Of course, if you possess (or, even, control) product and if people can find you, they will be able to watch your product and pay you for it—if they are interested. The democracy of the Web provides the opportunity for everyone to be a channel, but it is this very democracy that will continue to push production costs down as audiences for single works become smaller, something evident on network broadcast television today: the major networks (ABC, CBS, NBC) in 1996 had less than 60 percent of the viewers on many evenings. By offering more choices, technology is continuing to split the market into smaller pieces. In business terms, this is diversification to the nth degree.

The Web offers the user the opportunity to watch programs whenever and wherever. Why watch a series show every week when it can be watched on the weekend anytime? Why bother even setting the VCR timer? Time-shifting is made obsolete. Picking a schedule of programs to watch from the five to hundreds of choices viewers will have becomes unnecessary when the infinity of ALL programs becomes possible. Sports events in real time are possible but, like the stock exchange quotes, why not watch the show later for less? The possibilities of the Web are staggering, for it will enable users to select moving image materials from vast libraries at low costs (per viewing) and at will. With millions of titles out there, what will people choose to watch? What will be the economic factors to drive their decisions? Will sponsored programs (from whatever advertisers) be given away "free" in exchange for viewership (infomercials)? The Web also invites people to give themselves their very own fifteen minutes of fame. I suspect we could see people doing horrible acts of violence on the Web, all in support of some "cause." The "bank robbery" film could become the suicide video in real time. Censorship will become a very real possibility as acts of violence and sex staged for viewers become parts of the nonfiction future. This is the terrifying possibility that true and open access provides.

The video box of today, holding the DVD or VHS copy of a work, will be replaced by a cable. How will that affect the video stores? And, if one has produced a nonfiction work, how will this change in delivery system influence the distribution process?

Ownership of product is the key. And yet, even with the legislated rights of ownership under the U.S. Copyright Act, all is not smooth sailing. There's the issue of "fair use," a growing demand by nonprofits, schools particularly, to "use" works even on the net without payment to the copyright owner (does that sound "fair"?). Little hope is seen in the statutory authority for the U.S. Copyright Office and the FBI to police the illegal performance of *This Land Is Your Land* by a summer camp group on skit night or the singing of "Happy Birthday" on *Oprah*; and neither is there much comfort in assuming the MPAA will hunt down a school librarian who purchased a copy of Jane Fonda's aerobics tape for $14.95 at K-Mart, only to screen it for the senior citizens group, a venue clearly requiring public performance rights absent from the personal–use only purchase at K-Mart. Nonetheless, to even begin to control the use and the life of a work requires ownership.

The questions for the future are the very ones that challenged the past: how will works be funded? How will the producer be paid? Who will control the wire (distribution and access)? How will copyrights be protected?

It would be simple to offer up, as conclusion to this discussion, a piece of advice to budding filmmakers: get out, while the getting's good. And to some extent, that would be sound counsel: forget about making serious works with the hope of making a living and realize that imagemaking is at best a mere job, at worst a hobby. In a game where little respect is given to creators of product—serving as pure fodder for cable and broadcast programmers to fill their schedules with works of appeal—the temptation is simply to refuse to play. And yet, are we willing to see a tradition that contains *The Sorrow and the Pity*, *Common Threads*, and so many other noteworthy hallmarks simply go down the drain? Given all the problems facing the future for imagemakers, there simply has to be some way to retain that passion and commitment from the documentary heritage. Or do we resign ourselves to the mean cinema of semistaged nonfiction that the networks and sponsors are willing to fund and that mass audiences will watch?

The future will reveal the answers to those questions.

Special acknowledgment and thanks to Tim Lyons, Betsy A. McLane and Joan von Herrmann for their thoughtful comments and assistance.

Mitchell W. Block is an Emmy Award-winning fiction and nonfiction filmmaker. He is the founder and president of Direct Cinema Limited, a specialized distribution company. Since 1979, he has been an adjunct professor for the School of Cinema Television at the University of Southern California, where he teaches independent producing and business. He is a member of the Academy of Motion Picture Arts and Sciences in the short films branch and has served on the documentary committee since 1979. He is also a member of the Television Academy and the British Academy of Film and Television Arts. He is a life member of the University Film and Video Association and, since 1994, has served on the board of the International Documentary Association.

PART VIII

TWO INTERVIEWS

Left to right: David Maysles, Albert Maysles. Far right: Paul Brennan in "Salesman".

AN INTERVIEW WITH FREDERICK WISEMAN

Michael Tobias   What really got you into nonfiction filmmaking?

Frederick Wiseman   I don't know the answer to the question other than that when I was living in Paris in the mid-fifties I shot a lot of films in 8mm, about street markets. Ordinary experience always interested me and trying to find ways of either writing about it or getting it on film. I felt that if you could capture daily life on film, you would have sequences that were dramatic, funny, sad and tragic, and that it would be possible to make dramatic documentary movies from this material. In the early sixties, I saw some of the documentaries that were being made in America. I realized that some film makers were beginning to do that and that there was no reason why I couldn't try.

MT   Were there any films in particular that you recall that stood out for you?

FW   Yes, there was a movie by Jim Lipscomb which is sometimes called *Football* and sometimes *Mooney vs. Fowl*. It's about two high school football teams getting ready for a championship game in Miami.

MT   What was it about it as a film that interested you?

FW   I realized somebody was working with a technique that I could adapt to my interests. Many of those early sync sound documentary films—not *Mooney vs. Fowl* but others—followed one person or one theme. What interested me was, and I don't know why, to make movies where the place would be the star rather than an individual. The result would give a sense of the institutional life or some aspect of community life without the restrictions of following one person. By having an intensive look at one place, there would be a possibility of finding traces of more general kinds of issues.

MT   Did you feel that there was a nonfiction place that would be appreciably different than the dramatic material that you were exposed to?

FW   When you are really lucky in a documentary film, you get sequences that you have to be a great writer to invent whereas in documentary, if you come across them and recognize them for what they are, you can use them. But you haven't written them in the way a writer invents them. The technological developments in the late 1950s, mainly portable cameras and sync sound, made it possible to record any experience where there was enough light.

MT   Frederick, I gather you're now working on your thirtieth film. But tell me about your first film.

FW   *Titicut Follies.*

MT   Why that film?

FW   Well, I had been teaching law and a course in legal medicine, and I was trying to make it more interesting, both for myself and for the students, so I began to take them on field trips to the kinds of places where their clients might end up. I was teaching at Boston University in the Law School and at that time a lot of the students became criminal defense lawyers, assistant district attorneys, or assistant U.S. attorneys. I thought the students should have a real sense of what the criminal justice system was like. Not just theoretically as described in books or appellate court decisions, but by visiting prisons, criminal trials, mental hospitals, and prisons for the mentally insane. One of the places I took the students was the Bridgewater Prison for the Criminally Insane. When I decided to stop teaching and make a documentary, since I knew Bridgewater, I thought it would make a good subject.

MT   How old were you when you made that film?

FW   Thirty-six.

MT   And the response to *Titicut Follies*?

FW   The critical response to *Titicut Follies* was very good, but the film was banned for twenty-five years.

MT   Banned in what sense?

FW   The Massachusetts Supreme Court initially banned the film from any showing and ordered the negative destroyed. On appeal, the Massachusetts Supreme Court ruled I could show the film but only to limited audiences of doctors, lawyers, legislatures, people interested in custodial care, and students in these and related fields, but not the merely curious general public. I could only show the film to people in these categories on condition that I gave the Court and the Attorney General's office a week's notice of any screening and then file an affidavit after the screening guaranteeing that from my personal knowledge that everyone who saw the film was within the class of people allowed to see it. It was rather restrictive.

MT   That's extraordinary.

FW   That condition was finally lifted in 1991 when a different Massachusetts judge said the film was protected under the First Amendment.

MT   But in all those years, didn't you fight it under the First Amendment?

FW   I fought it. The case went up to the U.S. Supreme Court which denied certiorari 4 to 3. For a number of years there was nothing I could do. Then in the mid-eighties I brought another action to have the injunction lifted and in 1991 it was, in fact, lifted.

MT   Were there other documentary filmmakers at that time who had similar censorship?

FW   Not as far as I know.

MT   And how would you characterize the reason you were singled out?

FW   Politics. Some people in the Massachusetts state government were embarrassed by the film so they raised the question of the privacy of the inmates as a way of trying to prevent the showing of the film. The state alleged that I had invaded the privacy of the inmates. My position was that the state had a conflict of interest. The conflict was that the state was responsible for the conditions shown in the film and, at the same time, they were using the inmate's right of privacy to prevent the public from knowing about those conditions. The worst thing about the case against the *Titicut Follies* was that some people who I thought were my friends turned against the film. Some people refused to talk to me or didn't defend the film even though they liked it. They were afraid that they were going to get in some kind of trouble themselves by being associated with me or the film. It was that sort of a personal betrayal that bothered me much more than the public aspect did. I thought the behavior of the state was high comedy.

MT   How would you relate the times then, vis-a-vis the Supreme Court decisions and the arena in which documentary filmmakers were working, versus now?

FW   I think the issues have been more completely litigated and there have been a lot more First Amendment cases that deal with similar issues, the most prominent example being the Pentagon papers case. However, the principle of first amendment protection was established in the mid-sixties in the case of the *New York Times v. Sullivan*. The public's right to know was found to be protected by the first amendment. However, after the Pentagon papers case writers or documentary filmmakers or journalists were more fully protected in their effort to report on governmental activities.

MT   Of course, then we got the Freedom of Information Act which certainly helped.

FW   Yes.

MT   Ok. So tell me about the post *Titicut Follies* period in your early career. You've gone on to do so many American social institution type films—*Zoo*, *High School*—what is it about that arena that moves you?

FW   I enjoy it and it's interesting and I get to travel and think about different subjects each year.

MT   I gather you make one film a year?

FW   Yes. Since 1966.

MT   And are most of these independent films?

FW   They're all independent.

MT   So you've never gone the route of advance financing from a network or distributor?

FW   Well, no, they're independent but I often get money from PBS and CPB. But, I never get full funding from them. The money comes from a combination of sources.

MT   How have you managed in lieu of complete funding to raise money?

FW   Well, there are only a limited number of sources in the world for money for documentaries. And all documentary filmmakers go to the same funding sources: the Corporation for Public Broadcasting (CPB), the Public Broadcasting Service (PBS), the National Endowment for the Arts (NEA), and the National Endowment for the Humanities (NEH). Also, from time to time, one or more European television networks. There are also some foundations that make grants.

MT   When you're making a film, are you full-time, I mean for that whole year?

FW   Yes. That's all that I do. Plus the occasional college lecture.

MT   I gather the film you're now working on concerns public housing. Another social institution. Have you ever done a film focusing upon an individual?

FW   Well, I did one fiction film. But otherwise, all the documentaries have been about institutions, public or private.

MT   I'm very intrigued by your recent *La Comédie Française*. I gather that you were the first person to ever be allowed to film that.

FW   That's right.

MT   How did it come about?

FW   I had the idea for a long time and there were some French producers that contacted me. I went to speak to the head of the Comédie Française and he gave me permission.

MT   That simple! Of course, your work is such a testament to sensitivity; the ability to really get inside and reveal the institution... When you are dealing with a palette of individuals where you've got a large canvas of different voices, different souls, so to speak, are there any specific preparatory techniques

335

that you find particularly worthwhile? When I asked a similar question, for example, to Albert Maysles, he said he never does research.

FW I don't either. I usually spend a day or two at the most at the place in advance. At La Comédie Française, I spent longer because I had to be there to deal with the various issues connected with getting permission. But, ordinarily I only spend a day or two because I like to be surprised. None of the events in the film are rehearsed or repeated. For me, every day is the first day from the point of view of surprise. I don't like to be doing research when something spectacular might be going on and I'm not prepared to get it.

MT But so many diverse filmmakers insist that research, research, research is key. That you can never do enough research.

FW My style is very instinctual. I just follow my nose and accumulate a lot of film and then figure it out in the editing. I don't figure it out in advance.

MT What kind of ratios do you typically shoot?

FW 30 to 1.

MT So not vast.

FW No.

MT That's pretty normal. Given the types of films you make, you obviously have a pretty strong nose.

FW So far.

MT What prognosis do you see with respect to true documentary?

FW I'm very bad at cultural generalizations. I would guess that there will always be some interest, a limited interest. There will always be some people who want to make documentaries. I can't say beyond that because I simply don't know.

MT Is there a role of documentary to highlight in your instance, for example, the abuses of a system?

FW   I don't think that's what I do. I don't view myself as somebody who makes exposé movies. Although *Titicut Follies* is considered an exposé movie, it is not just that and certainly the rest of my movies are not meant to be simple-minded exposés. I think it is important to show as wide a range of human activity as possible—good, bad, and indifferent. I think the subject is ordinary experience.

MT   What is that, what is ordinary?

FW   I mean just the day-to-day experience of people interests me in all the different subjects. Everybody passes through a hospital one way or another. Everybody's gone to high school. Forty or fifty million people have been in the army over the last fifty years, etc.

MT   And so for you it is an exploration of just the ordinary?

FW   It's an exploration of human behavior in its various manifestations and forms and expressions.

MT   Carl Jung once had a marvelous expression where he referred to the heroism of daily life.

FW   That's a good expression.

MT   For you, what would be a really great response to one of your films? Or, put differently, what do you hope people will get from your films?

FW   I don't. I hope they like it, but I don't think too much about it.

MT   Where's the moment for you?

FW   When I see the movie is coming together. All of editing isn't exciting, there are always three or four months of boring work getting the material in some kind of usable form. The most exciting time is the last couple months of editing. I begin to sense the movie and work to find it. That's very exciting.

MT   Your films tend to be longer than most. Is there a specific reason for that?

FW   Yes, I have a variety of obligations. There are a series of interlocking responsibilities—to the subject, to the people who've given me permission to film, and to myself.

MT   What does that all mean, responsibility?

FW   It means that the subjects are generally complex subjects and I think that I would be irresponsible if I shortened them to meet the demands of the network. My shortest film was seventy-three minutes and the longest film six hours. It is six hours not out of some wish to provoke but because I felt that was the appropriate length for the material I had. That was *Near Death*. And the seventy-three minute film was *High School*.

MT   Picasso once said that a work of art is a sum total of destruction and he said it right after he did that marvelous rendition of an anatomically correct bull in three lines. He had previously rendered countless sketches of bulls incorporating hundreds of lines to get it right. Over time he was able to hone the creature down. Do you have any sense of honing in? By that I mean, when you are in the editing process and you are honing in on your subject, how does something end up on an editing floor as opposed to in your film?

FW   Editing is a funny combination of rationality, nonrationality, and instinct. Every editor is constantly making judgments. Editing is function of the interaction of your eye, brain, and hand.

MT   You do all of your editing on film?

FW   Yes.

MT   Have you ever shot video?

FW   No.

MT   Do you ever think you will?

FW   No, not if I can help it.

MT   Why?

FW   I don't like the look of it.

MT   What about the onset of digital?

FW   I don't know what's going to happen with that. I like the idea of handling the film and I don't have the money to buy an Avid and I don't think that if I did, I would.

MT   Throughout the year, do you keep a small team that works with you?

FW   Well, no. I have an assistant who syncs up the rushes and helps with the preparation for the mix. I do all the editing myself.

MT   And I understand that in terms of music in your films you have some very strong views.

FW   Well, I don't necessarily have strong views. I don't use music that was not recorded in the context of making the film.

MT   Why is that?

FW   Because I like to be able to represent that everything that happened happened in the course of the shooting of the film.

MT   Do you ever, when you're directing, ask for retakes?

FW   No.

MT   And is there, when you are directing, is there any degree of coaching?

FW   None.

MT   And it's a one camera shoot?

FW   Right.

MT   What do you usually shoot with?

FW   An Aaton.

MT   And crew size when you are in these situations? How many people?

FW   Three.

MT   Just three. The Ansel Adams style of filmmaking.

FW   Yes, well, I mean you have to keep your crew small because you don't want
       to interfere with what is going on. And also you have to be prepared to
       move quickly. Documentary filmmaking is a sport and you have to be in shape.

MT   A shoot day is how long for you?

FW   Twelve to fourteen hours.

MT   Seven days a week?

FW   Seven days.

MT   And the duration of the shoot? *La Comédie Française*, for example?

FW   The shooting there (in Paris) was eleven weeks. That was the longest.
       Usually they're six or eight weeks.

MT   They are exhausting.

FW   Yes, they are.

MT   Do you lose weight?

FW   No. (And he adds—I never lose weight in Paris.)

MT   Are you looking at rushes when you are making your film?

FW   After about the third day of shooting you look at rushes every night.

MT   Is there one documentary that you've never made that you feel you must make?

FW   No. No, because I mean I always find each subject interesting. There are
       a lot of good subjects.

MT   Is there anything you would want to go back to and revise or look at again?

FW   Well, sure, when I look at some of the films I see mistakes that I made that I like to think I wouldn't repeat.

MT   How many of your films are available now?

FW   Thirty.

MT   They are in home video?

FW   No, they're not available in home video. But through school and college institutions.

MT   To the young aspirants who are fascinated by documentary, what would you urge them to consider if they were thinking of it as a career, or what caveats might you convey to them?

FW   Well, I'll answer that with a story. A number of years ago, a young documentary filmmaker who was about to graduate from an Ivy League college came to see me. He had written out all his questions which was very flattering and then when he asked the questions, he would write down my answers which I thought was even more flattering and his last question was, "If you have one bit of advice for a documentary filmmaker, what would it be?" I said, "Marry a rich girl." And he wrote down my answer, "Marry a rich girl."

MT   And did you?

FW   No.

AN INTERVIEW WITH ALBERT MAYSLES

Albert Maysles   Cinematography is in the worst state of affairs. It used to be you'd go to a movie for escape which is bad enough, right. We as documentary filmmakers are interested in presenting stuff that's inescapable. It's the connection and the possibilities for connection that make for life. But what we have now is distraction. You look at television, as people do for six hours. How do they do it? If you've got nothing to remember you can watch it endlessly. There's no content, nothing to wrestle with, nothing to ponder about. One of the things that excites me about documentaries is that we're trying to get, with exactitude, the heart and soul of what's going on. The peculiar thing about it is that on one level the documentary is really a surface phenomenon because it's filming reality. We don't have to go beyond reality. Reality is good enough. Get as close as you can to that, with exactitude; everything relevant to what's going on, with a keen sense of humanity.

Michael Tobias   What is the keen sense of humanity as you see it?

AM   Well, a lack of prejudice. I think that so much of the documentary has been spoiled by the prejudice of a point of view, which is an insult to the medium, although most documentary filmmakers wouldn't feel this way. That series on television—"Point of View." What a disgrace to have to use the expression POV as a marketing tool.

MT   Is it possible to be objective as a documentary filmmaker?

AM   You can get so caught up with the two extremes of being subjective versus objective that you get paralyzed so that you can't film. There are film schools that distinguish between anthropological film and subjective film, and the poor student is caught in a catch-22 situation. To my mind it's not total objectivity, but it's not partisanship. Maybe that's a better way to put it so if you are making a film where the issue, say, is abortion, we should be fair. Otherwise you're going to end up with something that's a piece of propaganda. There's a wonderful quote: The essence of tyranny is the denial of complexity. Okay. That's a beautiful thing for a documentary filmmaker to go by. It's only human to have a point of view, but do your damnedest to distance yourself from it.

MT   Conversely in the literary realm, everyone always is fond of citing a Hemingway or Camus for their simplicity.

AM   Somebody said in some wonderful advertising slogan that what we and our co-filmmakers do is so simple that nobody else knows how to do it.

MT   And Mark Twain said, "I'd shorten it if I had time."

AM   Right. A documentary filmmaker should be guided by some instinct, have a number of virtues. He should be charitable. He should approach a subject with love. You can say that's a point of view, but at the same time, it is so free and so encompassing of various elements that it doesn't bind you to a preconception. Sometimes you end up with a film that is so charitable and so nonpartisan and at the same time so perceptive—all these good things going for it—and somebody will say that *Primary* was about Kennedy and Humphrey, their primary election campaign, boy you sure had it in for Humphrey, didn't you? And then I have to tell them, to their great surprise, if you would ask us at the time who was our favorite candidate, it was Humphrey, but you don't want to control the preconceptions of the audience. I guess voters preferred Kennedy rather than Humphrey because they were impressed with Kennedy's charisma, his class, his Harvard degree, all these superficial things that Humphrey didn't have. Humphrey had the better voting record. Humphrey was more a man of the people. Humphrey was not a cold fish. I think people may be wrong about it, but if you're going to be a president, style is so important. And this is one of the things that's killing us now in our civilization. Everything is style, nothing is content. With communications today whether it's through computers, through film, through theater, or a brand of soap, whatever, there is this obsession with making everything new, innovative, just for innovation's sake.

MT   T.S. Elliott: everything derives.

AM   That's right. Documentary the way you and I make it goes back to Tolstoy. The idea came to him when in 1907 two Frenchmen came to his home and asked if they could film him on his porch. The new technology got him all excited so he said, sure. They looked at the footage later on and his comment was, now we don't have to invent stories any more. We can just go around Russia and film ordinary people.

MT   Tell me what triggered your interest in documentaries?

AM   My first desire to make a documentary came when I had the opportunity to go to Russia forty-two years ago. I thought that the news we were getting was too obsessed with what goes on behind the walls of the Kremlin. What about the grass roots, the real life of ordinary people? And, remember that wonderful *Life* magazine cover photograph by Henri Cartier Bresson of a Russian soldier eyeing a Russian woman. A very international sort of gesture. Well, then later on in 1959 there was the "Family of Man" photographs that were the sensation in Moscow. They roused more people than the automobiles and the kitchenware also on show at that time. Margaret Meade made the point that the number one need in the world then, and it's true today too, is for people to establish a common ground of understanding. It's true whether it's between Arabs and Israelis or neighbors in the same apartment building. So, I went to Russia hoping to make a film on mental hospitals. It was 1955. I borrowed a movie camera which I never even had seen before. I got it from CBS. They gave me some 100–foot rolls of film with the understanding that if they used any of the footage, they'd pay me a dollar a foot and that I would have access to the footage and eventual ownership of it. They used 14 feet, paid me $14. I then took the film that I put together to NBC and the program director, who was a friend, looked at it and said, "I suppose it has certain freak value."

MT   Freak value?

AM   Right, and then, of course, never showed it because it wasn't freaky enough. I shouldn't have been surprised because the quality of television then and now is pervaded by sensationalism, the guiding hand of a narrator.

MT   Eventually, I gather, you were able to edit a fifteen-version of your footage which was shown on WGBH Boston under the title *Psychiatry in Russia*.

AM   Yes, and then I traveled all over the Middle East with a guy from Chicago, Charles Sharpe, to retrace the travels of St. Paul. At that time, networks weren't prone to shooting anything on 16mm. It had to be 35. Anyway we shot it in 16.

MT   What were you recording the sound with?

AM   Didn't have any sound equipment. I had to—

MT   Narrate?

AM   Narrate. I didn't feel comfortable about that, but that's what I had to do. Then the big moment came in 1959.

MT   *Primary*.

AM   Yes.

MT   You recorded live sound?

AM   Yes, it was the first, I would say, uncontrolled piece of cinema where you didn't need a narration, you didn't need music. Where you could feel that you were actually there, nobody was directing. That was a big turning point, and I think it was the biggest turning point in the history of documentaries. Actually, in another way it was a step backward for me from *Psychiatry in Russia* because it was about celebrities and political events rather than things on the grass roots level.

MT   What did you hope to achieve by the film? What was your intention?

AM   There were four of us making the film and I contributed a major portion of the filming. Our intention was to take the *Life* magazine concept of a twosome: correspondent and photographer. Making the step into movies from there, you would have the actuality of a movie camera picking up more of a story without a caption or narration; more than a magazine could do. When that first stuff locked into sync and we saw it, we just were transformed. We said, this is—I guess I don't know what we said, but we knew that was to be our life.

MT   Was this the first time a documentary had gotten in sync like that?

AM   Yes. We could run around anywhere—on buses or anywhere anytime and without stopping, without having to say, repeat that, or I missed that. So we could get things as they happened. We developed new technology, so sound person and cameraman were in sync but without a connecting cable. Five long days filming, and then a month of twenty-two hour days editing. It got shown, I think, on a few stations that *Time* and *Life* happened to own, but not on network TV or in a movie theater.

MT And then?

AM My brother had lunch with the Capote's editor, Joe Fox at Random House, and posed the question, "What do you think would make a good nonfiction film?" Fox suggested door-to-door salesmen. My brother and I had done door-to-door selling: Fuller Brushes, Avon, encyclopedias, all that stuff. So we knew the possibilities. We began doing some research and found there were guys actually selling Bibles door-to-door. What could be more

Left to right: from "Salesman": Paul Brennan, David Maysles, Albert Maysles.

American than that? That's it. We found four guys in the New England area, and this is important, you have to be really vitally interested in the subject and in the people to make the best kind of documentary film, I think. So, going back a bit, there we were, Jewish kids, brought up in Dorchester, just outside of Boston. There wasn't a day in my youth that I didn't have to use my fists to defend myself, against some Irish kid. We were fascinated with the Irish-Jewish. We found that Mid-American Bible in Chicago had four guys working the New England territory, selling the Bible; four Irish guys from Boston and we thought, that's great. We'll get to know these guys. Again, I suppose this thing of establishing common ground between them and ourselves, that in the process we would discover friendship once we met these guys, upon whom we were about to stake our fortune. Not only staking our financial fortune, but our professional fortune as filmmakers. This meant a major investment in time as well.

MT How much did *Salesman* cost?

AM   Around $200,000.

MT   Huge budget for 1967.

AM   It would be like a million and a half today, I guess.

AM   We spent day and night, six weeks with them on the road.

MT   You raised the money yourselves?

AM   Oh, yeah. My mother was a schoolteacher, my father a postal clerk and my father had died some time before and she had put aside I think, $10,000 in life savings and we borrowed $1,000 from her.

MT   Did she ever get it back?

AM   Oh, yes. This is very important. We had a very strong trust in one another and we were brought up to trust other people, too. And if you have that kind of trust, and you deserve to be trusted, you don't fear that you're going to exploit people by exposing them to film, right? This is a very important thing. There are things that we do on film which are so totally honest and so necessary, and yet we get more criticism for doing them when others do the same in fiction. It's so odd. Filmmakers are so confused about this issue because it's a confusion that the culture has. We say, for example, we use the term brutally frank. Well, what's brutal about being frank? Is it kinder to be dishonest? Does kindness rest in being dishonest?

MT   People do fear the truth.

AM   Yes. When the Kubler-Ross book *Death and Dying* came out, I took the idea to PBS. They said no, the subject's too depressing. They wouldn't sponsor or show a film on that. Is reality by its very nature depressing? That's why I say civilization is dying. Well, twenty-five years later, in 1996, I made this film with Susan Froemke for HBO. It was called *Letting Go* and HBO took a chance that maybe no one would see it but it would certainly win awards, which it did.

AM   And PBS is getting more and more difficult.

MT   Have you ever had any good fortune with PBS in your work?

AM   Finally, after twenty-five years of pushing and prodding, I got PBS to show *Salesman*. They broke all their rules, one of which was not to show an older film even if it had never been shown on television. Even though, you know, this film has had an enormous influence on other filmmakers and on film students. There are 25,000 film students in America today and when they study documentary, they'll most likely be shown *Salesman*. It seems to me their obvious choice would be documentary over fiction because its inexpensive but more important, to me at least, is that left to its own devices, motion picture film would be documentary.

MT   Say that again, explain that.

AM   Left to its own devices, film or video would be documentary. Unleft to its own devices it becomes a borrowing from the theater, from commercialism, from all kinds of other things. The strength, the essential virtue and quality of documentary is the exactitude with which you can represent life as it is. And that's what nothing else can do but film. So left to its own devices, that would be the essential thing that you would go for.

MT   So you're referring, by other devices, to the temptations, financial greed.

AM   The superimposition of a point of view. The kind of entertainment that diverts, disengages. *Salesman* was not about an issue. Shakespeare was not about an issue, nor did it have a point of view. What Shakespeare tried to do was to distance himself from a point of view. That's why three-hundred years later the issues have changed but the plays remain universal. Well, it's been thirty years now and *Salesman* is as strong as ever. I would venture to say that there's hardly a documentary film course that doesn't include *Salesman*. That's going to be true of *Gimme Shelter* and it's going to be true of *Grey Gardens*, too. And that's part of the virtue of any well–made documentary, that it goes beyond what meets the eye of the ordinary observer. It even goes beyond repeated viewings because the camera is picking up so much stuff there's always more you didn't notice.

MT   What other documentaries do you greatly admire by other people?

AM   Haven't seen many. There are a lot that I don't like.

MT   What about the ones you do like? *Harlan County, USA?*

AM   Never saw it. Because it had that kind of—

MT   Good guy/bad guy?

AM   Once I heard that, I didn't want to see it.

MT   *Roger & Me?*

AM   Never saw it, hate it. Met the guy. That's not for me. Anything he might do is not for me. You know, I talk as a person who's wide open to almost just about anything, but at times I seem to talk as a person with a closed view. He said something, I saw a quote from him and he said, you know, you don't have to really kill anybody with what you're shooting, you just let them do it themselves, let them do it to themselves.

MT   And what don't you like about that comment?

AM   That's hate, not love and for a selfish purpose.

MT   For film aficionados of nonfiction, is being a voracious viewer of other documentaries a prerequisite?

AM   No.

MT   It isn't?

AM   I don't think you have to see another film.

MT   What is a prerequisite?

AM   The idea. And, the idea which has potential. Knowing that it has potential, it's probably going to be a better idea the more personal your engagement is with the idea and it's likely to be an extraordinarily good film if, somehow or other, it connects with an early image or experience that you may have had.

MT   So the past, one's own ontology, one's history, is a key?

AM   Yeah. But the peculiar thing is that I've been decrying the propagandistic nature of some films. At the same time, you need that passion for that particular idea on the subject to be dispassionate.

MT   I understand that.

AM   You have to end up with this as you're filming, as you're conceptualizing. It's a dispassionate process but passion, obsession has to go into it. But the obsession has to yield to dispassionate.

MT   Your films don't have interviews?

AM   No. Now there are sort of semi-interviews in sponsored films because you only have a certain amount of time because of the budget and so forth, but you won't find anything like that in *Salesman* or *Grey Gardens* which we financed and shot entirely on our own.

MT   The interview presupposes something that should already be there in the—

AM   It's a short-coming, it represents a failure to get "film" information.

AM   I love talking to strangers. About three or four weeks ago I'm at a reception for a discussion on cybernetics and I met an extraordinarily beautiful woman. I said, tell me about your father, just like that. She said, oh, I never met my father, not until last week.

MT   Until last week?

AM   So we exchanged cards and then about three days ago I called her up. I said, what's going on? Come on over. So she comes over and we sit there and we talked about what happened when she first met her father. She said, "Well, I was so scared that I'd be alone with him that I had a dozen of my friends in my apartment when he arrived." When I heard that I said to myself, "Jesus Christ, I should have been there." I was right. Next thing I knew her father repaired motorcycles and he was taking her back to her birthplace, Detroit from New York via motorcycle.

MT   That's a scene. But talking to strangers, is that a prerequisite?

AM   It's my way of doing things. Because it's, you know, it's love at first sight. It's got all that fascination on both sides.

MT   Is that something that documentary can pay tribute to or reflect upon that the dramatic films cannot?

AM   Yes. You use your presence to get closer to people; as close to the heart and soul of the scene, of the people, and so forth. You're not just a fly on the wall; that doesn't work because, for one thing, you are there so why deny it. I've seen documentary filmmakers, say don't pay any attention to the microphone. Make believe it's not there. Or the ludicrous statement, act natural. The thing is, it's not an act. It's life, that's what you're after.

MT   Well, if to any extent you do participate as a filmmaker in a situation, then obviously to some extent you're affecting them.

AM   Your participation is as a witness. And that's different...

MT   But there are different witnesses. There's the witness who stands behind a one–way mirror.

AM   I wouldn't shoot behind the one–way mirror. I want to be right in the thick of it and use my presence as a way of accepting and allowing. Because I know that I'm adept at using my presence in such a way that you could say that the Heisenberg effect is nullified.

MT   In the beginning of our discussion, you emphasized the approach to reality. Get as close as you can, but you also emphasized the nonmanipulative necessity of good documentary.

AM   That's right.

MT   What happens in a situation like the independence of Romania where it was the press, it was witnesses who were in the media, who in fact helped instigate, helped propagate, helped consummate the independence of a country. In a sense, if you are there in the room with the two women in the *Grey Garden*, are you not meddling with history?

AM   No, because, we never want to change anything for the film. I'm using all my curiosity to discover so as to recognize something that's vital in the other person and I try to bring that out by filming it. But to bring it out, shall we say, so uncontaminated that it may be a complete contradiction to what was anticipated.

MT   But this is what the Greeks thought of as catharsis, in a sense.

AM   Yes, yes.

MT   You have this welling need and are able to realize the satisfaction of that need by helping somehow, by paying witness to it outside of yourself. Is that the sense of it?

AM   Yes. This is how you can get things with their purity. Your presence is so important. If you can use your presence somehow or another, you can be silent. They may not say a thing, but somehow they feel that they're being recognized and if the film is an honest, truthful recognition—

MT   There's honor?

AM   Of them. Yes, right. And it also means things that are painful, things that are a bit awkward or whatever, that's okay. The two women felt it a celebration as well. But the ultimate confirmation of the rightfulness of what we were doing—

MT   As documentary filmmakers—

AM   Came when the mother was dying and the daughter turned to her and as she told us later on, said, "What more would you like to say?" And their mother said, "There's nothing more to say. It's all in the film."

MT   That's a tribute to you, indeed.

AM   And to the genre of documentary filmmaking.

MT   Is documentary filmmaking a therapeutic process?

AM   Yes, in the sense that it answers a need. For the filmmaker and those filmed, if it really works out right; the need for recognition which is so basic. And satisfaction for the filmmaker, in satisfying that need for the other person and making a film that really works. That's it.

MT   What really works?

AM   Well, what really works is if the people in the film can look at it and say well, there were moments, kind of embarrassing you know. But, on the whole, they can say, that's the way it was. When we made *Salesman* the salesmen didn't have the foggiest idea of how this could possibly be a film. How could anybody attach that much importance to their daily lives. And I guess it was true of their customers as well.

MT   Because that suggests that everybody could be a film?

AM   Just about. But also people are accustomed to think of film as featuring celebrities and not the lives of ordinary people.

MT   You've mentioned qualities like love, charity, getting close, giving trust, and hence deserving trust.

AM   These are all important elements. I think that even more than some of the words that I've used—love and charity and so forth—ah, Jesus, it almost makes me cry when I suddenly think about the kindness of strangers and, well, the kindness of filmmakers making a documentary film about strangers. Both kindnesses. How can you be kind to strangers when you don't even know them? How can strangers be kind to you and they don't even know you? And can you continue to be kind to one another when you really get to know the other person. How can you be kind to them? Because in kindness there's honesty and revelation.

MT   So the film, the process of making a film, of a documentary film is truly emotional catharsis.

AM   Yes...

MT   Any other qualities?

AM   The skills that make a good camera person.

MT   You've shot most of your film yourself?

AM   Yeah.

MT   Have you shot video?

AM   I'm just beginning to.

MT   How do you feel about that medium?

AM   It's great. I'm fooling around now with a Sony camera, it's called a "passport" camera. Take one of these little tapes, feel how big it is. Got half a dozen tapes, it's an hour. No stopping or changing. We're testing out the image to see whether it can go up to 35mm so we can show it in movie theaters. The technology is simply the servant which allows you to get closer to what you're really after.

MT   In the beginning of our conversation you mentioned the death of civilization. What's causing it, and how can documentary reverse the trend?

AM   (AM grins) The death of civilization. You know where it started? It started with *Sesame Street*, about twenty-five years ago.

MT   (I too am grinning) In what sense?

AM   In that they said, "Okay, this is going to be for kids. We love kids. We want to do right by them. They have short attention spans; we'll put everything in little pieces."

MT   And?

AM   So, they gave them short attention spans.

MT   MTV did the same thing with high school students and now Hollywood does the same thing with adults.

AM   That's right. The question is, having done that to the minds of those generations, is there any way back from that?

MT   You've described the difficulties confronting documentarians in reaching an audience. With the channelization of the media, 500 channels, it'll become 1,000 channels, and so on, do you think the narrow targeting of broadcasters will facilitate greater opportunities for the nonfiction filmmaker?

AM   There's some hope, bits and pieces when good documentaries get shown, but, uh, you know, it's like when people leave a house of worship where they've been given a stirring sermon, they leave and they shake hands with the minister and what do they do? They say... my God, do they say "I was moved to tears?" No, they say, "I enjoyed what you said. As if he were some sort of entertainer." But that's not what he meant and that's not what we mean to do. For us a film is not a diversion; just a way of passing time.

AM   I think what's killing movies today is the cinematography isn't genuine. There's no photography in it. Mostly expensive visual gymnastics. And no silences.

MT   Do you have a TV at home?

AM   No. And the kids have agreed to it.

MT   But you expressed enthusiasm for video. Do you actually believe, based on what you said, the lack of silences, of real photography, and so on, that a young aspirant who wants to make a documentary film and owns some video camera will be able to cultivate silences with that medium?

AM   You can.

MT   Truth?

AM   You can get at it.

MT   The medium is appropriate?

AM   Absolutely.

MT   How would you advise that young filmmaker?

AM   Make it observational. No interviews, no narration. Keep your eyes and ears open for scenes. Something actually taking place that will tell the story. You're not a fly on the wall, you're an observer but not an active participant except that your participation is in the kindness that is exchanged in the process of giving something to one another. You're giving them the film and they're giving you the film. You're witnessing, not judging. That's the main thing. And the other thing is to take pride in the exactitude in which you can exercise your profession. Available light.

MT   And if it gets too dark, you can add candles?

AM   Yes. Otherwise, if there is enough light, it's nature's contribution. It's nature, it's the human spirit, it's all these things which evolve around us. Lennon had it right, John Lennon, when he said, "let it be." That's the idea. Whereas the idea of creating something that is over and beyond reality is hostile to the whole idea of documentary film, I think. You're not trying to upstage reality. You're trying to get as close to reality as possible.

MT   And you think, to go back to the very beginning when I asked you about the death of civilization, this could be an antidote?

AM   Oh, yes. The more you know the real world, the more people can love one another. I think it's true. That's what we need more of. Truth, knowledge, love—they all go together.

PART IX

THE SPIRITUALITY

OF NON-FICTION

© Jeremy Norgarth

ZEN AND THE ART OF THE DOCUMENTARY

MICKEY LEMLE

Whenever I address an audience of young film students, I always answer the most important question, as I see it, whether it is asked or not.

"What is the most important single thing you have learned about making documentary films?" Sometimes I will ask myself aloud. Then I answer: Perhaps I am a slow learner, I begin. Because every time I go to make a new movie I must relearn the same fundamental lesson, and that is: TO LET GO OF MY PRECONCEIVED NOTIONS AND SEE WHAT IS REALLY GOING ON.

Not only do I have to relearn this lesson each time, but I also have to relearn this lesson at every phase of the filmmaking process. When you start the process of making a movie you must start out with an idea of what the movie is that you want to make. What is the story you want to tell? You cannot just go out and make a movie about "life." How would you decide where to point the camera? So you have your original idea, and then you start the research. But during the research process, you must let go of your "idea" of what the movie is about and really listen to the potential subjects of the movie. Open to what is really going on. Find out what the truly profound issues are.

When I set out to make *The Other Side of the Moon*, a movie about the spiritual

NASA photo.

experiences of the Apollo astronauts, my assumption was that anyone who flew 250,000 miles across space in a machine made by the lowest bidder in a government contract, and then stood on another heavenly body and watched the Earth rise, surrounded by the vast blackness of infinite space, would be affected by these experiences

361

in a profound way. What I found when I spoke to these men was that a lot of them claimed that they weren't really affected at all.

"Did it change you?" I would ask. "Nah," responded Charles "Pete" Conrad, the mission commander of Apollo 12 and the third man to walk on the moon. "It didn't change us at all. We trained for so long, it was what we expected." He became an important part of the movie which also featured seven other astronauts whose lives were profoundly changed.

I do extensive research. I try to cast the net as wide and far as possible in the initial stages of the process. When I meet possible subjects of my documentaries we just chat. I never use a tape recorder, nor do I take notes. We just have a friendly conversation. After I say good-bye, I drive around the block, pull over to the curb, and write down all of the "gems" that they said during the conversation.

Don't worry about forgetting the "gems." I remember reading an interview with Marshal Brickman, who cowrote *Annie Hall* with Woody Allen. According to the article, they would walk up and down Third Avenue trying to make each other laugh. Then after several hours, they would go back to Woody's apartment and write down the really great stuff. "Aren't you worried about forgetting the really great stuff?" the interviewer asked. "You never forget the really great stuff," Brickman replied.

Based on these preliminary interviews, I write the important "gems" on 3x5 cards and structure the movie on a bulletin board. For instance, when I was researching my movie about the life of the Dalai Lama, *Compassion in Exile: The Story of the 14th Dalai Lama*, I knew that a key turning point in his life was the night he left Lhasa, the capital of Tibet, and went over the Himalayas into exile in India. During my initial research conversation with the Dalai Lama, he told a funny story about that night. His younger brother, fourteen at the time of the escape, told me about that night in a very dramatic and compelling way.

I then located some rare 16mm footage of the actual escape that night on horseback. So I had the Dalai Lama's stories and his brother's stories on 3x5 cards as well as a note about the stock footage. I knew these elements would create a sequence in the movie, woven in some way.

One of the great lessons I learned in the process of editing documentaries when I was just starting out, is that movies are really about the structure of the movie.

The audience needs, and is entitled to, a firm guide who will take them on a journey. Subliminally they must have confidence in the structure, just as one must have confidence in the experience of a whitewater river guide. You may hit rapids, you may be scared or amused or emotionally opened, but someone is there to take you through the experience safely.

Most people see only the surface of movies—the acting, the lighting, the camera moves (they should never see the editing!). But good writers and directors see structure.

Mikhail Baryshnikov is one of the most beautiful dancers I have ever seen; his understanding and execution of movement are unsurpassed. But he isn't much of a choreographer in my opinion. George Balanchine on the other hand was not a great dancer, but he could see the structure of music, and he knew how to move bodies through space and time creating sequences that added up to a total aesthetically pleasing experience. Likewise, good movies are fundamentally about good structure.

So I figure out the structure, the flow of the storytelling, before I start to shoot. Based on the preliminary research interviews, I even write out approximately what I expect people will say on 3x5 cards, then into a script. This helps figure out how to maximize the usually limited shooting days, and usually limited financial resources.

Then I go out to shoot the movie. On location, I must once again learn the key lesson: TO LET GO OF MY PRECONCEIVED IDEAS OF WHAT THE MOVIE IS ABOUT AND SEE WHAT IS REALLY GOING ON.

When I interview people, I know what stories I hope to get, again based on the preliminary interviews and the themes of the movie. But in the course of an interview, if there is some energy in an answer that diverges from the preconceived path, I follow it. The interviews are conversations. As a director you are listening with an inner ear for a "gem" of a statement—one with life in it, well articulated, metaphoric, hopefully expressed as if the subject had just thought it up and was saying it for the first time. Also, you hope it is a full paragraph with a beginning topic sentence, a middle, and an end. These are the treasures for which you are searching. These are the moments that you see in a movie that just feel "true."

Remember, a movie is made up of a series of "gem" moments arrived at gracefully and left gracefully.

I always have a list of questions that I have written out on a pad before the interview. I only look at the list, however, when we are changing magazines. Otherwise, I have a conversation and don't read the questions off a list during the interview. Also, because I am interested in "gut" statements, I never ask subject what he or she "thinks" about anything. So I never asked any of the astronauts what they "thought" about going to the moon, which would place their response in their heads. Rather, I asked them, for example, to "tell me about a time you felt fear," or "Tell me about a time you felt awe." This placed the questions in their emotions (juicy) rather than in their intellects (dry). I try to make movies about human experiences rather than theories about experience. The movies are about people, not issues. Hopefully the subject's experiences and stories become metaphoric of the larger themes and issues of our shared human predicaments.

One astronaut, Rusty Schweikart of Apollo 9, had had an extraordinary five minutes floating in space outside the capsule with nothing to do. While Rusty was testing the portable backpack equipment, his partner Dave Scott was taking pictures of him. Dave Scott's camera jammed (I could relate to that) and Rusty was told by the mission commander to just "hang out for five minutes" while Dave went into the capsule to fix the camera. He was floating weightless in space, traveling over the surface of the Earth at 17,000 miles per hour. It was completely silent. This experience changed his relationship with the cosmos and changed his life. He couldn't wait to tell me about it on camera. He had told it thousands of times before. It was an essential part of his story and based on my knowledge of the story from the research, it was an essential part of the movie. In fact, it had been one of the motivating elements of the whole project.

But when Rusty told it, it sounded canned. I came back to the story later in the interview. Again it felt canned. After I had asked him most of my questions, and while we were changing magazines, I asked him to close his eyes and remember the physical sensations of his space walk. I asked him to remember the feeling of weightlessness in his body, remember the silence, remember the visual effects of seeing the Earth passing below him.

I looked over to the cameraman, my great friend Buddy Squires, who silently gave me the sign that he was ready. I silently responded by giving him the sign to roll. I sat down next to the camera and gently told Rusty that when he was ready, to open his eyes and describe the experience to me.

His tone changed completely. He was there, and because of that, that section of the movie vividly brings the audience "there." At another point during the research, I spoke to a remarkable astronaut named Al Bean who walked on the moon with Pete Conrad on Apollo 12. Now he spends his time as an artist, painting pictures of the lunar landscape.

"Did people change?" I asked him during our initial conversation. "No," he responded. "They just became more like they were on weekends." This was definitely one of the "gems" that I remembered and wrote down after I had left him and driven around the block. It made it onto a 3x5 card, onto the bulletin board, and into the script. During the actual on camera interview, I asked him again if people changed. He gave a very different answer. I came back to it several times, changing the question slightly so I didn't seem like a complete idiot. Finally, in desperation, I asked, "Would you say people became more like they were on weekends?" "No," he said, "I wouldn't say something like that."

Real life can be unpredictable. That is the source of joy and tribulation for the documentarian. Real people will say things you could never think up or write. They also won't say things you thought up or wrote. Sometimes they won't say things they said or wrote. Again, YOU MUST LET GO OF YOUR PRE-CONCEIVED IDEAS AND CONCEPTS AND BE OPEN TO WHAT IS REALLY THERE HAPPENING IN FRONT OF YOU.

After filming, let's say you have captured great stuff on camera. The movie takes on a new shape in your mind and with great expectations you look forward to seeing the rushes. Watching rushes to me is like going to the mailbox to find out that you have just won the Irish Sweepstakes and that your best friend has just died in a plane crash.

Shots are not as you remember them happening. Some great action happened off camera, or in a wide shot instead of a close-up (it was close-up in your mind when it happened). You ran out of film at a key moment, it''s out of focus, it's dark, there's scratch, the sound ran out, there was a plane overhead, there's a flare on the film—you name it, it has happened to me. If you stay in this business long enough, it will happen to you.

Then the process of watching rushes again becomes a process of letting go of preconceived ideas and concepts in order to be open to see what really went on in front of the camera. Cameras really do steal souls. They capture what is really going on in the moment. Sure, there is choice involved, manipulation. It isn't THE TRUTH, but it is a truth, even if part of that "truth" that was captured is the manipulation or lies.

Then comes the first stab at structure and the long editing process. I treat editing as a meditation practice. Each time the movie is going forward on the editing machine, I try to empty myself and see it for the first time—just like your audience will. What do you see in the frame? What do you feel? What do you want to see or hear next to keep the story going? Does it hold your interest and attention?

Of course I have an idea of what the movie is about, but the process of editing for me is the process of revealing deeper and deeper levels of the reality of the story. Deeper levels of truth, if you will. I feel like an Inuit or Eskimo carver, who will pick up a horn or a stone and ask, "What is in here?" And then they carve to reveal the form that they believe is already inherently there in the horn or in the stone. Likewise, my editing process is a process of revealing the best movie that is in the material. And like the Inuit carver, I must work to reveal by cutting things away and rearranging the order, the sounds, the images, the juxtapositions, the sequences, and thereby find the structure. Often it's not until I have been working on the movie for a while that I start to find that the deeper questions and issues emerge. This takes time. It also takes an ability to be open to it.

I asked Edgar Mitchell, lunar modular pilot of Apollo 14, why some of his fellow astronauts claimed to be unaffected by their journeys to the moon. Ed's life had changed radically. He had been an MIT-trained scientist, a career military pilot, raised in a fundamentalist Christian home. He came back from his trip to the moon with an overwhelming experience of a great intelligence in the universe, a true cosmic consciousness experience.

He came back and in the early seventies after leaving NASA, he started the Institute of Noetic Sciences which has studied ESP, clairvoyance, psychokinesis, precognition, mind–body relationships—to say the least, Ed had changed.

"How is it that some of your colleagues that went to the moon claim that it didn't affect them at all?" I asked Ed.

"It's a little like bouncing a ball off a wall," Ed said. "If you weren't open to the experience," he continued, "you didn't have it."

Likewise as a filmmaker, if you aren't open to the deeper truths in the story you are telling, you might not find them. What usually gets in the way is your idea or concept of how it was supposed to be.

When I started out as a filmmaker at WGBH, the public television station in Boston, for about a week or two every year I would fill in for the guys who shot and edited the local nightly news when they went on vacation. This was in the old days of shooting and editing film. We would have a story meeting in the morning and decide which story was going to be the "film story," and go out to shoot it that morning. It had to be shot and in the lab by 2:00 p.m. The film came back by 4:00 p.m., I edited it, and by 7:00 it was on the air. Often we would decide on "the story" on our way to the story. The tendency would be to shoot our preconceived ideas of what the story was and if the images diverged from the story, the reporter would cover it with voice-over.

Years later, I made a movie on photography called *Media Probes* for a series I did with my friend Kit Laybourne. The theme of the show was this notion of the preconceived image. For one sequence, I spent the day with a young woman photographer for the New York Daily News as she rode around in a radio car waiting for the dispatcher to tell her to go photograph a fast-breaking news story. At that time the Daily News had several of these cars cruising around New York because it was and is so hard to get around town at rush hour.

As the dispatcher radioed the story to our young photographer, and she took off toward the location, I would ask her, "Do you have an idea about the photograph you will take?" As she drove through the traffic, she would describe the photograph she was going to take when she got to the breaking news story. She had already preconceived the image in her mind.

I truly believe that one reason why so much of television today is disposable is because people are showing their ideas of how it is supposed to be rather then revealing how life is. I believe that which time goes into in the research phase and the shooting and the editing phase will last over time. For then the deeper truths have a chance to be revealed and I believe that every one of us, every member of the audience has within them an "honest witness" which knows when someone on the screen is telling the truth of their experience. Creating that resonance in the hearts and minds of the audience is what our work is truly about.

ANSWERS IN BLUE

Vanessa H. Smith

I was born in San Pedro, California, twenty miles south of Los Angeles in 1957.

I think the seeds of my documentary filmmaking were sown in a rose garden thirty years ago. When I was a little girl, one of my household chores was to water the roses which I would do in the evening as the sun was setting. I would always take a book with me. My favorite choices were biographies and fairy tales from around the world. I would read standing up and watering. I would dream of other people's lives and deeds and about what I would become when I grew up. These books and my dreams made me intensely curious about the world.

Some years ago I read a short book about Robert Rauschenberg. He said that the weather had always been the most important thing to him. The same was true for me. Growing up I always wanted days to be dark, cloudy, moody, and rainy. I felt this so strongly that, in large part because of the light, I moved to New York from Los Angeles in 1985. I was never able to see properly in the California sun. I always preferred to see colors pop from the darkness. I find that most filmmakers are obsessed with light. They love it and actually live through it. I most definitely prefer low light. It makes one stretch to see more.

In California the natural and man–made forms influenced the way I see. Important to me: tall eucalyptus trees, silhouettes of palm trees, billowy pillow clouds, strong green sunsets with cherry and violet coloured streaks of punctuation, the very wet green grasses of April, and the languid music of the beach. In my filmmaking I often seek to include these images.

As a typical girl growing up in filmic L.A., I watched Fred Astaire movies and animated shorts. I always liked old black and white films and scary programs like Chiller, (a sixties B–grade black and white horror program which played on Saturday afternoons.) My other favorite shows were dance programs called *Shindig* and *Hulaballoo*. I also had an intense interest in James Bond films partly because I wasn't allowed to watch them. Two specific scenes I saw on TV still haunt me. I saw Victor Mature stripped naked and wearing only glitter, while being lowered into the earth on a wooden plank, to be buried alive. The other scene was a mad scientist suffocating a little person with a cotton ball.

In real life as opposed to in-the-movies, I have been most inspired by people who are able to make quick and difficult decisions with integrity. I have always been attracted to documentary filmmaking which explores the lives of dynamic and inspiring individuals.

I moved from California to New York in 1985 and then to New Delhi, India, in 1992 where I have lived with my husband, Don Weeden for five years. My first  week in India I met a man named K.S. Kulkarni. K.S., a well–known Indian artist and teacher, was to become my mentor until his death in 1994. He also possessed all of the qualities I look for in a documentary subject: strength of character, talent, drive, intelligence, humor, and humility. I had begun to tape our talks together almost as soon as we met and decided that at some point I might like to make a documentary about him. He liked the idea saying that he hoped to meet someone who would appreciate what he had to say. At the age of seventy-four he was indeed a man of impressive accomplishments, having been instrumental in the formation of many of India's premiere art institutions as well as heading up several faculties at major art schools. He had exhibited widely and received many awards and honors.

In February 1994, K.S. exhibited in two shows where he was scheduled to give talks on his ideas about creativity and transcendental thinking. Just as the shows were opening I began to film K.S. talking, painting, and basically just doing all the things that he did everyday. He became ill very soon thereafter. The talks were re-scheduled for later that year but K.S. died somewhat suddenly in October after several bouts with various illnesses. I later realized how lucky I was to have come into contact with K.S. when I did and, secondly, that I had jumped on the urge to film him soon after meeting him.

I have completed the documentary about K.S. I pored over hundreds of his works and traveled to the place in Pune where he spent his youth and met his wife of forty-nine years. There was a carnival going on in Pune as I was filming and I took a Hi 8 camera onto one of the rides with K.S.'s close friend, Vijay Kowshik. We were scooped high into the sky. Ahead of us was a woman in a long blue sari and her young son. I filmed the edge of their feet and then panned up into the sky as they rode in the carriage ahead. I used this as the last shot of the film which dissolved into a single star in the sky. I felt that this was a very appropriate ending for K.S. I also found archival film footage from the thirties at Prabat studios near Pune. I found a single shot of a man who resembled K.S.'s tall, slim good looks. The man was swinging on a rope swing into tall trees.

Documentary filmmakers never create in a vacuum. I was influenced in making *K.S.*, the documentary, by a superb selection of documentaries on painters which I had seen at the French Cultural Center in New Delhi. One of the films was about Picasso, which probably rates as my favorite documentary. In it Picasso stands alone in a dark room in front of a large glass palette illuminated by two spotlights. He draws on the glass with a fat grease stick. We see his painting being born before us, worked and reworked many times. It is a magical film about the process of creativity and discovery. It is also a film about a lonely genius. I most appreciate the film because it allows one to experience the act of creation, the transcendental experience of both making art and knowing it from the outside.

While in India I have also become quite involved in the Tibetan community, traveling to Dharamasala, the seat of the Tibetan government–in–exile and home of

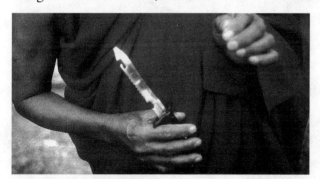

His Holiness the Dalai Lama, numerous times. I was hired to work on the feature–length documentary about the making of Martin Scorcese's *Kundun*. *Kundun* is the Dalai Lama's story of his flight from Tibet in 1959. Palden Gyatso, a Tibetan monk who suffered through years in Chinese prisons and torture, was photographed for the documentary. He shows some of the torture instruments that he was able to smuggle out. One knife in particular interested me. It is a knife with a blade about 6 inches long by 2 inches wide, very much like any other knife except for the fact that it has curved notches grooved out at two points. These notches allow the knife to extract chunks of flesh as the knife is pulled out of the victim. The knife shows the sadness and cruelty of torture. I responded to this last trip to Dharamsala by writing these lines.

DOCUMENT FOR TIBET

perhaps all of history is captured in smelling time
land that has guts and members that grasp
moving politics and allowing little fish to swim in open waters

the smell of warm old books, the dead
the winds of summer, burden, tsampa
dusty carpets, damp earth, and ancient answers

One other interview I did recently was with a four-year-old boy who has just left Tibet to live in India. He came with his father by bus. His father had already left to rejoin the rest of the family in Tibet when we had the interview. The little boy does not know why he is in India. He only knows that his parents wanted him to get a good education. In India he will be able to study Tibetan language in freedom. He knows that he lives in the same country as His Holiness the Dalai Lama.

As I filmed I was happy for this little boy for he will have better opportunities for Tibetan language education in India than he would have in Tibet. I was also sad for him at the same time, being so young and separated from his family. After meeting this little boy I wrote these lines about people and character.

IDENTITY

identity is not to be expected
it gets loose over time, naturally,
as clothes on a lover

identity should never be simple to find

its form is process not object

identity has to be unlimited
if not, it is a boundary or stopping point
that life needs to be lived up into

and

in proportion to what you call your soul
you possibly have no one thing to identify at all

when you have left and you are outside

As filmmakers we are led to certain subject matter for various reasons. I have felt fortunate to have been able to spend some time in India with the Tibetan community at an important point in their struggle for autonomy. His Holiness the Dalai Lama and the entire community have taught me that people need to learn and listen to one another with heart as well as mind. I feel that as the world becomes increasingly more populated and therefore complicated, that we are going to need to live more compassionately. The Tibetans are great reminders to the world of the power and effectiveness of gentleness.

I will close these thoughts with a favorite film image of a yak mother and baby on a Tibetan hillside in the 1940s. A bush of pink flowers blows in the wind on the

right while fog and a single cloud brush past in a very violet gray sky. The baby feeds from its mother. For me this image is full of knowing.

I hope that my next project involves poetry and the link between abstract thought and where we are going in the next century with our world.

IN SEARCH OF SOUL

JOHN SWINDELLS

"One way or another, we all have to find what best
fosters the flowering of our humanity in this
contemporary life, and dedicate ourselves to that."
Joseph Campbell, *The Power of Myth*

Joseph Campbell, the famous mythologist, once said (something to the effect) that there is the transcendent, there is what we think is happening, and then there is our attempt to articulate it. As far back as I can remember I have always been fascinated by the transcendent, not so much as something to marvel at or adore, but by the way in which it manifests in everyday life, how it appears (or does not appear) in our humanity. Although it may be a futile exercise to try and articulate it, this hasn't stopped thousands of artists, poets, novelists, musicians, composers, singers, photographers and filmmakers from attempting to articulate what springs from their souls.

I can remember being awestruck by the transcendent moments in Peter Weir's films *Witness* and *Dead Poets Society*. I can remember being totally captivated by the "feel" of *Matter of Heart*, a documentary on the life of Carl Jung. I had been taken into Jung's world and came away feeling that I had experienced something of him. I can remember watching *Thirty-Two Short Films About Glenn Gould* and being fascinated by the realization that a biographical documentary can be like a sketchbook. It need not be cohesive; after all many lives are not cohesive, but complex, fractured, and held together by a few thin threads. In all of these examples, I think the filmmakers had recognized something and had worked towards documenting or re-creating what they had seen or experienced.

At the risk of sounding pretentious, this process of recognizing something extraordinary (or should I say extraordinarily ordinary) and the excruciating hunger to give it a voice has haunted me for many years. Perhaps I am driven by the need to expunge something, to put it out there in order to free myself of the burden of carrying it around.

This can be very dangerous terrain. The other side of this passion is the abject terror that goes with it—the fear that an audience will not "get it" or worse, that I was totally deluded about what I thought I had seen.

Several years ago, I was making a documentary about the experience of a young man, Stephen, who was living with episodic schizophrenia. During postproduction, we were trying to replicate the sound of the voices that Stephen would hear in his head when he was ill. Felicity Fox, a very talented composer, had sampled some voices and sounds based on Stephen's verbal description. Within seconds of listening to the tape, Stephen pulled the headphones off and was looking horrified. After he regained his composure, he was able to tell us that these sounds were disturbingly close to the voices of his own demons and he would be uncomfortable with us using them in the film. What then transpired was quite unbelievable. Stephen allowed us to play the tape again through the speaker system so that we could all hear it together.

Stephen's incredible vulnerability and bravery in letting us share this with him was very moving. He could now share this experience of the "voices" from inside his head in the company of other people. We were seeing a certain liberation occurring through the release of something caught inside Stephen's tortured soul.

Recently, I made a film about a former merchant sailor and trade unionist, Henry Spira, who became one of the most effective activists in the American animal liberation movement. What motivated this very tough guy to fight for the rights of lab rats and cats who were being cruelly abused for the sake of medical and product testing? At first, it seemed incongruous, but after spending a few days with Henry, the extent of his own emotional fragility and isolation became apparent. For many years, Henry had lived alone with his cat in his home/office surrounded by hanging racks, filing cabinets, and computer equipment. Here was a man with no sentimentality or introspection. When I did try to discuss his emotional life with him, he would shut me out completely. We decided that the best way to tell his personal story and establish him as a character was to film him at work, going about his daily life in his apartment and on the streets of New York. In some cases, so much can be said by what is not said.

I truly believe that everyone would like to think that their life has been worthwhile in some way and would like to tell their story, given the opportunity. As a result of this focus, (or perhaps obsession) most of my work has tended to be character driven. I guess I am a bit anthropological, having always been fascinated by the way in which an organism (namely, a human being) finds its own truth, its balance, its integrity in its own particular universe. What most fascinates me is the way in which people have dealt with the challenges, milestones, and turning points in their lives.

Wisdom for me comes from a life full of passion, experience, humility, and emotional bravery—a journey towards a profound personal understanding of one's own humanity. This need not be a dogmatic path, or even a rational one, but there should be some peace and grace at the end of the road.

I can remember having a conversation with a good friend when we were in our early twenties about what we admired in people. She said that there was no one that she would describe as being "inspirational." I was quite upset by this, but had no idea at the time why. More than ten years later I was working on my first film, *A Human Search*, the biography of Bede Griffiths, an Oxford-educated Benedictine monk and one of the greatest mystics of this century—a man who I found so inspirational that I felt compelled to document his life. If someone were to ask me what it was about him that moved me so, it would be impossible for me to find words that would come close. The power of his being could only be conveyed through film.

Having been what could possibly be described as an eclectic agnostic with mystical sympathies, I still find it quite extraordinary that I would have taken a film crew to India to document the life of a Christian monk. Belonging to a generation that grew up to be cynical of religious dogma and institutional intentions, I had very little time for organized religion. I would often defer to scientific rationalism to find answers to puzzling questions; and if there remained any doubts, I would become very busy, finding distractions from my concerns.

I became fascinated with Bede's story after reading an article entitled "East Meets West in the Venerable Bede" in a Sydney newspaper. The image of this frail old man sitting beneath a tree haunted me. He looked unreal, like the archetypal wise old man - Merlin, Moses, or Ben Kenobi from *Star Wars*.

Curious things soon began to happen. I called the newspaper to find out if they had any more information about Bede's public engagements, but they were unable to help me. I then contacted a local religious and spiritual bookstore to find out if they had any of Bede's books. The clerk agreed to put some aside for me. When I asked him if he knew where Bede would be appearing in Sydney, he informed me that Bede had just walked into the store. A chill went down my spine.

Several nights later, I found myself in a large civic hall in Sydney's northern sub-
urbs awaiting Bede's arrival. A tall, frail old man dressed in saffron robes with
well-groomed long silver hair and beard took the stage. He began to speak in a
kind, gentle voice, with a fine Oxford accent. I was overwhelmed with a sense of
mission and urgency. I turned to my friend Robin and told her that I had to document this man's journey and try to capture some of his grace on film. Over the
next few months, I read everything I could find that Bede had written and that had
been written about him. I started to collect photos of Bede in his Indian ashram,
and throughout his life. I gathered music that seemed to touch on places where
he had been within his own consciousness—ranging from southern black spirituals
to classical Gregorian chants to sacred Indian music.

Within a month, I had prepared an outline for a one-hour documentary and went
about trying to raise the necessary funds. Bede's advanced age and frail health made
it very difficult to proceed through the normal fund-raising and distribution channels.
My own limited experience as a filmmaker at this time, combined with the fact that
we would be shooting on location in India, also issued an enormous challenge.

My enthusiasm must have been infectious. Within five months of coming across
Bede, a private investor had agreed to put up the necessary funds and we were
shooting a documentary at Bede's home in southern India. I truly believe that I
was "called" into service on this project to assist in documenting Bede's life for
posterity so that his wisdom could be shared by a wider audience.

In my opinion, my craft as a filmmaker is still relatively untrained and quite naive. I
believe my talent lies in recognizing interesting subjects and in assembling a team of
very talented people in order to give the subject of the documentary a voice. I see
myself as more of a facilitator or perhaps collaborator, bringing together the elements,
each with their own unique contribution—the production manager, cinematographer,
sound recordist, editor, composer, and many others. I tend to provide the initial
passion and enthusiasm for the subject and enroll the others into the project.

I think the most important thing in doing a biography, particularly an oral
biography, is to create an atmosphere on the set that will enable the person
being interviewed to "show up"—to feel safe enough to open up in the interview
and reveal something of who they truly are. I believe real storytelling must be
grounded in truth and for people to tell the truth, they need to feel safe. This
also involves spending time up front developing a good working relationship
with the key people in the film. I try to discuss with them what I want to shoot

and what I ultimately would like to put in the film. I do believe that a film works better through this kind of relationship. (Of course it depends ultimately on the people involved, what their own agenda are, and whether it is possible to establish this level of trust.)

Having done an enormous amount of research, I usually script my films—to establish a working structure for the film, the interview questions, the visual images required, the range of locations and activities we need to shoot—so that we are clear on our basic coverage. (I feel a certain responsibility to make sure that we always come back with something that will cut into a film.) This is then broken down into a shooting schedule. I try to plan it so that we get the coverage in about 70-75 percent of our time (and stock), leaving us with plenty of opportunity to get those spontaneous gems, extra moments that will give us the film.

The film really starts to take shape in the editing room. For me, this is the most intense time. It is like putting together this amazing puzzle. It becomes a balance of form and essence. You are shaping the material, carefully trying to reduce it down by a factor of sometimes ten or twenty or thirty or forty times! At the same time you are trying to hold onto the story as well as those nice moments during which you get an insight into the subject. When I was making *A Human Search* (AHS), I felt so immersed in the material, I sometimes felt the material was talking to me, telling me what to keep and what to discard. We had shot at a ratio of about 16:1 and most of it was compelling interview material, more than half of that with Bede Griffiths, the hero of the film (who was incidentally a "one-take wonder").

Perhaps it is bizarre to describe a film in terms of the "feel" of the material, but for me the process is so much about the intuitive response. (Maybe it's because I am so attracted to the resonance of the subject that I am drawn to the material that is infused with this resonance.)

Being quite a cerebral character, I am always challenged by the need to make my work more visual, more "filmic." "Talking heads" fascinate me, but turn off many people (including network programmers). With AHS, we were particularly challenged by the need to create some dramatic tension around the major turning points in Bede's life. There was some very important information in the original interview material during which Bede was describing his *Dark Night*. There is great pathos and humility in his story, but in the interview his manner was unsentimental, so modest and so unembellished that the significance of this experience to the rest of his life is lost in the subtlety of his delivery. The editor,

Laura Zusters, and I decided to slow it down—cut it to a piece of music and intercut some poetic abstract images as he related his experience. We found a piece of music from Mahler's Symphony No.4 in G major that added just enough vulnerability and melancholy to the moment without being too obtrusive. We then cut up the dialogue to give it some space and what we ended up with, I hope, was a more dramatic telling of the story, but still true to the original material.

I don't think a film is ever truly objective or observational. There is always a point of view and a degree of subjectivity. If the material is edited or has been shot from one point of view, it has been affected by someone's judgement. I do, though, believe that a filmmaker can give breath to the subject, some space for people to "show up" and reveal something of themselves.

There are two questions that I always labour over when contemplating a project: (1) What is it about? and (2) Why do I want to make it? (Or more accurately, Where is my attachment/projection in this?) The first question forces me to get clear on what the film is about and how the story will be told. The second question requires taking responsibility for my involvement in the project. What is it that appeals to me personally? Where is my investment? What am I projecting into this that could affect a reasonable degree of objectivity in my handling of the subject? As I have said, nothing is truly objective, but if we can take responsibility for our perspective in covering a subject, then we will make a better film. With Bede, I think I had finally found a wise old man who spoke from the heart and at the same time had a brilliant mind and profound knowledge; a man who warranted enormous respect. The challenge for me was to keep the film even, documenting his charisma and wisdom, but also his humanity and his foibles. Ultimately, we ended up with a significant film which has been widely distributed and acclaimed throughout the world, thanks to the poetic camera work of Tony Gailey, and Laura Zusters's elegant and graceful edit.

The greatest learning for me as a director on this project was and continues to be the challenge of communicating my vision to these highly talented crafts people. The onus is on me to tell them what I see and feel and what I want from them. They can then use their skills to bring this vision into being.

Although this type of filmmaking is so personally rewarding, it is a very hard road to follow. With so much focus on the commercial imperative, it feels somewhat self-indulgent sometimes to aspire to poetic or artistic expression independent of a market attachment. The television arena is so formulaic, dictated by programming strands, time slots, and the agenda of sponsors and advertisers. In order to do this type of filmmaking you have to be prepared to make a film on a shoestring budget, relentlessly chase alternative funding sources, hope that broadcasters and distributors will acquire your finished film, and that people will want to see it. But I can tell you that there is nothing like the feeling of seeing your work completed and being appreciated by an audience around the world who are taking the journey with your hero.

For the future, I hope to continue my exploration of the lives of other fascinating and brave individuals. I am currently developing several projects, including an exploration of the relationship between mental illness and spirituality, the experience of autism, and a meditation on the various types of human relationships. The search for Soul continues.

John Swindells, an Australian/Canadian filmmaker has written, produced, and directed numerous documentaries, corporate videos, multimedia programs, and commissioned works on subjects ranging from Christian mysticism to schizophrenia, environmentalism to animal rights. Born in Toronto, Canada, John emigrated to Australia with his family while in his teens. After a brief career in computer engineering and marketing, he decided to follow his heart and began making films five years ago. The majority of his work has been in the area of oral history/biography. John Swindells's documentaries include *A Human Search—The Life of Fr. Bede Griffiths* (1993), *Dreamer of the Earth—The Life of Thomas Berry* (1994), *One in Five—Living With A Mental Illness* (1995, a young man's experience of living with schizophrenia), and *Henry—One Man's Way* (1997, a biography of animal rights activist, Henry Spira).

THE EYE SWIMS IN THE CANALE GRANDE

Eduard Schreiber
Translation by Georg Hartmann

At first sight, this landscape is a sanitary landfill in northern Berlin: a place where you dump furniture, status symbols and symbols of state, love letters, military uniforms and an accordion. It's the fall of 1990. Right now a state is about to vanish—the German Democratic Republic, East Germany. With a hectic movement, many people get rid of these seemingly unnecessary items, collected in forty years of history, to make room for new things. A one-of-a-kind historical event, happening with an unbelievable speed. It remains a picture of a growing scene of devastation.

The orange-colored garbage trucks almost look like ghostly ships on the Canale Grande, floating accompanied by a Neapolitan song performed by Enrico Caruso. And here the film *Eastern Landscapes* leaves the boundaries of reality, as they have been drawn by history, far behind. The thirteen-minute film does not use words. There is only the wind, the low humming of the cars and again silence, interrupted by music coming from the instruments that are found in the pile of garbage.

And there are hardly any people present. At the beginning, a young disposal worker points the way for the incoming trucks with a silent gesture. Later on an old worker is standing right in front of the camera, holding the accordion, trying to lure a few sounds out of this broken instrument. Nobody speaks, nobody is asked. The closeness to the people that distinguished many East German documentaries seems to have transformed into a mute, speechless distance.

What was fascinating me about this course of events I was experiencing day in and day out at the landfill was history taking its turn without mercy, with indifference, and it became my challenge to capture this with my eye only, with the eye of the camera.

Up to this moment, my experience had grown from working on films that told life stories, that gave individuals room for growth, room to articulate their thoughts, to show their gestures, even opposed to or at least avoiding the established, ideologized image structures. My pictures wanted to create a world that did not appear in government statements. My images were connected to the individual, with all the problems coming with this approach. Of course it was occupying (remark: in a sense of the act of filming occupying the object that the film is capturing), but the individual was never uncovered, abused, or informed against.

These pictures had room for humans; they were mostly long, steady shots in a classic format, strongly influenced by the gesture of photography. These were shots with an "echo," an experience every documentary filmmaker knows—the important movement, the important word, the glimpse of a gesture summing it all up—often pointing towards the speechlessness that happens when the camera stops rolling. Because most of the time people in this society were speechless, which served the medium film, but not the ideology of the establishment. Silent gestures have always been suspicious to the establishment, and so they were suspicious here, too. (That explains why television, a medium that does not know the silent gesture, turns into the tool of trade for the establishment in every society.) And because of that, a take often was not cut, when the action seemed to be over.

These pictures were arranged by montage, they were put in an order that was ruled by slowness. Something that had vanished from the field of vision had to be captured; the audience was asked to look twice, to discover something. Maybe this was an illusion, because the slowness of this society meant inflexibility as well, portliness and boredom. Still you couldn't overlook a certain care, precision, and honesty. Cynicism was a stranger to a certain kind of documentaries. The pictures determined the montage, so films progressed in a linear fashion, which did not fully use the possibilities the medium was offering.

The course of events that I was able to observe at the landfill was happening on different levels. The garbage of a city was brought here, a city that called itself the capital of a state, though it only was half of a city. What are people liberating themselves from when consideration and fear disappear? Did they want to hide all traces of a past betrayal, everything that could tell that they had been obvious partygoers of a system that suffered a breakdown? Or do they just want to create space for the newer, more colorful, long desired items of the affluent society now come upon them? Or was it simply garbage, always being dumped here, no matter what the political climate was like? The leftovers of an affluent society?

I am interested in the layers that now came to light. I was interested in the question, what images do I find and how does a cinematic structure come into being, a structure describing a political downfall and a downfall of civilization without obviously connecting these two events? I was interested in how to escape from the atmosphere that had banned these pictures, depicting garbage.

The edited images are describing the garbage of a society; they reflect an atmosphere of finality; they show the euphoric act of throwing things away, up to the

Photo: Sebastian Richter

extreme sequence showing love letters whirled up by the wind, letting us read the sweet talk on the sheets of paper. What a time is this, when you say goodbye to your most intimate past like this.

If one observes as a documentary filmmaker, keeping track of everyday events, one's eye ready to discover the moment that shows a social structure, a human motion, a condition of society, one is often led to images that can't be replaced by skillful editing or "staging." It is the faith in the event, the instinct of the documentary filmmaker. Something is coming to him.

At a sanitary landfill, stuff is not only brought but also picked up. There are people who think some found items are valuable, people with a different set of values, resulting from being poor, being ethical, or being obsessed. This persistence created the shot of the Russian soldier, who, while his army and his country are deteriorating, finds a suitcase that he first eyes indecisively. Then he is picking up the suitcase, again waiting clueless, and finally he takes off with the suitcase. The camera follows his movements, follows his hesitation and his walking away, being surprised by what it sees. The camera is not hiding, the soldier simply does not see it.

It is an invitation to the eye to take a closer look, to recognize the dimension of an event, the rulings of hope and doubt, joyfulness and pride, to discover something with the eye that does not have a place in the media, that are swamped by a flood of pictures. In this shot the dilemma of a huge country becomes an image.

Images like this are the images I searched for, but no frame is staged. In this sense the pictures are documentary style and because they are not edited along someone's biographical data, the forms, colors, and signs can sometimes turn into symbols. But this depends on the audience's point of view and its involvement in the events, or in other words, how close or how far away from these events the viewer is standing.

I had to push the things I'd seen away from my mind, I had to mobilize my self-critical potential—I had lived and made films in this city, too—I had to make these images mine once more, in order to find a functioning form of montage. Now I was freed from the course of events that I had observed, free from the items in the garbage that had caused me surprise, upset, and creativity. Now I was able to handle time in a different way, the seasons were mixing, the brown dust of the fall storms and the ice crystals of the approaching winter. That is how montage creates historic time, the all-important thing in films.

Of course I wasn't completely free from the historic background. This led me to stage a scene at the end of the film. A young man dumps a suitcase, then his clothes, and disappears at the horizon, naked as he is, with the screams of ravens that circle the sky above the landfill. At this point in time, at the time of creation, this was an act of complete polemics, also provocation, targeted at the films of a country that had disappeared. It also was a metaphor for a chain of events that affected the East Germans. I was more fascinated by the emotionally strong image, the young man's disappearance accompanied by a song of Caruso.

The final sequence is only the climax of the action at the landfill and does not point at the East Germans in a superficial manner. In an absurd way it points at the consuming, crazed lifestyle and the destructive mentality of the people living in a society where every piece of art was oppressed, as soon as it even came close to showing a catastrophic scenario. It was of course also of psychological value to free oneself from these pressures, to catch up with something that was no longer of interest for my colleagues from other countries.

Today this film is seen with different eyes. The film is no longer emotionally charged. Today it's more of an advance from the edges towards the center of things. It's the appearance of images, shapes and colors, it is decay and destruction— and all in all it is an image of plenty, born by comparison of the world's different standards. This film "speaks" about an immoral event and it delivers the images, depicting why this society did not make sense, from the inside out. It tells a tale, but it also creates something that did not actually happen, the appearance of the young man, and in that way it anticipates the future.

Eduard Schreiber, born 1939 in Obernitz, Boehmen, CSSR; studied public relations and literature in Leipzig; received his Doctorate Degree for a thesis about Egon Erwin Kirsch. From 1971 to 1991 he worked as a writer and director of documentaries at the DEFA Studios. From 1991 to 1992 he was a guest professor at the University of Hamburg, teaching documentary filmmaking. Currently he works as a freelance writer/director. His films have been shown on festivals in Leipzig, Neubrandenburg, Krakau, Moskov, Oberhausen, Duisburg, Tampere, Uppsala, Berlin, Mannheim, Clemont-Ferrat, Bornholm, Montevideo, Odense, Paris, and Edinburgh. He was awarded in Oberhausen and Tampere. He wrote numerous articles about the history and theory of film, as well as reviews on literature and film. He is the coauthor of the book *B/W and Color - DEFA Documentaries from 1942-1992.*

Translation by Georg Hartmann, filmmaker and screenwriter, Los Angeles, CA. ghartmann@earthlink.net

© R. Radin

Michael Tobias is the author of 25 books, and has written, directed and produced more than 100 documentaries and docudramas. His works have been read and/or viewed in over 80 countries. In 1996 Tobias received the "Courage of Conscience Award" from the Pacifist Memorial/Peace Abbey in Sherborn, Massachusetts.

Michael Tobias
c/o Michael Wiese Productions
11288 Ventura Blvd, Suite 821
Studio City, CA 91604

CONSULTING SERVICES

MICHAEL WIESE PRODUCTIONS offers a consulting service to producers, directors, writers, media creators, distributors, suppliers, publishers and others to provide expert advice and strategies for film, video and television program development, marketing, production and distribution.

MWP works with a limited number of consulting clients at any one time. Only those clients where MWP feels that a real value will be added to their endeavors will be selected.

Both large and small clients may be considered. Rates include a one-time, initial consultation rate or an on-going monthly retainer.

Clients include:
NATIONAL GEOGRAPHIC
THE SMITHSONIAN INSTITUTION
BUCKMINSTER FULLER INSTITUTE
THE AMERICAN FILM INSTITUTE
MYSTIC FIRE VIDEO
PACIFIC ARTS VIDEO
PBS HOME VIDEO
KING WORLD TELEVISION
REPUBLIC PICTURES
WNET-PBS-NEW YORK
KCET-PBS– LOS ANGELES
THE APOLLO THEATER PRODUCTIONS

Consulting areas include program development, financing structure, budgeting, licensing, production, marketing strategy, sales, promotion, outreach, release planning, sponsorship and more.

For information or an appointment call (818) 379-8799 or fax (818) 986-3408.

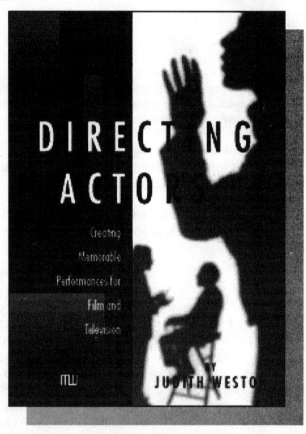

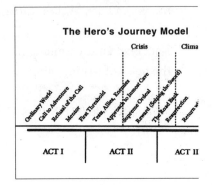

ORDER FORM

Four ways to order:

#1 Call 1-800-379-8808
#2 Fax (818) 986-3408
#3 E-mail: mwpsales@earthlink.net
#4 Copy and mail this order form to:

MICHAEL WIESE PRODUCTIONS
11288 Ventura Blvd., Suite 821
Studio City, CA 91604
1-818-379-8799

CREDIT CARD ORDERS

**CALL
1-800-833-5738**

OR **FAX
818 986-3408**

OR E-MAIL
mwpsales@earthlink.net

BOOKS:

_____	$_____
_____	$_____
_____	$_____
_____	$_____

Subtotal $_____
Shipping $_____
8.25% Sales Tax (Ca Only) $_____

TOTAL ENCLOSED_____

SHIPPING

1ST CLASS MAIL
One Book - $7.00
Two Books - $9.00
For each additional
book, add $1.00.

AIRBORNE EXPRESS
3 Business Day Delivery
Add an additional
$15.00 per order.

OVERSEAS (PREPAID)
Surface - $15.00 ea. book
Airmail - $30.00 ea. book

Please make check or money order payable to
Michael Wiese Productions
(Check one) ___ Master Card ___Visa _____Amex
Company PO#_____

Credit Card Number_____
Expiration Date_____
Cardholder's Name_____
Cardholder's Signature_____

SHIP TO:
Name_____
Address_____
City_____State_____Zip_____
Country_____Telephone_____

Ask about our free catalog.

VISIT OUR HOME PAGE at http://www.mwp.com

Please allow 2-3 weeks for delivery.
All prices subject to change without notice.